Imperial Russia's Muslims

Imperial Russia's Muslims offers an exploration of social and cultural change among the Muslim communities of Central Eurasia from the late eighteenth century through to the outbreak of the First World War. Drawing from a wealth of Russian and Turkic sources, Mustafa Tuna surveys the roles of Islam, social networks, state interventions, infrastructural changes, and the globalization of European modernity in transforming imperial Russia's oldest Muslim community: the Volga-Ural Muslims. Shifting between local, imperial, and transregional frameworks, Tuna reveals how the Russian state sought to manage Muslim communities, the ways in which both the state and Muslim society were transformed by European modernity, and the extent to which the long nineteenth century either fused Russia's Muslims and the tsarist state or drew them apart. The book raises questions about imperial governance, diversity, minorities, and Islamic reform, and in doing so proposes a new theoretical model for the study of imperial situations.

MUSTAFA TUNA is Andrew W. Mellon Assistant Professor of Slavic and Eurasian Studies and History at Duke University.

Critical Perspectives on Empire

Editors

Professor Catherine Hall
University College London

Professor Mrinalini Sinha
University of Michigan

Professor Kathleen Wilson
State University of New York, Stony Brook

Critical Perspectives on Empire is a major series of ambitious, cross-disciplinary works in the emerging field of critical imperial studies. Books in the series explore the connections, exchanges, and mediations at the heart of national and global histories, the contributions of local as well as metropolitan knowledge, and the flows of people, ideas and identities facilitated by colonial contact. To that end, the series not only offers a space for outstanding scholars working at the intersection of several disciplines to bring to wider attention the impact of their work; it also takes a leading role in reconfiguring contemporary historical and critical knowledge, of the past and of ourselves.

A full list of titles published in the series can be found at: www.cambridge.org/cpempire

Imperial Russia's Muslims

Islam, Empire, and European Modernity, 1788–1914

Mustafa Tuna

Duke University

CAMBRIDGE
UNIVERSITY PRESS

CAMBRIDGE
UNIVERSITY PRESS

University Printing House, Cambridge CB2 8BS, United Kingdom

Cambridge University Press is part of the University of Cambridge.

It furthers the University's mission by disseminating knowledge in the pursuit of education, learning and research at the highest international levels of excellence.

www.cambridge.org
Information on this title: www.cambridge.org/9781107032491

© Mustafa Tuna 2015

First published 2015

Printed in the United States of America by Sheridan Books, Inc.

A catalogue record for this publication is available from the British Library

Library of Congress Cataloguing in Publication Data
Tuna, Mustafa Özgür, 1976-
Imperial Russia's Muslims: Islam, Empire, and European Modernity, 1788–1914 / Mustafa Tuna (Duke University).
    pages   cm. –   (Critical perspectives on empire)
Includes bibliographical references.
ISBN 978-1-107-03249-1 (Hardback)
1. Muslims–Russia (Federation)–Volga-Ural Region–History.
2. Muslims–Russia (Federation)–Volga-Ural Region–Social conditions.
3. Community life–Russia (Federation)–Volga-Ural Region–History.
4. Islam–Social aspects–Russia (Federation)–Volga-Ural Region–History.
5. Social change–Russia (Federation)–Volga-Ural Region–History.
6. Volga-Ural Region (Russia)–Ethnic relations.   7. Volga-Ural Region (Russia)–Social conditions.   8. Muslims–Russia–History.   9. Imperialism–Social aspects–Russia–History.   10. Russia–History–1801–1917.   I. Title.
DK511.V65T86 2015
305.6′970947409034–dc23
2014046690

ISBN 978-1-107-03249-1 Hardback

To the memory of Emine and Hüseyin Tuna,
the teachers

Contents

List of figures   *page* viii
Acknowledgments   x
Notes on transliteration and dates   xii

Introduction   1

1   A world of Muslims   18

2   Connecting Volga-Ural Muslims to the Russian state   37

3   Russification: Unmediated governance and the
    empire's quest for ideal subjects   57

4   Peasant responses: Protecting the inviolability of the
    Muslim domain   79

5   Russia's great transformation in the second half of the
    long nineteenth century (1860–1914)   103

6   The wealthy: Prospering with the sea-change and
    giving back   125

7   The cult of progress   146

8   Alienation of the Muslim intelligentsia   171

9   Imperial paranoia   195

10 Flexibility of the imperial domain and the limits
    of integration   217

    Conclusion   237

    Bibliography   244
    Index   271

Figures

1 Rızâeddin bin Fahreddin. Courtesy of İbrahim Maraş.   *page* 3
2 The cover of *Tercüman*'s first issue, published on April 10, 1883. Image published with permission of ProQuest LLC. Further reproduction is prohibited without permission.   118
3 An advert for hair ointment that ran in Russian Muslim periodicals frequently after 1904. Image published with permission of ProQuest LLC. Further reproduction is prohibited without permission.   121
4 İsmâ'îl Bey Gasprinskiy.   150
5 Prominent authors and publishers of the Volga-Ural Muslim press between 1905 and 1915: Ğayaz İshâqî, Seyyidgiray Alkin, Ahmed-Hâdi Maqsûdî, Şeher Şeref, and Burhan Şeref. *Añ*, 1916 (1): 6–7, 10–11, and 13. Courtesy of İbrahim Maraş.   157
6 Prominent authors and publishers of the Volga-Ural Muslim press between 1905 and 1915: Rızâeddin bin Fahreddin, Ğatâullah Ahund Bayezidof, Zâkir Ramiyef, Şâkir Ramiyef, and Fâtih Kerîmî. *Añ*, 1916 (1): 6–7, 10–11, and 13. Courtesy of İbrahim Maraş.   158
7 Prominent authors and publishers of the Volga-Ural Muslim press between 1905 and 1915: Mahmûd Fu'âd Tuqtaref, Muhammedcan Seydaşef, Ahmedcan Seydaşef, Ahmed Urmançıyef, Hâris Feyzi, and Ğaliasgar Kemâl. *Añ*, 1916 (1): 6–7, 10–11, and 13. Courtesy of İbrahim Maraş.   159
8 Prominent authors and publishers of the Volga-Ural Muslim press between 1905 and 1915: Fâtih Murtazîn, Ğabdurrahman Ğumerof, Kemâl Tuhfetullin, Habîburrahman Ğaniyef, Timurşah Salavyof, and Kelîmullah Hüseyinof. *Añ*, 1916 (1): 6–7, 10–11, and 13. Courtesy of İbrahim Maraş.   160

9 Prominent authors and publishers of the Volga-Ural Muslim
  press between 1905 and 1915: Şerefüddîn Şehîdullin,
  Ya'qûb Halîlî, Fahrulislâm Âgiyef, Mahmûd Mercânî,
  Ğibâdullah Ğusmanof, and Zâkir Qâdirî. *Añ*, 1916 (1): 6–7,
  10–11, and 13. Courtesy of İbrahim Maraş.   161
10 The cover of the 41st issue of *Molla Nasreddin* in 1911.
  Image published with permission of ProQuest LLC. Further
  reproduction is prohibited without permission.   190
11 Şihâbuddin Mercânî.   191

Acknowledgments

The contributions and support of many individuals and institutions made this book possible.

I appreciate my teachers in history: Nejdet Gök, Hakan Kırımlı, Norman Stone, and Hasan Ünal at Bilkent University in Turkey; Ben Eklof, Hiroaki Kuromiya, and David Ransel at Indiana University; Stephen Kotkin, Jeremy Adelman, Linda Colley, Molly Greene, Şükrü Hanioğlu, Olga Litvak, Philip Nord, Robert Tignor, and John R. Willis at Princeton University. As I first conceptualized this project in Kazan in the 2001–2 academic year, Azat Ahundov, Alper Alp, Nadir Arslan, Lalä Hasanşina, İbrahim Maraş, Cävdät Miñnullin, Räfik Möhämmätşin, Süleyman Rähimov, Asiyä Rähimova, Rezeda Safiullina, İsmail Türkoğlu, Dilara Usmanova, and Cämil Zäynullin helped me with their knowledge and assistance. My advisor, Stephen Kotkin, Cemil Aydın, Jane Burbank, Bob Crews, Wayne Dowler, Rozaliya Garipova, Mona Hassan, Nora Fisher-Onar, Allen Frank, Molly Greene, Agnes Kefeli Clay, Adeeb Khalid, Anna Krylova, Bruce Lawrence, Gil Merkx, Martin Miller, Ben Nathans, Ekaterina Pravilova, Don Raleigh, Michael Reynolds, Uli Schamiloglu, Eric Taggliacozzo, Frank Wcislo, Erik Zitser, and two anonymous reviewers of Cambridge University Press read all or parts of my work at its various stages and helped me improve it with generous comments.

The Foundation for the Dissemination of Knowledge in Turkey funded my initial research in Kazan, and Princeton University's Graduate School enabled another trip to St. Petersburg. A timely donation from the Münir Ertegün Turkish Studies Fund to Princeton University Library provided me with easy access to an important collection of Turkic periodicals from the Russian empire. Awards from Duke University and from the Eurasia Program of the Social Science Research Council with funds provided by the State Department under the Program for Research and Training on Eastern Europe and the Independent States of the Former Soviet Union (Title VIII) enabled me to take research leave and focus on writing in the 2012–13 academic year.

My sister Ülkü Çetinkanat and brother-in-law Haldun Çetinkanat, their children Başak and Kutay, "*hocam*" Nejdet Gök and his family, my lifelong roommate Mehmet Ali Doğan, college comrades Faruk Bostancı, Murat Cemrek, Tahir Kaplan, Nurettin Kilci, Çağrı Özer, Mirat Satoğlu, and Hasan Şen, and numerous others blessed me with their friendship and support. My colleagues at the Slavic and Eurasian Studies Department of Duke University gave me a welcoming academic home. My wife Mona Hassan completed my life by also being my best friend and colleague, our two sons Hüseyin-Abdullah and Abdullatif gave us joy and strength, and my mother-in-law Afifa Afifi patiently helped us at each step, as we carried on through the long haul of our demanding projects.

I am grateful to them all.

Notes on transliteration and dates

The choice of characters in transliterating and transcribing the languages or dialects of the former Soviet Union's Turkic-speaking Muslim peoples is a politicized task. Muslims in the Russian empire and Transoxiana used the Arabic script until the advent of the Soviet regime. Although they had no common orthography and the spelling of words was hardly standardized in any particular Turkic language or dialect, the absence of vowels in the Arabic script (despite their prominence in Turkic languages) concealed many of the differences in local pronunciation. This situation changed in the 1920s, when the governments of Turkic Soviet republics introduced Latin-based alphabets for their titular nationalities, and again in the 1930s, when they were replaced with Cyrillic ones, in an attempt to bring the Union's Turkic peoples closer to the Russian core while simultaneously distancing them from Turkey. The vowels and many cumbersome diacritical marks in these Cyrillic alphabets marked the Soviet Union's designated Turkic nationalities from one another by highlighting and sometimes exaggerating differences in local pronunciation. Finally, since the Soviet Union's disintegration in 1992, some of those Turkic peoples have switched back to Latin-based alphabets, which partly continue to reflect the problems of the earlier Cyrillic ones. In the end, the artificial and politically charged nature of these changes leaves no standard and politically neutral way to transliterate the Arabic-script Turkic texts produced by imperial Russia's Muslims. One has to make an inevitably subjective choice.

In the footnotes and bibliography of this book, I used the Latin characters that I thought would best facilitate the identification of Turkic sources. In the main text, however, I transliterated Turkic words written in the Arabic script with a modified version of characters from the modern Turkish alphabet, with which I feel most comfortable. For people who lived both in the tsarist and Soviet periods, I transliterated from the Arabic-script version of their names. In spelling out words, I made an effort to maintain simplicity while also reflecting sharp differences in local pronunciation. When there was more than one option for pronunciation, I relied on modern Tatar unless the word was used in a text from outside of the Volga-Ural region, such as the Crimea or South Caucasus. I left some Turkic or Arabic words that are commonly used in the English-language literature, such as "madrasa" or "sheikh," in their conventionally accepted forms.

To transliterate texts or names from the Arabic or Persian languages, I used common standard transliteration systems. I did the same for Russian words and names, but I converted texts written with the old Russian alphabet to the modern Russian alphabet before transliteration.

Readers who are not familiar with Turkic alphabets may find the following helpful in reading the main text of the book:

A/a – "a" as in father
E/e – "e" as in pen or engine, or "a" as in pan
I/ı – no equivalent in English, similar to "e" in open
İ/i – "i" as in pin or in
O/o – "o" as in more or open
Ö/ö – "u" as in turn or urge
U/u – "oo" as in room but short
Ü/ü – similar to "u" in "cube" but short
C/c – "j" as in joy
Ç/ç – "ch" as in chair
Ğ/ğ – no equivalent in English, indicates "ع" (ʿayn) in Arabic and is similar to the French "r" at the beginning of a Turkic word as pronounced in the Volga-Ural region; elsewhere, either silent but prolongs the preceding vowel or similar to but less pronounced than the French "r"
ʿ – indicates Arabic "ع" (ʿayn), no equivalent in English, pronounced by constricting the throat and vibrating the vocal cords with an expulsion of breath, does not exist in Turkic words but is common in Arabic-origin Turkic names
K/k – "k" in key, indicates "ك" in Arabic
Ñ – nasal "n" similar to "ng" in "English"
Ş/ş – "sh" as in ship
Q/q – "q" in queen, indicates "ق" in Arabic
ˆ on â, û, and î – indicates prolonged vowels which are common in Arabic-origin words

I did not convert Julian calendar dates into Gregorian dates, but left them as they appeared in the original sources. I converted Hijri and Rumi calendar dates into Gregorian dates.

Introduction

It was winter in the early 1860s. The residents of a Muslim village in the Samara Gubernia of the Russian empire's Volga-Ural region winnowed grain in the cold morning wind. A young boy watched small pieces of chaff float through the air and disappear into the bright rays of the rising sun. He asked his older sister where the chaff went. "To Mekerye," she responded dismissively. Volga-Ural Muslims referred to Nizhny Novgorod's famous annual trade fair as "Mekerye," in reference to the name of the small monastic town Makar'ev, downstream from Nizhny Novgorod on the Volga River, where the fair had first started in the seventeenth century. The wind blew the chaff to the east while Nizhny Novgorod was located hundreds of miles to the west of the young boy's village in Samara. But this did not matter to him on that cold winter day. He did not know where Nizhny Novgorod was anyway. He had never been there and the Muslim peasants in his community typically did not have access to printed maps that could have otherwise allowed him to ascribe significance to the geographic direction of a market town. By the turn of the twentieth century, however, this young boy, whose name was Rızâeddin bin Fahreddin (1858–1936), would become a prominent communal leader and an erudite Islamic scholar with encyclopedic knowledge of world affairs. He would remember the short exchange with his sister from that morning with surprise, as a frustrating sign of the ignorance of his fellow Muslims in the Russian empire, which he believed had to change along with a world itself changing with rapidity.[1]

This book investigates the entangled transformations of Russia's Muslim communities in the Volga-Ural region, the tsarist administration, and the transregional vectors of exchange and interaction in the

---

[1] Raif Märdanov, Ramil Miñnullin, and Süläyman Räximov eds., *Rizaetdin Fähretdin: Fänni-biografik jentik* (Kazan: Ruhiyat, 1999), 10–11. In addition to this collection of materials on Rızâeddin bin Fahreddin, see İsmail Türkoğlu, *Rusya Türkleri Arasında Yenileşme Hareketinin Öncülerinden Rızaeddin Fahreddin* (Istanbul: Ötüken Neşriyat, 2000); and G. Kh. Abdrafikova and V. Iu. Gabidullina eds., *Materialy k biobibliografii Rizy Fakhretdinova* (Ufa: IIIaL UNTs RAN, 2010).

long-nineteenth century (1789–1914) with a focus on that rapid pace of the tsarist empire's latter decades. This is an inherently messy story, as imperial situations often are.[2] The power that made Fahreddin's villagers spare a portion of their produce every year to pay taxes to the imperial state emanated from St. Petersburg, but when his sister needed a point of geographic reference beyond the small boundaries of their village, she chose a closer market town, not the empire's capital. Fahreddin did not know which way Nizhny Novgorod was located and possibly neither did his sister, but they certainly knew where their parents turned to face the Kaaba in Mecca when they prayed. Fahreddin completed his studies without leaving the Volga-Ural region, but when he contemplated traveling to seek higher knowledge early in his student life, he wanted to go to the madrasas of Bukhara in Transoxiana, not to one of the prominent universities of the Russian empire, such as the ones in St. Petersburg, Moscow, or nearby Kazan. Yet, upon graduating from the madrasa, he traveled to Ufa to receive certification at an institution that the tsarist state had founded in the late eighteenth century to regulate religious and certain civic affairs of Muslims in the empire (the Orenburg Spiritual Assembly), and he soon took a prominent position at that assembly too. The dynamics that defined the lives of Volga-Ural Muslims in the Russian empire as well as the lives of the empire's other subjects were complex, sometimes seemingly paradoxical, and always multifaceted.

Rather than attempting to organize this potentially confusing mess into a tidy yet oversimplified structure for the sake of false argumentative clarity, this book makes a sustained effort to engage the complexity of its subject matter in search of greater historical understanding. The through-line that strings together the resulting multilayered narrative is a focus on the intricate interplay of local, imperial, and transregional influences that shaped the experiences of Volga-Ural Muslims in the Russian empire. Therefore, this book offers first and foremost an informed recognition of the complexity of imperial situations like that of the Russian empire. An effort to identify conceptual tools to make sense of that complexity emanates from this recognition. And the narrative employs those tools to process a broad spectrum of historical data – ranging from macroeconomic indicators to newspaper advertisements, and from highbrow interpretations of a world in change to peasant

---

[2] Jane Burbank and Mark von Hagen, "Coming into the Territory: Uncertainty and Empire," in *Russian Empire: Space, People, Power, 1700–1930*, ed. Jane Burbank, Mark von Hagen and Anatoly Remnev (Bloomington: Indiana University Press, 2002), 1–29, highlights this point well.

Figure 1 Rızâeddin bin Fahreddin.

rumors – thereby painting a holistic picture of the experiences of imperial Russia's Muslims. The resulting historical account presents insights not only to those interested in the Russian empire and its Muslim subjects but also to a broader audience involving the students of empires in general, Islamic studies, world history, and post-colonial studies.

Subject matter and arguments

The primary protagonists of this book are the Volga-Ural Muslims, roughly consisting of the Turkic-speaking Muslim population of the lands to the north of the Caspian Sea and their wide diaspora. The Volga-Ural Muslims represent the northernmost reach of Islam in the premodern world: a status challenged only by the diasporic expansion of Muslim communities in the modern era. More importantly though, having been incorporated into the emerging Russian empire in the mid sixteenth century, the Volga-Ural Muslims have had the longest experience of living as subjects of a conquering non-Muslim power and – with a few exceptional periods – surviving under regimes hostile to Islam to this day. Only the Hui Muslims in China have a comparable and, in fact, longer experience of living under non-Muslim powers, but their communities emerged through immigration and conversion, without the shock of imperial conquest that the Volga-Ural Muslims faced in the mid sixteenth century.[3]

In the centuries following their incorporation into the Russian empire, the Volga-Ural Muslims dispersed over a wide area stretching from St. Petersburg in the west to Kashgaria in eastern China. Moreover, they maintained intense cultural exchange with other Muslim communities in Transoxiana, the Kazakh Steppes, the Caucasus, the Crimea, and increasingly in the late nineteenth century, the Ottoman territories. Between the mid eighteenth and the mid nineteenth centuries, the Russian state encouraged this exchange in order to utilize Volga-Ural Muslims to extend tsarist influence over other Muslim peoples in the empire's borderlands. Yet, in the late-nineteenth century, tsarist agents also problematized the Volga-Ural Muslims' broad reach by suspecting them of being sympathizers and potential collaborators of the Ottoman Empire and by restricting their contacts with Muslims elsewhere in Russia, especially the Kazakhs. As a result, thanks to the diasporic expansion and wide cultural reach of the Volga-Ural Muslims, the scope of this book extends from the Volga-Ural region to a broader Muslim-inhabited geography, to the Russian empire itself, to Europe, and eventually to a global web of relations. As such, the history of Volga-Ural Muslims in the Russian empire provides a revealing case to study many historiographically significant questions, from the vitality of empires to the dynamics of imperial situations and from the expansion of European modernity in colonial or imperial settings to the integration of Muslims in non-Muslim societies.

Today, a contemporary map would identify at least two Muslim "nations" – Tatars and the Bashkirs – in the Volga-Ural region, but this should be considered the outcome of many layers of tsarist, Soviet, and post-Soviet identity politics, with limited relevance for the pre-revolutionary period. Nationalist ideas emerged among Volga-Ural Muslims only in the last decades of the tsarist regime and did not produce fully fledged nations before the Soviet era. I use "Volga-Ural Muslim" as a relatively neutral designation with more historical validity for the tsarist era, while turning to various other ethnic and tribal categories – such as Tatar, Bashkir, Noghay, Mishar, and Tipter – that existed among Volga-Ural Muslims to distinguish between those categories when necessary or to

---

[3] Michael Dillon, *China's Muslim Hui Community: Migration, Settlement and Sects* (London: Curzon Press, 1999).

reflect their usage in specific sources. Russian and European observers used "Tatar" to refer to Volga-Ural Muslims in general too, but the term had broader connotations, designating Muslims in a wider geography, including the Crimea, South Caucasus, and Siberia, and even non-Muslims, such as the Kräshens, also known as the "Baptized Tatars."[4]

We also need to qualify the term "imperial Russia," for it simultaneously refers to the tsarist state and its agents, the territories and peoples ruled by the tsarist state, and the institutions that the tsarist regime created and employed to govern. Even after we differentiate between such aspects of empire, we still need to recognize that these entities interacted in different ways in different imperial contexts and periods. The "imperial turn" since the end of the Cold War provided us with excellently nuanced histories of empires, but ironically, the cumulative upshot of this new attention to empire has been an essentialist assertion of the superiority of empires over nation-states in accommodating human diversity.[5] Empires did not possess an essential nature; they were evolving structures with multiple faces. The Volga-Ural Muslims remember their subjection to the Russian empire before the mid eighteenth century as a horrendous experience characterized by forced conversions and expulsion from fertile lands. Catherine II (r. 1762–96) altered these circumstances as she built an imperial model based on governing through intermediaries. However, yet another model based on unmediated governance emerged from the Great Reforms of Alexander II's reign (1855–81).[6] In short, the Russian empire revealed many faces in different phases of its history. *Imperial Russia's Muslims* analyzes how the shifts between these phases affected Volga-Ural Muslims in the late nineteenth and early twentieth centuries.

Beneath the overarching trends of imperial governance, the interventions of particular imperial institutions or agents could affect an empire's subjects in diverse ways too. Different ministries of the tsarist government had different priorities, and their policies regarding Muslims did not necessarily agree. More notably, the institution of *zemstvos* as local

---

[4] Allen J. Frank, *Islamic Historiography and "Bulghar" Identity among the Tatars and Bashkirs of Russia* (Boston: Brill, 1998), 42–43.

[5] Among many sources on the "imperial turn," see Ilya Gerasimov, "In Search of a New Imperial History," *Ab Imperio*, 2005 (1): 33–56; Michael David-Fox, Alexander M. Martin, and Peter Holquist, "The Imperial Turn," *Kritika: Explorations in Russian and Eurasian History*, 2006 7(4): 705–12; Alan Mikhail and Christine M. Philliou, "The Ottoman Empire and the Imperial Turn," *Comparative Studies in Society and History*, 2012 54(4): 721–45.

[6] Charles Robert Steinwedel, "Invisible Threads of Empire: State, Religion, and Ethnicity in Tsarist Bashkiria, 1773–1917" (Ph.D. Dissertation, Columbia University, 1999), especially 4–5, provides a similar argument.

bodies of governance in the Great Reforms era (1861–81) and the increased involvement of Muslims in other local administrative forums in the late nineteenth and early twentieth centuries created ample room for variations between central state policies and the acts of local administrative organs. These variations moderated the Volga-Ural Muslims' overall experience as subjects of the late Russian empire, even though a survey of central state policies alone would present the bleak picture of an assimilationist government attempting to limit the cultural livelihood of its Muslim subjects.

Finally, a more complete understanding of the Volga-Ural Muslims' overall experience in late imperial Russia requires an examination of their mundane circumstances and encounters, which were admittedly shaped by but not limited to the binary of state–subject relations. The world surrounding an average Volga-Ural Muslim's daily experiences changed exceedingly fast in the last decades of the long nineteenth century. This was part of a global transformation marked by the acceleration of time, reduction of distances, industrialization of production, and supposed human victories over nature – by railways and steamboats, telegraphy and print media, machinery and cash crops, and penicillin and public health projects.[7] "Modernity," or more precisely "European modernity,"[8] is a shorthand for these processes (the list of which may well be expanded) as they emerged and evolved in western Europe – with North America in its wake – and spread to other parts of the world at varying degrees, speeds, and forms.[9] However, "modernity" is a loaded term with multiple connotations, including references to much earlier and much later phenomena.[10] Therefore, I choose to use it sparingly throughout this book and instead, focus on describing the processes of transformation at play in various contexts.

These processes of transformation moved from Europe outward, as Europe provided the models, technology, and, sometimes the push for change. Antonio Gramsci's theory of "cultural hegemony" may be a

---

[7] For an insightful analysis of this process, see Stephen Kotkin, "Modern Times: The Soviet Union and the Interwar Conjuncture," *Kritika: Explorations in Russian and Eurasian History*, 2001 2(1): 111–64.

[8] For a Eurocentric definition of modernity, see Anthony Giddens, *The Consequences of Modernity* (Stanford: Stanford University Press, 1990), 1–2.

[9] An inspiring account regarding the nature of this spread is Fernando Ortiz, *Cuban Counterpoint: Tobacco and Sugar* (New York: A. A. Knopf, 1947) along with Fernando Coronil, "Introduction: Transculturation and the Politics of Theory: Countering the Center, Cuban Counterpoint," in *Cuban Counterpoint: Tobacco and Sugar* (Durham: Duke University Press, 1995).

[10] Among many sources, see *Daedalus: Early Modernities*, 1998 127(3); and *Daedalus: Multiple Modernities*, 2000 129(1).

useful way to consider this process if we imagine hegemony on a global scale, with Europe's (and later North America's) cultural frame gradually defining the "norm" in the rest of the world.[11] This seemed spontaneous as Europe's cultural frame spread to various regions of the world, claiming legitimacy primarily through the mediation of intellectual networks, but it also involved and eventually produced a significant level of coercion that materialized not only in physical force, as in the "opening" of China to free trade, but also in emulative pressure, as in the deliberate choice of Meiji reformists to transform Japan in the image of Europe in the late nineteenth century.

European modernity affected the Russian empire's western borderlands first and proceeded rapidly in an eastward direction following the railway lines that covered European Russia in a dense web by the turn of the twentieth century. But this transformative process faded beyond the Ural Mountains, as only a single railway line sliced through Siberia. Two Russias emerged in the end: one in the lands to the west of the Ural Mountains and one to their east. The Volga-Ural Muslims inhabited the frontier zone between these two worlds. With a sharp comparative perspective resulting from their in-betweenness, some of them looked up to Europe as a model of emulation and down upon their coreligionists as ignorant masses to be molded in Europe's image: a project in the making. This book carefully distinguishes that intellectual project (often referred to as "Jadidism" in the literature) from the actual processes of transformation that shaped the everyday lives of Volga-Ural Muslims in late imperial Russia, thereby revising conventional historiography's tendency to equate the experience of Volga-Ural Muslims with the ideas and efforts of progressive intellectuals among them.[12]

---

[11] Antonio Gramsci, *Selections from the Prison Notebooks of Antonio Gramsci*, ed. Quintin Hoare and Geoffrey Nowell-Smith (New York: International Publishers, 1971), 12.

[12] For examples of works that read Volga-Ural Muslim history through the lens of progressive intellectuals, see Cafer Seydahmet Kırımer, *Gaspıralı İsmail Bey* (Istanbul: Türk Anonim Şirketi, 1934); Serge A. Zenkovsky, *Pan-Turkism and Islam in Russia* (Cambridge, MA: Harvard University Press, 1960); Alexandre Bennigsen and Chantal Lemercier-Quelquejay, *La presse et le mouvement national chez les musulmans de Russie avant 1920* (Paris: Mouton, 1964); Akdes Nimet Kurat, "Kazan Türklerinde 'Medeni Uyanış' Devri," *Ankara Üniversitesi Dil ve Tarih-Coğrafya Fakültesi Dergisi*, 1966 24 (3–4): 95–194; Abdullah Battal-Taymas, *Kazan Türkleri: Türk Tarihinin Hazin Yaprakları* (Ankara: Türk Kültürünü Araştırma Enstitüsü, 1966); Khusain Khasanovich Khasanov, *Formirovanie tatarskoi burzhuaznoi natsii* (Kazan: Tatarskoe knizhnoe izdatel'stvo, 1977); Ayşe Azade-Rorlich, *The Volga Tatars: A Profile in National Resilience* (Stanford: Hoover Institution Press, 1986); and Christian Noack, *Muslimischer Nationalismus im russischen Reich: Nationsbildung und Nationalbewegung bei Tataren und Baschkiren: 1861–1917* (Stuttgart: Franz Steiner Verlag, 2000).

Since the Cold War the literature on the history of Volga-Ural Muslims in tsarist Russia has improved significantly beyond this conventional historiography and made important contributions to the "imperial turn." Some of the best studies in the field sifted through dusty files in the archives to explore the views, predicaments, anxieties, and policies of Russian imperial agents and institutions about the presence of Muslims in *their* empire.[13] Others provided us with detailed accounts of religious debates, institutions, and to some extent, daily life among Volga-Ural Muslims primarily by looking at the previously little explored writings (mostly manuscripts) of Islamic scholars.[14] Still others combined archival data with insights from late imperial Russia's Turkic press to reveal the social, cultural, and economic transformation of Volga-Ural Muslim communities in ways underexplored before.[15] And finally, a few scholars focused on the interaction of Russia's Muslims with the tsarist state beyond a more conventional resistance paradigm.[16]

---

[13] Some outstanding works in this category are Steinwedel, "Invisible"; Robert P. Geraci, *Window on the East: National and Imperial Identities in Late Tsarist Russia* (Ithaca: Cornell University Press, 2001), especially 86–157 and 264–308; Paul W. Werth, *At the Margins of Orthodoxy: Mission, Governance, and Confessional Politics in Russia's Volga-Kama Region, 1827–1905* (Ithaca: Cornell University Press, 2002), especially 177–99; Wayne Dowler, *Classroom and Empire: the Politics of Schooling Russia's Eastern Nationalities, 860–1917* (Montreal: McGill-Queen's University Pess, 2001), especially 120–49; and Elena I. Campbell, *Muslim Question and Russian Imperial Governance* (Bloomington: Indiana University Press, 2015).

[14] See, for instance, Michael Kemper, *Sufis und Gelehrte in Tatarien und Baschkirien, 1789–1889: der islamische Diskurs unter russischer Herrschaft* (Berlin: K. Schwarz, 1998); Frank, *Islamic Historiography*; Daniel Damirovich Azamatov, *Orenburgskoe Magometanskoe Dukhovnoe Sobranie v kontse XVIII–XIX vv.* (Ufa: Gilem, 1999); Allen J. Frank, *Muslim Religious Institutions in Imperial Russia: The Islamic World of Novouzensk District and the Kazakh Inner Horde, 1780–1910* (Leiden: Brill, 2001); Rafik Muhammetshin, *Tatarskii traditsionalizm: osobennosti i formy proiavleniia* (Kazan: Meddok, 2005); Allen J. Frank, *Bukhara and the Muslims of Russia: Sufism, Education, and the Paradox of Islamic Prestige* (Leiden: Brill, 2012); Rozaliya Garipova, "The Transformation of the Ulama and the Shari'a in the Volga-Ural Muslim Community under Russian Imperial Rule" (Ph.D. Dissertation, Princeton University, 2013).

[15] See, for instance, Noack, *Muslimischer*; and Radik Salikhov, *Tatarskaia burzhuaziia Kazani i natsional'nye reformy vtoroi poloviny XIX-nachala XX v.* (Kazan: Izdatel'stvo Master Lain, 2000). Many works in this category remain in dissertation format. See Agnès Kefeli-Clay, "Kräshen Apostasy: Popular Religion, Education, and the Contest over Tatar Identity (1856–1917)" (Ph.D. Dissertation, Arizona State U., 2001); James H. Meyer, "Turkic Worlds: Community Representation and Collective Identity in the Russian and Ottoman Empires, 1870–1914" (Ph.D. Dissertation, Brown University, 2007); Danielle M. Ross, "From the Minbar to the Barricades: The Transformation of the Volga-Ural `Ulama into a Revolutionary Intelligentsia" (Ph.D. Dissertation, University of Wisconsin, Madison, 2011); and Madina V. Goldberg, "Russian Empire-Tatar Theater: The Politics of Culture in Late Imperial Kazan" (Ph.D. Dissertation, University of Michigan, 2009).

[16] Azamatov, *Orenburgskoe*; Robert D. Crews, *For Prophet and Tsar: Islam and Empire in Russia and Central Asia* (Cambridge, MA: Harvard University Press, 2006); Norihiro

In this last group, Robert Crews' treatment of the tsarist state's "policy of toleration" toward Islam (which involved not only letting the Muslims be, but also transforming their religious institutions into instruments of imperial rule) especially resonated and found broad acclaim among the students of the imperial turn.[17] Yet, most specialists on Russia's Muslims have criticized (sometimes even dismissed) Crews' argument as overly favorable to the tsarist state, disregarding of regional and periodic differences, and poor in representing Muslim points of view beyond what might be gleaned from the records of adjudicated conflict situations.[18] Beneath this criticism lies an objection to the rosy image of empires, and especially the Russian empire, which has evolved from the imperial turn and, according to Adeeb Khalid, has become "absurd" taken to an "extreme."[19]

Imperial Russia's Muslims intervenes in this debate and argues that the Russian imperial situation, which involved multiple layers of human interaction at the local, governmental, and transregional levels, was too complex and multifaceted to provide a definitive answer to the question of empires' abilities in accommodating difference, especially as an indicator of their endurance.[20] Instead, *Imperial Russia's Muslims* highlights

Naganawa, "Molding the Muslim Community through the Tsarist Administration: Mahalla under the Jurisdiction of the Orenburg Muhammedan Spiritual Assembly after 1905," *Acta Slavica Iaponica*, 2006 (23): 101–23; Norihiro Naganawa, "Holidays in Kazan: The Public Sphere and the Politics of Religious Authority among Tatars in 1914," *Slavic Review*, 2012 71(1): 25–48; and Stefan B. Kirmse, "Law and Empire in Late Tsarist Russia: Muslim Tatars Go to Court," *Slavic Review*, 2013 72(4): 778–801.

[17] Crews, *For Prophet*. Also see Robert Crews, "Empire and the Confessional State: Islam and Religious Politics in Nineteenth-Century Russia," in *American Historical Review*, 2003 108(1): 50–83. For examples of Crews' reception, see Mikhail Dolbilov, "Russifying Bureaucracy and the Politics of Jewish Education in the Russian Empire's Northwest Region (1860s-1870s)," in *Acta Slavica Iaponica*, 2007 (24): 112–43; Karen Barkey, *Empire of Difference: The Ottomans in Comparative Perspective* (Cambridge ; New York: Cambridge University Press, 2008), 112; and Eugene M. Avrutin, *Jews and the Imperial State: Identification Politics in Tsarist Russia* (Ithaca: Cornell University Press, 2010), 35.

[18] See, for instance, Michael Kemper, "Review of *For Prophet and Tsar: Islam and Empire in Russia and Central Asia*," *Die Welt des Islams*, 2007 47(1): 126–129; Adeeb Khalid, "'Tolerating Islam' review of For Prophet and Tsar: Islam and empire in Russia and Central Asia," *London Review of Books*, 24 May 2007; Michael Khodarkovsky, "Review of *For Prophet and Tsar: Islam and Empire in Russia and Central Asia*," *The American Historical Review*, 2007 112(5): 1491–1493; and Alexander Morrison, "Review of *For Prophet and Tsar: Islam and Empire in Russia and Central Asia*," *The Slavonic and East European Review*, 2008 86(3): 553–557. Rozaliya Garipova's recent dissertation offers a fresh revision of many of Crews' analyses as well. Garipova, "The Transformation."

[19] Khalid, "Tolerating Islam". Also see Adeeb Khalid's objection to a similarly pro-empire argument in Adeeb Khalid, "Russian History and the Debate over Orientalism," *Kritika: Explorations in Russian and Eurasian History*, 2000 1(4): 691–99.

[20] Two important and inspiring works dealing with this question are Barkey, *Empire*; and Jane Burbank and Frederick Cooper, *Empires in World History: Power and Politics of Difference* (Princeton: Princeton University Press, 2010).

the complexity and inherent ambiguity of imperial situations in the case of the Russian empire. It builds on the insights that the divergent vantage points of the earlier literature offer, and with the benefit of fresh evidence from various source categories, it constructs a new conceptual model for studying multiple layers of human interaction in imperial contexts.

Domains: A conceptual model for writing history

Two diametrically opposite forces work against each other in the process of historical writing. While things, humans, events, and institutions relate to one another in inseparable and often unpredictable ways, historians observe snapshots of past reality and convey observations and ideas through framed categories that the human intellect needs in order to process data. Therefore, writing history requires creating a coherent narrative with a beginning and an end from snapshots of seemingly unending webs of relations. Some level of distortion remains inevitable as the historian chooses what to include and what not to include in the resulting narrative, therefore, further delimiting what is already limited by the available snapshots of past reality.[21] With this predicament in mind and in an effort to preserve the intricate and elusive nature of history as much as possible, even as it is cast in the molds of textual narrative, I chose to follow a fluid model of delimitation that focuses on a particular area, like eyesight, and moves as needed while constantly maintaining a gradually dimming view of the rest of the visible universe.

To put that eyesight model into practice, I introduce the term "domains" as a conceptual tool highlighting certain patterns and connections in history while maintaining a sense of their actual fluidity. This concept emerged in the early stages of my research on the Volga-Ural Muslims as I compared their experiences with those of Russia's Jewish communities for which the outstanding work of Benjamin Nathans on "the crossing of visible and invisible boundaries" by Jews in the late Russian empire served as a primary reference.[22] Beginning in the 1790s, Russian imperial law confined the residence of Jews to the visible boundaries of the Pale of Permanent Jewish Settlement in Russia's

---

[21] For an inspiring discussion of the process of delimitation in writing, see Edward W. Said, *Orientalism* (New York: Vintage Books, 1994), 15–16. For another work that has inspired my search for a new model of inquiry that transcends the limits of purely regional, confessional, or ethnic categories, see Alexei Miller, "Between Local and Inter-imperial: Russian Imperial History in Search of Scope and Paradigm," *Kritika*, 2004 5(1):7–26.

[22] Benjamin Nathans, *Beyond the Pale: The Jewish Encounter with Late Imperial Russia* (Berkeley: University of California Press, 2002), quote on 1.

western borderlands. The Volga-Ural Muslims were not confined to any particular region in the nineteenth century, and in fact, they were remarkably mobile. Yet, the more I became familiar with their voices, the more I was convinced about the enduring presence of an invisibly delineated world where they interacted primarily with other Volga-Ural Muslims and felt at home. The idea of "domains" emerged from the need to speak about this and other invisibly delineated worlds that shaped the experiences of Volga-Ural Muslims, or human experience in general.

"Domains," in the context of this book, refer to constructed instruments of social analysis that prioritize exchange relations in identifying human categories. This prioritization does not disregard shared (or presumably shared) qualifiers, such as identity, culture, or religion, but evaluates the nature and functions of those qualifiers as they shape and are shaped by exchange relations.[23] Like Pierre Bourdieu's idea of "fields," a "domain" would best be understood as an "open concept" that is recognizable yet malleable, that is defined by the interaction of its particulars rather than defining its particulars, and that can be redefined to reflect changes in its particulars.[24] Domains designate "metatopical common spaces," as articulated by Charles Taylor, transcending topical – i.e. physical – spaces and assembling people into a recognizable universe through a sustained experience of exchange and sharing.[25] This exchange and sharing can relate to a locale, such as a region or trans-regional area, in one way or another and that locale can even impact the nature of the ongoing exchange, but it is the patterns of exchange that define the emerging universe, not the locale. For the existence of a domain, this experience of sharing and exchange has to attain sufficient intensity to offer a shared cultural frame and comfort zone to its participants, although the comfort level of each participant can vary significantly. The participants of a domain sacrifice the familiarity of this comfort zone

[23] For an exploration of the potentials of the concept of "exchange" in analyzing imperial and inter-imperial contexts, see Stephen Kotkin, "Mongol Commonwealth? Exchange and Governance across the Post-Mongol Space," *Kritika: Explorations in Russian and Eurasian History*, 2007 8(3): 487–531.

[24] For Bourdieu's definition of "fields" as "open concepts," see Pierre Bourdieu and Loïc J. D. Wacquant, *An Invitation to Reflexive Sociology* (Chicago: The University of Chicago Press, 1992), 94–115; and David Schwarz, *Culture & Power: The Sociology of Pierre Bourdieu* (Chicago: The University of Chicago Press, 1997), 118–19.

[25] Charles Taylor, "Modernity and the Rise of the Public Sphere," in *The Tanner Lectures on Human Values, vol. 14*, ed. Grethe B. Peterson (Salt Lake City: University of Utah Press, 1993), especially 229; and Charles Taylor, *Modern Social Imaginaries* (Durham: Duke University Press, 2004), 86.

when they leave their domain to interact in a different one, even if they are already informed about the new domain's cultural frame.

Although Taylor offers the concept of "metatopical common space" as a way to build on Habermas' idea of "public sphere," which itself has proven fruitful in the historiography of the Russian empire,[26] the usage of "domains" as a conceptual tool in this book should not be confused with the "public sphere." The "public sphere," as outlined by Habermas, is an institution of democratic nation states, or at the minimum, an institution that emerges in the process of the formation of democratic nation states.[27] One can think of "reading publics" in the Russian empire or imagine its Russian-speaking, educated elites – the "*obshchestvo*" – analogous to Habermas' public sphere. But the study of multiple layers of human interaction, particularly in an imperial situation involving several linguistic and confessional population groups, unequal estates, and multiple co-existing legal systems, requires a more sophisticated model of analysis.

Some aspects of the concept of "domains" that may contribute to the construction of such a model include the following:

(1) Domains, as open concepts, can intermingle, encompass smaller domains, or be subsumed in larger domains. A person can simultaneously interact in more than one domain with varying levels of comfort in each.

(2) The formation and existence of domains are not dependent on a certain type of exchange that we may recognize as "modern," such as the print media or the internet, although changes in the modes of exchange would affect the nature of a domain.

(3) Domains function in "higher time," merging multiple time frames, as opposed to in "profane time," here and now.[28] Therefore, the

---

[26] For some excellent works that explore the concept of "public sphere" in the history of the Russian empire, see Daniel R. Brower, *The Russian City between Tradition and Modernity, 1850–1900* (Berkeley: University of California Press, 1990); Louise McReynolds, *The News under Russia's Old Regime: The Development of a Mass-Circulation Press* (Princeton, NJ: Princeton University Press, 1991); Douglas Smith, "Freemasonry and the Public in Eighteenth Century Russia," in *Imperial Russia: New Histories for the Empire* ed. Jane Burbank and David L. Ransel (Bloomington: Indiana University Press, 1998), 281–304; and Jane Burbank, *Russian Peasants Go to Court: Legal Culture in the Countryside, 1905–1917* (Bloomington: Indiana University Press, 2004), 147–53, and especially 265–67.

[27] In addition to Jürgen Habermas, *The Structural Transformation of the Public Sphere: An Inquiry into a Category of Bourgeois Society*, trans. Thomas Bürger and Frederick Lawrence (Cambridge: Polity Press, 1992); see Nancy Fraser, "Transnationalizing the Public Sphere: On the Legitimacy and Efficacy of Public Opinion in a Post-Westphalian World," *Theory, Culture, and Society*, 2007 24(4): 7–30.

[28] For a discussion of these concepts, see Charles Taylor, *A Secular Age* (Cambridge, MA: The Belknap Press of Harvard University Press, 2007), 54–59 and 192–196.

transmission of ideas and values across many generations can be a defining aspect of a domain.

(4) Secularity is not essential to the existence of domains. They can, although do not have to, take shape around religion, defined as "discursive tradition" following Talal Asad's example, and therefore build on connections in higher time.[29]

In *Imperial Russia's Muslims*, I have identified the following four domains as: (1) the transregional Muslim domain; (2) the Volga-Ural Muslim domain; (3) the Russian imperial domain; and (4) the pan-European domain. The transregional Muslim domain refers to the wide cultural exchange system that connected Volga-Ural Muslims to other Muslims in other parts of the world, especially in Transoxiana, the Caucasus, the Crimea, and the Ottoman lands. The Volga-Ural Muslim domain indicates the more localized patterns of exchange and sharing among Volga-Ural Muslims as subjects of the Russian empire, but with references in higher time to an earlier history including the Golden Horde of the thirteenth and fourteenth centuries and extending as far back as the Bulghar Khanate in the Middle Volga Basin, which officially adopted Islam in the tenth century. The Russian imperial domain refers to the totality of exchange that took place among subjects of the Russian empire. Subject-state relations were an aspect of this exchange and took place predominantly through the mediation of imperial elites and local intermediaries. We should also note that the Russian imperial domain transformed significantly in the last decades of the tsarist regime, as more inclusive channels of contact and communication opened between both the Russian state and its subjects and among the empire's subjects themselves. The Russian imperial domain hosted an ethnic Russian domain – or potentially domains – too. While examining the tsarist empire's ethnic Russian communities remains beyond the scope of this study, we will pay close attention to the Russian educated elites who occupied a space between those communities and the imperial domain,[30]

---

[29] Talal Asad, *The Idea of an Anthropology of Islam* (Washington, DC: Georgetown University Center for Contemporary Arab Studies, 1986).

[30] Wayne Dowler, *Russia in 1913* (DeKalb: Northern Illinois Press, 2010), 90–189 provides an up-to-date study of the Russian educated elites and their relations with the tsarist state. The ability of these elites to represent the broader ethnic Russian population and to lead them into nationhood has been the subject of an ongoing debate. Geoffrey Hosking considers ethnic Russian nationalism a failed cause primarily due to the burden of maintaining a multi-national empire. Nathaniel Knight adds the alienation of Russian intellectuals from the Russian "nation" as another factor in this failure. Alexei Miller, on the other hand, suggests that ethnic Russian nationalism could coexist with the imperial cause and indeed evolved in the direction of building a Russian nationhood in late

for the increasingly nationalistic interventions of these elites guided – and sometimes misguided – government policies toward Muslims, especially after the revolutionary tide of 1905.[31] Finally, the pan-European domain should bring to mind the metatopical common space that became starkly recognizable in the late nineteenth century as ideas, products, technologies, and practices with European origins altered the experiences of the inhabitants of many areas around the world, including the Russian empire, therefore, connecting them "all" (hence the suffix "pan-") to a European sphere of influence. This should not be interpreted as Europe's (or the West's) unilateral impact on the rest but rather, as a recognition of how Europe's gargantuan weight warped the world's otherwise multi-directional vectors of exchange and interaction in the late nineteenth century.

That being said, since a domain is defined by its particulars rather than defining its particulars, the nature of each of these four domains should become clearer to the reader as the content of many chapters reveal those particulars. The above explanations provide advance guidelines to help in identifying the functions of each domain in the narrative but should not be taken as comprehensive definitions.

Chapter outline

Imperial Russia's Muslims is organized into ten chapters that progress thematically while also following a chronological order from the late eighteenth century to the end of the tsarist regime. As they build toward a holistic narrative of "Islam, empire, and European modernity," the gaze of these chapters pans over many agents, from Muslim scholars, peasants, merchants, and intellectuals to tsarist officials and provincial notables, and intently follows their interactions in contexts ranging from personal meetings and markets to official correspondence and the print media. The first chapter introduces the Volga-Ural Muslim domain primarily through the life stories of Islamic scholars who lived among peasants, played a central role in shaping their shared norms and imaginaries, and also connected them to the larger world, especially to the transregional Muslim domain. The second chapter explains how the

---

imperial Russia. See Geoffrey A. Hosking, *Russia: People and Empire, 1552–1917* (Cambridge, MA: Harvard University Press, 1997); Nathaniel Knight, "Was the Intelligentsia Part of the Nation? Visions of Society in Post-Emancipation Russia", *Kritika*, 2006 7(4): 733–58; Alexei Miller, *The Romanov Empire and Nationalism* (Budapest: Central European University, 2008), especially 161–79.

[31] For a comprehensive study of the attitudes of Russian state agents toward Muslims, see Campbell, *Muslim Question.*

Volga-Ural Muslim domain was embedded in the Russian empire and how the tsarist state's use of Islamic scholars as intermediaries to access and manage Muslim communities, especially between the late eighteenth and mid nineteenth centuries, helped Volga-Ural Muslims maintain a mediated distance from the state. The insulated safe space that this mediated distance created for the conduct of intra-Muslim affairs was one of the well-functioning aspects of the Catherinian imperial model and helped the accomodation of Volga-Ural Muslims in the Russian empire.

Nonetheless, in the second half of the nineteenth century, as the Russian imperial domain expanded with improvements in transportation and communications and the emancipation of serfs in 1861, the Russian state started to transition to a new imperial model based on unmediated governance. Faced with the challenge of managing an expanding imperial domain, in an environment of inter-imperial competition and rising nationalisms, Russian imperial agents aspired to create ideal subjects for the empire by "enlightening" Russian peasants and "russifying" non-Russians through various schooling projects, which often took shape with the involvement of Orthodox missionaries. The third chapter explains this transition to a new imperial model and presents the background to the tsarist state's initiatives to russify Muslims, primarily through schooling. The fourth chapter describes the responses of Volga-Ural Muslims, especially the peasants among them, to such initiatives between the 1870s and 1890s. While the Muslim peasants' responses varied from resistance – which was more common – to cooperation and functionalization (i.e. using government schools for purposes unintended by their founders), their primary objective remained the preservation of the Volga-Ural Muslim domain's insulated safe space.

However, as the fifth chapter demonstrates, the effects of an expanding pan-European domain, which often revealed itself with economic growth and market integrations, altered the Volga-Ural Muslims' insistence on the preservation of a mediated distance from the tsarist state, or from Russians in general. The sea-change effect of the empire's great and uneven transformations in the late nineteenth century offered new possibilities and brought new challenges to the Volga-Ural Muslims. The sixth chapter turns to the few but influential wealthy Muslims in the region ("*bay*s" in Tatar) who encountered this sea-change firsthand, as they traded in the ethnically and religiously mixed markets of the empire, beyond the comfort zone of insulated Muslim communities. *Imperial Russia's Muslims* presents the entrepreneurship and philanthropy of these wealthy Muslims as two important sources of access to the imperial and pan-European domains for the Volga-Ural Muslims. But it also challenges the more conventional interpretation of their activities as a form of "bourgeois nationalism."[32] In the fifth and sixth chapters, we also observe among Volga-Ural Muslims new attitudes about resistance to Russian influences. While they generally continued to insist on protecting the inviolability of intra-Muslim affairs, some among them started to learn Russian and willingly sent their children to government schools, especially in relatively urbanized areas.

To turn to the emergence and influence of nationalism and other pan-European ideologies among Volga-Ural Muslims, the seventh chapter brings in the Volga-Ural Muslim intelligentsia as a new status group that emerged around the turn of the twentieth century, when European forms of education became more readily available to Volga-Ural Muslims. The Muslim intellectuals constituted a motley group but were loosely united by a secular "idea of progress," which was built on comparative evaluations of the conditions of Muslims in Russia and of Russia among European empires, as such comparisons became possible for increasingly more Volga-Ural Muslims in the late nineteenth century. The progressive Volga-Ural Muslim intellectuals wanted to "enlighten" their coreligionists and help them "progress" in ways inspired by the examples of Europe, the educated Russian elites, and the Ottoman Westernizers. As products of the new modern era, they used print media remarkably effectively, especially after the 1950 Revolution when censorship was abolished. And they invested substantial effort in developing a new system of Muslim education that would constitute an alternative to the traditional and nearly ubiquitous Muslim educational institutions (maktabs and madrasas) where Islamic scholars taught. Yet, as the eighth chapter suggests, the progressive intellectuals eventually marginalized themselves among the broader Muslim population by turning against Islamic scholars as a rival influence on society and censoriously questioning many of the region's Islamic traditions.

The progressive reformist intellectuals were unlikely to be the catalysts of large-scale social mobilization or cultural revival among Volga-Ural Muslims under these circumstances, but their efforts were consequential in other ways. Although they enjoyed little authority among the broader Muslim population, they voiced and pursued aspirations rivaling those of the tsarist officials and Orthodox missionaries. Hence, the ninth chapter demonstrates how an alliance of officials and missionaries followed Muslim affairs from the writings of progressive Muslim intellectuals especially after 1905, confused the intellectuals' aspirations and

---

[32] A representative work for this approach is Salikhov, *Tatarskaia burzhuaziia*.

pursuits with actual mobilization, and attempted to suppress that presumed mobilization with heavy-handed and obscurantist measures in a state of paranoia. This paranoia completed the break from the Catherinian imperial model and created a conspicuous sense of bitterness in the central tsarist state establishment's relations with most of the empire's Muslim subjects. However, the tenth and final chapter zooms out of the tension-ridden binary of these state–subject relations to reveal still existing opportunities of cooperation, which moderated the experiences of Volga-Ural Muslims in the imperial domain, and probes the limits of those opportunities on the eve of the First World War.

1　A world of Muslims

The number of books that I have copied has reached two hundred
twenty three volumes with this one. I started copying books when
I was twenty. Now I have reached the age of ninety-five. I never wore
glasses. I burned burning sticks and wrote. Indeed, something called
"candle" has become available nowadays, but I don't have the money to
buy even one night's supply of candles. I have gotten old now; maybe
I won't have the power to write after this![1]　　　an Islamic scholar from a
village in the Cheliabinsk District, died in 1841

İşmuhammed bin Zâhid was born in 1740 in a Muslim village located
midway between the cities of Orenburg and Kazan. He led a vagrant life
as a young man. His voice was beautiful. He liked to sing, dance, and
drink. He made a name for himself with his singing and dancing at the
drinking parties that he frequented, but he remained an inauspicious
figure – the Volga-Ural Muslims at best tolerated the habitual drinker
and merrymaker that he was.[2] He married around the age of twenty-two,
and one day, shortly after getting married, he walked away from his
village without informing anybody. None could have guessed what
happened to him until he returned as a learned scholar of Islam
twenty-five years later. He had first gone to Mecca and performed the
Hajj. Following this, he had studied in the madrasas of Cairo for eight
years, and then traveled and studied in various other cities of the Ottoman
Empire for several years. Finally, he had decided that it was time to settle
down, and here he was, back in his village. We don't know what happened

[1] Rızâeddin bin Fahreddin, Âsar: Üz Memleketimizde Ulgan İslâm 'Âlimleriniñ Tercüme ve
Tabaqaları, 2 vols. (Kazan: Tipo-litografiia imperatorskogo universiteta, 1900–8), vol. 1,
456.
[2] On the attitudes of Volga-Ural Muslims about drinking, see National Archive of the
Republic of Tatarstan (NART), f. 1, op. 3, d. 7797, ll. 1–6; Fahreddin, Âsar, vol. 1,
233 and 376–77 and vol. 2, 200–01, 337–38, 357–58, and 384–86, Sbornik tsirkuliarov i
inykh rukovodiashikh rasporiazhenii po okrugu Orenburgskogo Magometanskogo dukhovnogo
sobraniia 1841–1901 g., Russian-language part ed. (Ufa, 1902), 95–97, and Ğabdürreşîd
İbrâhîmof, Tercüme-yi Hâlim yaki Başıma Kilenler (St. Petersburg: Elektro-pechati A. O.
Ibragimova), 3.

to his first wife. He married a second time after his return and had several children. He earned his living by reciting the Qur'an in religious gatherings and by teaching. He became famous in the Volga-Ural region as an accomplished Islamic scholar and reciter. All of his four sons became scholars following their father's example, and his daughters married either scholars or notable persons. He died in 1840 at the age of one hundred.[3]

İşmuhammed bin Zâhid's remarkable transformation while away from his village catapulted him from the Volga-Ural Muslims' boundaries of tolerance to a model, ideal figure: an Islamic scholar. When he left for Mecca, he traveled away from the physical space where his community was located, but he moved closer to the center of an extra-spatial medium of exchange, a Muslim domain, where Muslims connected to one another across time and space and negotiated their shared norms and imaginaries. Islamic scholars had a central role in this exchange as its primary negotiators thanks to their skills and privileges in transmitting, interpreting, and authorizing the Islamic traditions and their ability to connect otherwise insulated Muslim communities to other Muslims in distant locations.

The ability of Islamic scholars to connect to a broader Muslim universe had a critical significance for the Volga-Ural Muslims due to the absence or paucity of other agents who could have shared in this role. The Volga-Ural Muslims were the subjects of an Orthodox Christian-ruled empire, their nobility was incapacitated by the Russian occupation, and they had very few big merchants until the late nineteenth century. They predominantly lived in the countryside as agricultural peasants or seasonal nomads until the collectivization campaigns of the early Soviet period,[4] and they rarely ventured beyond the surrounding area of their villages or market towns.[5] Islamic scholars, on the other hand, traveled extensively, especially during their years of education as

[3] Fahreddin, *Âsar*, vol. 1, 448–53.
[4] See the statistics in Henning Bauer, Andreas Kappeler, and Brigitte Roth, *Die Nationalitäten des Russischen Reiches in der Volkszählung von 1897*, vol. 1 (Stuttgart: F. Steiner, 1991), Table 1, pp. 69–72, Table 6, pp. 77–78, and Table 40, pp. 214–230; and Noack, *Muslimischer*, 49–54.
[5] A few possible exceptions to this rule were Hajj trips for a select group of Muslims who could afford it, occasional visits to shrines, marrying men from distant places and moving to their communities for some women, and military service for a very small number of male Muslims although most of the conscripts never returned due to the long duration of service. See Battal-Taymas, *Kazan Türkleri*, 69; Allen J. Frank, "Islamic Shrine Catalogues and Communal Geography in The Volga-Ural Region: 1788–1917," *Journal of Islamic Studies*, 1996 7(2): 265–86; and Kefeli-Clay, "Kräshen Apostasy", 206–29.

madrasa students. Mobility and the long years of camaraderie in madrasa hostels enabled them to forge lasting connections with each other. They weaved these connections into scholarly networks through kinship ties, letters, Sufi associations, and debates over the controversial issues of religion. And they tapped into a broader, transregional network of Islamic scholars that extended primarily to Transoxiana but also to Daghestan, Afghanistan, India, and, increasingly in the late nineteenth century, to the Ottoman territories and Egypt. It was mainly the Islamic scholars who reached beyond local Muslim communities in the Volga-Ural region, and the extent of their reach played a decisive role in shaping the way Volga-Ural Muslims interpreted and responded to the larger world until the Soviet regime liquidated Islamic scholars in the 1930s.[6] Hence, tracing the stories of these scholars can open windows into the experience and imaginaries of Volga-Ural Muslims, and thankfully, we have a number of biographical dictionaries, *ṭabaqāt* books as they are commonly known in the Islamic literature, that provide us those stories.[7]

A remarkably comprehensive biographical dictionary written in the Volga-Ural region is the work of Rızâeddin bin Fahreddin.[8] With a profound interest in history, Fahreddin had organized the archive and library of the Orenburg Spiritual Assembly while working there as a high-ranking official (*qadi*) in the 1890s. The works and official records of thousands of scholars that had accumulated at the building of this institution in Ufa since its foundation in the late eighteenth century provided Fahreddin with the initial material he needed to start working on a biographical dictionary. In 1900, he prepared a short fascicule with thirty entries and published it under the title *Âsar*, meaning "traces." Shortly after this fascicule appeared in the bookstores and market stalls of the Volga-Ural region, he started receiving letters from Muslims in various parts of the Russian empire with further information and documents about other scholars to be included in the following fascicules of

---

[6] On the "ulama," see *Encyclopedia of Islam*, New Edition, s.v. "ulama"; R. Stephen Humphreys, *Islamic History: A Framework for Inquiry* (Princeton, NJ: Princeton University Press, 1991), 187–88; Frank, *Islamic Historiography*, 21–46; and Frank, *Muslim Religious Institutions*, 106–50.

[7] On a general discussion of biographical dictionaries in Islamic historiography, see Humphreys, *Islamic History*, 186–208. On a short note about biographical dictionaries written in the Volga-Ural region, see, Allen J. Frank and Mirkasyim A. Usmanov eds., *An Islamic Biographical Dictionary of the Eastern Kazakh Steppe, 1770–1912* (Boston: Brill, 2005), xviii–xx.

[8] On the assembly, see Alan W. Fisher, "Enlightened Despotism and Islam under Catherine II," *Slavic Review*, 1968 (4): 542–53; Azamatov, *Orenburgskoe*; and Crews, *For Prophet*. Later, in the Soviet period, Fahreddin would serve as the head (*mufti*) of this assembly too.

the dictionary. As a result, what started as Fahreddin's personal project turned into a collective effort among Volga-Ural Muslims to document the lives of their past scholars and, occasionally, a few prominent lay persons. Fahreddin painstakingly compiled and published his fascicules for eight years. He organized the entries according to the death dates of the scholars. By 1908, he had published 565 entries and reached the 1870s. Many of his entries included copies of personal letters, notes, or legal opinions (*fatwas*) written by various scholars, in addition to biographical information about their genealogies, marriages, children, teachers, students, and places of study or residence.[9] What follows in this chapter is an outline of some of the central exchange relations that shaped the Volga-Ural Muslims' world from the mid eighteenth to the late nineteenth centuries as those relations emerge primarily from this extraordinary compilation of biographies. It cannot do justice to the individual experiences of millions of Muslims who lived and died in that world, but it provides a look, albeit a telescopic one, into the contours of their collective experience.[10]

The geography of studying

As among most other Muslim peoples, Muslims of the Volga-Ural region had a widespread system of elementary religious education. Mosque imams, or "*mullahs*" in Volga-Ural Turkic, taught the boys in their neighborhood while their wives taught the girls. If the children were young enough, either the mullah or his wife could teach both sexes too. Sometimes, the parents constructed a separate building for instruction, but in many cases, the mosque or the mullah's house served that purpose. Almost all Muslim children studied subjects such as the basics of Islam and Qur'anic recitation for a few years in these classes known as

---

[9] Liliia Baibulatova, *Asar Rizy Fakhreddina: istochnikovaia osnova i znachenie svoda* (Kazan: Tatar. kn. izd-vo, 2006) is a useful introduction to *Âsar*. 260 more biographical entries that Rızâeddin bin Fahreddin wrote after 1908 remained unpublished. The manuscripts of these entries are preserved at the Scientific Archive of the Ufa Scientific Center of the Russian Academy of Sciences in Ufa. An earlier biographical dictionary by Şihâbuddin Mercânî is also worth mentioning here: Şehabeddin Mercani, *Müstefad'ül-Ahbar Fi Ahval-i Kazan ve Bulgar*, 2 vols. (1900; reprint Ankara: Türk Kültürünü Araştırma Enstitüsü Yayınları, 1997). However, I relied primarily on *Âsar* because of the collective effort involved in its production and because Fahreddin had partly incorporated *Mustafād al-akhbār* in *Âsar*.

[10] My purpose in this chapter is to outline exchange relations and not to provide an ethnographic description of the world of the Volga-Ural Muslims. Two helpful sources for more ethnographic insight are Frank, *Muslim Religious Institutions*; and Kefeli-Clay, "Kräshen Apostasy", especially 93–234. For major issues of debate among the region's Islamic scholars, see Kemper, *Sufis und Gelehrte*.

maktabs. Then, a small number of male students who wanted to acquire a degree of knowledge that would entitle them to be recognized as scholars continued their studies in higher educational institutions, called madrasas, for approximately fifteen to twenty years.[11]

Madrasas of the Volga-Ural region were often small, poor, and short-lived. In Muslim-ruled countries, such as the Ottoman Empire or the Bukharan Emirate, charitable endowments protected by law, called *waqfs*, provided stable income and organizational continuity to the madrasas.[12] The Russian administration, however, destroyed the Volga-Ural Muslims' waqfs following the invasion of Kazan in 1552.[13] One could still endow the building of a village mosque, a few shops, some land, or even books, but these small endowments were not protected by law, and they did not compare with the large, income-producing waqfs of the Muslim-ruled countries.[14] Only in the nineteenth century did the registering of waqfs officially become possible in the Volga-Ural region and, paralleling the improvements in the Muslim population's economic conditions, only in the last decades of the imperial regime did wealthy Muslims start to create large endowments.[15] Until then, a madrasa in the Volga-Ural region was usually comprised of a scholar who offered regular

---

[11] For a short description of Volga-Ural maktabs and madrasas, see NART, f. 142, op. 1, d. 39. Also see Iakov Dmitrievich Koblov, *Konfessional'nyia shkoly kazanskikh tatar* (Kazan: Tsentral'naia tip., 1916).

[12] On the role of charitable endowments in Muslim-ruled countries, see Jonathan Porter Berkey, *The Transmission of Knowledge in Medieval Cairo: A Social History of Islamic Education* (Princeton: Princeton University Press, 1992), 6–9 and 44–94; Hasan Akgündüz, *Klasik Dönem Osmanlı Medrese Sistemi* (Istanbul: Ulusal Yayınları, 1997), 349–50, 472–74, and 479–92; and Adeeb Khalid, *The Politics of Muslim Cultural Reform: Jadidism in Central Asia* (Berkeley: University of California Press, 1998), 31–32.

[13] For the destruction of Muslim political elites and religious institutions after 1552 and the incorporation of Transoxiana into the Russian empire in the nineteenth century, see Rızâeddin bin Fahreddin, "Millî Matbu'âtımız," *Şûra*, 1908 (10): 324–26, and (17): 525–27; Ravil Emirhan, *İmanga Tugrlık* (Kazan: Tatarstan Kitap Neşriyatı, 1997), 17–26; Frank T. McCarthy, "The Kazan Missionary Congress," *Cahiers du monde russe et soviétique*, 1973 14(3): 311; Michael Khodarkovsky, "'Not by Word Alone': Missionary Policies and Religious Conversion in Early Modern Russia," *Comparative Studies in Society and History*, 1996 38(2): 274–279; Türkoğlu, *Rızaeddin Fahreddin*, 26–30; Frank, *Muslim Religious Institutions*, 165–76; and Khalid, *Jadidism*, 83–84.

[14] For examples of such small endowments, see Fahreddin, *Âsar*, vol. 1, 298–309 and vol. 2, 47–49, 457–59, and 494–95; Noack, *Muslimischer*, 75–76; Frank, *Muslim Religious Institutions*, 232–36; and Liudmila M. Sverdlova, *Kazanskoe kupechestvo: sotsial'no-ekonomicheskii portret* (Kazan: Tatarskoe Knizhnoe Izdatel'stvo, 2011), 276–78.

[15] Daniel D. Azamatov, *Iz istorii musul'manskoi blagotvoritel'nosti: vakufy na territorii evropeiskoi chasti Rossii i Sibiri v kontse XIX – nachale XX veka* (Ufa: Bashkir University, 2000), 4–24; and Daniel D. Azamatov, "Waqfs in the European Part of Russia and Siberia in the Beginning of the XXth Century," in *Islamic Civilisation in the Volga-Ural Region*, ed. Ali Çaksu and Rafik Muhammetshin (Istanbul: Organisation of the Islamic Conference, 2004), 257–60.

instruction at the madrasa level and, perhaps, some boarding arrangements for the students. Only rarely did the continuing support of a village congregation or wealthy family provide some sort of organizational continuity to the Volga-Ural madrasas.[16]

Madrasas of the Volga-Ural region followed a curriculum that was commonly used by the scholars of the Hanafi legal school.[17] While the institutionalized madrasas in Muslim-ruled countries could employ several instructors and offer advanced courses for the entire Hanafi curriculum, or at least for a majority of its subjects, most of the madrasas in the Volga-Ural region had only one instructor. No matter how erudite this single scholar was, it was practically impossible for him to provide training in all fields of Islamic scholarship. Each scholar specialized in teaching one or a few subjects and, sometimes, just a single book.[18] Some scholars did not hold classes at all. They assigned books to their students, the students read these books on their own or with other students, and the scholar reviewed the progress of each student on the assigned book from time to time.[19] An ambitious student who wanted to excel in one of the fields not offered at the advanced level at his current madrasa would have to find the specialist of that field and move on to *his* madrasa.

The need to seek different instructors in order to cover all fields of study required students to move from one madrasa to another as they advanced in their studies. Cârullah bin Bikmuhammed (1796–1869), for instance, changed locations seven times before he finished studying and found a job as a village mullah.[20] Sometimes, a student could finish his studies without changing madrasas so frequently, especially if he entered the madrasa of a relatively more knowledgeable scholar early in his

---

[16] For helpful descriptions of Volga-Ural madrasas, see NART, f. 92, op. 1, d. 10464, ll. 16–22 and İbrâhîmof, *Tercüme-yi Hâlim*, 4–15. For the makeshift nature of Muslim educational institutions in the Volga-Ural region, see NART, f. 92, op. 1, d. 10464, ll. 4–9, 16–22, and 51–59 and NART, f. 322, o. 1, d. 46. For two examples of scholars opening their madrasas see Fahreddin, *Âsar*, vol. 1, 330–31 and vol. 2, 72–74. On three major villages with a tradition of scholarship, see Muhammed Şakir Mahdum Tuqayef, *Tarih-i İsterlibaş* (Kazan: B. L. Dombrovskogo Tipografiyası, 1899); Zäki Zäynullin, "Ästärlebaş Mädräsäse," in *Mädräsälärdä Kitap Kiştäse*, ed. Röstäm Mähdiev (Kazan: Tatarstan Kitap Näşriyatı, 1992), 175–85; Mutahhir ibn Mulla Mir Haydar, *İski Qışqı Tarihi* (Orenburg: Din ve Ma'îşet Matbaası, 1911), 17–21 and 41–42; Gasim Lotfi, "Kışkar Mädräsäse," in *Mädräsälärdä Kitap Kiştäse*, ed. Röstäm Mähdiyäv (Kazan: Tatarstan Kitap Näşriyatı, 1992), 150–71; and İbrâhîmof, *Tercüme-yi Hâlim*, 11–15.

[17] Muhammed Kemal Muzafferof, "Bizde Şâkirdler Sabırlılar," *Şûra*, 1912 (18): 568–69; Kemper, *Sufis und Gelehrte*, 215–17; and Frank, *Muslim Religious Institutions*, 243–46.

[18] For examples of scholars specializing in the instruction of specific texts or topics, see Fahreddin, *Âsar*, vol. 1, 272–75 and vol. 2, 41–42, 313, 400–02. İsterlibaş Madrasa provided comprehensive instruction in the Hanafi curriculum, but this was one of the exceptions that proved the rule. See Tuqayef, *Tarih-i İsterlibaş*, 10–11.

[19] İbrâhîmof, *Tercüme-yi Hâlim*, 11–15.   [20] Fahreddin, *Âsar*, vol. 2, 488–89.

educational career. Rızâeddin bin Fahreddin, for instance, never switched madrasas,[21] but in general, students traveled as they studied. While most of them circulated among Volga-Ural madrasas, a small group of students who could afford long-distance travel went to major centers of Islamic scholarship outside of the Russian empire too.

The Bukharan Emirate in Transoxiana was the most familiar and preferred destination for students from the Volga-Ural region until the late nineteenth century. They went to other Transoxianian cities like Samarqand and Khiva too, but Bukhara was a more prominent and revered center of scholarship, and Russia's Muslims used its name to refer to the Transoxianian scholarly traditions in general.[22] The descendants of a seventeenth-century scholar, Yûnus bin İvanay (b. 1636), claimed that their ancestor was the first scholar from the Volga-Ural region who had studied in Bukhara. Since the Russian invasions following the fall of Kazan in 1552 seem to have interrupted the transmission of knowledge among the Volga-Ural ulama, it is possible for scholars like Yûnus bin İvanay to have revived Islamic scholarship in the region after an interlude, and the madrasas, libraries, and traditions of Bukhara are likely to have guided them in this restoration.[23]

Yet, going to Bukhara was a demanding enterprise. One had to cross the Qizilqum Desert. Every year, merchants organized caravans between Bukhara and major cities in eastern Russia, such as Petropavl, Troitsk, and Orenburg. Nizhny Novgorod's large trade fair, located about 250 miles to the east of Moscow, was also connected to Bukhara through caravans.[24] Students from the Volga-Ural region had to wait for the travel season and join a caravan in order to go to Bukhara or return from it. The journey from Orenburg to Bukhara took one to two months. Therefore, depending on where a student started his journey, he would have to travel up to several months in order to reach Bukhara. This was an expensive trip. One had to save money for the road and the expenses

---

[21] Türkoğlu, *Rızaeddin Fahreddin*, 26–30. Also see Fahreddin, *Âsar*, vol. 2, 229–30.

[22] Frank, *Bukhara*, especially 27–75.

[23] Fahreddin, *Âsar*, vol. 1, 38–40 and vol. 2, 479–81. For other examples of the scholars who studied in Bukhara, see Fahreddin, *Âsar*, vol. 1, 32, 38–40, 44, 249, 250, 258–60, 272, 414–15, 458–69, and 471–72 and vol. 2, 7, 105, 114–15, 120, 162–63, 177–79, 192, 203, 209–10, 216–17, 218–20, 236, 239–40, 248–49, 254–56, 258–59, 265–66, 290, 312, 326, 333–35, 393, 397, 402–4, 443, 450, and 461.

[24] On Bukharan merchants at the Nizhny Novgorod Fair, see "Mekerye Bazarından Mektub," *Tercüman*, 25 August 1883. For trade between Transoxiana and Russian towns in general, see Ahmed Zeki Velidi Togan, *Bugünkü Türkili: Türkistan ve Yakın Tarihi* (Istanbul: Arkadaş, Ibrahim Horoz ve Güven Basımevleri, 1942), 212–13 and Audrey Burton, *Bukharan Trade, 1558–1718* (Bloomington: Indiana University, Research Institute for Inner Asian Studies, 1993), 6–8 and 66–85.

in Bukhara or else find support from a benefactor. Many of the scholars who studied in Bukhara initially worked as village mullahs and saved some money before they could take the long journey.[25]

Once in Bukhara, students needed to find connections and settle in one of the madrasas of this town. Many of them earned their livelihood by working at ad hoc jobs as they studied. Additionally, local rulers and notables offered scholarships and charity money, and from the late eighteenth century on, the cells that students could rent or purchase in Bukharan madrasas entitled them to a share of the institution's *waqf* income.[26] Yet, finding a cell was not easy, even if one had the money to rent or purchase it. Typically, students who traveled to Bukhara from Russia would first need to find an acquaintance who had come earlier. This acquaintance would then help them locate a cell and join the classes of a madrasa instructor.[27]

Since Islamic scholarship in the Volga-Ural region was modeled after Bukharan scholarship, education in the madrasas of Bukhara was not too different from that of the Volga-Ural madrasas. The books used in Islamic education were predominantly in Arabic, both in Russia and in Transoxiana, and the Turkic dialects spoken in both places were mutually intelligible to their speakers although not identical. Students in Transoxiana had to familiarize themselves with Persian too since this was the predominant language in the urban centers of the region. Some madrasa instructors gave regular lectures, that is, one of the students read from a book, and the instructor commented as he deemed necessary or supervised a discussion of the topic by the students. Other instructors did not give lectures but only assigned books to the students and coached them as they read through those books. Students progressed at their own pace. Attendance was not required, and students could attend the lectures of any instructor who accepted them to his class, often in return for a small gift.[28]

However, Bukhara also offered opportunities that were not available in the Volga-Ural region such as the agglomeration of several madrasas and instructors in a single city and the availability of a large collection of

---

[25] For a detailed account of the Volga-Ural Muslims' relations with Bukhara, see Frank, *Bukhara*, 95–150. For examples of individual scholars traveling to Bukhara, see Fahreddin, *Âsar*, vol. 1, 453–56 and vol. 2, 497–502; Rızâeddin bin Fahreddin ed. *İsmâ'îl Seyahati* (Kazan: Tipo-Litografiia İ. N. Kharitonova, 1903), 7; and İbrâhîmof, *Tercüme-yi Hâlim*, v. The Transcaspian railway, constructed in the 1880s, shortened the travel time to Bukhara from Russia, but it was mainly used for state purposes. See Seymour Becker, *Russia's Protectorates in Central Asia: Bukhara and Khiva, 1865–1924* (Cambridge, MA: Harvard University Press, 1968), 125–28 and 188–91.

[26] Khalid, *Jadidism*, 31–32, and Sadriddin Aini, *Pages From My Own Story* (Moscow: Foreign Languages Pub. House, 1958), 29–66.

[27] Fahreddin, *Âsar*, vol. 1, 453–55. [28] Khalid, *Jadidism*, 29–31, and Aini, *Pages*, 12.

books in the libraries, private collections, and markets of the emirate for reading, copying, and purchasing. The gathering of several instructors and a high number of students in the same location created an environment of scholarship that encouraged the students to study intensively and also allowed them to follow the lectures of different instructors without having to move from one place to another. The availability of a variety of books was also crucial for the scholarly development of a student at a time when copying by hand was the only way to reproduce books. Obtaining books attracted both students and older scholars to Bukhara.[29] Books printed in Egyptian and Ottoman print houses as well as in Kazan and St. Petersburg became increasingly more available in the Russian empire throughout the nineteenth century and changed the intellectual range of its Muslims, but copying by hand never lost its scholarly importance.[30]

Afghanistan and India were also within the geographical scope of the Volga-Ural Muslims. A significant number of students either studied in Kabul or spent some time there while studying in Bukhara. It seems that the Sufi circles of Afghanistan, especially the famous Naqshbandi Sheikh Fayḍhan bin Hiḍrkhan of Kabul (d. 1802), attracted Muslims from the Russian empire in the late eighteenth and early nineteenth centuries.[31] The relations between Bukharan and Indian Muslims were crucial in connecting the Islamic scholars of the Volga-Ural region to India. Indian Muslim students came to Bukhara to study, as caravans regularly traveled between India and Transoxiana, and Russian Muslims also organized caravans to trade with India.[32] Some students who went to

---

[29] For the availability of books in Bukhara see Fahreddin, *Âsar*, vol. 1, 453–55 and vol. 2, 457–59. For the scholarly environment of Bukhara, see Munir Yusupov, *Galimdzhan Barudi* (Kazan: Tatarskoe Knizhnoe Izdatel'stvo, 2003), 34–43. For the importance and difficulty of copying and collecting books, see Fahreddin, *Âsar*, vol. 1, 267–68, 279–81, and 394–95 and vol. 2, 255, 64–65, and 443.

[30] Fahreddin, *Âsar*, vol. 1, 303 and vol. 2, 375–78, 440–43, 457–59. On the development of a Muslim print media and the circulation of Ottoman and Egyptian publications in the Volga-Ural region, see Muhamed Kh. Gainullin, *Tatarskaia literatura XIX veka* (Kazan: Tatarskoe Knizhnoe Izdatel'stvo, 1975); Gainullin, *Tatarskaia literatura*, 183–88; A[brar] G. Karimullin, *U istokov tatarskoi knigi: ot nachala do 60-kh godov XIX veka* (Kazan: Tatarskoe Knizhnoe Izdatel'stvo, 1992); Türkoğlu, *Rızaeddin Fahreddin*, 41–42; and R[ezeda] R. Safiullina, *Istoriia knigopechataniia na arabskom iazyke v Rossii i musulman Povolzh'ia.* (Kazan 2003), http://www.tataroved.ru/publication/nacobr/7.

[31] For examples of Volga-Ural Islamic scholars with Sufi connections to Afghanistan, see Fahreddin, *Âsar*, vol. 1, 67, 140, 146–49, 177–79, 183–84, 207–8, 219, 272–75, 317, 327–28, and 471–72 and vol. 2, 203, 344, and 389–92. Also see Kemper, *Sufis und Gelehrte*, 92–97; and Crews, *For Prophet*, 32–33.

[32] İbrâhîmof, *Tercüme-yi Hâlim*, v and Togan, *Bugünkü Türkili*, 110–13 and 223–24. Scott Cameron Levi, *The Indian Diaspora in Central Asia and Its Trade, 1550–1900* (Leiden: Brill, 2002) is an informative work on Indian merchants in Transoxiana.

Bukhara from the Russian empire in order to study continued on to India mostly to seek Sufi guidance or to travel further to Hijaz via the sea.[33] The number of students from the Volga-Ural region that are recorded in *Âsar* as having studied in India is low.[34] But even though a small number of Islamic scholars from the Volga-Ural region seem to have maintained direct contact with India in the nineteenth century, the influence of Indian Muslims on the Muslims of the Volga-Ural region can hardly be exaggerated, considering the prominent role of the Indian-origin Mujaddidi branch of the Naqshbandi Sufi order in the Volga-Ural region.[35]

Daghestan was another well-known center of scholarship for Islamic scholars from the Volga-Ural region. At least one Daghestani scholar, Muhammed bin 'Ali el-Daghestani (d. 1795), settled in Orenburg in the early nineteenth century and taught in what Fahreddin calls the "Daghestani way."[36] Fahreddin also records five Volga-Ural scholars who had traveled to Daghestan in the early nineteenth century to study. Interestingly, four of them continued further after Daghestan to the Ottoman territories.[37] The Daghestani scholar Nadhīr al-Durgilī (1891–1935) mentions three more scholars from the Volga-Ural region in his biographical dictionary of Daghestan, and he explains that students from the Volga-Ural region went to Daghestan especially to improve their Arabic-language skills.[38] Finally, the Russian state exiled a number of Daghestani Sufi *sheikh*s to the Volga-Ural region in the late nineteenth century, which also fostered connections between the Islamic scholars of the Volga-Ural region and Daghestan.[39]

The Ottoman territories were also a part of the Volga-Ural Muslims' geographical imagination. Hijaz was definitely their most important destination in the Ottoman Empire. Muslims from all over the world, including Russia, went to Hijaz in the Arabian Peninsula to perform the Hajj in Mecca and visit the tomb of the Prophet Muhammad in

---

[33] Fahreddin, *Âsar*, vol. 1, 178–79, and 272–75 and vol. 2, 267–79, 393–95, and 487; İbrâhîmof, *Tercüme-yi Hâlim*, 68–69; and Togan, *Bugünkü Türkili*, 223–24.

[34] Fahreddin, *Âsar*, vol. 1, 178–79, and 272–75 and vol. 2, 267–79, 393–95, and 487. This might partly be due to the weakening of trade relations between India and Transoxiana after the conquest of Transoxiana by the Russian empire. See Levi, *Indian Diaspora*, 223–60.

[35] See Kemper, *Sufis und Gelehrte*, 81–212.   [36] Fahreddin, *Âsar*, vol. 1, 66–68.

[37] Fahreddin, *Âsar*, vol. 1, 226, 231–33, 238–40, 337–38, and 412.

[38] Michael Kemper, *Muslim Culture in Russia and Central Asia. Vol. 4, Die Islamgelehrten Daghestans und ihre arabischen Weke* (Berlin: Schwarz, 2004), 34–35.

[39] Frank, *Muslim Religious Institutions*, 156–57 and Michael Kemper, "Dahestani Shaykhs and Scholars in Russian Exile: Networks of Sufism, Fatwas and Poetry," in *Daghestan and the World of Islam*, ed. Moshe Gammer and David J. Wasserstein (Helsinki: Academia Scientiarum Fennica, 2006), 95–107.

Medina.[40] Many scholars whose biographies are recorded in Fahreddin's *Âsar* also took this journey.[41] However, before at least the second half of the nineteenth century the Hajj journey or going to the Ottoman territories to study were even more arduous and expensive enterprises than traveling to Bukhara. As scholars and lay Muslims who performed the Hajj related their experience back in Russia, Ottoman madrasas entered within the range of options for Muslim students from the Volga-Ural region, but few students actually traveled there to study until the late nineteenth century.

By the late 1800s, steamboats carrying passengers between the Russian port cities and Istanbul or even Jeddah made traveling to the Ottoman territories significantly easier for Russia's Muslims. This increased the number of students and Hajj travelers from the Volga-Ural region who traveled to the Ottoman Empire so much that special hostels were opened for them in Istanbul, Mecca, and Medina. While going to Medina in 1879, as a young and poor student, Ğabdurreşîd İbrâhîm (1857–1944), who would later become a prominent political activist among Russia's Muslims, stayed in one of these hostels for about fifty days. He did not have to pay for his room. The caretaker of the hostel, Muhammed Efendi from Kazan, even provided him with food and clothing.[42] When Ğabdurreşîd İbrâhîm arrived in Medina, there were four hostels for Russian Muslims in the city, and İbrâhîm wrote that there were hostels located in Mecca as well. The hostels in Medina filled during the Hajj season, but when the Hajj travelers left, only four married Russian Muslims and fourteen single students, including Ğabdurreşîd İbrâhîm, remained behind.[43]

---

[40] See Daniel Brower, "Russian Roads to Mecca," *Slavic Review*, 1996 55(3): 567–84; and Alexandre Papas, Thomas Welsford, and Thierry Zarcone eds., *Central Asian Pilgrims: Hajj Routes and Pious Visits between Central Asia and Hijaz* (Berlin: Klaus Schwarz Verlag, 2012); especially Norihiro Naganawa, "The Hajj Making Geopolitics, Empire and Local Politics: A View from the Volga Ural Region at the Turn of the Nineteenth and Twentieth Centuries," in *Central Asian Pilgrims: Hajj Routes and Pious Visits between Central Asia and Hijaz*, ed. Alexandre Papas, Thomas Welsford, and Thierry Zarcone (Berlin: Klaus Schwarz Verlag, 2012), 168–98.

[41] For some examples, see Fahreddin, *Âsar*, vol. 1, 26, 31, 33–36, 38–40, 89, 150, 200–1, 213–14, 297, 299, 334–35, and 414–15 and vol. 2, 119–20, 143–44, 175–76, 179, 218–19, 222, 239–40, 252, 254, 326, 344, 393–95, 397, 399–400, 404–5, 410–12, and 461.

[42] İbrâhîmof, *Tercüme-yi Hâlim*, 56–59. While Ğabdurreşîd İbrâhîm stayed in this *tekke*, a wealthy businessman from Kazan, İshaq Hacı Apanayef, came to Istanbul and bought another building to endow as a hostel for Russian Muslims. For information about another *tekke* purchased in Istanbul in 1877 for Russian Muslims, see Fahreddin, *Âsar*, vol. 2, 319–20. About the increase in the number of Hajj travelers from the Russian empire, see Brower, "Russian Roads", 571–73.

[43] İbrâhîmof, *Tercüme-yi Hâlim*, 68–69 and 95. Also see Fahreddin, *Âsar*, vol. 2, 247.

Students coming from the Russian empire could study in a variety
of places in the Ottoman territories. One early example, Ğabdulhâlıq bin
Ğabdulkerîm (1771–1844) from the Ufa Gubernia, went to Istanbul in
1798 with the apparent intention of performing the Hajj. He indeed
wanted to perform the Hajj, but his real plan was to study in a Muslim-
ruled country. From Istanbul, he wrote to his relatives that he considered
the options for a long time and decided to go to the famous Hâdim
Madrasa in Konya to study with the city's mufti, Muhammed Emin
Hâdimî. After studying there for six years and also receiving initiation
into the Naqshbandi Sufi order, he went to Mecca to perform the Hajj.
He did not leave Mecca right away but remained there for a while
to study. Following this, he traveled to Medina, Cairo, Jerusalem,
and Damascus, studying with the scholars of these cities too. Finally,
he returned to Ufa in 1808 and opened his own madrasa.[44] The cities
that Ğabdulhâlıq bin Ğabdulkerîm visited, as well as some others like
Diyarbakır and Baghdad, in the Ottoman territories, were all common
destinations for Muslim students from the Volga-Ural region.[45]

Ulama as network

Traveling was only one of the ways in which Islamic scholars covered a wide
geography and connected their fellow Muslims to the larger world. Once
students finished studying and settled in particular locations as scholars,
they traveled significantly less, and some of them did not travel at all. But
they still remained connected beyond their local communities through
kinship ties, letters, Sufi associations, and debates over the controversial
issues of religion both within Volga-Ural scholarly networks and beyond,
extending to a broader area that paralleled the students' geographical range
of study.[46] While the mobility of scholars, especially in their student
years, was crucial in determining the scope of their geographic reach, their
participation in scholarly networks gave permanence to their connectivity.

When a madrasa student finished his studies, he would typically start
looking for a position as the mullah of a mosque. Graduates of Bukhara
and other prominent centers of Islamic scholarship often found good jobs
in mosques with wealthy congregations. Those with better qualifications
could open madrasas and start training students in addition to serving

[44] Fahreddin, *Âsar*, vol. 2, 96–102.
[45] For other examples, some of whom are from later dates, see Fahreddin, *Âsar*, vol. 1, 226,
292, 412, 448–53, 455–56, and 476–78 and vol. 2, 96–102, 163–75, 188, 213, 267–79,
389–92, 457–59, and 461.
[46] Crews, *For Prophet*, 105–6 examines some of these connections among the ulama.

as mullahs, and those with the best credentials could even forego the position of mullah and focus on teaching alone.[47] Those who left their education at a relatively early stage could still take up positions as adhan callers.[48] And finally, since the region had more madrasa graduates than needed, especially in the late nineteenth and early twentieth centuries, some students could never find religious positions upon finishing their studies.[49] They would continue their lives as clerks, peasants, merchants, or something else that the possibilities of the region allowed.[50]

Regardless of the position that a madrasa graduate took, the knowledge that he accumulated provided him with a distinctive and respected status in the Muslim community.[51] He became an *'ālim*, or "scholar" as it is often translated, which literally means, in its Arabic origin "one who knows." "Ulama (*'Ulamā'*)" is the plural of "*'ālim*," but it implies more than "scholars" in the plural. It is a collective name for the network that the Islamic scholars constituted – not only at a given time and place, through personal connections, as we shall see below, but also across time and space, through the transmission of knowledge. Thus, by becoming an Islamic scholar, the madrasa graduates would acquire the authority of both the knowledge that they had accumulated and of the "ulama" as an influential and respected segment of the Muslim Ummah.

Several factors forged the aggregate of individual Islamic scholars into a cohesive network in the Russian empire. The mobility of madrasa students helped them meet many other students and scholars. When they switched to a more stable way of life upon finishing their studies, they continued to communicate with some of their acquaintances through occasional visits and letters. For instance, İbrâhîm bin Hocaş (d. 1825) had studied in Daghestan and Anatolia before settling in Bugulma. As a scholar, he continued to communicate with other scholars in these two regions and asked their opinions about controversial issues of religion, such as the performance of night prayers in northern territories where the sun did not set during summer nights.[52] In a society where functional literacy was a rarity, the ability to read and, more importantly, to write was a distinguishing quality. It helped members of the ulama to

---

[47] Most scholars mentioned in *Âsar* opened their own madrasas.

[48] Frank, *Muslim Religious Institutions*, 146–51; and Mir Haydar, *İski Qışqı*, 40–43.

[49] Iakov Dmitrievich Koblov, *O magometanskikh mullakh: religiozno-bytovoi ocherk* (Kazan: Izdatel'stvo Iman, 1907; reprint 1998), 6; and "Mullalıkdan Künil Suvunuvı ve İşbu Haqda Sualler," *Şûra*, 1914 (1): 18–20 and (2): 47.

[50] For examples of a few scholars who *chose* not to take religious positions, see Fahreddin, *Âsar*, vol. 1, 422–24 and vol. 2, 189–90, 204, and 331–32.

[51] İşmuhammed bin Zâhid's story is an illustrative example of how knowledge earned respect and status. Fahreddin, *Âsar*, vol. 1, 448–53.

[52] Fahreddin, *Âsar*, vol. 1, 227.

keep in touch with the wider world, especially with other scholars in distant locations, through letters.[53]

Until the end of the nineteenth century most of these scholars relied on the services of occasional travelers rather than the imperial postal system to convey their letters.[54] It seems that there were enough travelers among Russia's Muslims to enable the emergence of reliable communication patterns as early as the beginnings of the eighteenth century. The letters that a scholar from Kazan, Seyfeddin bin Ebubekir, exchanged during his Hajj journey in 1824 with Ercümend Kirmanî of Ufa are revealing in this respect. According to the arrangement between Seyfeddin and Kirmanî, Kirmanî would move to Kazan and maintain Seyfeddin's madrasa during the latter's Hajj journey. Seyfeddin started his journey from the city of Kazan. When he arrived in Astrakhan, he received a letter from Kirmanî. Seyfeddin did not have an address in Astrakhan, but apparently a contact person in this city received letters and parcels coming from other parts of the Volga-Ural region, and travelers went to this person in order to check if there was anything sent in their name. Seyfeddin responded to Kirmanî's letter from Astrakhan and instructed him to send his next letter to Anapa with other Hajj travelers. It seems that these patterns were so reliable that Seyfeddin could comfortably expect to receive in another city on his route a letter that Kirmanî would give to Hajj travelers from Ufa or Kazan.[55] Similarly, hostels that Volga-Ural Muslims maintained in Istanbul, as well as a few individual Volga-Ural Muslims who resided in this city, facilitated communication for travelers. For instance a certain Muhammed Kerîm from Kazan, who had settled in Istanbul in the 1850s, served as the contact person for the Volga-Ural Muslims who traveled to Istanbul in the 1860s.[56]

Kinship was another factor that contributed to the existence of an ulama network. The sons of scholars often adopted the profession of their fathers.[57] This was such a common practice that the inability of a scholar's son to become a scholar as well or his choice not to become one

[53] For sample letters or information about letters, see Fahreddin, *Âsar*, vol. 1, 34–35, 140, 224–25, 268, and 375–420 and vol. 2, 96–102, 339–43, and 472–78. For an explanation of functional literacy and how it could be separate from the ability to write, see Khalid, *Jadidism*, 24–25.

[54] Toward the end of the nineteenth century, the Russian state permitted Islamic scholars to use the imperial postage system free of charge in their official correspondence. *Sbornik tsirkuliarov*[Russian section], 63.

[55] Fahreddin, *Âsar*, vol. 1, 224–25.   [56] Fahreddin, *Âsar*, vol. 2, 410–12 and 62–69.

[57] For some examples see Fahreddin, *Âsar*, vol. 1, 161–173, 252–55, 262, 297, 427–29, 448–53, 458–69, and 469–70 and vol. 2, 72–74, 108–9, 121, 152, 162–63, 175–76, 203, 205–6, 221–22, 226, 235–36, 310, 312, 334–35, 337–38, 345, 405–7, 431–32, and 478.

would trouble the father.[58] Moreover, many scholars arranged marriages between their daughters and promising students.[59] While these kinship connections did not grow into a caste system and scholarship remained open to all who were willing and able to acquire knowledge, they did create an environment where a scholar was very likely to have other scholars among his relatives. As a result, the familial relations of these scholar relatives simultaneously intensified interactions among the ulama.

Sufism also played a significant role in weaving scholarly networks in the Volga-Ural region. The practice of Sufism, by nature, connects individuals through submission to a sheikh and membership in a brotherhood. Until the utilization of printed and audiovisual mass media in the twentieth century,[60] personal training for initiation into an order and visits thereafter were the essential forms of relations between Sufi sheikhs and their followers.[61] Not all scholars were Sufis, but many were, and they kept traveling to visit their sheikhs. Sufism connected scholars of the same Sufi order (tarīqah) closely to one another as well as to the lay affiliates of that order since lay Muslims could also partake in the Sufi practice.

The Naqshbandi Sufi order had an especially noticeable presence among the scholars of the Volga-Ural region in the nineteenth century. It is difficult to estimate when and how this order entered the region, but Fahreddin records several Volga-Ural scholars as having received initiation into the Mujaddidi branch of the Naqshbandi Sufi order from Fayḍhan bin Hiḍrkhan of Kabul or Sheikh Niyazqul el-Türkmânî of Bukhara (d. 1820) in the late eighteenth and early nineteenth centuries. This, it seems, was key in the evolution of the Volga-Ural region's Sufi networks in the early nineteenth century.[62] Then, a new branch of the

---

[58] Fahreddin, Âsar, vol. 2, 104–7 and 219–20; and "Mullalıkdan Künil", 1913 (20): 622–23.

[59] For examples, see Fahreddin, Âsar, vol. 1, 275, 327–29, and 458–69 and vol. 2, 72–74, 121, 146, 152, 205–6, 312, 337–38, 396, 402, 406, 471.

[60] Carl W. Ernst, "Ideological and Technological Transformations of Contemporary Sufism," in Muslim Networks from Hajj to Hip Hop, ed. Miriam Cooke and Bruce B. Lawrence (Chapel Hill: The University of North Carolina Press, 2005), 191–207.

[61] This was the situation for the many scholars who are recorded to have Sufi connections in Fahreddin's Âsar. Zeki Velidi Togan relates his father's annual visits to his sheikhs too. Zeki Velidi Togan, Hatıralar: Türkistan ve Diğer Müslüman Doğu Türklerinin Milli Varlık ve Kültür Mücadeleleri (Ankara: Türkiye Diyanet Vakfı Yayınları, 1999), 30–31.

[62] For disciples of Niyazqul el-Türkmânî, see Fahreddin, Âsar, vol. 1, 124, 280–91, and 476–78 and vol. 2, 77–93, 108–9, 140–42, 180–81, 250, 264, and 333–34. Especially Devletşah bin Ğadilşah (died in 1812), one of Türkmânî's disciples, became very famous in the Volga-Ural region and initiated many other disciples. See Fahreddin, Âsar, vol. 1, 280–91 and vol. 2, 176–77 and 211–12. For other Russian Muslim scholars who entered

Naqshbandi Sufi order, the Khalidiyya, also entered the region in the second part of the nineteenth century. The first Khalidis came from Daghestan, but it was the disciples of Ahmed Ziyaüddin Gümüşhânevî from Istanbul (1819–99) who really made a significant impact.[63] One of Gümüşhânevî's disciples in particular, Sheikh Zeynullah Rasûlî of Troitsk (1835–1917), gathered a huge following; three thousand of his disciples were reported to have assembled in Troitsk to see him in one event. Fearing the size of his following, imperial authorities exiled Rasûlî to Siberia in 1873. But when he ultimately returned to Troitsk in the 1880s, the number of his disciples grew still higher, and he became one of the most popular Sufi sheikhs in the region.[64]

Finally, debates over controversial religious questions, especially theological problems, also helped coalesce Russia's Islamic scholars – both as allies and opponents. Some issues of controversy were the necessity of

Sufism in Bukhara, see Fahreddin, *Âsar*, vol. 1, 295 and vol. 2, 114, 162–63, 203–4, 266–67, and 326. For disciples of Fayḍhan bin Hiḍrkhan, see Fahreddin, *Âsar*, vol. 1, 67, 140, 177–79, 183–84, 207–8, 219, 272–75, 317, 327–28, and 471–72 and vol. 2, 203, 344, and 389–92. Also see Hamid Algar, "The Naqshbandi Order: A Preliminary Survey of Its History and Significance," *Studia Islamica*, 1976 (44): 123–52; Kemper, *Sufis und Gelehrte*, 82–98; Baxtiyor M. Babadžanov, "On the History of the Naqšbandīya Muğaddidīya in Central Māwaräannahr in the Late 18th and Early 19th Centuries," in *Muslim Culture in Russia and Central Asia from the 18th to the Early 20th Centuries*, ed. Michael Kemper, Anke von Kügelgen, and Dmitriy Yermakov (Berlin: Klaus Schwarz Verlag, 1996), 386–413; Michael Kemper, "The History of Sufism in the Volga-Urals," in *Islamic Civilisation in the Volga-Ural Region*, ed. Ali Çaksu and Rafik Muhammetshin (Istanbul: Organisation of the Islamic Conference, 2004); Azamatov, *Orenburgskoe*, 22; and Khalid, *Jadidism*, 32.

[63] On the Khalidi sub-branch of the Naqshbandi Sufi order in the Ottoman lands, see Butrus Abu-Manneh, "The Naqshbandiyya-Mujaddidiyya in the Ottoman Lands in the Early 19th Century," *Die Welt des Islam*, 1982 22(1): 1–36; and Hür Mahmut Yücer, *Osmanlı Toplumunda Tasavvuf [19. Yüzyıl]* (Istanbul: İnsan Yayınları, 2003), 73 and 853. On Gümüşhânevî, see İrfan Gündüz, *Gümüşhânevî Ahmed Ziyâüddin (ks): Hayatı-Eserleri-Tarîkat Anlayışı ve Hâlidiyye Tarîkatı* (Ankara: Seha Neşriyat, 1984). On Gümüşhânevî's impact in the Volga-Ural region, see Mustafa Kara, "Ahmed Ziyaüddin-i Gümüşhanevî'nin Halifeleri," in *Ahmed Ziyaüddin Gümüşhanevî Sempozyum Bildirileri*, ed. Necdet Yılmaz (İstanbul: Seha Neşriyat, 1992), 121–29; and Frank, *Muslim Religious Institutions*, 152–53.

[64] Hamid Algar, "Shaykh Zaynullah Rasulev: The Last Great Naqshbandi Shaykh of the Volga-Ural Region," in *Muslims in Central Asia*, ed. Jo-Ann Gross (Durham: Duke University Press, 1992), 112–33; İbrahim Maraş, "İdil-Ural Bölgesinin Cedidci Dinî Lideri Zeynullah Rasûlî'nin Hayatı ve Görüşleri," in *Dinî Araştırmalar*, 1998 1(1): 76–92; Azamatov, *Orenburgskoe*, 173–75; and I. R. Nasyrova ed. *Sheikh Zeinulla Rasuli (Rasulev) an-Nakshbandi: izbrannye proizvedeniia* (Ufa, 2001). In addition to being a popular Sufi sheikh, Zeynullah Rasûlî was a strong supporter of educational reform. In addition to the above cited sources, see Zeynullah Rasûlî, *Troyski Gulemasu ve Usûl-i Cedîde* (Orenburg: Kerimof Hüseynof Matba'ası, 1907). For examples of other Sufi sheikhs with a considerable following in the Volga-Ural region, see Fahreddin, *Âsar*, vol. 1, 177–81, 249–50, 280–91, and 335–36 and vol. 2, 180–81, 389–92, and 487; and Frank, *Muslim Religious Institutions*, 153–57.

performing night prayers during the short summer nights, the relation of
God's attributes to God's self, the possibility of considering the Russian
empire as "land of Islam" (*dār al-Islām*), and related to this last question,
the conditions of performing the congregational Friday prayers.[65] Some
scholars, such as Ebunnasr Ğabdunnasîr el-Qursâvî (1776–1812) and
Ğabdurrahîm bin Ğusman Utız İmenî (1754–1835), were so forceful
in their treatment of these issues that whether a scholar supported or
opposed their views came to clarify that scholar's position among
the ulama of the Volga-Ural region.[66] Qursâvî especially, who criticized
the theologians of Bukhara and wrote a number of thought-provoking
treatises, inspired many scholars among Volga-Ural Muslims. His ideas
would have a strong influence on the proponents of renovation in religious thinking in the latter part of the nineteenth century too.[67] Utız
İmenî was also proficient at writing and distributing short but compelling
pamphlets about controversial subjects.[68] Throughout the nineteenth
century many other scholars wrote pamphlets (*risâle*s) on these issues.
Their works circulated in the region mostly in handwritten manuscripts
and helped the members of the ulama to engage in a regional debate.[69]

Conclusion

In his memoirs, Ğabdürreşîd İbrâhîm narrates how in his youth he saw a
camel for the first time while traveling south in the snow-covered Kazakh
Steppe on a moony night and how he was awed thinking that this was a
genie. Then, he comments that had he had access to books with pictures,
he could have recognized the camel.[70] Maps, pictures, photographs, and

---

[65] See Fahreddin, *Âsar*, vol. 1, 261–62, 305–16, 331, and 467 and vol. 2, 72, 193–94, 234,
267–68, and 479–81.

[66] For Ebunnasr Ğabdunnasîr el-Qursâvî see Fahreddin, *Âsar*, vol. 1, 95–130 and for
Ğabdurrahîm bin Ğusman Utız İmenî see Fahreddin, *Âsar*, vol. 1, 300–316. Also see
Michael Kemper, "Entre Boukhara et la Moyenne-Volga: 'Abd an-Naṣīr al-Qursāwī
(1776–1812) en conflit avec les oulémas traditionalistes," *Cahiers du Monde Russe*,
1996 37(1–2): 41–51; and Kemper, *Sufis und Gelehrte*, 172–212 and 225–13.

[67] Some scholars who supported Ebunnasr el-Qursâvî's ideas are recorded in *Âsar* as
follows: Fahreddin, *Âsar*, vol. 1, 290, 469–70, and 476–78 and vol. 2, 75, 105,
146–51, 218, 267–79, 320, 341, 432, 461, and 471. For some of his opponents see
Fahreddin, *Âsar*, vol. 2, 15–16, 72, 234, 393–95, and 407–8. Also see Michael Kemper,
"Šihābaddīn al-Marğānī über Abū n-Naṣr Qūrsāwīs Koflikt mit den Gelehrten
Bucharas," in *Muslim Culture in Russia and Central Asia: Arabic Persian and Turkic
Manuscripts (15th–19th Centuries)*, ed. Anke von Kügelgen, Aširbek Muminov, and
Michael Kemper (Berlin: Klaus Schwarz Verlag, 2000), 353–71.

[68] Fahreddin gives a list of Utız İmenî's supporters: Fahreddin, *Âsar*, vol. 1, 331.

[69] For two very good analyses of these debates, see Kemper, *Sufis und Gelehrte*; and İbrahim
Maraş, *Türk Dünyasında Dinî Yenileşme, 1850–1917* (Istanbul: Ötüken, 2002).

[70] İbrâhîmof, *Tercüme-yi Hâlim*, 35–36.

journalistic descriptions of different phenomena from around the globe became available in mass print to the Volga-Ural Muslims at the turn of the twentieth century, and the popularization of this material continued into the Soviet period. Until then, the region's Muslims imagined the larger world based on the oral traditions of past generations, the narratives of those who traveled and actually saw far-away places, and occasionally, on a limited number of mostly religious texts. Typically, Muslim communities in the Volga-Ural region turned to Islamic scholars for the transmission and interpretation of those narrations and texts. The Islamic scholars were literate, they had the skills and privilege to authorize Islamic traditions, and they were actually connected beyond their local Muslim communities.[71] All of these distinctions located Islamic scholars at the center of an exchange of ideas and influence among Volga-Ural Muslims as well as between the Volga-Ural Muslims and the larger world. From that exchange emerged a transregional Muslim domain: a metaspace belonging primarily to Muslims: a world where Muslims felt familiar and comfortable.

One can find parallels to the above-explained patterns of travel, communication, and interconnectivity among many other Muslim communities, and therefore these patterns indicate the involvement of Volga-Ural Muslims in a characteristically Muslim domain that did not owe its existence to the Russian empire. However, it would still be misleading to assume that the ulama or the Muslim communities of the Volga-Ural region existed in isolation from the Russian state. At least since the late sixteenth century, the mosques in which the Islamic scholars of the Volga-Ural region served as mullahs existed under the jurisdiction of Russian imperial laws or they were destroyed as a result of the decisions of Russian imperial authorities.[72] Imperial authorities did not establish or control Sufi networks, but they still influenced them by measures such as exiling Daghestani Sufi sheikhs to the Volga-Ural region. It was the Russian state that destroyed income-producing *waqfs* in the Volga-Ural region. The steamboats that carried Hajj travelers and students from Russian Black Sea ports to Istanbul and Jeddah belonged to companies that were incorporated according to Russian imperial laws.[73] And finally, aside from

---

[71] Merchants and lay intellectuals would start to rival Islamic scholars in these regards in the late nineteenth century. See Chapters 5–8.

[72] On mosques in the Volga-Ural regions, see Efimii Malov, "O tatarskikh mechetiakh v Rossii," in *Pravoslavnyi sobesednik*, 1867 (3): 285–320 and 1868 (1): 3–45; and Frank, *Muslim Religious Institutions*, 163–83.

[73] See "Russian Steamship Transportation and Trade Company," *Tercüman/Perevodchik*, 25 January 1902 and 20 December 1902; "Hajj Steamship," *Tercüman/Perevodchik*, 30 September 1905 and 16 October 1907.

these limited and indirect sources of influence, imperial authorities directly contacted and tried to regulate Islamic scholars in the Russian empire with the purpose of benefiting from their services in the administration of the empire's Muslim communities.[74] Indeed, as we shall see in the next chapter, a process that Catherine II initiated in the 1780s created an institutionalized bond between Volga-Ural Muslims and the Russian state by incorporating the region's Islamic scholars into the imperial state apparatus.

[74] For early examples of this cooperation, which involved primarily the employment of scholars from the Volga-Ural region to manage Kazakh tribes further east, see Gulmira S. Sultangalieva, "The Russian Empire and the Intermediary Role of Tatars in Kazakhstan: The Politics of Cooperation and Rejection," in *Asiatic Russia: Imperial Power in Regional and International Contexts*, ed. Tomohiko Uyama (New York: Routledge, 2012), 58–62.

2   Connecting Volga-Ural Muslims to the Russian state

> I, the mufti of Muslims at this time by the grace of the all-knowing Lord, Gabdusselâm, son of the deceased Mulla Ğabdurrahîm, wrote down narrations and passages from the oft-used and well-respected books of our Shariah, and herein I am sending this piece of advice to all the *ahund*s, mosque supervisors, and Islamic scholars. May they each read and explain this [compilation] to the congregations of the mosques in their neighborhoods, may they advise and moralize their congregations at the Friday and holiday prayers, and may they enjoin good and forbid evil so that the people may be persistent in their worship of God, Blessed and Exalted is He.[1]   Mufti of the Orenburg Spiritual Assembly, 1840

The Russian invasion of the Volga-Ural region following the fall of the Kazan Khanate in 1552 ushered in a period of debilitation for Muslims in the Volga basin and to some extent in the Ural region. The attitude of Russian state agents, especially the state-endorsed missionaries, toward Muslims remained generally restrictive and even antagonistic for a long while.[2] Nevertheless, this situation changed significantly beginning in the mid eighteenth century and especially during the reign of Catherine II. By the early nineteenth century, the Volga-Ural Muslims had started to enjoy a rather peaceful and even prosperous existence in the Russian empire. In addition to the policy of confessional tolerance that Catherine II introduced in the 1770s,[3] her incorporation of the Volga-Ural ulama into the imperial state apparatus through the foundation of the Orenburg Spiritual Assembly had an important share in this improvement.

It is conventional to think of the ulama among Sunni Muslims without a hierarchical structure, but this assumption, which is largely based on a reading of legal texts, disregards the mundane power relations among

---

[1] Fahreddin, *Âsar*, vol. 1, 256.

[2] Said Murza Kniaz' Enikeev, *Ocherk istorii tatarskogo dvorianstva* (Ufa: Izdatel'stvo Gilem, 1999), 57–121; Ravil Bukharaev, *Islam in Russia: The Four Seasons* (New York: St. Martin's Press, 2000), 285–304; and Andreas Kappeler, *The Russian Empire: A Multiethnic History* (Harlow: Longman, 2001), 21–32.

[3] Crews, "Empire", 1–51.

Islamic scholars. The biographies in *Âsar* indicate that some sort of ranking system was already in existence among the Volga-Ural ulama by the mid eighteenth century. Factors such as a scholar's age, erudition, number of students, and following as a Sufi master promoted him to a higher status. When imperial officials decided to contact Islamic scholars to benefit from their services in the administration of Muslims, they first targeted those scholars who already enjoyed a perceivable prominence. And it seems that many of those prominent scholars further bolstered their influence by agreeing to cooperate with the imperial authorities and thereby putting the state's muscles behind their charismatic authority. The resulting transformation in the power relations among the Volga-Ural ulama rendered the region's scholarly networks increasingly more hierarchical in the course of the late eighteenth century, and the foundation of the Orenburg Spiritual Assembly in 1788 formalized this hierarchy.

The authority structure that emerged with the creation of the Orenburg Spiritual Assembly actually carried a noteworthy potential for controversy. The muftis who headed the assembly were always chosen from among prominent Muslims, mostly scholars, but they remained the subjects of an Orthodox Christian monarch and served under the jurisdiction of the Russian minister of internal affairs. Yet, barring a few marginal exceptions, the Volga-Ural Muslims perceived this situation not as an affront to religious freedom but as an opportunity to maintain a mediated distance from the imperial state that created an insulated safe space for intra-Muslim affairs.[4] From the point of view of the imperial administration, the assembly transformed the Volga-Ural ulama into a cheap, albeit inefficient, instrument of surveillance and regulation, similar to the position of the Orthodox clergy since the establishment by Peter I of the Holy Synod as a supervising state organ.[5] While the Orthodox Church still maintained some level of autonomy, as Gregory Freeze argues, and never became a mere "handmaiden of the state,"[6] its clergy helped the tsarist state connect to and gather information about the empire's Orthodox subjects, especially the manorial serfs, more directly.[7]

---

[4] Allen Frank has suggested the term "insulated" as opposed to "isolated" to describe this situation. Frank, *Muslim Religious Institutions*, 314–15.

[5] Crews, *For Prophet*, especially 92–191, provides an elaboration of this argument.

[6] See Gregory L. Freeze, *The Parish Clergy in Nineteenth-Century Russia: Crisis, Reform, Counter-Reform* (Princeton: Princeton University Press, 1983); and Gregory L. Freeze, "Handmaiden of the State? The Church in Imperial Russia Reconsidered," *Journal of Ecclesiastical History*, 1985 36(1): 82–102.

[7] Gregory L. Freeze, "Bringing Order to the Russian Family: Marriage and Divorce in Imperial Russia, 1760–1860," *The Journal of Modern History*, 1990 62(4): 709–46; and Charles Robert Steinwedel, "Making Social Groups, One Person at a Time: The Identification of

The ulama, in its turn, helped the tsarist state reach out to and survey its Muslim subjects, but with crucially different implications resulting from the mediating role of the spiritual assembly between Muslim communities and various government organs. Since the overwhelming majority of Volga-Ural Muslims had never been enserfed, manorial lords did not mediate their interactions with the tsarist state. The intercession of the muftis of the spiritual assembly, however, still allowed them to imagine themselves living in an insulated Muslim domain, where they could follow the leadership of Muslim authorities and practice Islam without conspicuous external interference despite their status as the subjects of a Christian monarch. They did not live in an isolated world apart, as Crews emphasizes,[8] but they could still maintain enough distance from the imperial state to avoid facing constant and pervasive intervention in their daily and especially religious affairs.

Ulama in state service

The Volga-Ural Muslims distinguished those Islamic scholars with the highest standing in the region's scholarly networks with the rank of *ahund*.[9] Already by the early eighteenth century, several ahunds appear to have been wielding some level of administrative authority among the region's Muslim communities as a corollary of their charismatic influence but without necessarily an official mandate.[10] The imperial authorities who wanted to benefit from the prominent Islamic scholars' influence over Muslim communities initially tried to control these scholars by turning the rank of ahund into an official title, limiting their number, and therefore determining who would or would not become an ahund. Imperial authorities also supported those Islamic scholars who cooperated with the state by enforcing their judgments among the

---

Individuals by Estate, Religious Confession, and Ethnicity in Late Imperial Russia," in *Documenting Individual Identity: The Development of State Practices in the Modern World*, ed. Jane Caplan and John Torpey (Princeton: Princeton University Press, 2001), 69–72. The so-called "crown rabbis" would assume a similar role with regard to Jewish communities. See Avrutin, *Jews and the Imperial State*, 34–38, and 72.

[8] Crews, *For Prophet*, 9 and 299.

[9] On ahunds, see Frank, *Muslim Religious Institutions*, 109–10; Garipova, "The Transformation", 220–64; Nathan Spannaus, "The Decline of the Ākhūnd and the Transformation of Islamic Law under the Russian Empire," *Islamic Law and Society*, 2013 20(3): 202–41.

[10] Danil' D. Azamatov, "Russian Administration and Islam in Bashkiria (18th–19th Centuries)," in *Muslim Culture in Russia and Central Asia from the 18th to the Early 20th Centuries*, ed. Anke von Kügelgen, Michael Kemper, and Dmitriy Yermakov (Berlin: Klaus Schwarz Verlag, 1996), 95–99; and Frank, *Muslim Religious Institutions*, 109.

region's Muslims.[11] Additionally, material remunerations, such as decorations, robes, money, and especially land grants, were available for the most prominent and cooperative scholars.[12] An early example of an Islamic scholar who cooperated with the imperial authorities was Ğabdullah Müslim (d. 1794/95). In a letter that he wrote in 1771 and that is reproduced in *Âsar*, Müslim appoints a certain Ulmazqul Hucamquloğlu as the mullah of a village, upon the village elders' demand, with the authority to lead Friday and holiday prayers as well as to judge according to the Shariah. Interestingly, Müslim's signature at the end of this letter indicates him to be an "ahund and *deputat*." "Deputat" is a Russian term corresponding to "deputy" in English, and its usage in this context implies that Müslim had received the title of deputy from the Russian state in addition to his recognition as an ahund.[13] Another scholar recorded in *Âsar* with credentials similar to those of Ğabdullah Müslim was Velîd bin Maqsûd (d. 1794/95) from İsterlitamaq. He served as a judge for major conflicts in his vicinity and also appointed mullahs with the authority to lead Friday prayers.[14]

The strategy of selectively cooperating with scholars of a higher stature yielded mixed results for the Russian state throughout the eighteenth century. Moreover, this cooperation was mostly tuned to improve Russian influence among the nomadic Bashkirs and Kazakhs[15] without significantly contributing to the experience of sedentary Muslims in the Volga-Ural region. Here, the relations between Russian state agents and the Muslim communities were particularly tense between the 1730s and 1764, when St. Petersburg officially supported or at least condoned the zealous efforts of Orthodox missionaries to coerce the region's non-Russian inhabitants, including Muslims, to receive baptism *en masse*.[16]

---

[11] See Azamatov, "Russian Administration," 95–99; and Azamatov, *Orenburgskoe*, 16–18. This engagement with the tsarist state would erode the authority of the region's ahunds in the long run. See Spannaus, "The Decline"; and Garipova, "The Transformation," 220–64.

[12] Fahreddin, *Âsar*, vol. 1, 64–65 and 182–184.   [13] Fahreddin, *Âsar*, vol. 1, 65–66.

[14] Fahreddin, *Âsar*, vol. 1, 61–62. For other examples of cooperation between Islamic scholars of the Volga-Ural region and Russian state officials, see Fahreddin, *Âsar*, vol. 1, 158 and 182–83.

[15] Sultangalieva, "Russian Empire"; and Spannaus, "The Decline," 211–19.

[16] On the conversion campaigns, see Chantal Lemercier-Quelquejay, "Les missions orthodoxes en pays musulmans de moyenne-et basse-Volga, 1552–1865," *Cahiers du Monde Russe et Soviétique*, 1967 8(3): 369–403; and İskhak M. Lotfullin and F. G. Islaev, *Dzhikhad tatarskogo naroda* (Kazan, 1998). Paul Werth complicates this matter by questioning who ordered or perpetrated coercive violence or whether it preceded or followed conversion, but he too grants the existence of coercive violence. Paul W. Werth, "Coercion and Conversion: Violence and the Mass Baptism of the Volga Peoples, 1740–55," *Kritika: Explorations in Russian and Eurasian History*, 2003 4(3): 543–69.

Lay imperial authorities struggled to establish administrative control over Islamic scholars while the baptism campaigns of the missionaries still held sway. These early efforts to control the ulama were successful to some extent in the Volga Basin, where Russian rule had deeper roots and the ulama network had grown weak as a result of the gradual exile and emigration of prominent scholars from the area in the preceding centuries. However, further east, in the Ural region, a series of rebellions that were partly incited by religious oppression limited the influence of Russian state initiatives.[17] Most significantly, the Bashkir rebellion of 1855 in which a prominent Islamic scholar, Batırşah ʿAli, played a leading role made it clear, especially to the lay imperial authorities, that the tensions resulting from religious coercion in the region had to decrease for the sake of administrative efficiency and the empire's very integrity.[18]

Reducing tension required an accommodating approach to the administration of Muslims, and this approach found its champion in the person of Catherine II. Born as a German princess, the empress was originally raised a Lutheran. She had received Orthodox baptism as a requirement of her royal marriage to Peter III, and she did not pursue Orthodoxy with a missionary zeal. Moreover, she was fascinated with the ideas of Enlightenment philosophes, such as Voltaire and Diderot, who dissociated themselves from organized religion and promoted religious tolerance.[19] Thus, in 1764, two years after she came to power, Catherine II closed the Office of New Converts, the institution that had been organizing the forced baptism campaigns since the 1730s.[20] In 1773, she issued "the Toleration of all Faiths" edict primarily as a response to the complaints of her Muslim subjects.[21] When she annexed the Crimean khanate in 1783, upon the recommendation of her advisor on Muslim affairs Baron Osip A. Igel'strom, she recognized the existing religious establishment of the khanate and paid the salaries of its leaders.[22] And in 1788, again

---

[17] See Azamatov, "Russian Administration," 95–99; and Frank, *Islamic Historiography*, 26–35.

[18] On the Batırşah rebellion, see Danielle M. Ross, "In Dialogue with the Shadow of God: Imperial Mobilization, Islamic Revival and the Evolution of an Administrative System for the Tatars, Bashkirs and Mishars of Eighteenth-Century" (MA Thesis, University of Wisconsin-Madison, 2007).

[19] Catherine II, *The Memoirs of Catherine the Great*, ed. Moura Budberg and Dominique Maroger (New York: Collier Books, 1961), especially 78.

[20] Lemercier-Quelquejay, "Les missions," 390; F. G. Islaev, *Islam i pravoslavie v Povolzh'e XVIII stoletiia ot konfrontatsii k terpimosti* (Kazan: Kazan University Press, 2001), 85 and 176–77; and Khodarkovsky, "Not by Word," 272.

[21] For the text of this edict, see D. Iu. Arapov ed. *Islam v Rossiiskoi Imperii (Zakonadatel'na'ia akty, opisaniia, statistika)* (Moscow: Akademkniga, 2001), 45–46.

[22] Abdürreşid İbrâhîmof, *Çoban Yıldızı* (St. Petersburg: Abdürreşid İbrâhîmof Elektrik Basmahanesi, 1907), 17–18; Fisher, "Enlightened Despotism," 547; and Hakan

upon the recommendation of Baron Igel'strom, who had now carried his experience to the Ural region as the vicegerent of the Ufa and Simbirsk gubernias, she founded a Muslim assembly to carry the ad hoc measures of selectively cooperating with prominent Islamic scholars to an institutional level. The assembly opened in Ufa, a city that served as the administrative center of the Ural region but hosted only a few dozen Muslims. In 1792, it moved to Orenburg and from then on came to be known as the "Orenburg Spiritual Assembly" although it moved back to Ufa in 1802.[23] Shortly after its foundation, Baron Igel'strom prepared a draft law to clarify the assembly's status and functions. The draft was never approved officially, but it remained in effect until several other edicts and Senate decisions gradually framed the legal status of the Orenburg Spiritual Assembly over the course of the nineteenth century.[24] Initially, the assembly answered to Baron Igel'strom, but then it was placed under the jurisdiction of the Ministry of Internal Affairs (MVD).[25]

Catherine II appointed Muhammedcan bin el-Hüseyin (1758–1824), an ahund who had already been of service to the Russian state in its dealings with the Muslim population of the Orenburg borderland, as the first mufti of the Orenburg Spiritual Assembly.[26] Until 1917, seven other muftis headed the assembly, and they were all appointed from St. Petersburg. The assembly also continued to function under the Soviet regime for a while. In 1917 and 1923, Muslim congresses elected the mufti. Being elected to this position in 1923, Rızâeddin bin Fahreddin served until his death in 1936, but the institution had lost all practical

Kırımlı, *National Movements and National Identity among the Crimean Tatars, 1905–1916* (Leiden: Brill, 1996), 14–17. For a description of the Crimean ulama before Russian occupation, see Barbara Kellner-Heinkele, "Crimean Tatar and Nogay Scholars of the 18th Century," in *Muslim Culture in Russia and Central Asia from the 18th to the Early 20th Centuries*, ed. Michael Kemper, Anke von Kügelgen, and Dmitriy Yermakov (Berlin: Klaus Schwarz Verlag, 1996).

23 On the foundation of the Orenburg Spiritual Assembly, among other sources, see Fisher, "Enlightened Despotism," 542–53; Azamatov, *Orenburgskoe*; and Crews, *For Prophet*, 31–60. The name of this institution was *"Orenburg Mahkeme-yi Şer'iyesi"* in Turkic and *Orenburgskoe Dukhovnoe Sobranie* in Russian. Catherine II's edict founding the assembly can be found in *Pol'noe sobranie zakonov Rossiiskoi Imperii: sobranie tret'e* (St. Petersburg: Gosudarstvennaia Tipografiia, 1885–1916), vol. 22, 1107–8; and Arapov ed. *Islam*, 50–51.

24 *Materialy po istorii Bashkirskoi ASSR*, vol. 5 (Moskva, Izd-vo Akademii nauk SSSR, 1960); Azamatov, *Orenburgskoe*, 26–35; and Türkoğlu, *Rızaeddin Fahreddin*, 84–94.

25 Türkoğlu, *Rızaeddin Fahreddin*, 84–88.

26 On Mufti Muhammedcan bin el-Hüseyin, see Fahreddin, *Âsar*, vol. 1, 182–86; Türkoğlu, *Rızaeddin Fahreddin*, 158–60; Kemper, *Sufis und Gelehrte*, 50–65; and Crews, *For Prophet*, 52–60.

influence by this time.[27] Aside from the mufti, the Orenburg Spiritual Assembly had three members who participated in its decision-making processes and assisted the mufti in his bureaucratic duties. According to Catherine II's edict from 1788, these three members, called *qadis*, would be chosen from among the scholars of the city of Kazan for three-year terms. Igel'strom's draft law did not clarify whether they would be elected or appointed, but in practice, the notables of the city of Kazan elected them until 1889, in which year the mufti started to appoint the qadis.[28] Additionally, the spiritual assembly had six (later nine) administrative employees who served as managers, secretaries, scribes, and translators. Most of these administrative employees were non-Muslim Russian-speakers in the beginning. Gradually, Muslims who could speak, read, and write in the Russian language took over all positions in the assembly.[29]

In the course of the nineteenth century, the Orenburg Spiritual Assembly evolved into the administrative center of the ulama network in most of Siberia, the Volga-Ural region, and the central Russian lands.[30] A measure in Baron Igel'strom's draft law that required Islamic scholars first to be certified as "ahunds, mullahs, and in other religious positions" by the spiritual assembly and then to be appointed in their positions by local government officials was crucial in this development.[31] Originally, village or neighborhood elders would meet and decide whether to employ a madrasa graduate as the mullah or adhan caller of their mosque or not. In some places, this was the end of the process – the licenses that students received from their teachers were sufficient for their recognition

---

[27] Türkoğlu, *Rızaeddin Fahreddin*, 157–91, 263–66, and 282–86. For a survey of the history of Islamic institutions in the Soviet Union, see Yaacov Ro'i, *Islam in the Soviet Union: From the Second World War to Gorbachev* (London: Hurst & Co., 2000), 9–286.

[28] İbrâhîmof, *Çoban*, 22; and Khasanov, *Formirovanie*, 59; and Daniel D. Azamatov, "The Muftis of the Orenburg Spiritual Assembly in the 18th and 19th Centuries: The Struggle for Power in Russia's Muslim Institution," in *Muslim Culture in Russia and Central Asia from the 18th to the Early 20th Centuries*, ed. Anke von Kügelgen, Michael Kemper, and Allen J. Frank (Berlin: Klaus Schwarz Verlag, 1998), 355–84; and Türkoğlu, *Rızaeddin Fahreddin*, 84–88.

[29] İbrâhîmof, *Çoban*, 17–19; and Crews, *For Prophet*, 56. The terms "mufti" and "qadi" as used in this historical context should not be confused with their general usage in Islamic terminology. Baron Igel'strom seems to have borrowed these terms from the religious establishment that he found in Crimea after its annexation, but the terms acquired new connotations in the Russian imperial context.

[30] Separate assemblies were instituted in the Crimea and the South Caucasus. The Kazakhs remained under the jurisdiction of the Orenburg Spiritual Assembly until 1867, but then, with the exception of the Kazakh Inner Horde, they were separated from the assembly. See Kırımlı, *National Movements*, 14; Türkoğlu, *Rızaeddin Fahreddin*, 101; and NART, f. 1370, op. 1, d. 2, ll. 1–3.

[31] *Materialy po istorii Bashkirskoi ASSR*, vol. 5, 563–64.

as bearers of knowledge. They could start in their positions without further requirements, although ahunds and local government authorities gradually increased their involvement in the appointment process throughout the eighteenth century. After 1788, a madrasa graduate, who agreed with the elders of a village or neighborhood to serve as their mullah or adhan caller, first had to obtain a passport from the authorities of the administrative unit where he was registered. Then he traveled to Orenburg and took an oral exam at the spiritual assembly. If he passed the exam, the mufti or one of the qadis gave him a certificate to submit to the local government officials that oversaw the village or neighborhood where he intended to work. Finally, these officials appointed him to his new position.[32]

Since several fires destroyed the early documents of the Orenburg Spiritual Assembly, we do not have precise information about the process of certification in its initial years. It seems that many scholars who already held a position or managed to secure one from the members of a congregation did not bother to go to Orenburg and apply for certification at the beginning. According to surviving data, 1,921 scholars took the exam by 1800 (an average of 160 exams per year),[33] and only 2,527 scholars took it between 1804 and 1836 (an average of 80 exams per year).[34] Yet, aside from the occasional objections of certain Islamic scholars about the authority of particular muftis, both the Islamic scholars of the Volga-Ural region and imperial authorities, some of whom initially hesitated about sharing power with an Islamic institution, gradually accepted the existence and functions of the Orenburg Spiritual Assembly.[35] The biographies recorded in *Âsar* give the impression that going to Orenburg for certification had become an almost universal practice among the Volga-Ural ulama by the mid nineteenth century. One could still find a scholar or two who led prayers without appointment, but these were the

---

[32] Türkoğlu, *Rızaeddin Fahreddin*, 88–91. It seems that the certification requirement was dropped for adhan callers by 1891. *Sbornik tsirkuliarov i inykh rukovodiashikh rasporiazhenii po okrugu Orenburgskogo Magometanskogo dukhovnogo sobraniia 1841–1901 g.*, Russian-language part (Ufa, 1902), 24.

[33] *Materialy po istorii Bashkirskoi ASSR*, vol. 5, 684. For an example of an Islamic scholar who worked without certification, see Fahreddin, *Âsar*, vol. 2, 425–26.

[34] Türkoğlu, *Rızaeddin Fahreddin*, 96.

[35] See Frank, *Islamic Historiography*, 37–38; Kemper, *Sufis und Gelehrte*, 57–61; Crews, *For Prophet*, 58–66. One significant yet still marginal exception was the Vaisov Movement in the late nineteenth and early twentieth centuries. See Chantal Quelquejay, "Le 'Vaisisme' a Kazan. Contribution a l'etude des confreries musulmanes chez les tatars de la volga," *Die Welt des Islams*, 1959 6(1/2): 91–112; Kemper, *Sufis und Gelehrte*, 393–428; and Diliara Usmanova, *Musul'manskoe "sektantstvo" v Rossiiskoi imperii: "Vaisovskii Bozhii polk staroverov-musul'man" 1862–1916 gg* (Kazan: Fen, 2009).

exceptions that proved the rule.[36] In general, the efficient enforcement of the law and certain advantages that accompanied certification, such as job security in officially recognized positions or, until 1870, exemption from conscription and corporal punishment, led Islamic scholars in the Volga-Ural region to seek certification from the Orenburg Spiritual Assembly.[37]

Being certified by the assembly and appointed by local imperial authorities placed the loosely ranked ulama network of the Volga-Ural region into a hierarchical system where power emanated from the MVD and disseminated through the mufti. The mufti's powers over mullahs increased gradually over the course of the nineteenth century. In addition to the once-in-a-lifetime certification process, the assembly started to supervise Islamic scholars on a permanent basis through the mediation of ahunds, and, later, when the position of ahund lost its significance, through the mediation of mosque supervisors, called *muhtasibs*.[38]

By connecting the ulama to its state establishment on a permanent basis, St. Petersburg acquired a bureaucratic apparatus capable of reaching the empire's Muslim subjects without incurring any expenses other than the small sums spent on the salaries of a mufti, three qadis, and a few employees in a stone building in Ufa. Almost every Muslim village in the empire had a mosque (unless the village was divided into more than one neighborhood, called *mahalles*, and therefore had multiple mosques), and almost every mosque had a mullah. According to the system that evolved after the foundation of the spiritual assembly, every mullah received orders from the mufti and was answerable to him through the mediation of ahunds or muhtasibs.[39] The resulting system did not amount to a perfect chain of command in which the mullahs executed the mufti's orders minutely. At times, the mullahs evaded regulations and ignored orders coming from the spiritual assembly. They continued their duties as they deemed necessary and, sometimes, neglected them too.[40] However, despite its flaws, the molding of the Volga-Ural region's scholarly networks into a hierarchical structure with the foundation of the Orenburg Spiritual Assembly

---

[36] For an example, see Fahreddin, *Âsar*, vol. 2, 14.

[37] See İbrâhîmof, *Çoban*, 22; and Crews, *For Prophet*, 108. The exemption from military service and corporal punishment would end in 1870.

[38] Räfyq Möhämmätshin, "The Tatar Intelligentsia and the Clergy, 1917–1937," in *In Devout Societies vs. Impious States?*, ed. Stéphane A. Dudoignon (Berlin: Klaus Schwarz Verlag, 2004), 36.

[39] Mûsa Cârullah Bigiyef, *Islâhat Esasları* (Petrograd: Tipografiia M-A Maksutova, 1915), 36–39; and Türkoğlu, *Rızaeddin Fahreddin*, 88–89.

[40] For examples of neglect and evasion, see Fahreddin, *Âsar*, vol. 1, 425 and vol. 2, 14, 75, 199–200, and 425–26; and İbrâhîmof, *Çoban*, 23–24.

enabled the Russian state to rely on the services of the ulama in governing the region's Muslim communities.

Ulama as judges

One of the services that the ulama provided under the jurisdiction of the Orenburg Spiritual Assembly was judging certain civil law cases. Islamic scholars have traditionally served as arbiters and judges of their communities thanks to their expertise in interpreting the rulings and principles of Islamic jurisprudence. In the Volga-Ural region, they had been rendering this service through local Shariah courts long before the establishment of the Orenburg Spiritual Assembly. During the eighteenth century, Russian authorities tried to restrict the influence of Shariah courts,[41] but once the Orenburg Spiritual Assembly incorporated Islamic scholars into the Russian state establishment, incorporating their judicial powers into the imperial judiciary seemed feasible as well. Thus, Igel'strom's draft law recognized the ulama as the legal authority to pass judgment on most aspects of civil law – especially family law, crimes against religion, and the issues of inheritance.[42]

This was a tricky situation for the ulama. On the one hand, becoming a part of the state establishment was empowering, because the state could enforce their decisions. On the other hand, it was restrictive, because the official recognition of their authority to judge certain cases simultaneously meant that they were not allowed to judge other cases. For instance, when a man beat his wife and caused injury, the scholars had to consider it a criminal case and refer the matter to the police rather than passing judgment on their own.[43] Or, according to a circular from 1891, when the heirs of a dead Muslim could not agree on the distribution of his or her estate that involved agriculturally productive or immovable property, the scholars had to refer the case to the respective village administration rather than apportioning the inheritance according to Islamic law.[44] Even when an Islamic scholar was able to pass judgment on a specific case without having to involve Russian imperial authorities, the willingness of the imperial authorities to enforce his judgment determined the outcome of the case. For instance, if the parties involved in the conflict were not registered in a place that was geographically under the jurisdiction of the judging scholar, the imperial authorities could refuse to enforce his judgment.[45]

---

[41] Azamatov, "Russian Administration," 92–93; and Azamatov, *Orenburgskoe*, 18.
[42] *Materialy po istorii Bashkirskoi ASSR*, vol. 5, 564–66 and Azamatov, *Orenburgskoe*, 27–28.
[43] Fahreddin, *Âsar*, vol. 2, 352–55.   [44] *Sbornik tsirkuliarov* [Russian section], 32.
[45] Ibid. 33–34 and 36.

Moreover, as Muslims developed familiarity with the administrative organs of the empire, they started to take advantage of alternative judicial institutions whenever they did not like the judgment of an individual scholar. In one illustrative case from the early 1830s in the Kazan region, a man named Neziroğlu, before setting out on a Hajj journey, had authorized his wife to divorce him in case he did not return. When he did not return for a long time, his wife Ğumerqızı asked a local mullah named Muhammed İbrahimoğlu Hocaşef to register her divorce, which the mullah did after listening to witnesses. Then, she married another man named Maqsûdoğlu. Two years later the first husband, Neziroğlu, came back from his journey. He asked Maqsûdoğlu to return Ğumerqızı to him. Maqsûdoğlu refused on the grounds that Ğumerqızı's divorce from Neziroğlu and marriage to himself were already recognized by Hocaşef. Then, Neziroğlu applied to a local government court in Kazan, but unable to support his case at the court, he admitted to having authorized Ğumerqızı for divorce and promised to write a statement of divorce himself.

Once the trial was over, however, instead of producing a divorce statement, Neziroğlu applied to the region's military governor without mentioning his first trial at the local court. The governor authorized Ahund Ğabdunnâsır Rahmanqul to resolve the situation. Seeing that Rahmanqul would decide in favor of Neziroğlu, Maqsûdoğlu also applied to the military governor and obtained an order for Rahmanqul to judge the case together with an elder ahund, Fethullah bin el-Hüseyin. However, Rahmanqul refused to cooperate with Ahund Fethullah and ruled that Ğumerqızı was still married to Neziroğlu. When Ahund Fethullah forced Rahmanqul to an arbitration meeting in the presence of other ahunds, Ahund Rahmanqul protested that his decision as an ahund could not be reviewed by another ahund. He purported that even the spiritual assembly could not intervene in this case for Neziroğlu had already carried it beyond the assembly's jurisdiction. Moreover, he claimed that the assembly's responsibility should be limited to certifying men of religion anyway. Thus, Fethullah bin el-Hüseyin also evaluated the case individually and ruled that Ğumerqızı's divorce from Neziroğlu and, therefore, marriage to Maqsûdoğlu were both valid. He informed the military governor about his decision and forwarded the documentation of the case to the spiritual assembly, it seems, in expectation of a reprimand to Ahund Rahmanqul.[46]

Unfortunately, the documents in *Âsar* do not indicate the final outcome of this dispute, but the case is revealing about the complex power

[46] Fahreddin, *Âsar*, vol. 2, 20–23.

relations among the Russian imperial authorities, Islamic scholars, and ordinary Muslims in the Volga-Ural region after the foundation of the Orenburg Spiritual Assembly. In the absence of a disputing party, the local mullah was able to divorce Ğumerqızı from her husband and open the way for her second marriage with Maqsûdoğlu easily. Yet, when Neziroğlu refused to accept the mullah's judgment after his return and the resolution of the situation required enforcement, he went to the local government court rather than a mullah or ahund. Once Neziroğlu carried the case beyond the purview of the ulama, Maqsûdoğlu followed him first to the local court and then to the military governor. The military governor could not judge the case, but he could choose and appoint the Islamic scholar who would. At all stages of the dispute the Russian authorities and Islamic scholars who were involved acted with a shared understanding about the ulama's right and authority to judge divorce and marriage cases. However, the ulama were dependent on the Russian imperial authorities to enforce their judgments. This restricted their authority as judges and also enabled the Russian imperial authorities to influence the outcome of cases that were otherwise left to the ulama's jurisdiction.

Ulama as registrars

Another service that the Russian state required from Islamic scholars was the keeping of civil registry books. According to a law that passed in 1828, mullahs would receive two empty books every year and enter births, marriages, divorces, and deaths in these books. At the end of the year, they would send one of the books to the spiritual assembly and keep the other one in their possession. These books and other occasional records that the mullahs kept served as a major source of statistical data for the imperial authorities. In July 1890, the mufti, Muhammedyâr Sultanof, ordered the mullahs to enter in their books the cause of death from various sicknesses as indicated by medical inspectors.[47] The following year, he asked the mullahs of the Ufa Gubernia to provide a list of births in their congregations to the zemstvo administrations.[48] And, in 1895 and 1896, he instructed the mullahs to send the passports of those lower-rank reserve soldiers who died to the related authorities.[49] The mullahs' records served as legal reference in cases of marriage, inheritance, and conscription too. As a result, the civil registry books that they kept acquired tremendous importance both for the Russian

---

[47] *Sbornik tsirkuliarov* [Russian section], 23.   [48] Ibid. 28.
[49] Ibid. 73–74 and 80; for other conscription-related circulars, see 68 and 78.

state and the Muslim population. A wrong entry in the book could save one Muslim man from military service and send another one to the army in his place. Failure to register the birth of a child with the mullah could deprive the child of his or her inheritance. Or, since the legal age for marriage was eighteen for boys and sixteen for girls, the accuracy of the entry in the civil registry book could affect young Muslims' ability to marry.[50]

Mullahs traditionally oversaw the major life events of the members of their congregations, such as birth, marriage, and death, and they performed the religious rites, such as naming babies, performing marriages, and leading funeral prayers, at these events. They also received a small fee or gift in return for their performances, which sometimes comprised an important part of their income.[51] To the Russian bureaucrats, recording these life events in civil registry books seemed like an easily manageable addition to the mullahs' conventional obligations. Yet the mullahs were not trained in bookkeeping, and they generally handled the civil registry books very poorly. Despite the spiritual assembly's repeated efforts to improve the situation, civil registry books remained insufficiently or inaccurately filled even into the early twentieth century.[52] Most mullahs did not record the events right away but kept them in mind in order to write all at once when the books were due to the spiritual assembly at the end of the year. Consequently, they confused or forgot many things. Their handwriting was rarely legible, and they often omitted necessary information. Some of the mullahs were even unable to write properly. They went to a nearby madrasa at the end of the year and dictated what was left in their memory to one of the madrasa students in return for a fee.[53]

Nevertheless, even though the mullahs were negligent about keeping civil registry books, they were not defiant. Their bookkeeping skills were inadequate, but they still filled out a civil registry book every year and kept the imperial legal system functioning with the information they recorded in these books. By the 1870s, the responsibility of mullahs to keep civil registry books had become such a normal part of their duties

---

[50] İbrâhîmof, *Çoban*, 23–24; *Sbornik tsirkuliarov*[Russian section], 37–42.

[51] İbrâhîmof, *Çoban*, 23–24; Türkoğlu, *Rızaeddin Fahreddin*, 94–96.

[52] For the repeated circulars of the spiritual assembly to the imams about the civil registry books, see *Sbornik tsirkuliarov* [Russian section], 3–5, 8–9, 37–42, 45–46, 64–67, 69–71, and 103–10.

[53] İbrâhîmof, *Çoban*, 23–24. Ğabdürreşîd İbrâhîm worked in the Orenburg Spiritual Assembly as a qadi in 1891–93, and he had first-hand experience of the assembly's efforts to organize civil registry books and of the consequences of the imams' inability or unwillingness to keep them properly. İsmail Türkoğlu, *Sibiryalı Meşhur Seyyah Abdürreşid İbrahim* (Ankara: Türkiye Diyanet Vakfı Yayınları, 1997), 18–19.

from the point of view of the Russian administration that the MVD
decided to require Islamic scholars to learn Russian in order to fulfill
their functions in the imperial state apparatus better.[54]

Ulama as messengers

A third service that the Russian state expected from the ulama was
providing a channel of communication between imperial authorities
and the local Muslim communities. During the nineteenth century,
muftis of the Orenburg Spiritual Assembly penned several circulars on
various issues ranging from religious practice to disease control and
instructed the Muslim men of religion under their jurisdiction to convey
the content of these circulars to their congregations. More often than
not, Russian authorities were also involved in the preparation of these
circulars, either to standardize the religious and customary practices of
the Muslim population and integrate them into imperial law, or to use
the authorities of the spiritual assembly and Islamic scholars to influence
the Muslim population.[55]

One good example of how the spiritual assembly's circulars were
used to influence the empire's Muslim population is an appeal by Mufti
Gabdulvâhid bin Süleyman to the Muslims in the east of Russia during
the Crimean War, when the Russian empire fought against the Ottoman
Empire and its European allies. In summary, the mufti wrote that
Muslims had been living in the Russian empire under the sovereignty
of compassionate tsars as equal members of a huge imperial family. The
tsars, he continued, had treated Muslims as their children, helped them
in times of difficulty such as famine and plague, and given them food,
medicine, and seeds for cultivation. Beneath the tsar, imperial bureaucrats had treated the Muslims as their younger brothers, according to the
mufti. Therefore, he invited the Muslims to pray for the continuation of
the Russian empire and the royal family. In a convoluted twist of facts, he
presented the Crimean War as Russia's endeavor to rescue the Ottoman
Empire from the domination of European powers and asked Muslims
to volunteer in order to serve in the "compassionate Tsar's army."
He also urged the Muslims to keep their promise of loyalty to the Tsar

---

[54] See NART, f. 92, op. 1, d. 21060. For other considerations involved in this decision and
its implementation, see Chapters 3 and 4.

[55] For examples, see Fahreddin, *Âsar*, vol. 1, 356; *Sbornik tsirkuliarov*, [Russian section]12,
30–31, 43, 47–53, 55, 61, 86–90, and 97; and Azamatov, *Orenburgskoe*, 123–25. Also see
Crews, *For Prophet*, especially 175–91.

and exhorted them to be thankful for being able to perform their religious obligations safely away from the front.[56]

Another example dates from 1894 when rumors about a forced Christianization campaign against Muslims spread in the Orenburg Gubernia and at least 200 Muslim families left the gubernia to migrate to the Ottoman Empire.[57] The mufti of the time, Muhammedyâr Sultanof, sent a circular to the Orenburg ulama explaining that the rumors were unfounded:

The Government has no intention to baptize us. On the contrary, it allows us to practice Islam openly, without restrictions on performing the rites of our belief or on constructing mosques for prayer. The rumors ... come from foolish or malicious people who are not worth believing, but the dark people believe them. Some people sell off their property in order to go to Turkey, and ill-willed individuals take advantage of this situation by purchasing every last piece of property from the naïve folks in return for nothing or by collecting money from them pretending that the money will be used for their resettlement expenses.[58]

When provocative rumors like this one spread in the region, police chiefs would generally visit Muslim villages one by one and try to convince the villagers that what they heard was unfounded,[59] but a letter from the mufti read in the mosque during the Friday prayer by the village mullah was far more effective. It was the Russian officials, including the police chiefs, whom the Muslims feared as the potential agents of forced Christianization, after all.

The circulars of the Orenburg Spiritual Assembly helped Russian officials in more mundane situations such as enforcing public health regulations too. In 1850, the mufti, Ğabdulvâhid bin Süleyman, warned the Muslims of the Orenburg, Viatka, and Perm gubernias about leprosy and syphilis. He told them to be careful about hygiene, to wash their bodies every Friday, to keep their houses clean, to consult medical doctors when they had indications of leprosy or syphilis, to take prescribed medicines, and not to marry if they had one of these diseases. He also instructed the mullahs to have the parents of brides and grooms witness before registering a marriage that their children did not have leprosy or syphilis.[60] And, in another example, in April 1891, the spiritual assembly instructed the ulama of the Ufa Gubernia to inform the

---

[56] Fahreddin, Âsar, vol. 2, 369–73.

[57] Osmanlı Belgelerinde Kazan (Ankara: Başbakanlık Devlet Arşivleri Genel Müdürlüğü, 2005), 81–82.

[58] Sbornik tsirkuliarov [Russian section], 72. Also quoted in Meyer, "Turkic Worlds," 47–48. Translation mine.

[59] See Chapter 4.

[60] Fahreddin, Âsar, vol. 2, 366–69, and for a similar instruction, see 364.

members of their congregations about the measures that could be used in preventing the spread of smallpox among children.[61]

We do not know to what extent the ulama followed these instructions or conveyed them to their congregations. It is difficult to imagine that the modernizing projects of Russian authorities, such as plague prevention campaigns or gathering statistics, could be realized by sending instructions to the mullahs alone without repeated visits by police chiefs, health officials, and surveyors to the Muslim villages. However, the very possibility of using scholars to read circulars in each Muslim village or to collect information from those villages was an asset that the empire acquired with the foundation of the spiritual assembly and its evolution into the administrative center of the ulama network. Aside from technical assistance, the Russian administration needed the ulama's moral authority to influence the empire's Muslim population. As a legacy of the coercive Christianization attempts of the earlier centuries, the Volga-Ural Muslims were highly suspicious about the intervention of state officials in their daily lives. Therefore, it was crucial for the Russian administration to receive the ulama's support if it wanted the Muslims to take medication for syphilis, receive vaccination for smallpox, bury their dead in certain ways, provide statistical data, or even remain loyal to the tsar.[62]

Two vantage points

In the century following the foundation of the Orenburg Spiritual Assembly, a complex relationship developed between the Russian state and the ulama of the Volga-Ural region. The spiritual assembly molded the ulama network into a hierarchical structure and connected it to the imperial bureaucracy. Instances such as certification by the spiritual assembly, appointment by local imperial authorities, and receiving instructions from the mufti, who was under the jurisdiction of the MVD, gradually transformed Islamic scholars into civil servants.[63] This transformation had several advantages for the Islamic scholars, such as exemption from conscription and corporal punishment, official recognition in religious positions, and the enforcement of their judgments by

---

[61] *Sbornik tsirkuliarov* [Russian section], 26; for similar public-health related instructions see 25, 54, 57, 83, and 91–92.

[62] For the suspicions of the Muslim population of the Volga-Ural region during the 1897 census, see I. K. Zagidullin, *Perepis' 1897 goda i Tatary Kazanskoi Gubernii* (Kazan: Tatarskoe Knizhnoe Izdatel'stvo, 2000), especially 166–88.

[63] For an overview of Islamic scholars' duties in the imperial system of governance, especially in the late nineteenth and early twentieth centuries, see Naganawa, "Molding the Muslim Community," especially 105–8.

imperial authorities. But it also subjected them to regulations, obligations, and restrictions imposed by the imperial state. Through the mediation of the spiritual assembly, the Russian state oversaw the judicial
functions of Islamic scholars, held mullahs responsible for keeping civil
registry books, and sent circulars to the ulama network to mobilize it for
government projects or in support of the empire. By the mid nineteenth
century, viewed from St. Petersburg, the ulama looked like a subordinate
division of the imperial state apparatus.[64]

Nevertheless, Islamic scholars were never reduced to the status of
the conveyor belts of imperial authority. The ulama hierarchy that the
Russian state endorsed and consolidated provided a legal basis for permanent supervision over mullahs but not the control mechanisms that
one would expect from rationalized bureaucracies or even premodern
patronage systems.[65] The examination for certification occurred once
in a lifetime. Circulars reached Muslim villages only rarely, and neither
the mufti nor other imperial authorities had the ability to control whether
the mullahs conveyed the instructions in these circulars to their congregations or not. Islamic scholars continued to read what they used to
read, to study where they used to study, and to preach what they deemed
important without large-scale intervention from the Russian state.
They became dependent on the imperial state for their titles but not for
their livelihood. The state paid the salaries of the mufti, the qadis, and the
imams of a few major mosques. It also bestowed occasional grants to
a few prominent ahunds, but it did not pay for the mullahs, the adhan
callers, and the majority of ahunds. The Muslim congregations supported
the ulama with charities and gifts on a daily basis, and therefore, the local
dynamics and moral economy of their respective congregations mattered
to Islamic scholars significantly more than government priorities.

This primacy of things local is important from the point of view
of Muslim congregations too. Viewed from village mosques, Islamic
scholars continued to serve primarily as the representatives of religion
and bearers of religious knowledge. True, the ulama's dependence on
government forces to implement their decisions and the possibility of

---

[64] Garipova, "The Transformation," and Spannaus, "The Decline" both emphasize the
detrimental effect of tsarist rule on the authority and capacities of the ulama, especially
the ahunds.

[65] On "rational bureaucracy," see Max Weber, *The Theory of Social and Economic
Organization*, trans. A. M. Henderson and Talcott Parsons, ed. Talcott Parsons (New
York: Oxford University Press, 1947), 328–41. For an excellent description of the
Ottoman patronage system, see Cornell H. Fleischer, *Bureaucrat and Intellectual in the
Ottoman Empire: The Historian Mustafa Ali (1541–1600)* (Princeton: Princeton
University Press, 1986).

carrying intra-Muslim conflicts outside of the Muslim domain to government institutions provided leverage to the imperial state in the affairs of the region's Muslim communities.[66] However, only when an Islamic scholar had to judge between conflicting parties, and one of those parties refused to abide by his arbitration, would the scholar's authority go on trial and he would become dependent on the executive powers of the state. Furthermore, even though the state provided extra-communal venues for conflict resolution, such as government courts, individual Muslims had to negotiate their way to these venues in the moral economy of their respective communities first. Therefore, we need to approach the archival material that documents the utilization of those venues by individual Muslims as records of limited interaction between the Russian state and local Muslim communities. They can shed light on the interaction per se but not necessarily on the Volga-Ural Muslims' daily experiences that did not push the boundaries of the moral economy of their respective communities.[67] Conflicts produce more documents and are more likely to attract the historians' attention, but the quotidian relations between Islamic scholars and Muslim peasants were more decisive in determining the position of the ulama among Volga-Ural Muslims. In the realm of everyday relations, Islamic scholars remained the main source and interpreters of information for Muslim peasants about religion and the larger world. In the meantime, relying on Islamic scholars for a number of limited government functions saved the imperial state from having to invest in extending the branches of its bureaucratic institutions into Muslim communities for direct governance.

Conclusion

In the decades following the foundation of the Orenburg Spiritual Assembly, the Russian imperial state gradually incorporated Islamic scholars into its governing apparatus while the scholars continued to preserve their centrality in the mechanisms of exchange that brought about the Muslim domain. The ulama assumed a dual function as communal leaders of the Volga-Ural Muslim domain and local agents of the imperial state. This dual function placed them at the junction where the Russian state met the Volga-Ural Muslim domain, and it

---

[66] For discussions of this leverage, see Crews, *For Prophet*; and Stefan B. Kirmse, "Dealing with Crime in Late Tsarist Russia: Muslim Tatars Go to Court," in *One Law for All?: Western Models and Local Practices in (Post-)Imperial Contexts*, ed. Stefan B. Kirmse (Frankfurt: Campus Verlag, 2012), 209–41.

[67] Stefan Kirmse recognizes this limitation in theory. See Kirmse, "Dealing with Crime," 232–33.

created an institutional bond between the imperial state apparatus and the Muslim communities of the Volga-Ural region.

Yet sometimes, the two functions of the ulama conflicted, for the scholars represented the authority of religion in their local communities but they also received orders from non-Muslim power holders. The intercession of the Orenburg Spiritual Assembly helped the Islamic scholars and ordinary Muslims to reconcile this conflict by creating a perception of mediated distance. When surveyors or health officials sought the assistance of mullahs, they did not contact the mullahs directly but wrote to the spiritual assembly as an imperial institution overseeing the affairs of Islamic scholars. When the spiritual assembly passed those inquiries to the mullahs, it wrote not only as an imperial institution but also as a religious authority, thus in the process transforming an obligation coming from the imperial state apparatus into a religious obligation.

Not all Islamic scholars accepted the transformation of imperial authority into religious authority through the intercession of the Orenburg Spiritual Assembly. Some of them refused to obey orders coming from the spiritual assembly, especially when the muftis failed to project an image compatible with the status of their position.[68] Some others obeyed the orders of the assembly and/or the Russian state but envisioned their obedience as an unavoidable, therefore permissible, necessity under dire circumstances (*darūrah* in Islamic terminology).[69] And most scholars either accepted the transformation in a conscious way[70] or availed themselves of the comfort offered by this transformation without publicly questioning it.

The Russian state did not intervene extensively in the daily lives of the empire's Muslim subjects in the Volga-Ural region in the nineteenth century at least until the 1870s. When it did intervene for small-scale projects, such as maintaining public health, gathering statistical data, or conscripting soldiers, it sought the ulama's assistance in realizing those projects through the mediation of the Orenburg Spiritual Assembly. The assembly's mediation kept the imperial state and the Muslim communities of the Volga-Ural region distant from one another but still connected. The resulting perception of freedom and inviolability in religious and to some extent intra-communal affairs helped Volga-Ural

---

[68] Kemper, *Sufis und Gelehrte*, 57–61 and 393–428; Frank, *Muslim Religious Institutions*, 103–5; and Crews, *For Prophet*, 58–66.

[69] Fahreddin, *Âsar*, vol. 2, 162.

[70] Kemper, *Sufis und Gelehrte*, 368–92. Also see the above-quoted circular of Mufti Ğabdulvâhid bin Süleyman during the Crimean War. Fahreddin, *Âsar*, vol. 2, 369–73.

Muslims maintain a generally peaceful existence in the Russian empire. Territorially, they lived on Russian soil and politically they were the subjects of an Orthodox Christian monarch, but culturally, the long-established patterns of Muslim exchange – whether transregional or confined to the Volga-Ural region – continued to define the contours of their shared imaginaries and way of life in the insulated safe space of the Volga-Ural Muslim domain.

3   Russification
Unmediated governance and the empire's quest for ideal subjects

> In this way, the Russian language will constitute an imperceptible but effective link gradually pulling the Tatars to the governmental center, to Russia ... wherever there is a link of words and comprehension, there springs up the links of ideas and convictions over time, and the tribal estrangement fades away.[1]   Count Dmitrii A. Tolstoi, Minister of Public Enlightenment to Alexander II, 1867

The imperial model that Catherine II instituted in the late eighteenth century, based on indirect governance through intermediaries, initiated a period of relative peace and normalcy between the Russian state and its Muslim subjects in the Volga-Ural region.[2] However, by the 1860s, the Romanov court, tsarist officials, and parts of the ever-expanding Russian public grew uneasy about this seemingly well-functioning model and the position of Muslims in it. Many factors contributed to their reservation: revolutions and the emergence of nation-states in Europe and the Americas, decades of Muslim resistance to Russian rule in the Caucasus, Polish rebellions, Russia's embarrassing defeat at the Crimean War, and repeated demands from the recently Christianized non-Russian peoples of the Volga-Ural region to be recognized as Muslims. Yet, underneath the veneer of these troubling events, it was the substantial growth, if not emergence, of what we may call an "imperial domain" that fundamentally challenged the model of indirect imperial governance and provoked the anxiety of St. Petersburg and its agents in the Great Reforms era. With a defensive attitude born out of this anxiety, tsarist officials attempted to establish mechanisms for closer control and direct management of Russia's subject peoples, including the Volga-Ural Muslims. This chapter outlines how tsarist officials, or Russia's ruling elite in general, started to see Muslims, especially in the Volga-Ural region, as a threat in the

---

[1] Dmitrii A. Tolstoi, "Po voprosu ob obrazovanii inorodtsev," in *Sbornik dokumentov i statei po voprosu ob obrazovanii inorodtsev*, ed. Ministerstvo narodnogo prosveshcheniia (St. Petersburg: V Tip. T-va Obshchestvennaia Pol'za, 1869), 160.

[2] On the Catherinian imperial model, see Crews, *For Prophet*.

growing imperial domain of the late tsarist period and how they resorted to schooling as an instrument to transform Muslims – as well as other population groups – into more manageable subjects.

Ideal subjects for the imperial domain

The imperial domain grew in the late Russian empire, as hikes in literacy, print volume, social mobility, civil rights, and other democratizing factors extended some of the otherwise exclusive privileges and functions of the *obshchestvo* (the elite minority whose opinions and legitimate interventions directly impacted local and imperial governance) to broader segments of the subject population. The gentry by and large filled the *obshchestvo*'s ranks until the end of the eighteenth century while a trickle of educated professionals started to join them during the reigns of Alexander I (1801–25) and Nicholas I (1825–55).[3] Peasants, the overwhelming majority of Russia's subjects, typically remained excluded from governance until the emancipation of serfs in 1861. Before then, the Russian state ruled peasants through intermediaries: the serf-owning gentry and, in the case of state peasants who were not serfs, communal leaders such as Islamic scholars and tribal chiefs.[4] The Great Reforms rendered intermediaries less significant in the governance of peasants, although not defunct. They also enabled vertical social mobility at formerly unprecedented levels and eliminated many of the structural barriers that kept peasants from enjoying at least some of the privileges of the *obshchestvo*.[5] The emancipation did not enfranchise or politically empower the peasants,[6] but gradually, what the peasants thought and wanted in aggregate did become a primary component of the empire's decision-making processes.

---

[3] W. Bruce Lincoln, *In the Vanguard of Reform: Russia's Enlightened Bureaucrats, 1825–1861* (DeKalb: Northern Illinois University Press, 1982); and Abbott Gleason, "The Terms of Russian Social History," in *Between Tsar and People: Educated Society and the Quest for Public Identity in Late Imperial Russia*, ed. Edith W. Clowes, Samuel D. Kassow, and James L. West (Princeton: Princeton University Press, 1991).

[4] For an excellent outline of the gentry's intermediary role, see David Moon, "Reassessing Russian Serfdom," *European History Quarterly*, 1996 26(4): 483–526. Kappeler, *Russian Empire* provides an overview of other intermediaries in the Russian empire. For a general analysis of the role of intermediaries in empires, see the various discussions on this topic in Burbank and Cooper, *Empires*, especially 13–14.

[5] For a concise analysis of the legal and societal continuity and change that accompanied the Great Reforms, see Gregory L. Freeze, "The Soslovie (Estate) Paradigm and Russian Social History," *The American Historical Review*, 1986 91(1): 11–36, especially 33. For peasant involvement, see Burbank, *Russian Peasants*.

[6] Burbank, *Russian Peasants*, 266–67.

Gone were the days when Catherine II could mock and dismiss the inklings of opposition that emerged in secretive and exclusive Freemason clubs, which served as venues for socially and politically significant discussion beyond the Court's direct control.[7] Will and skill started to trump status as the prerequisites of participation in local and imperial governance. Theoretically, Russia's monarchs remained absolute autocrats until 1917, but a romantic appeal to the people tempered their will even in the seemingly conservative "Orthodoxy, autocracy, populism (*narodnost'*)" trio of the Official Nationality doctrine that Nicholas I had embraced for himself and for his successors. After the emancipation, Russia's emperors felt the need to build their legitimacy on the approval of their subjects through careful management of what we would today call "public relations."[8] Improvements in the publication industry further consolidated this process. By the mid nineteenth century, the volume of Russian-language print media increased so much that the government had to switch from preventive to punitive censorship: from the advance evaluation and authorization of what could or could not be published to reviewing already published texts for possible sanctions.[9] Gradually, the *obshchestvo* lost its exclusivist function and there evolved a broader "imperial public," *obshchestvennost'* as some referred to this new phenomenon at the time,[10] or "civil society" according to Wayne Dowler's interpretation.[11]

Nevertheless, the imperial domain was still larger than the imperial public. Given the late nineteenth and early twentieth century discord between the radical intelligentsia and tsarist officialdom, which culminated in the Bolshevik Revolution in 1917, one may be tempted to explain Russia's imperial situation as an oppositional stalemate between the tsarist state and the imperial public, as represented by the intelligentsia.[12]

---

[7] Smith, "Freemasonry," 284–95.

[8] For an excellent analysis of this change in the tsarist strategies of constructing legitimacy, see Richard Wortman, *Scenarios of Power: Myth and Ceremony in Russian Monarchy*, 2 vols., vol. 2 (Princeton: Princeton University Press, 1995). On the evolution of the Official Nationality doctrine, see Nicholas V. Riasanovsky, *Nicholas I and Official Nationality in Russia, 1825–1855* (Berkeley: University of California Press, 1959).

[9] W. Bruce Lincoln, *The Great Reforms: Autocracy, Bureaucracy, and the Politics of Change in Imperial Russia* (DeKalb: Northern Illinois University Press, 1990), 122–33; and McReynolds, *The News*, especially 25.

[10] Several chapters in Edith W. Clowes, Samuel D. Kassow, and James L. West eds., *Between Tsar and People: Educated Society and the Quest for Public Identity in Late Imperial Russia* (Princeton: Princeton University Press, 1991); especially Gleason, "Terms," 21–22 explore this issue.

[11] Dowler, *Russia in 1913*, 91–93.

[12] See Gleason, "Terms," 21–22; and Nicholas V. Riasanovsky, *A Parting of Ways: Government and the Educated Public in Russia, 1801–1855* (Oxford: Clarendon Press, 1976).

However, the radical intelligentsia was only a small, albeit vocal, part of the imperial public.[13] And more significantly, at a deeper level, the tsarist state and the imperial public both became participants of a broader sphere of exchange where shared norms and imaginaries emerged from the exchange itself rather than being defined by and imposed from St. Petersburg. We will refer to this extraspatial marketplace of ideas and influence as the "imperial domain." Different from Jürgen Habermas' idea of the "public sphere," which is largely based on a democratic nation-state model where the societal structure can be neatly categorized into the private and public spheres along with the sphere of public authority, Russia's "imperial domain" grew in a multilayered and somewhat cacophonic imperial situation that defies easy dissection.[14] Its growth was a very slow and at times frustrating process – for those who aspired to join it. The Romanov court continued to claim, and arguably exercise, monopoly over the consideration of all political matters, or even non-political matters that transcended local and communal concerns. Yet, the exchange mechanisms in Russia gradually evolved to give access to increasingly more people who ranked lower in the empire's estate (soslovie) or legally sanctioned social stratification system.[15] Many legal and institutional obstacles barred many of Russia's subject peoples, especially the peasants, from direct participation in governance even after 1905. Yet, by the late nineteenth century, the growing imperial public owed its clout not to its relative strength vis-à-vis the tsarist state but to the almost universal expectation that each opinion in the empire, even those of the state representatives, had to seek validation in the imperial domain. The slow and invisible mechanisms of this validation process involved even the peasants and, although at varying degrees, the non-Russian minorities.

The architects of the Great Reforms, the "enlightened bureaucrats" as Bruce Lincoln has identified them, expected such validation to empower Russia by rallying peasants behind the centrally defined goals of the tsarist authorities.[16] Yet validation could be restrictive too, for the

---

[13] Dowler, *Russia in 1913*, 190.

[14] See Habermas, *Structural Transformation*. Taylor builds his discussion of "metatopical common space" partly on Jürgen Habermas' idea of the "public sphere" but keeps it more ambiguous and, therefore, more compatible with imperial situations.

[15] Andrew Verner, "Discursive Strategies in the 1905 Revolution: Peasant Petitions from Vladimir Province," *Russian Review*, 1995 54(1): 66. Also see Theodore R. Weeks, "Russification: Word and Practice 1863–1914," *Proceedings of the American Philosophical Society*, 2004 148(4): 476.

[16] See Alfred J. Rieber, "Alexander II: A Revisionist View," *The Journal of Modern History*, 1971 43(1): 42–58; W. Bruce Lincoln, "The Genesis of an Enlightened Bureaucracy in Russia," *Jahrbücher für Gesichte Osteuropas*, 1972 20(3): especially 326; and Lincoln, *Great Reforms*, 38–39, and 117.

authorities now had to negotiate their decisions in the imperial domain. They had to hear the opinions and try to realize the demands of the empire's subjects. Nonetheless, as the reforms started to unfold, events like the Polish Uprising of 1863 and Dmitrii Vladimirovich Karakazov's attempt on Alexander II's life in 1866 cast a long shadow on the enlightened bureaucrats' liberal optimism.[17] Not satisfied with the demands that were now publicly expressed in the name of the people (*narod*) and unable to stop the democratizing forces already set in motion in the imperial domain, Alexander II started to emphasize creating ideal subjects who would identify with the tsarist regime, share Romanov ideals, willingly follow imperial directives, and demand – when they demanded – what would please the tsar and his retinue.

Remaking societies seemed possible to many statesmen in the late nineteenth century – not only in Russia but around the world. They banked their hopes on popular education as a promising instrument toward this end.[18] Alexander II appointed a strikingly conservative statesman, Count Dmitrii Andreevich Tolstoi, as the over-procurator of the Holy Synod in 1865 and simultaneously as the minister of public enlightenment in 1866. In 1866, the tsar also announced the mission of education in Russia as preserving the existing political system and, to this end, strengthening "religion – notably Orthodoxy – among the people." In 1882, following the assassination of Alexander II, Nicholas II appointed Count Tolstoi as the minister of internal affairs while Count Tolstoi's long-time assistant Ivan Davydovich Delianov took charge of the Ministry of Public Enlightenment (MNP) until 1897.[19]

It was these conservative statesmen and their protégés in the officialdom, and not the liberal-minded enlightened bureaucrats, who planned and implemented educational policies at an imperial level in Russia until the turn of the twentieth century. Their schooling projects for the Volga-Ural Muslims, which may be considered the Russian state's first comprehensive response to the potential inclusion of Muslims in the growing imperial domain, evolved in the context of a broader reliance upon schooling as a means to cope with the social and political

---

[17] Claudia Verhoeven, *The Odd Man Karakozov: Imperial Russia, Modernity, and the Birth of Terrorism* (Ithaca: Cornell University Press, 2009) reflects the moment of this transition.

[18] Selim Deringil, *The Well-Protected Domains: Ideology and the Legitimation of Power in the Ottoman Empire, 1876–1909* (New York: I.B. Tauris, 1998), 93.

[19] Ben Eklof, *Russian Peasant Schools: Officialdom, Village Culture, and Popular Pedagogy, 1861–1914* (Berkeley: University of California Press, 1986), 64; and Dowler, *Classroom and Empire*, 63. On Count Tolstoi, see James Cobb Mills, *"Dmitrii Tolstoi as Minister of Education in Russia, 1866–1880"* (Ph. D. Dissertation, Indiana University, 1967); and Allen Sinel, *The Classroom and the Chancellery: State Educational Reform in Russia under Count Dmitry Tolstoi* (Cambridge, MA: Harvard University Press, 1973).

transformations of the Great Reforms era.[20] The initiatives of this conservative faction in the Russian government and bureaucracy were
indeed reformative, but they still parted from the logic of the Great
Reforms at a fundamental level. In the Catherinian imperial model,
regularity and universally applicable norms were not necessary or even
desirable components of the system. Imperial governance was based
on the recognition or creation and management of societal categories –
estates, confessions, and ethnic groups – with unequal privileges
bestowed from St. Petersburg.[21] This paradigm never disappeared completely, but the Great Reforms still gave way to an increasingly more
mobile and equalizing, though not egalitarian, social environment.
While the equalizing impact of the Great Reforms seemed to align with
the enlightened bureaucrats' hopes for increased governmental efficiency
resulting from reduced diversity, anxieties related to the growing inclu-
siveness of the imperial domain stimulated nationalist visions among
Russian elites about the primacy of a core Russian nation.[22] Count
Tolstoi and his advisors probably shared these nascent nationalist sentiments and visions, but more importantly, in the shaky atmosphere of
the empire after 1866, they were more concerned with stability and
the continuity of the fundamental principles and power structures of
Romanov rule than with efficiency.

Hence, the interventions of Count Tolstoi and his advisors in
schooling matters aimed to counter the potentially destabilizing consequences of social mobility in the Great Reforms era by molding the
empire's subjects in ways that would preserve St. Petersburg's preroga-
tive to determine the power matrixes among Russia's many peoples and
the primacy of Great Russians among them. With regard to schooling the
Great Russian peasants, this mission translated into "enlightenment"
(*prosveshchenie*), "intellectual and moral improvement through sound
education,"[23] or what Alexander Etkind has suggestively called "internal

---

[20] For excellent studies of these broader initiatives as well as the independent life that
popular education acquired in the hands of the Russian educated society and peasants,
see Sinel, *The Classroom*; Eklof, *Russian Peasant Schools*; and Jeffrey Brooks, *When Russia
Learned to Read: Literacy and Popular Literature, 1861–1917* (Evanston: Northwestern
University Press, 2003).

[21] Freeze, "The Soslovie Paradigm," 11–36; Kappeler, *Russian Empire*; Steinwedel,
"Making Social," 67–82; and Crews, "Empire".

[22] See Miller's comments on the writings of Mikhail Nikiforovich Katkov and Petr
Berngardovich Struve in Miller, *The Romanov Empire and Nationalism*, 170–73.

[23] *Sbornik dokumentov i statei po voprosu ob obrazovanii inorodtsev*, ed. Ministerstvo
narodnogo prosveshcheniia (St. Petersburg: Tip. T-va Obshchestvennaia Pol'za,
1869), 5 and 9.

colonization."[24] With regard to non-Russians, Count Tolstoi had to experiment and figure out what the goals of stability and of the preservation of Romanov rule implied in their schooling.

Debate over schooling non-Russians

One of Count Tolstoi's early challenges as the simultaneous overprocurator of the Holy Synod and the minister of public enlightenment was the demand of about 11,000 baptized Tatars in the Kazan region to forsake Christianity and be recognized as Muslims.[25] Soon after his appointment, he traveled to Kazan and toured the region to investigate this issue. There, he met a young Orientalist and lay missionary, Nikolai Ivanovich Il'minskii (1822–91).[26] In the early 1860s, Il'minskii and another activist in the region, Nikolai Ivanovich Zolotnitskii (1829–80), – both graduates of the Kazan Ecclesiastical Academy – had simultaneously but independently developed elementary schools that utilized the students' native tongues to educate baptized non-Russian children as devout Christians.[27] Count Tolstoi was impressed, especially with Il'minskii's school for baptized Tatars in Kazan. He adopted Il'minskii as a trusted consultant on issues related to the non-Russian peoples of Russia's eastern borderlands, and Delianov later inherited this relationship when he replaced Tolstoi as the minister of

---

[24] Aleksandr Etkind, *Internal Colonization: Russia's Imperial Experience* (Malden: Polity Press, 2011).

[25] The reconversion movements in the Volga basin in the nineteenth century constitute the subject of several studies. Especially see Lemercier-Quelquejay, "Les missions", 369–403; Khodarkovsky, "Not by Word", 267–93; Lotfullin and Islaev, *Dzhikhad*; Kefeli-Clay, "Kräshen Apostasy"; Islaev, *Islam i pravoslavie*; and Werth, *At the Margins*, especially 44–73.

[26] Many of the missionary activists of the Volga-Ural region, including Nikolai Ivanovich Il'minskii, were lay people, but they devoted their energies to Orthodox proselytization and established institutions with missionary objectives. Therefore, here and throughout this chapter, I will use the word "missionary" without necessarily referring to an institutional affiliation with the Russian Orthodox Church establishment.

[27] On the life, work, and legacy of Il'minskii, see Isabelle Teitz Kreindler, *"Educational Policies Toward the Eastern Nationalities in Tsarist Russia: A Study of Il'minskii's System"* (Ph.D. Dissertation, Columbia University, 1969); Geraci, *Window*, especially 47–85; and Michael W. Johnson, *"Imperial Commission or Orthodox Mission: Nikolai Il'minskii's Work among the Tatars of Kazan, 1862–1891"* (Ph.D. Dissertation, University of Illinois at Chicago, 2005). For an account of Count Tolstoi's visit to Kazan by Nikolai Ivanovich Il'minskii, see Nikolai I. Il'minskii, "Otkrytie uchitel'skoi seminarii v Kazani," in *Nikolai Ivanovich Il'minskii: izbrannye mesta iz pedagogicheskikh sochinenii, nekotorye svedeniia o ego geiatel'nosti i o poslednykh dniakh ego zhizni.* (Kazan': Tipografiia imperatorskogo universiteta, 1892): 41–44. On Zolotnitskii's work, see *Sbornik obrazovanii inorodtsev*, 8–9 and 276.

public enlightenment.[28] Following his tour, Count Tolstoi submitted a
report to Alexander II "On the Question of Educating Non-Russians."
The new minister of public enlightenment was optimistic. He wrote:

In my opinion, enlightening the non-Russians, bringing them closer to the
Russian spirit and to Russia gradually, is a task with utmost political
significance for the future. It is necessary to direct the activities of the clergy
as well as the efforts of the Ministry of Public Enlightenment's provincial
functionaries to this goal.

He then described Il'minskii's school and informed the tsar of plans
for opening similar schools for baptized non-Russian peoples in other
parts of the Volga-Ural region as well. However, it seems that Count
Tolstoi had not yet considered an elaborate program for educating
Muslims. The one measure he mentioned regarding Muslim affairs was
opening a new mission targeting Muslims in the Samara Gubernia.[29]

Meanwhile, Count Tolstoi also spearheaded a discussion among
experts and officials about what to do for schooling the empire's non-
Russian peoples.[30] Many of the rather substantial and noteworthy contributions to this discussion are preserved in an edited volume that the
MNP collated in 1869, probably as reference material for the statesmen
who worked on preparing regulations for schooling non-Russians in
Russia's eastern borderlands.[31] The content preserved in this volume
suggests that Count Tolstoi and most of his advisors looked at schooling
as an opportunity to convince the empire's non-Russian peoples about
"the moral *superiority of the Russian nationality (narodnost')*" and to assimi-
late them "into [Russia's] first-coming (*pervenstvuiushchii*) people," the
Great Russians, who constituted the Romanov state's "primary source of
strength."[32] An editorial in the official *Journal of the Ministry of Popular
Enlightenment* wrote in 1867 that in this way:

The Russian state will fulfill its mission as a Christian and European-educated
power and render a genuine service to the Christian church as well as to general
civilization ... The enlightenment of non-Russian children in the Christian spirit
and their complete russification has to be the goal of these schools. Everybody
agrees on this.[33]

---

[28] Il'minskii's correspondence with Count Tolstoi and I. D. Delianov can be accessed in
NART, f. 968, op. 1, d. 6.
[29] *Sbornik obrazovanii inorodtsev*, 157–58.
[30] For an outline of these discussions, see Dowler, *Classroom and Empire*, especially
62–84.
[31] *Sbornik obrazovanii inorodtsev*, 1–469.
[32] *Sbornik obrazovanii inorodtsev*, 5 and 9. Emphasis in the original.
[33] *Sbornik obrazovanii inorodtsev*, 5.

The elusiveness of Muslim schooling and the urgency of control

Nevertheless, the Volga-Ural Muslims did not fit neatly into this boldly sketched picture. An acclaimed specialist on Muslim affairs, Vasilii Vasil'evich Grigor'ev, stated bluntly in a report to the MNP:

It is possible to annihilate Muslims or banish them out of the empire, if that is considered necessary, but radically transforming them is not possible. And what is not possible should not be pursued. The government cannot achieve this, no matter how much it is desired or may be desired.[34]

Other contributors were more optimistic, but when the discussion turned to the Volga-Ural Muslims, their emphasis almost invariably moved from the promises of cultural transformation through schooling to the vicissitudes of an ongoing power struggle between the imperial state and Muslim communities. In the early years of the Great Reforms era, the Volga-Ural Muslims were generally satisfied with the insulated existence of their local communities, and according to one contemporary observer, they often did not know enough Russian to interact beyond Muslim networks.[35] Therefore, they lacked the will and skill to claim their share in the imperial domain. Nonetheless, when seen from St. Petersburg, they still appeared as a quite affluent and dynamic population group. They were more literate, more rooted, better organized, and more cohesive than the other non-Russian – mostly animist and recently baptized – peoples in their vicinity.[36] They could be compared to the Poles of Russia's Western borderlands in this regard.[37] Having witnessed the Poles rebel with demands of independence in 1863, Count Tolstoi, who was directly involved in the suppression of the Polish Rebellion,[38] and his advisors could not imagine why the Muslims would not at least ask for equal consideration in imperial governance instead of being acquiescent recipients of the "Russian enlightenment." Moreover, the frequent attempts of baptized but not fully Christianized non-Russian

---

[34] *Sbornik obrazovanii inorodtsev*, 205. On Vasilii V. Grigor'ev, see Nathaniel Knight, "Grigor'ev in Orenburg, 1851–1862: Russian Orientalism in the Service of Empire?," *Slavic Review*, 2000 59(1): 74–100.

[35] See Karl Fuks, *Kazanskie Tatary v statisticheskom i etnograficheskom otnosheniiakh* (1844; reprint Kazan: Fond TIaK, 1991), 139.

[36] For one among many examples of this view, see *Sbornik obrazovanii inorodtsev*, 27–29. Also see the descriptions of contemporary European observers, such as Baron von Haxthausen, *The Russian Empire: Its People, Institutions, and Resources*, trans. Robert Farie, 2 vols. (London: Chapman and Hall, 1856), 323–28; and Robert Gordon Latham, *Russian and Turk* (London: William H. Allen and Co., 1878), 226.

[37] On Poles in the Western borderlands, see Theodore R. Weeks, "Russification and the Lithuanians, 1863–1905," *Slavic Review*, 2001 60(1): especially 99–102.

[38] Mills, "Dmitrii Tolstoi", 21–36.

peoples in the Volga-Ural region to be recognized as Muslims, including the movement in 1866, put the Orthodox Church, which Tolstoi supervized as the over-procurator of the Holy Synod, in a defensive position vis-à-vis the Muslims.

Thus, from the very beginning, the Volga-Ural Muslims appeared as not only the targets but also the rivals of St. Petersburg's aspirations and efforts to mold ideal subjects from non-Russian peoples. The author of the aforementioned editorial in the *Journal of the Ministry of Public Enlightenment* wrote:

> Here [in the Volga-Ural region], Islam appears not as much a religion of tolerance with a submissive spirit but more among the militant religions that constantly strive for new conquests ... Thanks to their large numbers, prosperity, and boldness, they [the Muslim Tatars] have recently stolen away incredible successes in spreading Muhammadan enlightenment among their ranks, and they are ready to lure each and every one of the non-Russian peoples located in their vicinity into their sphere of influence. On the other hand, Russian-Christian enlightenment has until now remained completely weak and insignificant both among these same Tatars and among other non-Russian peoples, although the other non-Russian peoples do not approach the Russian-Christian influence aggressively and even show an inclination to accept it.[39]

While other non-Russian peoples in the region appeared to be culturally malleable, as the initiatives of Il'minskii and Zolotnitskii suggested, Count Tolstoi's advisors viewed Volga-Ural Muslims as "fanatics" in a state of "estrangement" (*otchuzhdenie*) from the Russian state and its ideals.[40]

Il'minskii was probably the most influential one among Count Tolstoi's advisors. Some of his later statements and correspondence suggest that he actually favored an obscurantist policy of non-interference regarding Muslim schooling for he considered Muslim educational institutions to be archaic and obsolete and therefore, preferred to avoid any initiatives to improve them lest such improvement would render Muslims more capable and assertive.[41] However, Il'minskii's approach to Muslim education was actually more complicated than reading those later statements at face value may indicate. The educational commissions in the Kazan Educational Circuit, where Il'minskii had a very strong influence, recommended Count Tolstoi to open special schools for

---

[39] *Sbornik obrazovanii inorodtsev*, 2–5.

[40] Werth, *At the Margins*, 184–97; and Campbell, *Muslim Question*, 26–31. For expressions of this view, see *Sbornik obrazovanii inorodtsev*, 1–5, 159–60, 175–76, 452, and 456–61.

[41] Kreindler, "Educational Policies," 172; Dowler, *Classroom and Empire*, 143–45; and Geraci, *Window*, 150–53. The first governor of Turkestan, Konstantin von Kaufman applied this policy in Turkestan in the 1870s, and Il'minskii approved it.

Muslims that would teach colloquial Tatar using the Cyrillic script (instead of literary Tatar using the Arabic script as in maktabs), basic calculation, the Russian language, and Russian history and geography. They advised against teaching Turkish, Arabic, or Persian to the Volga-Ural Muslims, as was done in some madrasas, "since these [had] no educational significance from a Russian-European point of view."[42] They also stated that it was desirable to introduce Russian-language classes in Muslim schools, maktabs, and madrasas, and to attract Muslims to government schools.[43] Some aspects of these recommendations actually suggest that Il'minskii was spearheading the discussion in Kazan's educational commissions. Using Cyrillic script for Muslim languages to make transitioning into Russian easier for Muslim students, for instance, was an idea that he had successfully applied among the Kazakhs.[44] He had also emphasized colloquial instead of literary Tatar among the baptized Tatars in hopes of distancing them from the influence and religious discourse of the Islamic scholars, who tended to use literary Tatar.[45]

As one of Grigorev's mentees, Il'minskii shared the old Orientalist's views about the difficulty of "radically transforming" Muslims.[46] However, what Grigor'ev implied by radical transformation in the above quote was turning Muslims into devout Christians who loyally identified with the Russian state, as Il'minskii and Zolotnitskii suggested was possible among other non-Russian peoples in the Volga-Ural region. Otherwise, Grigor'ev also wrote:

Measures to russify (*rusit'*) Muslim Tatars and gradually weaken the fanaticism of their spirits, which originates from Islam, can of course be found, if looked for, but those measures do not lie within the jurisdiction of the Ministry of Public Enlightenment.[47]

This was a reference to measures for curbing the influence of Islamic scholars in Muslim communities as maktab and madrasa instructors and the jurisdiction that the Orenburg Spiritual Assembly, hence the MVD, exercised over them as opposed to the MNP. Il'minskii agreed with

---

[42] *Sbornik obrazovanii inorodtsev*, 189–90.   [43] *Sbornik obrazovanii inorodtsev*, 450–51.

[44] A. Alektorov, "Iz istorii razvitiia obrazovaniia sredi Kirgizov Akmolinskoi i Semipalatinskoi Oblastei," in *Zhurnal Ministerstva Narodnogo Prosveshcheniia*, 1905 362 (December): 168.

[45] See a report that Il'minskii wrote on this issue in 1862 in NART, f. 968, op. 1, d. 6, ll. 1–3; as well as a later study by him, Nikolai Ivanovich Il'minskii, *Opyty perelozheniia khristianskikh verouchitel'nykh knig na Tatarskii i drugie inorodcheskie iazyki v nachale tekushchogo stoleiia* (Kazan: Tipografiia Imperatorskogo Universiteta, 1883).

[46] On Grigor'ev's influence on Il'minskii, see Kreindler, "Educational Policies," 56–59.

[47] *Sbornik obrazovanii inorodtsev*, 205.

Grigor'ev that it did not make sense to invest government money in Muslim schools while they remained outside of the MNP jurisdiction. Instead, he and his colleagues in Kazan's educational commissions suggested opening separate government schools for Muslims where Islam would be deemphasized, to the extent that this was possible without agitating Muslim communities, while the Russian language would be emphasized, as a draw to the empire's "governmental center" and a token of submission to it.[48]

As for the maktabs and madrasas, many of Count Tolstoi's advisors suggested introducing Russian-language classes in them and encouraging or requiring mullahs to learn Russian so that they would set an example for their congregations.[49] But intervening in the daily affairs of the maktabs and madrasas was an elusive task. First, the Russian state had until then recognized Muslim schools as exclusively religious institutions. Therefore, the empire's Muslim communities were likely to perceive intervention in their maktabs and madrasas as restricting the religious freedoms granted to them by Catherine II a long time ago. Second, as Il'minskii also worried, improving Muslim schools enough to give Muslim children a sense of their status as subjects of the Romanov emperors but stopping short of empowering Muslim communities too much in the imperial domain required an almost impossibly delicate balance.[50] And third, at the end of the 1860s, the Russian state neither knew about nor had the ability to control Muslim educational institutions in the empire. In early 1868, the archbishop of Kazan, Anton', requested the MNP to "establish control over Muhammadan schools maintained by mullahs in Tatar villages." Kazan's educational commissions responded negatively: "in the absence of any regularity in the internal life of these schools controlling them is generally not achievable."[51] Yet, Count Tolstoi and most of his advisors still favored establishing some sort of a jurisdiction over maktabs and madrasas, for leaving them unchecked, with the gates of the imperial domain potentially open for Muslims, appeared to them as neglecting a serious and imminent threat.

The anxiety arising from this perceived threat and the uncertainties associated with the imperial state's ability to deal with it turned control

---

[48] *Sbornik obrazovanii inorodtsev*, 189–90 and 450–51.

[49] For examples of this view, see *Sbornik obrazovanii inorodtsev*, 94–95, 159–60, 169–73, 175–77, 205, and 450.

[50] For similar concerns of French colonialists in Algeria, see Fanny Colonna, "Educating Conformity in French Colonial Algeria," in *Tensions of Empire: Colonial Cultures in a Bourgeois World*, ed. Frederick Cooper and Ann Laura Stoler (Berkeley: University of California Press, 1997), 346–70.

[51] *Sbornik obrazovanii inorodtsev*, 550–51.

into the central goal of the government's interventions in Muslim schooling. The response of the trustee of the Odessa Educational Circuit, Markov, to the report of two Crimean Muslim noblemen, Arslanbey Taşçıoğlu and Abdulveli Karaşayskiy, about Muslim education in the Crimea highlights this point. Taşçıoğlu and Karaşayskiy diagnosed Russia's Muslims with the problem of backwardness "in a primitive state of darkness, not knowing what [was] going on in the world." They asked for the opening of government schools for Muslims that would teach the Russian language as a "means by which ignorance could be suppressed and education could be introduced." The two noblemen preferred maktabs to be left alone as exclusively religious institutions, but they wanted the government to introduce Russian-language classes taught by Muslim teachers in madrasas. And most importantly, they wanted these classes to be financed, therefore controlled, by religious endowments that still existed in the Crimea.[52] In response, Markov approved the idea of introducing Russian-language classes in the madrasas, but he did not want teacher positions to be restricted to Muslims only. He also cautioned against leaving the initiative in the hands of Muslim nobles and mullahs. Instead, he suggested that the government treasury should provide the money and have jurisdiction over the matter.[53] Although the Crimean and Volga-Ural Muslim experiences differed in many ways, the two peoples still shared enough commonalities to warrant comparisons, and the MNP officials tended to treat them similarly. Therefore, Markov's position in this exchange parallels that of many other officials and unofficial advisors who corresponded with Count Tolstoi regarding the schooling of Volga-Ural Muslims. An educational committee that convened in St. Petersburg in 1867, for instance, agreed that the Russification of Tatars could not be achieved through the agency of Islamic scholars.[54]

To be fair, not all of Tolstoi's advisors tried to exclude Muslims from the planning of Muslim schooling. For instance, the director of schools in the Orenburg Gubernia, Popov, shared the concerns of other advisors about the Muslims' "fanaticism" and influence over other non-Russians, but in a way similar to the approach of small-deeds liberals who worked among Russian peasants, he sought ways of cooperating with the Islamic scholars in order to introduce "European civilization" and the Russian language to Muslim communities. He even suggested the possibility of introducing Russian-language classes at the İsterlibaş Madrasa in Sterlitamak, for, he explained, the Muslims of the region and even of

---

[52] *Sbornik obrazovanii inorodtsev*, 134–36.   [53] *Sbornik obrazovanii inorodtsev*, 155–57.
[54] *Sbornik obrazovanii inorodtsev*, 169.

Russia respected the Islamic scholar who oversaw this madrasa so much so that they "considered him a saint."[55] Indeed, the İsterlibaş Madrasa was a prominent educational institution among Russia's Muslims and its chief instructor in the 1860s, Muhammed Hâris Hazret, was an influential Naqshbandi-Mujaddidi sheikh who had cooperated with the Russian government on many occasions. He had even advised his followers to learn languages and "inform themselves about world affairs."[56] Nevertheless, Popov's liberal approach put him in a marginal position among Count Tolstoi's advisors. In the end, the advisors' consensus would shift from an absolute rejection of Islamic scholars as agents of transforming the Muslims to utilizing them as models for their respective congregations. However, while Popov saw this as a matter of cooperation with the Islamic scholars, the hawkish majority perceived it as a matter of pressing, or at least encouraging, mullahs into submission.[57]

The Catherinian imperial model designated each societal category a more or less certain place within an imperial matrix of power relations. The equalizing pulse of the Great Reforms removed certainty from this matrix by creating an environment of social mobility and competition. Pandora's box had opened. Count Tolstoi and his advisors could not put everything back in and close the lid. Therefore, they focused on finding measures to maintain the matrix of existing power relations even as the empire's societal categories – estates, confessions, and ethnic groups – started to morph or move out of their former domains. Because the Russian state identified first and foremost with the Russian-speaking Orthodox peasants, it was necessary to improve the Russian peasants through "enlightenment" and make them factually superior. It was also necessary to convince the empire's other ethnic groups that the hierarchy of peoples and values the Romanov regime identified with or chose to promote was fair. In February 1870, Count Tolstoi convened a committee in St. Petersburg to boil down the years of discussion on non-Russian education to a set of regulations. The committee stipulated that "the purpose of the education of all non-Russians who live in the borders of our fatherland, without dispute, has to be russification (*obrusenie*) and bringing them closer to the Russian (*russkii*) people."[58] Russification did involve cultural transformation and, ideally, even identity shifts, as highlighted by many studies that examine the Russian state's relations with its non-Russian peoples in the late tsarist period within the framework of

---

[55] *Sbornik obrazovanii inorodtsev*, 453–62.   [56] Tuqayef, *Tarih-i İsterlibaş*, 9–14.
[57] For an example, see *Sbornik obrazovanii inorodtsev*, 205.
[58] I. L. Morozov and N. N. Semenova, *Agrarnyi vopros i krest'ianskoe dvizhenie 50–70x godov XIX v.* (Moscow: Izdatel'stvo Akademii Nauk SSSR, 1936), 285.

nationalism and identity.[59] However, an equally important aspect of Russification as "the purpose of the education" of non-Russians in Russia, was the attempt of the empire's conservative officials and self-employed agents to preserve the imperial matrix of power relations that they perceived to be melting away in the Great Reforms era.

Regulations and reality

Alexander II approved the regulations that Count Tolstoi's committee devised into law on 26 March 1870.[60] The law had two separate sections: one for Muslims and one for the animist and baptized non-Russian peoples of Russia's eastern borderlands. Thanks to Count Tolstoi's support, the section on animist and baptized non-Russians heavily reflected Il'minskii's views.[61] The section on Muslims, however, reflected a haphazard compromise among the many opinions presented to the MNP over the years. It authorized the ministry to open elementary schools for Muslims with Russian-language instruction. Either Muslims who spoke Russian or Russians who spoke Tatar could teach Russian in these institutions, which came to be known as "Russo-Muslim," "Russo-Tatar," or "Russo-Bashkir" schools in the Volga-Ural region. Separate teachers of Islam could offer regular maktab curricula too, but Muslim congregations would have to pay the expenses for that. Additionally, the MNP would open Russian-language classes in maktabs and madrasas, again to be paid for by Muslim congregations, and the opening of new maktabs and madrasas after 1870 would be contingent upon the allocation of funds for Russian-language classes by the Muslim communities. Inspectors of elementary public schools would supervise the Russo-Muslim schools and Russian-language classes in maktabs and madrasas while the spiritual assemblies in Orenburg and Tavrida (Crimea) would keep their jurisdiction over the actual maktabs and madrasas. And finally, the MNP would establish two teachers' schools for Muslims in the cities of Ufa and Aqmescit (Simferopol').

[59] For some good examples, see T. T. Tazhibaev, *Prosveshchenie i shkoly Kazakhstana vo vtoroi polovine XIX veka* (Alma-Ata: Kazakhskoe gosudarstvennoe izdatel'stvo politichesckoi literatury, 1962); Kreindler, "Educational Policies"; Z. T. Sharafuddinov and Iakub Iskhak Khanbikov, *Istoriia pedagogiki Tatarstana* (Kazan: Kazan State Pedagogical University, 1998); Theodore R. Weeks, *Nation and State in Late Imperial Russia: Nationalism and Russification on the Western Frontier, 1863–1914* (DeKalb: Northern Illinois University Press, 1996); and Geraci, *Window.*

[60] *Sbornik postanovlenii po ministerstvu narodnogo prosveshcheniia: tsarstvovanie imperatora Aleksandra II, 1865–70*, vol. 4 (St. Petersburg: Tipografiia imperatorskoi akademii nauk, 1871), 1556–66; and Dowler, *Classroom and Empire*, 62–84.

[61] For an analysis of this section, see Dowler, *Classroom and Empire*, 68–80.

Aside from these institutional arrangements, the Law of March 26 also introduced administrative measures to encourage Muslims to learn Russian. Here the focus moved to Islamic scholars as anticipated by earlier discussions. Islamic scholars would not be appointed to religious positions henceforth unless they demonstrated at least an elementary level of proficiency in Russian and the four arithmetical operations. Similarly, Muslims could join zemstvo boards and village councils only if they knew the Russian-language and the four arithmetical operations. Finally, the law authorized inspectors of elementary public schools or local county schools to administer Russian-language exams to Islamic scholars and other Muslims who needed to prove their proficiency in Russian.[62]

Nevertheless, the Muslim section of the Law of March 26 did not go into effect immediately. Count Tolstoi's committee had stipulated a grace period for implementing the new regulations about Muslim schooling and authorized the MVD to determine its duration. The over-optimism of the law became apparent from the beginning. Because the MNP did not have jurisdiction over mullahs or Muslim schools, it had to operate through the MVD and the spiritual assemblies in order to open Russian-language classes in maktabs and madrasas. Count Tolstoi wrote to the minister of internal affairs, Aleksandr Egorovich Timashev, and asked him to determine the grace period for Islamic scholars to learn Russian. Count Tolstoi also requested the MVD not to permit the opening of new maktabs and madrasas without accompanying Russian-language classes under the jurisdiction of the inspectors of elementary public schools. Timashev passed Count Tolstoi's requests to the then mufti of the Orenburg Spiritual Assembly, Selimgerey Tevkelef, but the mufti's response was discouraging. He wrote directly to Count Tolstoi and suggested the suspension of any changes in Muslim education until the establishment of a commission in the MVD to reorganize the affairs of the spiritual assemblies. Yet the reply came from Timashev, who ordered the mufti to cooperate with the MNP.[63] Himself a conservative statesman like Count Tolstoi, Timashev would not tolerate the mufti's failure to follow the Count's instructions.

Tevkelef appeared to comply by sending a Russian-language circular to the mullahs under his jurisdiction in which he explained the benefits of learning Russian,[64] but he also wrote a long report to Timashev in

---

[62] In addition to the text of the law as cited above, see NART, f. 92, op. 1, d. 10290.
[63] Rızâeddin bin Fahreddin, *İslâmlar Haqqında Hükûmet Tedbirleri*, vol. 1 (Orenburg: Kerimof, Hüseyinof ve Şürekâsı, 1907), 8–13.
[64] Fahreddin, *İslâmlar Haqqında*, 8–13.

order to spell out that the intended changes were not timely. The mufti explained that most maktabs and madrasas had a makeshift nature, meeting in mosque buildings or the mullahs' private homes. Therefore, establishing Russian-language classes in these institutions would require new equipment like desks and blackboards and, in many cases, even new buildings. The Muslim peasants were too poor to pay for such facilities. As a solution, the mufti recommended opening Russian-language classes with zemstvo money in places where a zemstvo existed but without requiring support from Muslim congregations. Additionally, he advised appointing Russian-language teachers from among the members of each Muslim community to increase the likelihood of their support.[65]

Count Tolstoi and Timashev forwarded Mufti Tevkelef's comments to the trustee of the Kazan Educational Circuit, Petr Dmitrievich Shestakov, whose educational commissions had already expressed their hesitation about attempting to take charge of maktabs and madrasas. Still, Shestakov forwarded Count Tolstoi's inquiry to experts in his region, and the experts did not offer much hope about the success of the new regulations either. They wrote that zemstvo support could be useful, as Tevkelef had recommended, but it was more important to earn the support of local Muslim congregations and mullahs. The experts were concerned that the mullahs would not want to share their influence over Muslim communities with the new Russian-language teachers. In that light, the experts found Mufti Tevkelef's suggestion about appointing Russian-language teachers from among the members of Muslim communities to be reasonable too. But there was one problem: there were no qualified Muslims to appoint. Instead, the experts suggested offering material incentives to the Islamic scholars to learn Russian as a long-term solution.

As for not permitting the establishment of new maktabs and madrasas without Russian-language classes, the experts agreed with Tevkelef that this was not a timely measure. If the government did not permit new maktabs and madrasas to open without Russian language classes, mullahs would simply teach without official permission. Moreover, maktabs and madrasas often functioned in mosques, and the MNP could not have jurisdiction over mosques. Cooperation with the spiritual assemblies could be useful in this respect, according to the experts, but even the assemblies did not have much power over maktabs and madrasas. Under the present circumstances, the expert reports concluded, the

---

[65] NART, f. 92, op. 1, d. 10464, ll. 1–2; and NART, f. 322, op. 1, d. 46.

MNP could at best control the relatively better-institutionalized madra-sas where students remained in residence throughout the year.[66]

An inspector to bend reality

These communications clarified that neither the MNP nor the spiritual assemblies as semi-autonomous institutions under the MVD had suffi-cient information about or control over Muslim schools to implement the Law of March 26. But that did not relieve tsarist officials from the obligation to implement the law. In 1869, the MNP had instituted the post of inspector to manage and improve Russian village schools. Another regulation in 1871 vested these inspectors with significantly expanded powers to establish fuller control over public education.[67] Seeing their utility in schooling Russians, Count Tolstoi decided to appoint an inspector to coordinate government efforts for taking Muslim schooling under control in the Volga-Ural region too. In November 1871, he established a post in Kazan titled the "Inspector of Tatar, Kazakh, and Bashkir Schools," and upon the recommendations of Shestakov and Il'minskii, he appointed to this post Wilhelm Radloff (1837–1918) – or Vasilii Vasil'evich Radlov, as he would sign his name in imperial Russian service – a German-born scholar of oriental lan-guages who had spent several years in Russia studying its Turkic peoples.[68]

The inspectorship turned Radloff, the German Orientalist, into the Russian state's chief agent of Russification among Muslims in the empire's eastern borderlands. The initial instructions of Count Tolstoi and Shestakov to Radloff give the impression that he was put on the spot to implement all the plans, which seemed unrealizable according to the earlier reports and correspondence. Among his duties were opening Russo-Muslim schools, preparing books and other materials for instruc-tion, opening Russian-language classes in the existing maktabs and madrasas, finding and appointing Russian-language teachers who spoke the Tatar language well, providing exact information about maktabs, madrasas, and Russo-Muslim schools to the MNP, and establishing a

---

[66] For the reports of the inspector of public schools in the Kazan Educational Circuit and the director of elementary schools in the Ufa Gubernia, see NART, f. 92, op. 1, d. 10464, ll. 4–9.

[67] Eklof, *Russian Peasant Schools*, 66.

[68] On the creation of this post and Radlov's appointment to it, see NART, f. 92, op. 1, d. 10290, ll. 1–2 and 5–6; NART, f. 92, op. 1, d. 11513, ll. 16–21; Geraci, *Window*, 139–40. For a biography of Radloff, see Ahmet Temir, *Türkoloji Tarihinde Wilhelm Radloff Devri: Hayatı, İlmî Kişiliği, Eserleri* (Ankara: Türk Dil Kurumu, 1991).

teachers' school for Muslims in Ufa. In order to realize these goals, he was authorized to publish books without censorship, certify Russian-language teachers for Muslim schools, contact Muslim communities in person, and demand information and assistance from police forces and mullahs.[69]

Radloff had a good command of the languages and cultures of Russia's Turkic-speaking Muslim peoples, but he had no administrative experience to carry out the gigantic mission with which he was charged. He assumed that the government would give him as much support as he needed and that the Muslims would readily follow his instructions. The right to demand information and assistance from mullahs and jurisdiction over Russian-language classes that were to be opened in maktabs and madrasas had already endowed him with some influence over existing Muslim educational institutions, but he found that insufficient. He asked for full jurisdiction over maktabs, madrasas, and their teachers – the mullahs. Muslim communities of the region, on the other hand, had already began showing uneasiness about the MNP's intrusion into the affairs of their schools, which they perceived to be purely religious institutions.

In March 1872, Radloff held a meeting with the head instructors of nine major madrasas in the city of Kazan in order to discuss the Law of March 26. The archives contain both the minutes of this meeting and Radloff's report about it. Interestingly, there are inconsistencies between the two documents. The discrepancy reveals the basic differences of opinion between Radloff and the instructors on the issues of Muslim education and autonomy in the empire. A reading of the minutes suggests that the instructors were fairly reserved about the law. They refused to establish Russian-language classes in their madrasas on the grounds that they did not have the necessary financial resources. When Radloff asked their opinion about how the Russian-language classes should be introduced if the government was to pay for them, they tried to keep the classes outside of their madrasas by demanding a separate building to be used jointly by the students of all madrasas. They also emphasized that the madrasas should not pay for this building or its teachers. Finally, the instructors seized the opportunity to ask if their students could travel to the madrasas with documentation from their local communities instead of official passports and with free tickets like the students of the MNP schools.

In his report, Radloff did not mention the reserved attitude of the instructors at all and presented the meeting as a constructive step.

[69] NART, f. 92, op. 1, d. 10290, ll. 1–9.

He wrote that he also supported the idea of a separate building, but since a new building only for Russian-language classes might not be worth the cost, he suggested the foundation of a teachers' school in the city of Kazan instead of, or in addition to, the one projected in Ufa. He wanted the school in Kazan to be used both to train Muslim teachers for elementary Russo-Muslim schools and to provide Russian-language education to the madrasa students. Interestingly, Radloff reported the instructors' request about easier travel arrangements for their students as a demand for transferring madrasas to the jurisdiction of the MNP. Then he added that this transfer could facilitate the introduction of Russian-language classes by enabling the ministry to make Russian language obligatory in all madrasas.[70]

Coming in the wake of the earlier discouraging reports, Radloff's optimism, as revealed in this document, eventually convinced the higher authorities of the possibility of realizing Count Tolstoi's project. In 1874, following negotiations between the MNP and MVD, the Council of Ministers recommended to Alexander II a second law to transfer all Muslim schools to the jurisdiction of the MNP.[71] The text of their recommendation points to Russia's new imperial model based on unmediated governance and reveals the perceptions of Russia's highest statesmen of the empire's Muslims at this critical moment in history. First of all, the ministers wanted the state to be in charge of all education in the empire. Leaving maktabs and madrasas outside of the jurisdiction of the MNP contradicted this principle, in their opinion. They declared the earlier assumption that all education in Muslim schools had a religious character wrong on the grounds that a considerably large number of Muslim schools taught subjects that reached far beyond the simple instruction of the Qur'an. Here, the ministers were referring to the long period of education in the madrasas that obviously included the study of several books aside from the Qur'an. In fact, the great majority of those books were religious too, but apparently, the ministers disregarded that point. The ministers were not happy with the mediation of Islamic scholars either. They complained that the absence of pedagogical programs in many Muslim schools enabled the education of students to be steered in whichever direction the mullahs deemed appropriate. The ministers suggested that leaving the schooling of Muslims to Islamic

---

[70] NART, f. 92, op. 1, d. 10464, ll. 16–22. Later in 1875, Radloff would relate this meeting and the developments following it in a different tone by emphasizing the opposition of the madrasa instructors and older madrasa students. NART, f. 92, op. 1, d. 10464, ll. 51–59.

[71] For Radloff's draft law about the transfer of the jurisdiction of Muslim schools to the MNP, see NART, f. 92, op. 1, d. 10464, ll. 27–28.

scholars any longer would be a grievous mistake. The condition of Tatars, in their opinion, proved that the existing nature of Muslim education was misguided. The Tatars had entered the empire as early as the sixteenth century, but they had still not cast off the remnants of their past. The ministers deemed this "abnormal" and lamented that the situation could have been corrected long ago had the Muslim children been educated properly. They wrote: "Unfortunately, however, the mullahs propagated enmity against all Russians and spread fanaticism, preventing the unification of Tatars with the empire's core people." Therefore, the Council of Ministers recommended the transfer of all Muslim schools to the jurisdiction of the MNP.[72]

Alexander II approved this transfer on 20 November 1874,[73] but apparently he was informed about the sensitivity of the issue too. He ordered Count Tolstoi to warn local authorities to exercise special caution in the affairs of Muslim schools and wanted the minister to prepare detailed instructions about the projected transfer. Count Tolstoi began to gather information in order to prepare these instructions. Although he was one of the proponents of the transfer law, he does not seem to have thought that it could be realized right away either. He wrote to Shestakov that Radloff should not exercise de facto control over Muslim schools before receiving detailed instructions from the ministry.[74] Theoretically, the law had transferred the jurisdiction of all Muslim schools to the MNP,[75] but the MNP was not ready to take them over. Count Tolstoi demanded experts like Radloff and Il'minskii to prepare draft instructions about the transfer,[76] but the issue got lost in red tape. The instructions never came out.[77]

Conclusion

In the Great Reforms era and after, Russian imperial statesmen aspired for a new imperial model, as opposed to the existing Catherinian model, that relied less on intermediaries and more on direct governance. This new model emerged from a process of experimentation and confusion

---

[72] NART, f. 92, op. 1, d. 11938, ll. 7–8.
[73] *Sbornik postanovlenii po ministerstvu narodnogo prosveshcheniia: tsarstvovanie imperatora Aleksandra II, 1874–76*, vol. 6 (St. Petersburg: Tipografiia imperatorskoi akademii nauk, 1878), 585–600.
[74] NART, f. 92, op. 1, d. 11938, ll. 1–6.
[75] Bashkir schools in the Orenburg Gubernia that belonged to the Ministry of War constituted the only exception. NART, f. 92, op. 1, d. 11938, l. 4.
[76] NART, f. 92, op. 1, d. 11938, ll. 11–20.
[77] NART, f. 1, op. 3, d. 6811. Also see NART, f. 92, op. 1, d. 12956.

riddled with ambition and improvisation as well as hesitation and frustration. The tsarist administration increasingly associated the empire's well-being with the popularization of a cultural frame that would presumably endorse and promote the Romanov regime's priorities. This cultural frame was theoretically open to all, but all had to rise to its level in order to claim their share in it. It did not exist in a neutral area neatly located at equal distance from the cultural frames of each subject population group, for the tsarist state associated mainly with the Great Russians and endorsed their culture as an ideal point of reference. As a result, although the definition of the Great Russian culture itself remained a moving target, the idea of Russification – however it might have been defined in any particular context – stimulated and legitimized many policies aimed at transforming the empire's subject population groups, including the Volga-Ural Muslims.

As in many other imperial contexts of the late nineteenth century, the Russian statesmen ambitiously turned to schooling in order to bring Muslims closer to the "empire's core people." Having included schooling among their tools of governance, they no longer considered the education of Muslims an exclusively religious affair to be left in the hands of local Muslim communities. However, their deliberations on developing concrete schooling projects for Muslims revealed how little they actually knew about the empire's Muslim subjects and how little leverage they had to transform them. After four years of discussions and another four years with a law in effect, the regulation of Muslim schooling remained an elusive task. And, as the coming chapter should illustrate, the response of the Muslim peasants in the following decades to government schooling initiatives would confirm this elusiveness.

4   Peasant responses
Protecting the inviolability of the Muslim domain

Let that inspector not interfere in the affairs of the Muslim maktabs and
madrasas, which exist for religious education alone, and let him not
interfere with the appointment of imams either.[1]   The peasants of a Tatar
village writing about Radloff to the governor of Kazan, 1883

This has nothing to do with intervening in their purely Islamic
(*musul'manskaia*) schools: they can study the Arabic scribble with their
mullahs and recite their Qur'an without understanding a word, but in
the school, they should learn the Russian language without any relation
to religion.[2]   Orientalist and Censorship Officer Vasilii D. Smirnov in the
Journal of the Ministry of Public Enlightenment, 1877

The Russian gentry and, later, the intelligentsia imagined and treated
Russian peasants with an infantilizing attitude, "as toys to be manipu-
lated at will" dwelling "in a stagnant, isolated, and unchanging world
of irrational tradition."[3] The attention of historians since the 1980s to the
"world the peasants made" has brought us a long way in breaking
through the vestiges of the prism of this elitist approach and building a
more nuanced view of the Russian peasantry.[4] The historiography on the
Volga-Ural Muslims – or Russia's non-Russian peoples in general – and
especially the peasant majority among them is still a different story. We
are yet to scratch beneath the veneer of state or elite-produced written

[1] NART, f. 1, op. 3, d. 5881, ll. 155–58.
[2] Vasilii D. Smirnov, "Neskol'ko slov ob uchebnikakh russkogo iazyka dlia tatarskikh
narodnykh shkol," in *Zhurnal Ministerstva Narodnogo Prosveshcheniia*, 1877 189(otd. 4): 2.
[3] Marc Raeff, *Origins of the Russian Intelligentsia: The Eighteenth-Century Nobility* (New York:
Harcourt Brace & Harvest, 1966), 123–26; Eklof, *Russian Peasant Schools*, 1–3; and Esther
Kingston-Mann, "Breaking the Silence: An Introduction," in *Peasant Economy, Culture, and
Politics of European Russia, 1800–1921*, ed. Jeffrey Burds, Esther Kingston-Mann, and
Timothy Mixter (Princeton: Princeton University Press, 1991), 6–9.
[4] Some noteworthy contributions are Ben Eklof, "Ways of Seeing: Recent Anglo-American
Studies of the Russian Peasant (1861–1914)," *Jahrbucher für Geschichte Osteuropas*, 1988
36(1): 57–79; Jeffrey Burds, Esther Kingston-Mann, and Timothy Mixter eds., *Peasant
Economy, Culture, and Politics of European Russia, 1800–1921* (Princeton: Princeton
University Press, 1991); David Moon, *The Russian Peasantry, 1600–1930: The World the
Peasants Made* (New York: Longman, 1999); and Burbank, *Russian Peasants*.

records to build a more refined understanding of the world that the Volga-Ural Muslim peasants made.[5] The debate, so far, oscillates between an epic picture of oppression and resilience versus a rosy picture of toleration and integration.[6] However, a look in this chapter at the responses of Muslim peasants, as well as elites, to the Russian state's schooling initiatives targeting their children offers examples of resistance and indifference along with meaningful episodes of cooperation and functionalization. That is, we see the utilization of state institutions by Muslims for purposes unforeseen by imperial agents. Simple though it may seem, recognizing the simultaneous possibility of these two forms of position-taking is liberating for it allows us to ask more nuanced questions about the anxieties, priorities, and strategies of Muslim peasants as individuals. Those questions also shed light on the nature of the multidirectional interactions among the Russian state agents, Muslim peasants, and Muslim elites.[7]

Most Volga-Ural Muslims refused to accommodate Russo-Muslim schools in their villages or Russian-language classes in their maktabs and madrasas. Neither did they like the newly introduced requirement for mullahs to learn Russian. The strategies of these Muslims to deal with pressuring imperial agents ranged from petition campaigns to small-scale disturbances and what James Scott has called the "everyday forms of peasant resistance."[8] However, some other Muslims welcomed the new government initiatives. Especially from the 1890s on, they started to see an economic and social utility in these schools and even demanded them.[9] The agents of the MNP, on the other hand, wanted Muslims to welcome government teachers and schools but were increasingly less willing to divert funds, which could otherwise be used for the education of Russian or baptized non-Russian peasants, to Muslim schooling. Zemstvos

---

[5] Frank, *Muslim Religious Institutions*; and Frank and Usmanov eds., *Islamic Biographical Dictionary* come closest to an exception to this situation.

[6] For representative examples of these two interpretations, see Azade-Rorlich, *Volga Tatars*; and Lotfullin and Islaev, *Dzhikhad*; versus Iakub I. Khanbikov, *Russkie pedagogi Tatarii* (Kazan: Kazan State Pedagogical Institute, 1968); Crews, *For Prophet*; and Kirmse, "Dealing with Crime" respectively.

[7] See Burbank, *Russian Peasants*, especially xiv on the individuality of peasants. See Meyer, "Turkic Worlds" for a study that recognizes the multidirectional nature of these interactions.

[8] James C. Scott, *Weapons of the Weak: The Everyday Forms of Peasant Resistance* (New Haven: Yale University Press, 1985). Moon, *Russian Peasantry*, 237–81 explores this idea in the context of the Russian peasantry.

[9] On comparable attitudes about the utility of gaining basic literacy and mathematical skills through schooling among ethnic Russians, see Eklof, *Russian Peasant Schools*, 263–82; and among baptized non-Russians in the Volga-Ural region, see Dowler, *Classroom and Empire*, 115.

gradually stepped in with their resources, especially after the turn of the twentieth century and in places where Muslim notables occasionally provided a liaison between Muslim communities and the institutions of local governance. Yet, without enthusiastic support from the MNP and with the experience of the unsuccessful initiatives of the previous decades in mind, the zemstvos were also hesitant to push for a widespread network of zemstvo schools for Muslims. Rather, they supported specific projects on a case-by-case basis after making sure that the affected Muslim community was certainly comfortable with a government school.

This was a story of mass social engineering that played out in many local contexts, with frequent twists and turns, second thoughts, hidden agendas, misconceptions, and false rumors yet it also informed decisions and reflexive position-taking where Muslims – peasants as well as elites – and tsarist officials constantly monitored and responded to each other's perceived intentions and power. A notably persistent trend within the chaos of these diverse experiences was that most Muslim peasants – and sometimes notables too – recognized what was at stake not as simply learning or not learning Russian but as the reconfiguration of power relations in tsarist Russia, as Russia transformed at a fast pace in the late nineteenth and early twentieth centuries. While Muslims did have (or developed) religiously motivated reservations about exposure to Russian as the language of Orthodoxy,[10] it was usually the nature of influence exchange between government officials and Muslim interlocutors that determined the outcomes of particular schooling initiatives. Muslim peasants could be accommodating when they felt safe about maintaining control over the internal affairs of their insulated Muslim domain. However, the environment of transition and uncertainty that accompanied new and experimental regulations usually revived memories of the pre-Catherinian times when Muslims were expelled from fertile lands and forced to accept baptism. Most Muslims, as a result, refused government involvement in the education of their children, fearing that the inviolability of their mediated distance from the imperial state was under threat.

Introducing the new imperial model

St. Petersburg's efforts to institute Russian-language education among Muslims marked the beginnings of the transition to a new imperial model based on unmediated governance for the Volga-Ural Muslims. The Orenburg Spiritual Assembly, as an institution of the old, Catherinian

---

[10] For an example, see Märdanov, Miñnullin, and Räximov, *Rizaetdin Fähretdin*, 21–22.

model was sidelined in the process, and consequently, it started to lose authority as the principal mediator between the tsarist state and its Muslim subjects in the Volga-Ural region. Mufti Tevkelef believed that learning Russian was useful for Muslims who lived in Russia, but he also believed that the government's recent policies to this end were misguided. In 1874, he once again complained to the minister of internal affairs, Timashev, that the local authorities were trying to force Russian-language education on the Muslim population without paying enough attention to their sensitivities. In one specific example, he wrote, the Viatka Zemstvo had opened Russian-language classes in a few villages, but it had put the Muslim villagers under the obligation to pay some of the expenses. These villagers were opposed to Russian-language education for religious reasons, not to mention concerns at covering its costs. Therefore, according to the mufti, the first step in teaching Russian to the Muslims had to be to convince them about the harmlessness and benefits of learning this language, but the current efforts were simply provoking more opposition. Under the current circumstances, Mufti Tevkelef declared, he was unable to influence the mullahs. The Muslims, he wrote, did not believe him any longer. Besides, he did not think that he had the right to intervene after the transfer of Muslim schools to the jurisdiction of the MNP in 1874 anyway.[11]

It seems that the MNP was actually aware of the Muslims' concerns at least in the early stages of its interventions in Muslim schooling. As it announced the Law of March 26 in 1870, it instructed local officials to plan in such a way that Muslim congregations themselves would take the initiative for Russian-language education.[12] Yet, this was easier said than done, and Radloff was hardly the person to do it. With a naïve confidence in the power of his official status to bring Muslims to compliance, he assumed a domineering attitude in his dealings with them from the very beginning.[13] Surely, he did open a number of Russo-Muslim schools in the Volga-Ural region. An overview of these cases, however, reveals that he was able to do so mostly thanks to another form of mediation: the involvement of cooperating Muslim agents who supported or at least approved Russian-language education for Muslims. These few Muslims, who already had access to the cosmopolitan culture of the emerging imperial domain thanks to circumstances that we shall discuss later,

---

[11] Fahreddin, *İslâmlar*, vol. 1, 15–19. Mufti Tevkelef and his successors would repeat this argument several times later on. Fahreddin, *İslâmlar*, vol. 1, 23, 28–29.

[12] Alta Kh Makhmutova, *Stanovlenie svetskogo obrazovaniia u tatar: bor'ba vokrug shkol'nogo voprosa, 1861–1917* (Kazan: Izd-vo Kazanskogo universiteta, 1982), 24.

[13] For an illustrative example of Radloff's attitude in this regard, see NART, f. 92, op. 1, d. 11513, ll. 5–8 and 16–21. Also see, Dowler, *Classroom and Empire*, 135.

found utility in making that culture accessible to other Muslims too.[14] Interestingly, the first Russo-Muslim school Radloff opened was a girls' school. Bîbicemal Ğusmanova, the widow of a prominent Muslim merchant and an educated woman who spoke Russian well, approached Radloff with a project for this school, and Radloff secured money for her from the MNP. Ğusmanova started teaching in 1873.[15] Finding her meager enrollments insufficient, however, the MNP closed the school the following year.[16] The Kazan City Duma sponsored another Russo-Muslim school in 1875. Among the contributors of the project were a Muslim student of the Kazan Imperial University who took the teacher position, a rising Muslim entrepreneur, Ahmedcan Seydaşef (1840–1912), who became the school's trustee, and another Muslim merchant who donated over three hundred books to establish a school library.[17] When Radloff opened Russo-Muslim schools outside of the city of Kazan, this usually involved the mediation of a Russian-educated Muslim with meaningful connections to a specific village or town who either wanted to sponsor a Russo-Muslim school or offered his services as a teacher in that location. Muhammed Safâ Bikkenin, for instance, was a mullah in a village of the Tetiushsk County to the south of Kazan. He enrolled at the newly opened Ufa Tatar Teachers' School in 1873. Then, in 1877, he graduated and applied to go back to his village, now, as a Russo-Muslim school teacher.[18] In another example, in 1882, a retired noncommissioned officer, Halîlullah İskenderof, donated his house in Astrakhan for what he called "a school of Russian and Tatar literacy." The school opened the same year and proved to be successful.[19]

In the absence of such intermediaries, however, Radloff often found himself in a losing battle with Muslim peasants over the establishment of

---

[14] İsmâ'il Gasprinskiy from the Crimea and Ğabdulqayyûm Nasırî of Kazan were two pioneering Russian Muslims in this regard. See Ismail Bei Gasprinskii, *Russkoe Musul'manstvo: mysli, zametki, nabliudenie musul'manina* (Simferopol: Spiro, 1881); and Xuçiäxmät Mäxmutov ed. *Kayum Nasıyri: Saylanma Äsärlär*, vol. 3 (Kazan: Tatarstan Kitap Näşriyatı, 2005), 323–35. Also see Edward J. Lazzerini, "Ismail Bey Gasprinskii and Muslim modernism in Russia, 1878–1914" (Ph. D. Dissertation, University of Washington, 1973); Saadet Çağatay, *Abd-ül-Qayyum Nasırî* (Ankara: Türk Tarih Kurumu, 1952); and more in Chapter 7.

[15] NART, f. 92, op. 1, d. 10972, ll. 1–3 and 26–27ob.

[16] Makhmutova, *Stanovlenie*, 26.

[17] N. N. Postnikovii ed. *Sistematicheskii sbornik postanovlenii Kazanskoi Gorodskoi Dumy za 22 goda* (Kazan: Kazanskaia Gorodskaia Uprava, 1898), 275–76.

[18] NART, f. 92, op. 1, d. 13147, ll. 6–13ob. For another school that opened thanks to the mediation of a mullah, see also NART, f. 92, op. 1, d. 13147, ll. 1–4ob.

[19] NART, f. 92, op. 1, d. 15086, ll. 1–7; and NART, f. 92, op. 1, d. 16902, ll. 1–2ob.

Russo-Muslim schools in their villages.[20] In the routinized practice of the empire since Catherine II, communications between the tsarist state and Muslim peasants typically took place through the mediation of the spiritual assemblies or with police chiefs visiting Muslim villages. Initially, the MNP authorized Radloff to contact mullahs and Muslim villagers directly. The MVD endorsed this decision and even asked Radloff not to resort to the mediation of police forces since the police were already busy.[21] However, Muslims refused to cooperate with an agent of the MNP directly on a sensitive issue like the upbringing of their children. As Crews elaborates, a social contract had evolved since the late eighteenth century between the tsarist state and its Muslim subjects according to which the Volga-Ural Muslims accepted the legitimacy of the tsars' sovereignty primarily in return for religious toleration.[22] In Mufti Ğabdulvâhid bin Süleyman's earlier-mentioned appeal to Russia's Muslims during the Crimean War, for instance, he suggested that the Muslims in Russia were treated even better than other Muslims in other parts of the world who lived under Muslim sovereigns.[23] Muhammedyar Sultanof, who also served as a mufti between 1886 and 1915, would evoke the same argument again in 1894 and exhort Volga-Ural Muslims to have confidence in the tsarist regime due to its long-established policy of allowing Muslims to practice Islam freely.[24] Yet, to the Muslim peasants, the visits to their villages of Radloff and occasional other school inspectors in order to introduce Russian-language education appeared as no less than a breach of this century-old social contract. Most mullahs even refused to furnish Radloff with statistical data, claiming that he had no right to ask for information from them. The imperial model that the Volga-Ural Muslims had internalized by now meant more to them than the new laws and regulations that they had just started to hear about. In 1875, in response to the escalating tension between school inspectors, especially Radloff, and the Muslim congregations, the MNP eventually ordered its agents not to contact Muslims directly lest this would cause large-scale dissent. From then on, Radloff and other inspectors had to rely on the mediation of police forces in order to contact Muslims. And this considerably narrowed their margin of movement.[25]

---

[20] For examples of several failed attempts, see NART, f. 92, op. 1, d. 11938; and Morozov and Semenova, *Agrarnyi vopros*, 308–21.

[21] NART, f. 92, op. 1, d. 10290, ll. 31–32.   [22] Crews, "Empire," 50–83.

[23] Fahreddin, *Âsar*, vol. 2, 369–70.

[24] *Sbornik tsirkuliarov* [Russian section], 72. For yet another pronouncement of the same argument later in 1912, see Anon., *Qazan Uyezdindeki Müslüman Avıllarında Rusça-Tatarça Mektebler Açuv Hususında* (Kazan: Beyanü'l-Haq Matbaası, 1912), 6.

[25] NART, f. 92, op. 1, d. 11938, ll. 58–73.

Negotiating the terms of the new imperial model

Most of the opposition to the opening of Russian-language classes in Muslim schools came from villages. Usually, resistance started in subtle forms without resorting to open confrontation. In the village of Satış in the Mamadysh County, for instance, the local zemstvo agreed to pay for the Russian-language class, and Radloff completed the official procedures for opening it in 1873. The zemstvo wanted to rent a building for this purpose in the village, but the villagers claimed that they did not have a suitable one. Then, the zemstvo authorities located an empty building, but the villagers refused to lease it on the grounds that it was the private property of a merchant who lived in Kazan. The zemstvo authorities tried to find this merchant, but it turned out that he was dead. So, they found his sons, but the sons had no idea about the building. Then, the zemstvo authorities turned to the mullah of the village for help, who said that he would not object if the zemstvo authorities found a proper way to enter the building but he could not break the lock on the property of a deceased person. In the end, the villagers refused to allow entry into the building, for, regardless of who had owned it previously, they had once performed prayers in this building and therefore considered it a religious space, and teaching Russian in a religious space would be sacrilegious in their opinion.[26]

When these subtle tactics failed, in Satış and elsewhere in similar circumstances, the situation could escalate into open confrontation too. Radloff and the zemstvo authorities insisted on opening a Russian-language class, found a venue, and sent a teacher, Ğumerbay Yusupof, to Satış in 1876. Yet, Yusupof was unable to perform his job because of the villagers' hostility. Shortly after his appointment, he reported that on one occasion approximately two hundred villagers had gathered to prevent him from teaching. He did not feel safe in Satış anymore. In a similar case, in the village of Qışqar, the villagers allowed the establishment of physical facilities for a Russian-language class, but they did not let the Russian-language teacher move into the village. The maktabs of both of these villages were established long before 1870, and the villagers did not have to pay for a Russian-language class according to the Law of March 26. However, the Mamadysh Zemstvo was willing to pay, and once established in their neighborhood, the law required the villagers to send their children to the Russian-language class. In the end, the local police asked for permission from the MVD to resort to punitive

---

[26] NART, f. 1, op. 3, d. 3712, ll. 1–13.

measures, but the MVD consulted the MNP and declined permission, referring to Alexander II's order to exercise caution in the affairs of Muslim schools.[27]

Both Count Tolstoi and Timashev were convinced that the mullahs led the opposition against Russian schooling among Muslims. Therefore, they decided to focus on the requirements meant to oblige mullahs and other Muslim notables to learn Russian.[28] Radloff supported this approach as well. He thought that the madrasa students would inevitably begin attending Russian-language classes if they were unable to take positions as mullahs without proficiency in Russian. He also reasoned that the mullahs would not instigate the Muslim population against Russian-language education if they went through the process of learning Russian themselves. And he hoped that the mullahs who learned Russian would set an example for other Muslims, thus weakening the propaganda against Russo-Muslim schools.[29] With these considerations in mind, Radloff and other MNP officials stopped insisting on opening Russian-language classes and Russo-Muslim schools in 1875.[30] The tension of the early 1870s subsided toward the end of the decade.

However, St. Petersburg's high-ranking statesmen returned to the task of creating ideal subjects for the empire with renewed anxiety following Alexander II's assassination in 1881. In 1882, Alexander III appointed Count Tolstoi as the minister of internal affairs and Tolstoi's protégé Ivan Davydovich Delianov as the minister of public enlightenment. Delianov prepared a set of new regulations about Muslim education to reinforce the earlier ones, and Alexander III signed them into law on February 5, 1882.[31] After repeating Alexander II's warning about exercising caution while dealing with Muslims, Delianov instructed MNP inspectors to establish jurisdiction over maktabs and madrasas gradually, to observe them closely, and to provide advice to local Muslim communities without raising discussions about the Law of March 26. He wanted the inspectors to start spreading Russian-language education among Muslims initially in places where Muslims lived side by side with Russians or baptized Tatars. Other Muslim communities, he thought, would follow suit. In this way, he hoped gradually to eliminate the Muslims' expectations about the inviolability of their educational institutions.[32]

---

[27] NART, f. 1, op. 3, d. 3712, ll. 14–17 and 68–82.
[28] NART, f. 92, op. 1, d. 10464, ll. 38–49.   [29] NART, f. 92, op. 1, d. 10464, ll. 51–59.
[30] Fahreddin, İslâmlar, vol. 1, 19.
[31] Sbornik postanovlenii po ministerstvu narodnogo prosveshcheniia: tsarstvovanie imperatora Aleksandra III, 1885–88, vol. 10 (St. Petersburg: Tipografiia "Obshchestvennaia pol'za", 1892), 459–64.
[32] Fahreddin, İslâmlar, vol. 1, 21.

Meanwhile, Vasilii Dmitrievich Smirnov, an enthusiastic, ethnic Russian Orientalist at St. Petersburg Imperial University and simultaneously a censor of Turkic-language publications and a rival of Radloff, put Radloff on the spot with an article in the *Journal of the Ministry of Public Enlightenment*, primarily for Radloff's approach to, and record in, promoting Russian-language education among Volga-Ural Muslims but also for his non-Russian origins.[33] The newly emerging imperial model based on unmediated governance called for preferably Russian officials on the government payroll to project the imperial state's authority to the tsars' subjects by contacting them directly at the individual level. High-ranking officials in St. Petersburg picked up on Smirnov's cue, and Radloff found himself under criticism for not having established jurisdiction over Muslim schools in his ten-plus years of service.[34] Delianov and the governor of Kazan, Leonid Ivanovich Cherkasov, shielded Radloff, affirming that the inspector had served the Russian state loyally and was able to correspond in Russian freely,[35] yet the German-born inspector's questionable success to that date still left him vulnerable to criticism.

Pressed between the growing frustration of authorities in St. Petersburg and with a renewed mandate in the Law of February 5 to take Muslim educational institutions under government control, Radloff dispatched a circular to Islamic scholars in Kazan's environs informing them of his jurisdiction over their maktabs and madrasas and asking for relevant statistical data. However, the scholars and their congregations considered this overture yet another unwelcome intrusion into Muslim affairs. Some scholars procrastinated by asking for copies of the instructions that Radloff had received from his superiors, which he could not produce due to the confidentiality of his correspondence. Others simply refused to comply. Once again, tension escalated in the region. In December 1882, Radloff and Governor Cherkasov toured Muslim villages together in order to convince their inhabitants to accept the law, but the protests of angry Muslim congregations met them everywhere.[36]

---

[33] Vasilii D. Smirnov, "Po voprosu o shkol'nom obrazovanii inorodtsev-musul'man," *Zhurnal' Ministerstva Narodnogo Prosveshcheniia*, 1882 222(otd. 3): 1–24; and Geraci, *Window*, 148. For the earlier rivalry between Radloff and Smirnov, see Smirnov, "Neskol'ko slov," 1–25; and Vasilii V. Radlov, "Eshche neskol'ko slov ob uchebnikakh russkogo iazyka dlia tatarskikh narodnykh shkol," *Zhurnal Ministerstva Narodnogo Prosveshcheniia*, 1877 194: 99–119.

[34] NART, f. 92, op. 1, d. 15539, ll. 1–3 and 24–25. Also see, Meyer, "Turkic Worlds," 80–81. Meyer suggests that Radlov had simply ignored instructions about establishing jurisdiction over Muslim institutions of education.

[35] NART, f. 92, op. 1, d. 15539, ll. 21–22ob and 24–25.

[36] NART, f. 92, op. 1, d. 15539, ll. 4–7; and Meyer, "Turkic Worlds," 81–82.

Then, a petition movement erupted in the Kazan Gubernia with thousands of Muslims asking for their educational institutions to be left alone.[37]

The first petition appeared in late March 1883.[38] When the movement began to subside in July 1883, Governor Cherkasov had determined 197 petitions in total.[39] This meant an estimated sum of about twenty thousand signatures.[40] The movement was mostly limited to five counties close to the city of Kazan, where Radloff had originally dispatched his circular, but participation within those counties was considerably high. Most of the petitions were copies of each other, indicating some sort of an organization, but there were some slight variation in their tone and the petitioners' demands.[41] Cherkasov suspected that most petitions were penned by a few individuals, possibly mullahs, spearheading the movement, but the police could not ascertain any individual mullah's responsibility judicially. They pointed to a certain Modest Suvorov, but he turned out to be a retired post office employee of Russian origin who wrote petitions for money.[42]

As Russia's peasants, including Muslim ones, often evoked the myth of a benevolent tsar who, if he knew, would remedy the wrongdoings of his subordinates,[43] the tsarist officials tended to draw upon what we may call the myth of "good but credulous peasants" who, had it not been for sinister agitators, would remain peaceful and obedient. Trying to understand the responses of Muslim peasants in the Volga-Ural region based on the observations of these officials may give the impression that whenever Muslim peasants were restless, unruly, or defiant, they acted out of ignorance about the larger picture and remained recalcitrant because of the unwillingness of "fanatic" mullahs to inform them duly. Peasants, however, were rarely so gullible,[44] and even when they acted based on false rumors, as they sometimes did, they could still be pursuing or protecting real interests. Moreover, what the tsarist officials judged as

[37] NART, f. 1, op. 3, d. 6811; and Fahreddin, İslâmlar, vol.1 23–24. For the petition movement see NART, f. 1, op. 3, d. 5881, NART, f. 1, op. 3, d. 5882, and NART, f. 1, op. 3, d. 5883.

[38] NART, f. 1, op. 3, d. 5881, ll. 21–22.   [39] NART, f. 1, op. 3, d. 5883, ll. 12–14.

[40] My estimate.

[41] The involved counties were Kazan, Laishevo, Mamadysh, Tetiushi, and Tsarevokokshaisk. There was one petition from Karmysh in the Ufa Gubernia too.

[42] NART, f. 1, op. 3, d. 5883, ll. 8–14.   [43] Dowler, Classroom and Empire, 132–33.

[44] For an interesting essay that emphasizes this point, see Timothy Mixter, "The Hiring Market as Workers' Turf: Migrant Agricultural Laborers and the Mobilization of Collective Action in the Steppe Grainbelt of European Russia, 1853–1913," in Peasant Economy, Culture, and Politics of European Russia, 1800–1921, ed. Jeffrey Burds, Esther Kingston-Mann, and Timothy Mixter (Princeton: Princeton University Press, 1991), 294–340.

the peasants' misunderstandings could actually represent differences between their own and the peasants' vantage points.

The tsarist officials' vantage point in the controversy over Muslim education was that the new and increasingly more rationalized categories of tsarist administration designated the MNP to regulate schooling and the Department of Spiritual Affairs in the MVD to deal with religions other than Orthodoxy.[45] Most officials secretly, and sometimes not so secretly, hoped that exposure to the Russian language and culture eventually would bring Muslims to the fold of Christianity, but otherwise, the immediate and official goal of the knowledge they wanted to impart upon Muslim children was to familiarize them with the cosmopolitan cultural codes of the emerging imperial domain where the Russian language served as the primary medium of exchange. Therefore, the bureaucrats who implemented the new regulations found it absurd that the Muslim peasants would perceive the transfer of Muslim schools to the MNP jurisdiction as restrictive of their religious freedom. Count Tolstoi, as the new minister of internal affairs, instructed Governor Cherkasov to inform petitioners about the "true intentions" of the regulations, and the governor sent county police chiefs to each petitioning village to correct their "misunderstandings."[46]

Yet, the petitioners of 1883 actually appear to have been considerably well informed about the impending changes, which they deduced from Radloff's circular and further communication with government authorities. Yes, they mixed memory and anticipation with present reality (as most people do),[47] and they worried that the instruction of "the Russian religion" would follow the instruction of the Russian language.[48] They suspected that the covert impetus behind introducing Russian-language education among Muslims was to weaken the position of Islam in Russia.[49] But the more fundamental problem from their vantage point was the preservation of the Volga-Ural Muslim domain's mediated distance. They considered the acquisition of knowledge (*'ilm*) to be first and foremost a religious and moral endeavor intended to draw young

---

[45] Alfred Rieber's caveat about the difficulty of building a rationalized and monolithic bureaucratic structure in the Russian empire is well taken, but it was, in Rieber's terms, the "ministerial interest groups," which came closest to a rationalized bureaucratic structure, that handled Muslim schooling in the Volga-Ural region in the late nineteenth century. See Alfred J. Rieber, "Bureaucratic Politics in Imperial Russia," *Social Science History*, 1978 2(4): 399–413.

[46] NART, f. 1, op. 3, d. 5883, ll. 12–14 and 21–22. Also see, Meyer, "Turkic Worlds," 79–80.

[47] Craig Calhoun *et al.* eds., *Contemporary Sociological Theory*, 2nd edn. (Malden, MA: Blackwell Publishing, 2008), 231–32.

[48] NART, f. 1, op. 3, d. 5881, l. 183.   [49] NART, f. 1, op. 3, d. 5881, ll. 270 and 284.

members of the Muslim community closer to God and to inculcate them in the community's proper modes of conduct. They considered all knowledge, including worldly knowledge needed for mundane sustenance, to be emanating from God, as Adeeb Khalid points out, but the Islamic tradition of the Volga-Ural region, as in most other Muslim contexts up until the modern times, still associated schooling first and foremost with religious knowledge and moral conduct.[50]

Therefore, it made perfect sense for the Muslim petitioners of 1883 to interpret the new regulations as an unwarranted restriction on their religious freedom, which, they liked to remind, was protected under the laws granted by Russian emperors. They viewed this restriction as an undeserved punishment since they had remained loyal and humble subjects of the emperors, they wrote, implying the possibility of an alternative line of conduct too.[51] They emphasized that the Muslim congregations or individual Muslims who financed maktabs and madrasas did so exclusively for the study of religion. They claimed that nobody would object to the study of other subjects in other schools, but they did not want subjects that were not required or allowed by Islam to be forced into Muslim educational institutions. Furthermore, they pleaded that the mullahs not be required to learn the Russian-language or other secular subjects lest this would prevent them from devoting their time to the study of Islam or to upholding religion among their congregations. Therefore, the petitioners demanded the transfer of maktabs and madrasas back to the jurisdiction of the Orenburg Spiritual Assembly, a ban on the appointment of public school graduates (such as the graduates of the recently opened Muslim teachers' schools) in mullah positions, and the abolition of the requirement that mullah candidates learn Russian.[52]

On the face of it, the tsarist government did not step back before these protests. Governor Cherkasov gave blunt replies to the petitioners, summarizing the new regulations and declining their demands.[53] But neither the MVD nor the MNP could press further to implement the law either. The MNP extended Radloff's appointment for five more years in 1884, but his powers and responsibilities had become too ambiguous by this time to allow him to function. After the troubles of the preceding two years, St. Petersburg had once again quit promoting Russian-language education among Volga-Ural Muslims, as evidenced by the MNP's

[50] See Khalid, *Jadidism*, 20–21 for a discussion of these issues in the Transoxianian Muslim context.
[51] This seems to be a common strategy in peasant petitions. See Verner, "Discursive Strategies," 70–71.
[52] NART, f. 1, op. 3, d. 5881; NART, f. 1, op. 3, d. 5882; and NART, f. 1, op. 3, d. 5883.
[53] NART, f. 1, op. 3, d. 5882, l. 50.

reluctance to finance Russo-Muslim schools in the following years.[54] Radloff left Kazan to join the St. Petersburg Academy of Sciences toward the end of 1884. The Ministry of Public Enlightenment temporarily appointed in his place Şahbazgiray Ahmerof, the Muslim director of the Kazan Tatar Teachers' School, who held a degree from the Kazan Imperial University.[55] Although a Russian-educated intellectual who hardly shared the social imaginary of the broader Muslim population,[56] Ahmerof, as a Muslim, was in a more advantageous position than Radloff to introduce Russian-language education among Muslim communities. When St. Petersburg revisited this issue later, however, its focus had completely shifted from opening government schools for Muslims to establishing jurisdiction over existing maktabs and madrasas.

In 1886, while reviewing the annual report on the Kazan Gubernia, Alexander III asked why none of the branches of the state had practical jurisdiction over "Tatar schools in mosques."[57] This started another round of correspondence in the imperial bureaucracy and led to the approval on July 16, 1888 of another law to establish educational standards for the mullahs and higher-ranking Muslim men of religion. The law required mullah candidates who would apply for certification after 1891 to be examined by county school commissions for basic Russian-language proficiency.[58] Upon Count Tolstoi's call for extreme caution in this matter, local officials in the Volga-Ural region proceeded to implement the law gradually and very carefully this time. They first discussed the matter with the Muslim notables of the city of Kazan in a meeting, which they tried to keep confidential lest its news reach and provoke ordinary Muslims. In the meantime, however, the Kazan Spiritual Consistory ordered its priests to gather statistical data about the number of Muslims in the mixed Tatar and Russian villages. Then, a priest in one of these villages asked the village mullah for a list of his

---

[54] For examples of this reluctance, see NART, f. 92, op. 1, d. 16039, ll. 9–10; NART, f. 92, op. 1, d. 16902, ll. 19–19ob; NART, f. 92, op. 1, d. 16903, ll. 14–14ob; NART, f. 92, op. 2, d. 14852, ll. 27–31ob. Also see, Makhmutova, *Stanovlenie*, 39–40; R. U. Amirkhanov, "Nekotorye osobennosti razvitiia narodnogo obrazovaniia u Tatar v dooktiabrskii period," in *Narodnoe prosveshcheniie u Tatar v dooktiabr'skii period*, ed. R. M. Amirkhanov and I. A. Giliazov (Kazan: Institut Iazyka, Literatury i Istorii im. G. Ibragimova, 1992), 31–33 and 222; Meyer, "Turkic Worlds," 40–41, which focus mostly in the period after 1905.

[55] NART, f. 92, op. 1, d. 16104; NART, f. 1, op. 3, d. 6811; Geraci, *Window*, 148–50; and Temir, *Türkoloji Tarihinde*, 34–35. For a report of Şahbazgiray Ahmerof from 1885, see NART, f. 92, op. 1, d. 16430, ll. 1–5ob.

[56] See more on the alienation of Muslim intellectuals in Chapter 8; and Mustafa Tuna, "Madrasa Reform as a Secularizing Process: A View from the Late Russian Empire," *Comparative Studies in Society and History*, 2011 53(3): 540–70.

[57] NART, f. 1, op. 3, d. 6881.　　[58] *Sbornik postanovlenii*, vol. 10, 1366–68.

congregation. The mullah refused and the affair quickly escalated into a conflict between the two men of religion. In December 1888, information about the confidential meeting in Kazan and this conflict started to travel through Muslim villages in the Kazan Gubernia, triggering one more petition movement.[59]

This time, however, the movement spread across the Volga-Ural region and continued for almost three years. The Orenburg Spiritual Assembly and various MVD offices in the region had received close to one thousand petitions by early 1891, when the movement started to subside, with occasional petitions continuing to arrive thereafter.[60] As in the 1883 movement, most petitions shared similar texts, and the copies of these texts reached various parts of the region at an impressive speed. As early as January 1889, the Spassk County police chief reported that he had found petitions in all Muslim villages in his area.[61] Later police reports from several counties point to mullahs and merchants as the movement's instigators and market fairs and personal connections as the main channels for its spread. Typically, merchants and mullahs were more mobile, better-connected, and better-informed than ordinary peasants and they tended to play an important role in swaying the opinions of the broader Muslim population.[62]

Once again, however, we need to take the tendency of tsarist officials to blame trouble on a few instigators with a pinch of salt. After investigating probably dozens of individuals, which sometimes included Russian scribes, between 1889 and 1891, for penning petitions or encouraging others to petition,[63] security forces were able to indict only a few Muslims as instigators, and even the activities of these few could hardly account for the scale of the ongoing movement.[64] Singling out and punishing individual Muslims with relatively more influence as troublemakers enabled the police to give the impression of having done

---

[59] NART, f. 1, op. 3, d. 7797, ll. 1–6 and 57–60.

[60] Some of these petitions and the correspondence about them are in NART, f. 1, op. 3, d. 7797–98 and 8137. Also see Fahreddin, *İslâmlar Haqqında*, v1, 33.

[61] NART, f. 1, op. 3, d. 7797, ll. 1–6 and 11.

[62] On the involvement of mullahs, see NART, f. 1, op. 3, d. 7797, ll. 1–6, 46–60, 115–18, 196–97, and 205–9; and NART, f. 1, op. 3, d. 8137, l. 1. On the involvement of merchants, see NART, f. 1, op. 3, d. 7797, ll. 196–210;NART, f. 1, op. 3, d. 7798, l. 60 and 112; Salikhov, *Tatarskaia burzhuaziia*, 24–26; Meyer, "Turkic Worlds", 83–84. In NART, f. 1, op. 3, d. 8137, ll. 12–27, I have not been able to confirm James Meyer's observation that "a total of one hundred ninety petitions" were found in the house of one peasant, named Hayrullah Seyfeddinof, as they were "being prepared for shipment to various tsarist officials."

[63] For examples of such investigations, see NART, f. 1, op. 3, d. 7797, ll. 1–6; and NART, f. 1, op. 3, d. 7798, ll. 133–34.

[64] NART, f. 1, op. 3, d. 8137, ll. 32–44, 62 and 79–85.

their job and, presumably, deterred other Muslims without the logistical hassles that implicating large groups of peasants could entail. Otherwise, ordinary Muslims could also learn in one way or another about the new regulations (especially the Russian-language requirement for mullahs), make a *rational* choice to take action, and urge their fellow villagers to petition. In fact, there were cases in which mullahs complained to the police for being forced by their villagers to prepare a petition against their own will.[65] The problem that tsarist officials faced, as they tried to push unmediated governance among Volga-Ural Muslims, was not the fictional propaganda of a few sinister instigators: it was the real concerns of Muslim peasants about maintaining a mediated distance from the tsarist state as the possibility of the closure of that distance revived residual memories of their pre-Catherinian troubles.

Yes, the police detected several false rumors that circulated in the region and prompted the Muslims' worries. In one illustrative example, the archpriest of a church in Buinsk gave a sermon about missionary activities among the animists of Siberia and asked for donations. After the service, some members of the congregation who possibly misinterpreted the sermon, began to talk about proselytization among Muslim Tatars. Four Muslim peasants from a nearby village overheard this conversation and carried the news to their own village from where the rumor spread to several other villages.[66] In due course, many Muslims in the region came to assume that the government was poised to establish Russian-language schools in all Muslim villages, force boys and girls to study together in the same classroom, and baptize them eventually.[67] Yet, Muslim peasants of the region already had enough anxiety about these issues to give credibility to such false assumptions.

Besides, the Volga-Ural Muslims did not necessarily need false rumors to incite defensive action. They had an issue with the content of the successive regulations since 1870 that targeted mullahs and the education of Muslim children, regardless of whether rumors distorted the lawmakers' intent or not. In March 1889, for instance, the MVD received information about a Tatar-language calendar that was distributed at a fair in the Yelabuga County of the Kazan Gubernia. According to the source of this information, the calendar claimed that archbishops would now have jurisdiction over mullahs.[68] The then governor of

---

[65] NART, f. 1, op. 3, d. 7798, ll. 47–50, 87, 95, 100–107.
[66] NART, f. 1, op. 3, d. 7797, ll. 57–60.
[67] NART, f. 1, op. 3, d. 7797, ll. 18–22, 48–60, and 131–37; and NART, f. 1, op. 3, d. 7798, ll. 14–15.
[68] NART, f. 1, op. 3, d. 7797, ll. 28–29.

Kazan, Petr Alekseevich Poltoratskii, investigated the issue and after collecting all of the Tatar-language calendars sold in the region, he found out that the calendars contained a correct translation of the Law of July 16 but no false information.[69] The Law of July 16 concerned only the Muslim men of religion, but despite their practical inapplicability, the earlier laws about Russian-language schools and MNP jurisdiction over maktabs and madrasas had continued to remain in effect and trouble the Muslim peasants. A circular that Radloff had dispatched to Islamic scholars in 1872 about the Law of March 26, for instance, still appeared among the petitioners' sources of information in 1889.[70]

Furthermore, the tsarist authorities had wanted to teach Russian to Muslims as a means of integrating them into the empire's broader exchange of ideas and influence, but this exchange was not at all sterilized to accommodate Muslim sensitivities. Many of the policy discussions that took place publicly, often in the empire's Russian-language print media where a Russian nationalist discourse had started to become commonplace, were sufficiently offensive to provoke the Muslim peasants' worry and ire. As they learned about such discussions in synaptic moments of contact with the imperial domain, they grew increasingly more anxious about protecting the inviolability of their religious and intra-communal affairs. In 1890, for instance, the police discovered two documents in the possession of two Muslim peasants who were involved in writing petitions. One of the documents was a copy of the Law of March 26 from the *Journal of the Ministry of Public Enlightenment*. It explained the purpose of the law as the Russification (*obrusenie*) of "Tatar-Muslims." The other document, an excerpt from the 1873 *Collection of the Works of the Kazan Theological Academy Students*, was more straightforward in its message. It argued that trying to influence better-learned Muslims who had stronger convictions about religion, such as the mullahs, was particularly necessary, because if a mullah decided that the Christian religion was better, others in his congregation would follow.[71] Having been exposed to such pieces of decontextualized information, it was difficult for Muslim peasants not to suspect the assurances of tsarist officials that there would follow no attempts for forced Christianization.

Once these rumors – true or false – arrived in Muslim villages, sometimes along with a sample petition text, the villagers began to consider

---

[69] NART, f. 1, op. 3, d. 7797, ll. 57–60. Muslim petitioners also cited another copy of this law that was published in *Kazanskii Listok*. See NART, f. 1, op. 3, d. 7797, ll. 21–22.
[70] NART, f. 1, op. 3, d. 7797, ll. 242–43; and NART, f. 1, op. 3, d. 7798, ll. 182–83.
[71] NART, f. 1, op. 3, d. 8137, ll. 32–41.

submitting their own petition. As an additional incentive, one rumor suggested that only the petitioning villages would be exempt from the new regulations.[72] Although their petitions had been declined time and again, they did not consider petitioning to be a vain effort. They knew that even the declined petitions produced effects and otherwise unavailable opportunities for negotiation, especially if petitions addressed to higher authorities pressured the lower ones to engage the petitioners in conversation before their pleas caused further nuisance and possible reprimands down the bureaucratic hierarchy. Thus, having decided to take action, the village elders elected and delegated a committee to petition on behalf of the village and also collected money for possible expenses, such as stamp money, the cost of a trip to deliver the petition, and the fee of a scribe if they needed one. Some villages wrote to the Orenburg Spiritual Assembly in Tatar, but most others prepared Russian-language petitions addressing the closest MVD authority in their area. As in earlier petition movements, the Muslim peasants demanded that their educational institutions be left alone and their men of religion not be required to learn Russian.[73]

Upon receiving these petitions, Governor Poltoratskii sent county police chiefs to Muslim villages to explain that while their petitions were declined, the Law of July 16 concerned only the mullahs and did not require Muslim children to attend Russian schools.[74] Mufti Sultanof also declined the petitions addressed to him on the grounds that he was not authorized to appeal to the tsar for changes in the law.[75] But then, in May 1889, the chief of the Gendarme Administration of the Kazan Gubernia informed Poltoratskii that some "instigators" in the region were planning to petition again if the authorities did not accommodate their demands by the time of the Nizhny Novgorod Fair in mid July.[76] A second round of petitions followed this warning. Police chiefs visited Muslim villages once again, but the petitioners would not desist easily this time. They started to question the police chiefs' credibility and demanded written proof that their petitions were actually declined. When police chiefs refused to produce such documentation due to confidentiality, the villagers began to write follow-up petitions.[77] In January 1890, the police

---

[72] NART, f. 1, op. 3, d. 7798, l. 87 and 197.
[73] On these petitions, see NART, f. 1, op. 3, d. 7797, ll. 1–8 and 48–57; and NART, f. 1, op. 3, d. 7798, ll. 5 and 14–15.
[74] NART, f. 1, op. 3, d. 7797, ll. 1–6, 48–60, 106, and 131–34; and NART, f. 1, op. 3, d. 7798, ll. 14–15, 24, 35–36, and 95.
[75] NART, f. 1, op. 3, d. 7797, ll. 92–93.
[76] NART, f. 1, op. 3, d. 7797, ll. 115–18 and 196–97.
[77] NART, f. 1, op. 3, d. 7798, l. 24 and 84; and NART, f. 1, op. 3, d. 8137, ll. 51–56.

chief of the Spassk County reported rumors about a mullah who had supposedly met Abdulhamid II in Istanbul and complained to him about the intervention of tsarist authorities in the religious affairs of Russia's Muslims. According to the rumors, the sultan had advised the mullah to try sending a delegation to the tsar and, if this also failed, to go back to Istanbul for further consultation.[78] We do not have evidence to verify a meeting of this sort, but we know that the Ottoman agents in St. Petersburg learned about the ongoing events from the Muslim residents of this city and followed the situation with concern. One of these agents may have raised the idea of a delegation to the tsar.[79] In any case, as local authorities declined their petitions, the Volga-Ural Muslims started to write to the tsar directly in 1890.[80] In March of that year, three of them were even caught in Chistopol' while boarding a train in order to go to St. Petersburg and appeal to the tsar in person.[81]

The escalation of the Muslims' protests to involve the tsar's name and possibly an international conflict put local authorities in the Volga-Ural region under tremendous pressure to stop the petition movement. In the earlier commotions, the MVD had usually urged local officials to limit their responses to mild measures, since excessive use of force could further agitate the Muslims. In some cases, it had even declined to permit the closure of certain madrasas or the exile of certain individuals whom the police had marked as troublemakers.[82] But as the stakes increased toward the end of 1890, the MVD started to introduce firmer measures such as the exile of instigators.[83]

The settlement

The petition movement began to subside by the first months of 1891, but since the police were only able to single out and punish a few individuals, the tightening of government measures is unlikely to have brought about this development. Plausibly, the Muslim villagers lost interest in struggling to change the Law of July 16 as they started to notice that three years after its promulgation, the law did not change their lives in a noticeable way. The exclusive right of the spiritual assemblies to examine and certify Muslim men of religion had already become a routine practice by the mid nineteenth century. Adding Russian-language exams to

---

[78] NART, f. 1, op. 3, d. 7798, l. 53.   [79] *Osmanlı Belgelerinde Kazan*, 11–29.
[80] NART, f. 1, op. 3, d. 7798, ll. 30–32; and 124 and NART, f. 1, op. 3, d. 8137, ll. 8–11.
[81] NART, f. 1, op. 3, d. 7798, ll. 164–67.
[82] NART, f. 1, op. 3, d. 3539. Also see NART, f. 1, op. 3, d. 3712.
[83] NART, f. 1, op. 3, d. 7798, l. 143; and NART, f. 1, op. 3, d. 8137, ll. 62 and 79–85.

the process was not as dramatic or visible a change as opening Russian-language schools in Muslim villages. Mullah candidates could study Russian for a few months before taking the exam, and once certified, they could forget about it. Between July 1888, when the new law that required Russian-language proficiency from mullahs was promulgated, and 1891, when it would take effect, the number of mullah candidates who applied to be certified at the Orenburg Spiritual Assembly increased so much that the assembly was unable to examine all applicants.[84] This was an attempt by the mullah candidates who were finishing their studies at the end of the 1880s to circumvent the law, but the increase in applications also shows that the madrasa students expected the law to stay, despite the petition movements.

In contrast, the issue of jurisdiction over maktabs and madrasas remained vague until the very end of the tsarist regime. The muftis of the Orenburg Spiritual Assembly had never attempted to regulate the educational functions of mullahs and madrasa instructors. In 1874, the law of November 20 gave Mufti Tevkelef an opportunity to wash his hands completely of this matter, even though the assembly continued to certify and regulate Muslim men of religion. By the end of the nineteenth century, public school inspectors had become the standard authority to grant official status to maktabs and madrassas,[85] though most maktabs and madrasas functioned unregistered anyway.[86] Another law restated the transfer of Muslim schools to the jurisdiction of the MNP in 1893, but establishing actual jurisdiction over maktabs and madrasas depended on the attitude and skills of individual public school inspectors in their respective regions.[87]

Opening Russo-Muslim schools and Russian-language classes in maktabs and madrasas proved to be the most difficult part of Tolstoi's project. In 1895, while reviewing the annual report on the Kazan Gubernia, Nicholas II wrote in the margins of the section about the spread of Russian-language education among Muslims: "I am fully convinced about this." Delianov saw the note and drew Governor Poltoratskii's attention to the issue with a report. The report noted that there were only eight Russo-Muslim schools and six Russian-language classes in the

---

[84] Anon, "Bugünki Meselemiz," *Şûra*, 1909 (8): 236–37; and Türkoğlu, *Rızaeddin Fahreddin*, 89.

[85] See NART, f. 92, op. 1, d. 13147; NART, f. 1, op. 3, d. 9606; NART, f. 1, op. 4, d. 886; NART, f. 1, op. 4, d. 3932; NART, f. 92, op. 2, d. 19435.

[86] Anon, *Orenburg Vilayetindeki Mektebler* (Orenburg: Orenburgskoe Gubernskoe Zemstvo, 1916), 10.

[87] Timurşah Salaviyof, *Mekteb ve Medreselerni Duhovniy Sobraniyege Birüv* (Orenburg: Kerimof, Hüseyinof, ve Şürekâsı, 1908), 3–9.

Kazan Gubernia for a population of 621,000 Muslims. The trustee of the Kazan Educational Circuit was demanding 25,000 rubles to open new Russo-Muslim schools, but this money could be used efficiently only if the governors and other administrative authorities in the region found a way to curb the Muslims' resistance.[88]

Poltoratskii responded to Delianov optimistically. Although the Muslims' overall resistance to Russian-language schools continued, he wrote, the children of well-to-do Muslim families often attended public schools. These students would eventually help in spreading Russian education among the Muslim population, but their significance went unnoticed since the MNP did not keep track of Muslim students in public schools.[89] A marginal minority of Volga-Ural Muslims, often the elites, had long sought Russian-language education, but Poltoratskii was still pointing to a new and important phenomenon in his report. Seeking Russian-language education began to lose its marginality among Volga-Ural Muslims in the last decades of the nineteenth century. Şahbazgiray Ahmerof had observed as early as 1885 that increasingly more Muslims in major cities and even provincial towns were recognizing the utility of Russian in their daily interactions and showing an unprecedented willingness to learn it.[90] Nonetheless, as we interpret Ahmerof's observation, we should also keep in mind that the urban-rural divide in the Volga-Ural region was extremely vague up until the twentieth century, and anecdotal information suggests that individual Muslims could develop a similar cosmopolitan attitude even in villages.[91]

This interest in learning Russian may seem counterintuitive given the preceding story of resistance to Russian-language education and Muslim concerns about conversion to Orthodoxy following Russian-language instruction. To add to the confusion, Gârifullah Gâziyef, a Muslim who was singled out by the Kazan police in 1891 for writing petitions against the Russian-language requirement for mullahs, was actually operating a private Russian-language school for Muslims in the city of Kazan in 1890.[92] Or take Ahmedcan Seydaşef, the Muslim trustee of the first Russo-Muslim school for boys that the Kazan City Duma opened in 1875. He too was a vocal opponent of the Russian-language requirement for mullahs or MNP jurisdiction over maktabs and madrasas.[93] But in

---

[88] NART, f. 1, op. 3, d. 9947, ll. 1–4.   [89] NART, f. 1, op. 3, d. 9947, ll. 5–9.

[90] NART, f. 92, op. 1, d. 16430, ll. 1–2. Also see NART, f. 92, op. 1, d. 24602.

[91] For examples of such anecdotal information, see Togan, *Hatıralar*, 1–55 and Märdanov, Miñnullin, and Räximov, *Rizaetdin Fähretdin*, 21–22.

[92] NART, f. 1, op. 3, d. 8137, l. 138.

[93] NART, f. 1, op. 3, d. 7797, ll. 196–210; NART, f. 1, op. 3, d. 7798, l. 60 and 112; Salikhov, *Tatarskaia burzhuaziia*, 24–26; and Meyer, "Turkic Worlds," 84.

the 1890s, he sponsored a new madrasa in Kazan that readily incorporated the Russian language into its curriculum.[94] Moreover, Ahmedcan
Seydaşef's son, Muhammedcan Seydaşef (1864–1914), was on record in
1912 criticizing the Kazan County Zemstvo for falling behind other
zemstvos in its efforts to open Russo-Muslim schools.[95]

To make sense of these seeming contradictions, we need to remember
that what was fundamentally at stake for Volga-Ural Muslims since the
early 1870s was not merely learning or not learning Russian but the
reconfiguration of power relations in tsarist Russia. In *Russian Peasant
Schools*, Ben Eklof observes a shift in the attitudes of the Russian public in
the 1890s from "the belief that 'because we are poor, we cannot afford
education' to the conviction that 'because we are poor, we must have
education.'"[96] Lying underneath this shift was a sea-change in Russia's
social and material conditions that followed the Great Reforms but also
took place in an environment of global market integration under Europe's preeminence.[97] The same sea-change moved an increasing number
of Muslims in the Russian empire from the position of defensively
avoiding all things Russian in order to protect their comfort zone in the
insulated Volga-Ural Muslim domain to actively engaging the Russian
imperial domain either to seek personal prosperity or to ensure communal vitality as various forms of social, economic, administrative, and
political integration rendered avoidance less effective or, perhaps, less
desirable.[98] Many Volga-Ural Muslims continued to avoid learning
Russian, or exposing themselves to the imperial domain's cosmopolitan
culture in general, as potentially dangerous and even impious acts. The
dreadful memory of the first mufti Muhammedcan bin el-Hüseyin's son
Mirza Ahmed, who had strayed away from the Muslim community and
lived with a Russian woman out of wedlock, still resonated in the region
in the early twentieth century.[99] Muslims who championed that their
coreligionists should learn Russian still had to back up their argument

[94] On this madrasa, see Ravil Ämirxan, "Möhämmädiyä Mädräsäse," in *Mädräsälärdä
Kitap Kiştäse*, ed. Röstäm Mähdiev (Kazan: Tatarstan Kitap Näşriyatı, 1992), 12–33.
[95] Anon., *Qazan Uyezdindeki*, 3.   [96] Eklof, *Russian Peasant Schools*, 114.
[97] On global market integrations in the late nineteenth and early twentieth centuries, see
Kevin H. O'Rourke and Jeffrey G. Williamson, *Globalization and History: The Evolution
of a Nineteenth-Century Atlantic Economy* (Cambridge, MA: MIT Press, 1999).
[98] See more on this in Chapters 5–8. A good example for the growing anxiety about
ensuring communal vitality in this period is Ayaz İshaki, *İki Yüz Yıldan Suñ İnqıraz*
(Kazan: I. N. Kharitopov Tipografiyası, 1904). Also see Musin Flun, *Gayaz İshaki*
(Kazan: Tatarstan Kitap Näşritatı, 1998), 28–35.
[99] Fahreddin, *Âsar*, vol. 1, 183–86.

with religious justifications.[100] Yet, from the 1890s on, one could observe a decline in the degree of overall resistance to learning Russian along with many instances of Muslims seeking and creating opportunities to learn it, which included attending not only the Russo-Muslim schools but indeed many madrasas with reformed programs, private Muslim schools, and regular government schools.[101]

The tsarist bureaucracy also revised its priorities concerning Muslim education in response to the social and economic transformations that altered Russia's power dynamics in the late nineteenth century. In addition to the MNP's growing reluctance to finance Muslim schools, its rather hawkish agents and advisors who maintained a particular concentration in the Kazan educational circuit responded to this change by trying to limit the opportunities that were available to Volga-Ural Muslims for learning Russian. These hawkish agents moved from the position of pushing Muslims to learn Russian so that the imperial state could access and influence them directly to the position of trying to prevent them from learning Russian so that they would not raise their voice in the imperial domain and create pressures on the administration. In 1914, a special commission on Muslim education that convened in St. Petersburg even advised "excluding the teaching of the Russian language from the programs of Muslim schools."[102] Giving Muslims access to the imperial domain's cosmopolitan culture, they reasoned, had not created ideal subjects for the empire but skilled advocates of Muslim interests. The MNP officials did not promote a similarly obscurantist policy among Kazakhs further east, whom tsarist specialists falsely assumed to be less Islamicized and therefore still salvageable,[103] but the Volga-Ural Muslims, and especially the sedentary Tatars, now appeared to many MNP agents and advisors as too fanatically Muslim to be russified in the foreseeable future.[104] The MNP could not face the moral burden of completely renouncing the ideal of russifying Volga-Ural

---

[100] For an example, see Niyaz Muhammed Süleymanof, *Mektublarım* (Orenburg: Kerimof, Hüseyinof ve Şürekâsı, 1908), 11–12.

[101] On this new attitude, see Makhmutova, *Stanovlenie*, 38; Röstäm Mähdiev ed. *Mädräsälärdä Kitap Kiştäse* (Kazan: Tatarstan Kitap Näşriyatı, 1992); Sharafuddinov and Khanbikov, *Istoriia pedagogiki*, especially 25–27; and Tuna, "Madrasa Reform," 540–70.

[102] Makhmutova, *Stanovlenie*, 39–40.

[103] Alektorov, "Iz istorii," 154–91. On the issue of the Islamicization of Kazakhs, see Frank, *Muslim Religious Institutions*, 274–312.

[104] For an example of this view, see Nikolai Bobronikov, "Sovremennoe polozhenie uchebnogo dela u inorodcheskikh plemen vostochnoi Rossii," *Zhurnal Ministerstva Narodnogo Prosveshcheniia*, 1917 novaia seriia 135 (May): 51–84.

Muslims and therefore, closing the region's Russo-Muslim schools, but it gradually stopped financing Muslim education.

Meanwhile, however, zemstvos and occasionally city administrations made their resources available for Russian-language education among Volga-Ural Muslims. To be clear, schooling Muslims usually ranked low among the priorities of the zemstvo boards. By 1914, for instance, most zemstvos in the Kazan educational circuit had partly or mostly fulfilled school plans for the non-Russian peoples in their areas, but not for Muslims.[105] But, this delay was primarily due to the apprehensions of zemstvo authorities about agitating Muslims. Otherwise, the small-deeds liberals who occupied the zemstvo boards tended to focus on getting the job done rather than preserving the established power dynamics of the Romanov regime.[106] When and where cosmopolitan Muslim notables, whose number and influence grew unprecedentedly by the early twentieth century, secured support from their coreligionists, the zemstvos were usually willing to pay for Russian-language education among Muslims.[107] An outstanding example of this situation was the Ufa Gubernia where Muslims constituted a significant portion of the overall population and received relatively more zemstvo subsidy for schooling.[108]

Conclusion

Studies that investigate the use of tsarist institutions, especially courts, by Russian as well as Muslim peasants suggest a process of gradual integration that transformed Russia's peasants and brought them closer to the tsarist state as the tsarist state made available more of such institutions to its peasant subjects in the nineteenth and early twentieth centuries.[109] This is a welcome contribution to the field for it opens room for multifaceted stories by undermining the misleading stereotypes of empires as

[105] See the zemstvo reports in NART, f. 92, op. 2, d. 17120, l. not paginated.
[106] See more on this in Chapter 10.
[107] NART, f. 92, op. 2, d. 14852, ll. 1–1ob and 8; NART, f. 92, op. 1, d. 23263, ll. 1–1ob and 4; NART, f. 92, op. 1, d. 24602; NART, f. 92, op. 2, d. 3100, ll. 1–3, 21–23, 29–34, and 41–47ob; NART, f. 1370, op. 1, d. 2; NART, f. 92, op. 2, d. 17120; and Anon., *Qazan Uyezdindeki.*
[108] See Makhmutova, *Stanovlenie*, 39–40; and Norihiro Naganawa, "Maktab or School? Introduction of Universal Primary Education among the Volga-Ural Muslims," in *Empire, Islam, and Politics in Central Eurasia*, ed. Tomohiko Uyama (Hokkaido: Slavic Research Center, 2007), 65–97. Also see NART, f. 1370, op. 1, d. 2, ll. 43–47, which illustrates the contrasting attitudes of the Ufa Zemstvo and the MNP on opening a Tatar teachers' seminary in Ufa. See more on this matter in Chapter 10.
[109] E.g. Burbank, *Russian Peasants*; Crews, *For Prophet*; and Kirmse, "Dealing with Crime."

evil and peasants as ever-resisting collectives.[110] Yet, the evidence
presented heretofore suggests that government efforts to transform the
lives of Volga-Ural Muslims actually caused a lot of tension, and the
Volga-Ural Muslims did resist. Yes, the Muslim peasants utilized state
institutions for various forms of conflict resolution as well as in search
of personal or communal prosperity, but we need to differentiate these
pursuits from the arrival of imperial agents in Muslim villages to introduce new and seemingly dangerous institutions and obligations into
the villagers' lives. In the first case, the imperial state provided an environment of expanded opportunities by creating new institutions, and its
Muslim subjects made individual decisions to use or not to use those
institutions. In the second case, the Muslims found themselves amid
uncalled-for faits accompli that deprived them of agency and created an
environment of uncertainty. Their immediate response was resistance
unless the mediation of a trusted liaison mitigated that uncertainty, and
their various forms of resistance usually worked in keeping the imperial
state at bay. Eventually, a major shift in Russia's social, economic, and
political structures – a sea-change – would force both the tsarist state and
its Muslim subjects to reconsider their strategies in this engagement
while both sides continued to hang on to their fundamentally conflicting
objectives.

---

[110] For a critique of historiographic prejudices on peasants, see Burbank, *Russian Peasants*,
xiv–xv and 46.

5   Russia's great transformation in the second half of the long nineteenth century (1860–1914)

It is said that a machine invented by a person named "Remifton" [Remington] makes it possible to write faster and better than with a pen. This machine resembles a sewing machine in appearance, and writing with it is like playing a piano. Although writing with this machine is good for the health of the body too, it is expensive for the time being, and it is made for writing with the Latin alphabet only.[1]   A news item in the Russian Muslim newspaper *Tercüman*, 1883

It is possible to designate the last century as the century of natural sciences. The inventions of the chemists, physicists, and biologists in the last sixty to seventy years have completely transformed the lives of the people who are alive today: wired and wireless telegraph, telephone, electric light, railways, automobiles, and so on; discoveries in the field of medicine: medication for various pains, etc., new techniques and machines for farmers ... these are only a percent of the inventions of our recent times.[2]   From a review of natural science books in the Kazan-based pedagogical journal *Mekteb*, 1913

The sea-change that engulfed Russia in the 1890s followed a long process of state-led structural improvements, going as far back as Peter the Great if not earlier,[3] but it swelled in the context of trans-imperial influences that reached a powerful crescendo in the latter parts of the long nineteenth century, and it radically altered human experiences around the world. Steam power in transportation and electric telegraphy in communications accelerated time and reduced distances. The unprecedented expansion of the "imperial repertoires" of power, such as global financial networks, industrial production, and powerful weapons, catapulted western Europe – with North America in its wake – toward the mastery of globally integrated markets and colonized populations.

---

[1] "Yazı Maşinası," *Tercüman*, 29 May 1883.
[2] 'Ayn. Fi., "Tabî'iyyattan Ders Kitablarıbız," *Mekteb*, 1913 1(12): 294.
[3] For an investigation of the origins of this process, see William L. Blackwell, *The Beginnings of Russian Industrialization, 1800–1860* (Princeton: Princeton University Press, 1968).

The alliance of technological innovation, industrial production, and effective distribution routinized change in the daily practice of most ordinary men and women. Positive science, which made possible all those innovations that bestowed power to states and comfort to individuals, claimed people's devotion as a source of guidance. The commercial use of print media created new and increasingly more egalitarian venues for the exchange of ideas and, therefore, influence. Many people in many parts of the world came to recognize their times as a historic moment of progress (*terakkî* in Turkic) for humanity. Filled with a sense of urgency so as not to be left behind, they turned to western Europe for benchmarks of progress against which to measure their own achievements, or lack thereof.[4]

States continued to regulate and sometimes mitigate these trans-imperial influences, but only partially, for the increased volume and accelerated means of global human exchange defied effective administrative controls. The repertoires of pressure in the hands of imperial subjects to influence – though not determine – the policies of their governments also expanded in this period. Change became a function of constant interaction between global, imperial, and local forces. However, these forces were not distributed equally across the globe. Western Europe and North America were far more powerful than the rest of the world to allow an egalitarian distribution of power. The West did not unilaterally shape the rest. "Vectors of influence" moved "in various directions," as Kenneth Pomeranz suggests in *The Great Divergence*,[5] and even new models of progress started to emerge, such as Japan at the turn of the twentieth century,[6] but the weight of those vectors favored the West as both non-European governments and societies felt pressured to emulate western Europe.

The Russian imperial state and elites had decisively oriented themselves to be a part of Europe at the turn of the eighteenth century, that is,

---

[4] For insightful studies of these transformations, see Wolfgang Schivelbusch, *The Railway Journey: The Industrialization of Time and Space in the 19th Century* (Berkeley: University of California Press, 1986); O'Rourke and Williamson, *Globalization and History*; Kotkin, "Modern Times," especially 156; Russell W. Burns, *Communications: An International History of the Formative Years* (London: Institute of Electrical Engineers, 2004), 93–164; Cristopher Alan Bayly, *The Birth of the Modern World, 1780–1914: Global Connections and Comparisons* (Malden: Blackwell Publications, 2004); and Burbank and Cooper, *Empires*, 287–330.

[5] Kenneth Pomeranz, *The Great Divergence: Europe, China, and the Making of the Modern World Economy* (Princeton: Princeton University Press, 2000), 10. For an exploration of the possibilities that the multi-directional nature of global exchange offers in the modern world, see Marwan Kraidy, *Hybridity, or the Cultural Logic of Globalization* (Philadelphia: Temple University Press, 2005).

[6] Bayly, *The Birth*, 12.

at least a century ahead of most other non-European states, such as the
Ottoman Empire or Japan. In 1815, having chased Napoleon's armies
back to Paris, Russia even joined Europe's geopolitical equilibrium as a
sovereign partner. However, in 1870, its per capita gross national product still remained at 39.8 percent of that of the United Kingdom and
further plummeted to about 23.2 percent by 1890, only to rise to 31.8
percent by 1910.[7] No doubt Russia's economic capacity did explode in
this period, especially after 1890,[8] but the United Kingdom and several
other industrialized countries in Europe started way ahead and grew even
faster. It would be an exaggeration to place Russia close to the extreme
other end from western Europe in the global economic divergence of the
nineteenth century, but the tsarist empire clearly did not make it into the
richest core either, remaining somewhere in between and perpetually
pushing, with a sense of urgency, to catch up.

That said, Russia's push for progress and the resulting improvements
in areas such as economy, infrastructure, access to knowledge, and
public health were not distributed equally within the empire either. Its
European parts enjoyed an incomparably larger share of those improvements than its Asian territories. This internal "divergence" further consolidated the sense of in-betweenness and urgency for the Volga-Ural
Muslims who physically as well as culturally stood at the crossroads
connecting Russia's East and West. In the late nineteenth century,
perceiving and making sense of the ongoing change entailed for the
Volga-Ural Muslims both temporal and spatial comparisons; between
memories of the past and experiences of the present as well as between
the contemporary experiences of various locations in their geographical
imaginary. This chapter will offer a broad view of the late nineteenth
century global changes that owed their origins and dissemination to the
example and direct influence of western Europe – or the globalization of
European modernity – as those changes unfolded in the Russian empire
and gradually transformed the experiences of Volga-Ural Muslims.

Three journeys to Mecca

In his madrasa years in the early 1870s, Rızâeddin bin Fahreddin had
come across and read a text about the mid-eighteenth-century journey

---

[7] Calculated based on Paul Bairoch, "Europe's Gross National Product: 1800–1975," *The
Journal of European Economic History*, 1976 5(2): 286.
[8] See Paul R. Gregory, *Russian National Income, 1885–1913* (Cambridge: Cambridge
University Press, 1982), 56–57 and 71; and Arkadius Kahan, *Russian Economic History:
The Nineteenth Century* (Chicago: University of Chicago Press, 1989), 1–90.

from Russia to Transoxiana, then to India, Hijaz, Damascus, Istanbul, and finally back to Russia of a Muslim man named "İsmâ'îl Efendi [Bekmuhammadof]." This turned out to be a curious find for Fahreddin since he had never heard detailed reports of such faraway places before. Later, in 1903, he decided to publish a critical edition of the text. He did not think that İsmâ'îl Efendi's travel notes were particularly informative, especially since other books in Turkic with more accurate information on distant parts of the world had already become available by this time. But he hoped that the text could inspire a sense of curiosity to the readers and provide a point of comparison about the changes in life since the mid eighteenth century.[9]

İsmâ'îl Efendi's trip started as a commercial expedition led by a Muslim merchant named Ya'qub Ağa from a suburb of Orenburg called "Qargali" (Kargala). In the late 1740s, the tsarist administration had settled Muslim merchants from the Kazan region in this suburb mainly to improve Russia's trade with the Muslim peoples of the Kazakh Steppes, Transoxiana, and Kashgaria.[10] Ya'qub Ağa's convoy arrived in Bukhara in a camel caravan after forty-one days, but İsmâ'îl Efendi offers almost no detail about this long walk. Such briefness, according to Fahreddin, was surprising in the light of the fact that Fahreddin's contemporaries, "who were used to traveling by train or steamboat," grumbled about the difficulties of travel even when they had to walk short distances. However, it seems that İsmâ'îl Efendi's real odyssey started after Bukhara, when his convoy continued through Afghanistan on to India where Mughal rule was disintegrating in the wake of Nadir Shah's invasions of the subcontinent. İsmâ'îl Efendi and his companions had to defend themselves against thugs as they walked thousands of miles from city to city with extended stays in some. When they reached the sea, they took a boat to Surat, but a pirate ship with twelve cannons caught up with them shortly before the journey's end. When they resisted, two of İsmâ'îl Efendi's fellow travelers were killed in the fight. Eventually, a European ship with fifty cannons gave protection to their boat, and İsmâ'îl Efendi and Ya'qub Ağa survived. After a few years of traveling on

[9] Rızâeddin bin Fahreddin ed. *İsmâ'îl Seyahati* (Kazan: Tipo-Litografiia İ. N. Kharitonova, 1903). The originality of the text of this travelogue has been questioned. See Michael Kemper, "Ismails Reisebuch als Genremischung," in *Istochniki i issledovaniia po istorii Tatarskogo naroda*, ed. Mirkasım A. Usmanov and Diliara M. Usmanonova (Kazan: Kazan State University, 2006), 318–30. However, even if the text has lost its originality, the travel of İsmâ'îl and his companions is confirmed in archival documents. See Mami Hamamato, "Tatarskaia Kargala in Russia's Eastern Policies," in *Asiatic Russia: Imperial Power in Regional and International Contexts*, ed. Tomohiko Uyama (New York: Routledge, 2012), 39.

[10] For a study of this settlement, see Hamamato, "Tatarskaia Kargala," 32–51.

the subcontinent and a meeting with the Mughal Sultan, Ya'qub Ağa decided to go back to Orenburg with İsmâ'îl Efendi in his retinue. However, the return route was blocked as a result of political turmoils. Unable to return home, they decided to go to Hijaz by the sea and perform the Hajj.[11]

Delayed by an eventful journey in which their boat caught an adverse wind and drifted off the route, they finally arrived in Mecca after several months. Here, they performed the Hajj and visited many holy sites including Prophet Muhammad's grave in Medina.[12] Then, they joined a caravan and went to Damascus, but Ya'qub Ağa got sick here. He bequeathed his property to someone named Murtaza Efendi before he died and entrusted İsmâ'îl Efendi to Murtaza Efendi's protection as well, but shortly after, Murtaza Efendi also died in a plague that hit Damascus. İsmâ'îl Efendi survived but was left without a benefactor. He took refuge in a madrasa. Then, at the end of the next Hajj season, he joined a group of Crimean Tatars on their way to Istanbul from Mecca. Together, they traveled by the sea and arrived in Istanbul after a month. İsmâ'îl Efendi settled here and studied at a madrasa for four years. About twenty more years would pass before he could finally find the opportunity to go back to Orenburg.[13]

If İsmâ'îl Efendi's story was curious and informative for Fahreddin in his adolescent years, representing a distant yet compelling reality in his imagination, it was simplistic and exotic by 1903, representing an obsolete world. The signs of this transition were already in place in the mid nineteenth century but not as obvious as they became within Fahreddin's lifetime. In 1908, Fahreddin published in Âsar the travel account of yet another Volga-Ural Muslim, Celâleddin bin Burhâneddin, who had performed the Hajj in 1864. As Celâleddin traveled, he regularly sent letters to his son back in Kazan narrating his experience. The physical conditions of Celâleddin's travel from Menzelinsk (to the east of Kazan) to Odessa were probably not too different from what İsmâ'îl Efendi might have witnessed a century before. Celâleddin and his companions traveled by a sledge troika on snow and, when the snow thawed, by coach through muddy land. When they reached Dnieper, they had to wait for the river to freeze before they could cross to the other side. It took them twenty-two days from Kazan to Odessa.[14] Of course they were benefiting from the facilities that the consolidated political power and investments of the Russian state provided on this track such as safety, more or less reliable provisions in consecutive towns and postal stations, and the

---

[11] Fahreddin ed. *İsmâ'îl*, 6–15.   [12] Ibid. 15–22.   [13] Ibid. 27–28.
[14] Fahreddin, *Âsar*, vol. 2, 462–66.

ability to send letters from those stations. None of that would have been available to İsmâʿîl Efendi, but otherwise, Celâleddin and his companions struggled with the same natural circumstances that troubled travelers a century before.[15] Yet, the experience of Celâleddin and his companions from Odessa onwards was considerably faster and easier to that of İsmâʿîl Efendi thanks to the introduction of steam power in long-distance transportation by this time.[16] They took a steamship to Istanbul in two days, another one to Alexandria in six days, a train to Cairo in four hours, another train to Suez within a day, and finally to Jeddah, by steamship, in five to six days. They were in Mecca thirty-eight days after leaving Odessa, but this included the time spent in various locations for rest and sightseeing. Otherwise, the travel time itself was only about two weeks.[17]

That was remarkable progress, but still outside of Russia's borders, not yet readily available to Fahreddin as he studied in a village of the Bugulma County, about 170 miles to the southeast of Kazan. Therefore, what actually struck Fahreddin in reading Celâleddin bin Burhâneddin's travel account was the progress he had witnessed within Russia since the 1860s. Elated by the surprise effect of this personal comparison, Fahreddin wrote that in a hundred to a hundred and fifty years, "if the world keeps progressing in this way and the entire nature subjects to the sons of Adam, there will come a time and ... traveling from Kazan to Holy Mecca will take probably less than one to two hours."[18]

What accounted for the futuristic optimism of this Muslim scholar who was born in a distant village of the Volga-Ural region in 1859 and did not leave the region until 1888 or Russia until 1926?[19] Perhaps, one way to capture the answer might be to imagine how increasingly more of the outside world became accessible to Rızâeddin bin Fahreddin

---

[15] İsmâʿîl Efendi's travel account does not include information about European Russia, but other sources may give an idea about what he may have witnessed here. For an example, see Jonas Hanway, *An Historical Account of the British Trade over the Caspian Sea: with a Journal of Travels from London through Russia into Persia; and Back Again through Russia, Germany and Holland* (London: Dodsley, 1753), 16–22 and 86–122.

[16] On the transformative effects of the use of steam power in industry and transportation, see William Rosen, *The Most Powerful Idea in the World: A Story of Steam, Industry, and Invention* (New York: Random House, 2010), especially 271–310. We should also mention that the Black Sea became open to international trade and transportation following the Crimean War. See Charles King, *The Black Sea: A History* (Oxford: Oxford University Press, 2004), 190–99.

[17] Fahreddin, *Âsar*, 466–69.   [18] Ibid. 469.

[19] Abdrafikova and Gabidullina, *Materialy*, 12 and 17.

and his contemporary Muslims in the towns and even villages of the Volga-Ural region in the late nineteenth century. Fahreddin's father performed the Hajj in 1879.[20] Although Fahreddin does not relate any details about this journey, we learn what his father may have related back home from the narrative of Ğabdürreşîd İbrâhîm's travel to Mecca and Medina in the same year. İbrâhîm started from Akmola in the Kazakh Steppes. He first rode a horse and then walked until Orenburg. From there on, however, his entire journey till Jeddah through Perm, Nizhny Novgorod, Moscow, Odessa, and Istanbul was by steamboat or by train, which he saw for the first time in Orenburg. Fifteen years after Celâleddin's trip, railways and steamboats on rivers had started to connect major towns in the Volga-Ural region to each other and to the urban hubs of European Russia such as Moscow and Odessa.[21]

The great transformation

Steam-powered transportation provided the infrastructure for Russia's transformation in the late nineteenth century. Sail boats, barges, and log driving continued to exist on its rivers through the end of the tsarist regime, but the proliferation of steamboats after the mid nineteenth century, coupled with waterway improvements, boosted the empire's volume of water transportation from 6 million tons of freight in 1861 to near 60 million tons by 1913.[22] The growth was huge, but water transportation still remained largely seasonal while railways could run year-round.[23] The length of Russia's railroads grew from 720 miles in 1857, when Alexander II issued a decree to launch large-scale railroad construction in the empire, to 11,300 miles in 1874. Construction slowed with the economic downturn of the 1870s but picked up again in the 1890s, under the leadership of the finance minister Count Sergei Witte (1893–1903). Russia's 19,500 miles of railroads in 1893 soared to 36,400 miles in 1903 and 43,900 miles in 1913. Even more striking than laying these lines was the surge in railway usage in the empire, with freight

---

[20] Ibid. *Materialy*, 6.   [21] İbrâhîmof, *Tercüme-yi Hâlim*, 51–61.

[22] Blackwell, *The Beginnings*, 262–69; John Norton Westwood, *A History of Russian Railways* (London: George Allen and Unwin Ltd., 1964), 18; Richard Mowbray Haywood, "The Development of Steamboats on the Volga River and Its Tributaries, 1817–1856," *Research in Economic History: A Research Annual*, ed. Paul Uselding (Greenwich: Jai Press, 1981), 142–86; E. G. Istomina, *Vodnye puti Rossii vo vtoroi polovine XVIII-nachale XIX veka* (Moscow: Nauka, 1982), 30–41; and Kahan, *Russian Economic*, 33.

[23] On the seasonality of waterways, see N. Peacock ed. *The Russian Year-Book: 1916* (London: Eyre and Spottiswoode, 1916), 283.

traffic rising from 14 to 158 million tons between 1874 and 1913 and passenger traffic from 32 to 244 million persons.[24]

These revolutionary changes in transportation concentrated in the lands to the west of the Ural Mountains, covering most of the Volga-Ural region, but left out many other Muslim-inhabited areas to the east. In 1910, for instance, 95 percent of Russia's water transportation took place on the network of rivers, canals, lakes, and sea routes in European Russia.[25] The Volga-Ural region was not abandoned though. It connected to the eastern edge of that network with the Volga and Kama Rivers.[26] Railway development in Russia also started in the west. Railroads reached Nizhny Novgorod as early as 1862 but did not extend further east until the 1870s. Then, in the late 1870s and early 1880s, construction began in the Urals region, mainly to take advantage of its iron reserves. This new grid joined the larger web to the west through Syzran in 1880 and Kazan in 1894, thus, integrating the Volga-Ural region into European Russia's transport revolution in the late nineteenth century.[27] Railways grew into a thickly woven web in European Russia by the turn of the twentieth century while single lines sliced through Siberia and the Kazakh Steppes.[28]

Postal stations and telegraph lines followed along railroad tracks and epitomized an equally important communications revolution. The Russian postal system expanded notably in the late nineteenth century as train stations started to provide postal services and county zemstvos opened their own postal stations. Russian postal services delivered approximately 593 million pieces of mail in 1896, 1.2 billion in 1903, and 2.2 billion in 1913.[29] The telegraph became a part of daily life in imperial Russia in its last decades as well. The length of its telegraph lines grew from about 11,000 miles in 1860 to 164,000 miles in 1910. Russian

---

[24] Anon., *Observations on the Objects and Prospects of the Russian Railway Enterprise* (London: T.F.A. Day, 1857); Theodore H. Von Laue, *Sergei Witte and the Industrialization of Russia* (New York: Columbia University Press, 1963), 22 and 33–89; and Westwood, *A History*, appendices 2, 5, and 6.

[25] Peacock, *The Russian Year-Book: 1916*, 287–88.

[26] Peacock, *The Russian Year-Book: 1916*, 283 and 287–88; and M. G. Mullagulov, *Bashkirskii narodnyi transport, xix-nachalo xx v.* (Ufa: Ural'skogo otdeleniia RAN, 1992), 32.

[27] See table in Westwood, *A History*, 302–3; and *Tatarskaia entsiklopediia*, s.v. "Zheleznodorozhnyi transport."

[28] See map in Westwood, *A History*, 24.

[29] *Entsiklopedicheskii Slovar'*, 1st edn., s.v. "Pochta"; *Entsiklopedicheskii Slovar'*, 2nd edn., s. v. "Pochta (dopolnenie k stat'e)"; Peacock, *The Russian Year-Book: 1916*, 102; and V. V. Mel'nikova, *Iz istorii razvitiia pochtovo-telegrafnoi sviazi v krae v XVIII-pervoi chetverti XX v.* (Volgograd: Volgogradskoe nauchnoe izdatel'stvo, 2004), 12–47. The numbers do not include Finland.

subjects would send close to 50 million telegraphs in 1913 alone.[30] Most postal stations started to handle telegraphs in addition to mail, and even telephones became available to Russia's subjects by this time, at least to those in more central locations.[31] Government investment in communications concentrated in western Russia too, but even those parts of the empire that were significantly distant from the central communications grid could potentially have some level of access to it.[32] A merchant in Kattakurgan, for instance, offered cargo services to the autonomous Bukharan Emirate in 1886, thereby connecting Transoxiana to the imperial postal system from Kattakurgan, although with a thin line.[33]

These improvements in transportation and communications both reflected and underpinned a process of regional market integration within Russia as the empire's overall economy itself became embedded in the fast-globalizing world markets of the late nineteenth century. The increase in world grain prices following the repeal of the British Corn Laws in 1846 provided a strong impetus for Russia to export grains, thus promoting the commercialization of its agriculture and plunging its economy into the ups and downs of global market fluctuations. Grain prices fell again in the 1870s as exports from the Americas boosted world supplies, but the dramatic reduction in transportation costs still allowed Russia to sell grains profitably through the end of the tsarist regime.[34]

Nevertheless, as Russia exported grains, European manufactured goods flooded its markets. Even trade in seasonal fairs, which represented a more traditional exchange system as opposed to urban markets, reflected this pattern. German, British, French, and Polish Jewish merchants brought European products to the famous Nizhny Novgorod Fair

---

[30] Kahan, *Russian Economic*, 34.

[31] *Entsiklopedicheskii Slovar'*, 1st edn., s.v. "Pochtas" and s.v. "Pochta (dopolnenie k stat'e)"; *Entsiklopedicheskii Slovar'*, 2nd edn., s.v. "Telegraf – ekonomicheskie znachenie (dopolnenie k stat'e)"; Peacock, *The Russian Year-Book: 1916*, 105.

[32] "Geçdi Zaman, Geldi Zaman," in *Tercüman*, October 29, 1904 .

[33] For an advertisement announcing this service, see "Iz Bukhary," *Tercüman*, February 28, 1886.

[34] Jacob Metzer, "Railroad Development and Market Integration: The Case of Tsarist Russia," *The Journal of Economic History*, 1974 34(3): especially 538; Evelyn B. Davidheiser, *"The World Economy and Mobilizational Dictatorship: Russia's Transition, 1846–1917"* (Ph.D. Dissertation, Duke University, 1990), 24; Kevin H. O'Rourke, "The European Grain Invasion, 1870–1913," *The Journal of Economic History*, 1997 57 (4): 775–801; O'Rourke and Williamson, *Globalization and History*, 33–36 and 47; Mette Ejrnæs, Karl Gunnar Persson, and Søren Rich, "Feeding the British: Convergence and Market Efficiency in the Nineteenth-Century Grain Trade," *The Economic History Review*, 2008 61(S1): 144.

in the early 1880s and set up stalls alongside the more familiar Iranians, Khivans, Bukharans, and Chinese.[35] French and Spanish wine came through Odessa and British silks through the Baltic ports. Agricultural machinery, medical and musical instruments, watches, and especially German sewing machines invaded the fair in the late nineteenth century.[36]

The profitability of Russia's grain exports appeared much less remarkable in light of the high profits that western Europe's industrialized economies made from the sale of manufactured products. Thus, beginning in the 1870s and especially the 1890s, the conductors of Russia's imperial economy started to concentrate on industrialization by raising protective tariffs, creating favorable conditions for foreign investment, and diverting revenues from grain exports to industrial investments.[37] Russia industrialized at an astonishing rate of about 5 percent annually in the late nineteenth century and over 8 percent in the 1890s.[38] State investments in heavy industry played an important role in this growth, but equally important was the growth of a robust consumer market that made smaller-scale investments profitable. Textiles and foodstuffs, for instance, accounted for half of the empire's industrial output in 1913.[39] The productions of cotton yarn and raw cotton cloth, primarily to be consumed domestically, tripled between 1890 and 1913.[40]

What made the growth of this consumer market possible were the consumers. Russia's population more than doubled between the 1860s and the First World War, primarily through natural increase in European

[35] "Mekerye Bazarından." On fairs and especially the Nizhny Novgorod Fair, see G. A. Dikhtiar, *Vnutrenniaia torgovlia v dorevoliutsionnoi Rossii* (Moscow: Izdatel'stvo Akademii Nauk SSSR, 1960), 140–47; Anne Lincoln Fitzpatrick, *The Great Russian Fair: Nizhnii Novgorod, 1840–90* (London: The Macmillan Press, 1990); and A. P. Mel'nikov, *Ocherki bytovoi istorii Nizhegorodskoi iarmarki (1817–1917)* (Nizhny Novgorod: Nizhegorodskii kompiuternyi tsentr, 1993).

[36] N. A. Bogoroditzkaia, "Torgovlia inostrannymi tovarami na Nizhegorodskoi iarmarke vo vtoroi polovine XIX-Nach. XX vv.," in *Makar'evsko-Nizhegorodskaia iarmarka: ocherki istorii*, ed. N. F. Filatov (Nizhnii Novgorod: Nizhegorodkii gosudarstvennii universitet, 1997), 135–38.

[37] On industrialization in late imperial Russia, see Von Laue, *Sergei Witte*; William L. Blackwell, *The Industrialization of Russia: An Historical Perspective* (New York: Crowell, 1970), 24–55; and Malcolm E. Falkus, *The Industrialisation of Russia, 1700–1914* (London: Macmillan, 1972), especially 44–74.

[38] Peter Gatrell, "The Meaning of the Great Reforms in Russian Economic History," in *Russia's Great Reforms, 1855–1881*, ed. Ben Eklof, John Bushnell, and Larisa Georgievna Zakharova (Bloomington: Indiana University Press, 1994), 85–86; and Kahan, *Russian Economic*, 13–26 and 36–38.

[39] Peter Gatrell, *The Tsarist Economy, 1850–1917* (New York: St. Martin's Press, 1986), 144.

[40] Kahan, *Russian Economic*, 16–18.

Russia.[41] A rapidly growing mass of people, mostly peasants, chose to procure a larger portion of their expanding needs and wants from the open market rather than from village economies or through household production.[42] Peasant poverty has long been an oft-visited trope of Russian historiography, and true, climate-related crop failures sporadically brought famine to the tsarist empire's villages. Yet, the crop failure of 1891 was the last in its history to trigger extended famine, as railways moved large quantities of foodstuff to hard-hit areas and nearly four million migrants from European Russia, who followed the Trans-Siberian Railroad, added their cultivation in Siberia to Russia's grain production.[43] In fact, rigorous scholarship suggests that the amount of land under cultivation, land productivity, and annual grain yields increased so much in the late nineteenth century that even as Russia exported grains to finance industry, its peasants had more to eat, save, and invest – primarily in land purchases.[44] According to one estimate, the average grain production per person in the Volga-Ural region increased from 690 pounds a year in 1864–1866 to 1040 pounds in 1883–1887.[45]

Moreover, although serfdom was already less of a barrier to the mobility of Russia's peasants by the 1860s, the emancipation and more flexible

[41] A. G. Rashin, *Naselenie Rossii za 100 let (1811–1913 gg.)* (Moscow: Gosudarstvennoe Staticheskoe Izdatel'stvo, 1956), 26.

[42] I have been inspired by Jan de Vries' ideas about "industrious revolution" in this section, although I do not consider the Russian experience in the late nineteenth century a repetition of the "industrious revolution" that de Vries describes in the contexts of Northwest Europe and North America. See Jan de Vries, "The Industrial Revolution and the Industrious Revolution," *The Journal of Economic History*, 1994 54(2): 249–270; and Jan de Vries, *The Industrious Revolution: Consumer Behavior and the Household Economy, 1650 to the Present* (Cambridge: Cambridge University Press, 2008).

[43] Gatrell, *Tsarist Economy*, 139–40; and N. M. Dronin and E. G. Bellinger, *Climate Dependence and Food Problems in Russia, 1900–1990: The Interaction of Climate and Agricultural Policy and Their Effect on Food Problems* (Budapest: Central European University Press, 2005), especially 53–66.

[44] Paul R. Gregory, "Grain Marketings and Peasant Consumption, Russia, 1885–1913," *Explorations in Economic History*, 1980 17(2): especially 147; Gatrell, *Tsarist Economy*, 130–40; Kahan, *Russian Economic*, 9; Elvira M. Wilbur, "Peasant Poverty in Theory and Practice: A View from Russia's 'Impoverished Center' at the End of the Nineteenth Century," in *Peasant Economy, Culture, and Politics of European Russia, 1800–1921*, ed. Jeffrey Burds, Esther Kingston-Mann, and Timothy Mixter (Princeton: Princeton University Press, 1991), 101–27; Gatrell, "The Meaning," 88; Barry K. Goodwin and Thomas J. Grennes, "Tsarist Russia and the World Wheat Market," *Explorations in Economic History*, 1998 35(4): 405–30; Boris Nikolaevich Mironov, *The Standard of Living and Revolutions in Russia, 1700–1917* (New York: Routledge, 2012); and Tracy Dennison and Steven Nafziger, "Living Standards in Nineteenth-Century Russia," *Journal of Interdisciplinary History*, 2013 43(3): 397–441.

[45] Khasanov, *Formirovanie*, 101–8 and 169. Also see Frank, *Muslim Religious Institutions*, 48.

internal passport requirements remarkably improved their ability to seek alternate or additional means of livelihood in different locations. Poorer peasants who wanted to supplement their budgets traveled to cities and urban towns to find employment as seasonal or permanent blue-collar workers. The tsarist empire's urban population quadrupled in its last half century,[46] but this only reflects the number of urban residents at census times, while the turnover of an even greater number of migrants who moved in and out of cities further accentuated Russia's urbanization experience. In many cases, even those new urbanites who permanently resided in cities and urban towns kept in touch with their relatives and fellow villagers back home through sustained communication and visits, therefore creating a liaison between the empire's urban centers and villages.[47]

Permanent urban markets that expanded in the late nineteenth century and dwarfed the trade volume of exchange in seasonal fairs, also contributed to the integration of markets in Russia. They emerged in cities and towns where railway lines intersected and sizeable urban populations concentrated. Skilled labor, business contacts, banks and other financial institutions, year-round shipment opportunities, and direct retailing to consumers were all available to entrepreneurs relatively easily in these urban hubs. The number of shops and stores in the empire's cities and urban towns increased dramatically, exceeding half a million by 1900 and adding another quarter of a million by the First World War.[48] European companies that wanted to sell agricultural machinery in Russia opened sales branches in cities, not in the country.[49]

Urban hubs, which were now connected to global markets through railways and telegraphy and to villages through peasant traffic and bazaar

---

[46] Gatrell, *Tsarist Economy*, 67.

[47] Thomas Stanley Fedor, *Patterns of Urban Growth in the Russian Empire during the Nineteenth Century* (Chicago: University of Chicago Dept. of Geography, 1975), especially 71–137 and 183–214; Joseph Bradley, *Muzhik and Muscovite: Urbanization in Late Imperial Russia* (Berkeley: University of California Press, 1985); Gatrell, *Tsarist Economy*, 67–69, 74, 89, 97, and 230; Brower, *Russian City*, especially 75–91; Jeffrey Burds, "The Social Control of Peasant Labor in Russia: The Response of Village Communities to Labor Migration in the Central Industrial Region, 1861–1905," in *Peasant Economy, Culture, and Politics of European Russia, 1800–1921*, ed. Jeffrey Burds, Esther Kingston-Mann, and Timothy Mixter (Princeton: Princeton University Press, 1991), 52–100; and Barbara Alpern Engel, *Between the Fields and the City: Women, Work, and Family in Russia, 1861–1914* (New York: Cambridge University Press, 1994), especially 64–165.

[48] Gatrell, *Tsarist Economy*, 157. On the evolution of Russia's financial markets after the Great Reforms, see Antoine E. Horn, "A History of Banking in the Russian Empire," in *A History of Banking in All the Leading Nations* (New York: The Journal of Commerce and Commercial Bulletin, 1896), especially 352–410.

[49] Bogoroditzkaia, "Torgovlia," 137.

networks served as loci where new ideas, products, consumption patterns, and aspirations made their appearance and became available for mass circulation. Newspapers too emerged in the big cities and thrived on street sales in addition to subscriptions.[50] Russian postal services delivered 425 million periodicals in 1910.[51] Russia's peasants and low-income urbanites learned to read and *did* read in this period.[52] As they read, albeit mostly cheap literature and tabloid journalism but also propaganda, they developed opinions.[53] Their opinions, in turn, reflected on the print media that they patronized, and once publicly available, their views started to acquire political significance.[54] Their ability to influence politics and governance directly remained limited, but both the *obshchestvo* and bureaucracy grew increasingly sensitive to what the peasants and low-income urbanites wanted.[55] As Witte emphasized in a report in 1892, it was *they* who paid the taxes after all.[56]

Without elective representation with legislative powers, Russia remained an autocracy through to the end of the tsarist regime, even after consultative representation became a part of its political system after 1905.[57] The empire's estate-based societal stratification did not break into an egalitarian citizenry or class hierarchy either. If anything, the estates adapted to new circumstances and proliferated.[58] However, especially in the lands to the west of the Ural Mountains, the world of caravans and seasonal fairs gradually morphed into a new world of railroads, wondrous and useful machines, electric communication, complicated financial transactions, innovative marketing strategies, newspapers, and even fashion and leisure for mass consumption.[59] This

---

[50] See McReynolds, *The News.*   [51] Peacock, *The Russian Year-Book: 1916,* 102.

[52] See Brooks, *When Russia.*

[53] For a personal account, see Semën Ivanovich Kanatchikov, *A Radical Worker in Tsarist Russia: The Autobiography of Semën Ivanovich Kanatchikov,* ed. Reginald E. Zelnik (Stanford: Stanford University Press, 1986), 33, 38, 44, 58–61, 69, 87–88, 127, 157, and 250.

[54] McReynolds, *The News,* especially 53–57.

[55] Burbank, *Russian Peasants,* 266–67; and Dowler, *Russia in 1913,* 90–140.

[56] Quoted in Von Laue, *Sergei Witte,* 34.

[57] On the persistence of autocracy after the Revolution of 1905, see Abraham Ascher, *The Revolution of 1905: Authority Restored* (Stanford, CA: Stanford University Press, 1992).

[58] Freeze, "The Soslovie Paradigm," 11–36; and Jane Burbank, "Thinking Like an Empire: Estate, Law, and Rights in the Early Twentieth Century," in *Russian Empire: Space, People, Power, 1700–1930,* ed. Jane Burbank, Mark von Hagen, and Anatoly Remnev (Bloomington: Indiana University Press, 2007), 196–217.

[59] See Halîl Sultanmuhammed, "Sevdagirlik," *Şûra* 1911(15): 461–62 for a contemporary observation of this transformation and Brower, *Russian City*; Louise McReynolds, *Russia at Play: Leisure Activities at the End of the Tsarist Era* (Ithaca: Cornell University Press, 2003); and Christine Ruane, *The Empire's New Clothes: A History of the Russian Fashion Industry, 1700–1917* (New Haven: Yale University Press, 2009) for in-depth studies on its various aspects.

was a sea-change in which multiple aspects of life were transformed simultaneously. Change revealed itself on a diminishing scale in the empire from west to east and from cities and urban towns to rural villages. But it elevated the fast-changing experiences of Russia's urban West into a model for the rest, thereby creating potential aspirations and challenges for even the most insulated imperial subjects. Moreover, as European products flooded Russia's markets and pushed their way into Russian households, transformations in the empire themselves became embedded within a global hierarchy where western Europe shone as the ultimate model of change or, as the contemporaries often saw it, of progress.

Muslims in Russia's great transformation

The advent of European modernity to the tsarist empire did not easily diminish the Volga-Ural Muslims' long-maintained distance from the imperial state and from things non-Muslim in general. Take the example of Ğabdurrahmân bin Ğatâullah el-Kazanî, a native of Kazan living in Eastern Turkestan as an imam. He traveled from Yarkend to Ufa, then to Kazan and Nizhny Novgorod, and then back to Yarkend in 1901. Despite his apparent open-mindedness and predilection for "progress," not once did he mention an interaction with non-Muslims when he later published an account of this three-month journey. However, the great transformations of the late nineteenth century still reflected on the experiences of Volga-Ural Muslims in noticeable ways. In Yarkend, Kazanî supplemented his income by trading in books that he mail-ordered from Kazan. When he traveled, he traveled by steamboat and train past Semipalatinsk. In Kazan, he phoned a steamboat company to purchase his ticket to Nizhny Novgorod, and in Nizhny Novgorod he attended horse races and a play, presumably in Russian, at the theater. He certainly encountered non-Muslims; he did not seem to identify with them, but he engaged them to exchange goods and services, if not in extended conversations and friendship.[60]

That being said, Muslims did not have to know Russian and interact with non-Muslims in order to witness the transformations of the late nineteenth century either. Fahreddin, for instance, lived within the confines of the Volga-Ural Muslim domain until the 1890s, but in 1884, one of his close friends introduced him to a Turkic-language newspaper called "*Tercüman.*" When he too subscribed to the newspaper by sharing

---

[60] Ğabdurrahmân bin Ğatâullah el-Kazanî, *Üç Aylık Seyahat* (Orenburg: Kerimof Matbaası, 1905).

the cost with a friend, little did he know that this printed periodical in Turkic – the first of its kind among Volga-Ural Muslims – would tremendously influence the evolution of his ideas.[61]

Published from the Crimea between 1883 and 1914 by İsmâ'îl Bey Gasprinskiy, who would later become famous as the founding father of progressive movements among Russia's Muslims, *Tercüman* was the only long-lived and Muslim-owned periodical in the Russian empire until many others appeared in print following press freedom in 1905 (see Figure 2). Its readership was large by Russian Muslim standards, reaching a peak of five thousand subscribers in the aftermath of the Revolution of 1905, but small in absolute terms, even if we keep in mind that newspapers were typically read and re-read by multiple people in this period. Yet, it circulated widely all around the Russian empire, especially the Volga-Ural region, and even in Eastern Turkestan and the Ottoman territories.[62] More importantly, in the absence of any other regular and widely circulating Muslim periodical until the Revolution of 1905, *Tercüman* provided a critical means of communication, especially for the progressive-minded Russian Muslims. Perhaps only a few read it, but many, even those who did not like Gasprinskiy's ideas, heard about it.[63]

Moreover, *Tercüman* and other periodicals published after 1905 did not only transmit information to their readers. They reflected the experiences of their readers and, although to a limited extent, of the broader Muslim population. A glance at the advertisements printed in the pages of *Tercüman* and one of those later periodicals – here we will pick *Vaqit* – may give an idea in this regard. *Vaqit* was published in the Volga-Ural region from Orenburg. It too had a relatively long life, lasting from 1906 until 1918, and a relatively wide circulation, a peak print count that reached around 5,000 in 1913. As a disclaimer, we should note that under the editorship of Rızâeddin Fahreddin's nephew Fâtih Kerimî (1870–1937), *Vaqit* addressed mostly progressive-minded

[61] Märdanov, Miñnullin, and Räximov, *Rizaetdin Fähretdin*, 19–20.

[62] İsmâ'îl Gasprinskiy, "Editorial," *Tercüman*, January 7, 1885; Bennigsen and Lemercier-Quelquejay, *La presse*; Edward J. Lazzerini, "Ismail Bey Gasprinskii's *Perevodchik/Tercüman*: A Clarion of Modernism," in *Central Asian Monuments*, ed. Hasan B. Paksoy (Istanbul: Isis Press, 1992), 143–56; Türkoğlu, *Rızaeddin Fahreddin*, 46; and Timur Kocaoğlu, "Tercüman Gazetesi'nin Dili ve Coğrafyası," in *İsmail Bey Gasrıralı İçin*, ed. Hakan Kırımlı (Ankara: Kırım Türkleri Kültür ve Yardımlaşma Derneği Yayınları, 2004), 215–27. Until 1905, censorship required Gasprinskiy to publish *Tercüman* simultaneously in Turkic and Russian. The Russian edition was named *Perevodchik*. Gasprinskiy's son continued the newspaper's publication until 1918.

[63] Kırımer, *Gasrıralı*, 62–63; Togan, *Bugünkü Türkili*, 556; Bennigsen and Lemercier-Quelquejay, *La presse*, 41–42; Lazzerini, "Ismail Bey Gasprinskii's *Perevodchik*," 154; and Kırımlı, *National Movements*, 35.

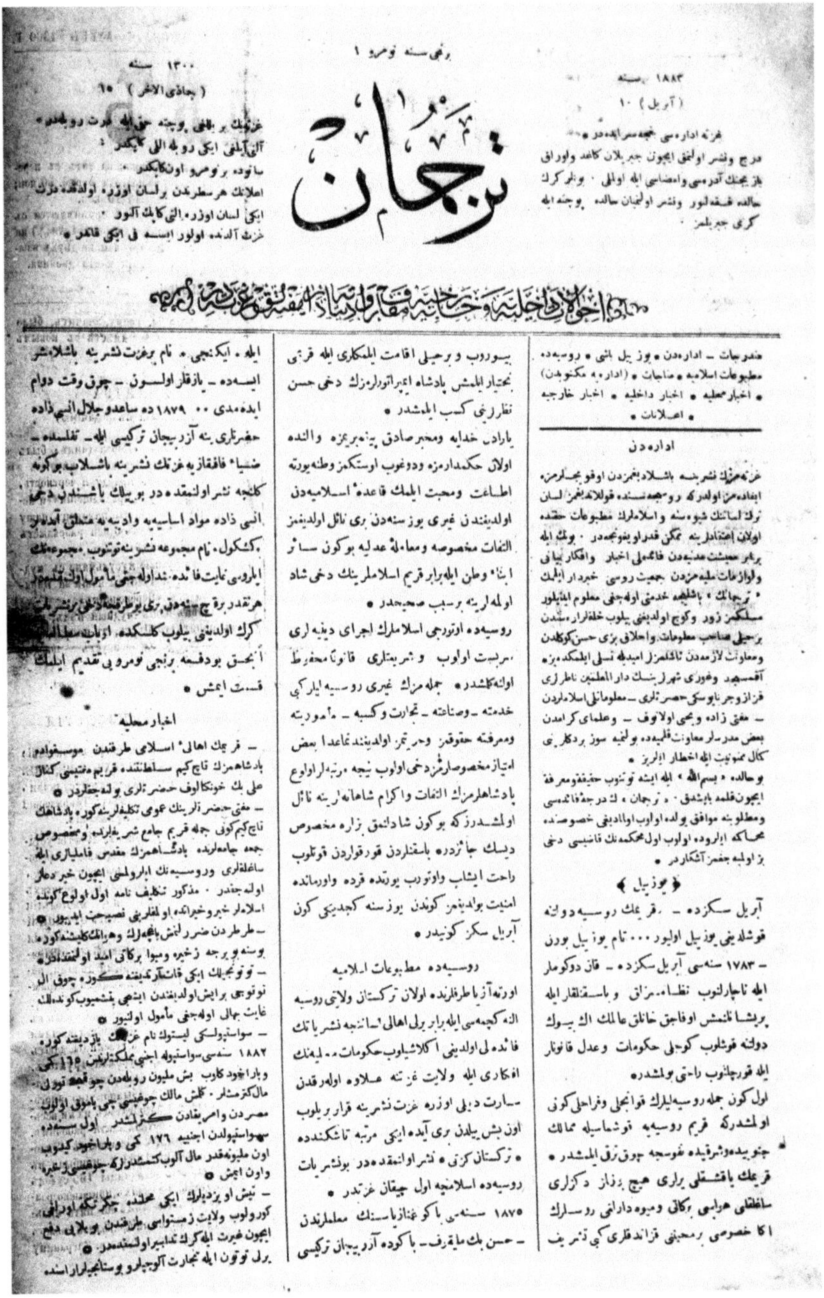
برنجی سنه نومرو ۱

ترجمان

۱۳۰۰ سنه

(جمادی الآخر ۱۵)

۱۸۸۳ سنه

(آپریل ۱۰)

اداره دن

اخبار محلیه

روسیه ده مطبوعات اسلامیه

یوزیل

Figure 2 The cover of *Tercüman*'s first issue published on April 10, 1883.

Russian Muslims too, but this is to be expected since progressive-minded Muslims largely dominated the Muslim press of the late Russian empire.[64]

The advertisements in *Tercüman* and *Vaqit* reflected the characteristics of an emerging consumer market where advertising typically introduced hitherto unknown or little-known products and services in an attempt to create demand for them rather than promoting the products of one brand among many in a competitive supplier market. Some of these products and services remained local to the region where either newspaper was published, perhaps indicating financial support for the progressive ideas of their publishers from personal acquaintances. However, a more substantial proportion of the advertisements came from various parts of Russia, especially the Volga-Ural region, and even from European countries like Germany and France. As such, they pointed to quotidian transformations in life that followed the commercial applications of technology, which usually hit Russia's markets as new European or American products.

To begin with, the advertisements in *Tercüman* and *Vaqit* reflected the expansion of travel options for Russia's Muslims that resulted from improvements in transportation. Shortly after the publication of its first issue, *Tercüman* started to receive advertisements about train services in Russia[65] and about steamships that shuttled between Black Sea ports or, later, that traveled to Jeddah.[66] Similar advertisements about train services regularly appeared in *Vaqit* too.[67] As the technology of transportation advanced, even the advertisement of an automobile with one horsepower found its way to the pages of *Tercüman* in 1914.[68]

---

[64] Diliara M. Usmanova, "K voprosu o tirazhakh musul'manskikh periodicheskikh izdanii Rossii nachala 20 veka" (paper presented at Ismail Gasprinskii – prosvetitel' naraodov Vostoka, k 150-letiiu co dnia rozhdeniia, Moscow, 2001), 212; and Raif F. Märdanov, "*Vakıt* gazetası," in *Bertugan Rämiyevlär: Fänni-biografik jientık*, ed. Liron Hämidullin, Raif Märdanov, and Ramil Miñnullin (Kazan: Ruhiyat, 2002), 161–63. On Fâtih Kerimî, see Raif Märdanov, Ramil Miñnullin. and Süläyman Räximov eds., *Fatih Kärimi* (Kazan: Ruhiyat, 2000).

[65] *Tercüman/Perevodchik*, November 25, 1883. For other examples see *Tercüman/Perevodchik*, December 23, 1883, March 14, 1884, September 26, 1885, and February 17, 1885.

[66] *Tercüman/Perevodchik*, May 29, 1883. The same advert continued to appear in *Tercüman* thereafter from time to time; e.g. November 4, 1883, December 23, 1883, and March 14, 1884. For repeated examples of advertisements about Hajj tours, see "Russian Steamship Transportation and Trade Company," *Tercüman/Perevodchik*, January 25, 1902 and December 20, 1902 and "Hajj Steamship," *Tercüman/Perevodchik*, September 30, 1905 and October 16, 1907.

[67] For two examples, see *Vaqit*, October 20, 1909 and January 22, 1916.

[68] *Tercüman/Perevodchik*, January 1, 1914.

Other advertisements point to the new ways Muslims could do business and deal with money in general. Banks, insurance companies, and other financial institutions frequently advertised, especially in *Tercüman*.[69] This, of course, was a sensitive issue for Muslims due to the Qur'anic sanction against usury.[70] And it sparked substantial discussions in the Russian Muslim periodical press, opening up what would have otherwise remained a matter of scholarly disputation to lay commentary in print media.[71]

New inventions from Europe and the United States, or novelties hitherto unknown to Russia's Muslims, took the largest share among the advertisements of *Tercüman* and *Vaqit*. *Tercüman*'s first issue advertised a store in Aqmescit specializing in agricultural instruments and machinery such as water pumps.[72] Sewing machines also proved a useful novelty; in 1894, a distributer claimed that every house needed one, and the advertisements of Singer sewing machines repeatedly appeared in both newspapers.[73] Nestlé advertised its milk supplement for babies in *Tercüman* starting in 1893,[74] and the advertisement of what the sellers called the "first milk chocolate in the world" appeared in *Vaqit* in 1910.[75] Chemical products such as medicinal solutions, pesticides, paints, various cleaning agents from perfumed soaps to water purifiers, and cosmetic items were also introduced to Russia's Muslims frequently in both newspapers. The advertisers generally claimed these products to be new inventions.[76] In 1904, a fictional character from Vienna, Anna Csillag, claimed that an ointment she invented made her hair grow over six feet in fourteen months. Customers could mail-order this ointment

---

[69] *Tercüman/Perevodchik*, January 31, 1885, October 3, 1885, February 17, 1886, February 28, 1886, June 17, 1907, January 2, 1909, and February 3, 1912.

[70] Qur'an 2: 275–80.

[71] For examples from one journal, see Anon., "Bankta Aqça Artuvu," *Şûra*, 1906 (6): 1; Zâkir Ayuhanof, "Ribâ Haqqında," *Şûra*, 1915 (1–19):; and Mustafa Seyfülmülükef, "İqtisâdî Tarihte Ribâ Meselesi," *Şûra*, 1915(14–24) and 1916(6–9) .

[72] *Tercüman/Perevodchik*, April 10, 1883. Also see *Tercüman/Perevodchik*, October 11, 1881 and *Vaqit*, October 20, 1909 and January 22, 1916.

[73] *Tercüman/Perevodchik*, May 26, 1894. For examples of other sewing machine advertisements, see February 6, 1904, October 9, 1907, June 4, 1910, January 1, 1914, and July 29, 1914 and *Vaqit*, January 8, 1908 and July 8, 1914.

[74] *Tercüman/Perevodchik*, January 9, 1893. Also see *Tercüman/Perevodchik*, May 3, 1905.

[75] *Vaqit*, January 1, 1910, February 23, 1910, and June 19, 1910.

[76] For examples, see *Tercüman/Perevodchik*, August 25, 1883, October 12, 1883, October 28, 1883, December 23, 1883, January 31, 1885, November 4, 1888, January 9, 1893, March 4, 1893, May 26, 1894, January 16, 1900, July 14, 1900, December 23, 1901, January 2, 1904, June 17, 1907, December 11, 1909, January 15, 1910, February 3, 1912, and February 3, 1912 and *Vaqit*, March 29, 1908, May 24, 1908, July 14, 1909, February 23, 1910, June 19, 1910, January 1, 1912, July 8, 1914, October 9, 1914, and April 20, 1916.

Figure 3 An advert for hair ointment that ran in Russian Muslim
periodicals frequently after 1904.

from a distributer in St. Petersburg. In three years, it became available for
store purchase in Orenburg too.[77]

Some of these new products were luxury items that rarely made their
way to local bazaars, nor did they become common household items
for the Muslims of the Volga-Ural region. They were generally available
only in specific stores in big cities, but mail order made them at least
potentially available for all interested customers. Among the near 2.2
billion pieces of mail handled by the imperial postal system in 1910 were
approximately 41.5 million money transfers, 19.8 million parcels and
packages with declared value, and 202.2 million ordinary parcels.[78] Many
products that were advertised in *Tercüman* and *Vaqit* were also available for
shipment to postal addresses. According to one advertisement in *Tercüman*

[77] *Tercüman/Perevodchik*, January 2, 1904 and *Vaqit*, January 5, 1908 and February 23,
1910. Togan writes that this was a fictional character: Togan, *Hatıralar*, 16.
[78] *The Russian Year-Book: 1916*, 102. Subscribed newspapers and Finnish mail are
excluded.

from 1885, a Moscow-based company took mail orders for various novelty items such as barometers, microscopes, steam machines, magic lanterns, and still cameras "with which one [could] take portraits and views."[79] A company in Warsaw sold gramophones,[80] another advertised "a gadget that could be carried in the pocket and used to light cigarettes,"[81] a Berlin-based seller offered cinematographs, gramophones, sewing machines, and similar "very new things,"[82] while a company in Paris introduced its "pocket typewriters" as the "newest invention"[83]: all available by mail.

Since they survived on subscriptions rather than street buyers, the readership of Muslim periodicals in Russia was not necessarily concentrated in cities and towns, but Muslim urbanites of the Volga-Ural region appear to have been more prone to adopting the novelties advertised in their pages. The appearance and gradual spread of European outfits in cities at the expense of the traditional Muslim clothing illustrates the propensity of urban Muslims to adjust their practices and to merge into what Christopher Bayly has called "global uniformities" that "create similarities on a larger scale," though not necessarily homogeneity.[84] Beginning in 1905, a company in Łódź, Poland, named "Progress," advertised, in both Tercüman and Vaqit, English and French fabrics for making men's suits.[85] In January 1912, a Muslim-owned store in Orenburg announced the shipment of Russian and foreign-manufactured items, especially women's clothes, for the winter.[86] And some Volga-Ural Muslims purchased and donned these foreign-manufactured clothes as one can follow from the photographs of some of the rather prominent Muslim families of the time.[87]

Yet, one should not assume that it was only a marginal group of Muslim notables who adopted European-inspired appearances. Once European style outfits became available through mail order or in urban specialty stores, whether or not to wear them became a choice to be made for many Muslims, especially the ones who lived in cities and towns

[79] Tercüman/Perevodchik, March 8, 1885. Also see March 11, 1894.
[80] Tercüman/Perevodchik, June 22, 1907.   [81] Tercüman/Perevodchik, February 3, 1912.
[82] Tercüman/Perevodchik, April 9, 1910. Also see Tercüman/Perevodchik, December 10, 1910.
[83] Tercüman/Perevodchik, December 10, 1910.   [84] Bayly, The Birth, 1 and 12–16.
[85] Tercüman/Perevodchik, May 3, 1905, February 22, 1906, June 17, 1907, and October 9, 1907 and Vaqit, February 9, 1908.
[86] Vaqit, January 1, 1912.
[87] Among many examples, see the photo entries in Märdanov, Miñnullin, and Räximov, Fatih Kärimi; Sälman Gobäydullin et al., Gaziz Gobäydullin (Kazan: Ruhiyat, 2002); Liron Hämidullin, Raif Märdanov, and Ramil Miñnullin eds., Bertugan Rämiyevlär: Fänni-biografik jientık (Kazan: Ruhiyat, 2002); and Nail' Tairov, Akchuriny (Kazan: Tatarskoe Knizhnoe Izdatel'stvo, 2002).

where the power of custom to limit options diminished as a result of cosmopolitan exposure. Fahreddin tackled this matter in a series of articles published in *Vaqit*'s biweekly appendix *Şûra* in 1915. He suggested that the change of outfits over time should be considered a natural process related to the cost, quality, and practicality of newly created garments, such as sturdy boots that even Muslim villagers purchased from Russian stores instead of traditional soft-leather shoes. However, Fahreddin also noted that the issue had escalated into a cause of tension among Volga-Ural Muslims as some of them changed their clothes to mark a preference for "progress" or "civilization" (*medeniyet*) and others found this ridiculous or, at times, even abominable.[88]

In 1908, Zeki Velidî Togan (1890–1970), the later Bashkir political leader and eventually an esteemed historian in Turkey, left his village in the southern Urals with the intention to study. He first went to Orenburg where a group of urbanized madrasa students made fun of his baggy Bashkir pants and gave him European-style trousers. He did not stay long in Orenburg though and continued to Kazan. As he spent a year in this city, he completely adapted to its cosmopolitan way of life and started to smoke too. Hence, when he visited his village next summer, it was his villagers' turn to laugh at his new appearance and tobacco smell. Not only displeased with the "Russian-like" clothes of their son but also sickened by the smell on them, his parents banished Togan's clothes to the attic until his departure in the fall.[89]

Conclusion

Change in imperial Russia in the late nineteenth century did not affect all of its subjects, including the Volga-Ural Muslims, equally, but the challenge was for all. Some Muslims celebrated this change as progress and believed in its ultimate promise to improve human conditions, as revealed in what they perceived to be the fruits of progress in Europe. In 1899, Fâtih Kerimî accompanied a prominent Muslim merchant from Orenburg, Şâkir Ramiyef (1857–1912), on a journey through Europe, including European Russia, and he published his observations in 1901. The highlight of Kerimî's account was the luster, industry, precision, hygiene, and grandeur of the cities on his route, which he narrated with

---

[88] Rızâeddin bin Fahreddin, "Kiyümler Haqqında," *Şûra*, (8): 225–28, (9): 258–60, and (10): 289–92. Also see Fâtih Kerimî, *Bir Şakird ile Bir Student* (Kazan: Tipografiia B. L. Dombrovskogo, 1903), 2–4. For a study of Fahreddin's ideas on this issue, see Ayşe Azade-Rorlich, "Rızaeddin Fahreddin and the Debate over 'Muslim Dress' among the Volga-Ural Muslims," *International Journal of Turkish Studies*, 2005 11(1–2): 95–105.
[89] Togan, *Hatıralar*, 42, 46–47, and 51–57.

an apparent sense of veneration that started in Moscow and St. Petersburg and escalated as he reached Berlin and Paris.[90]

Other Muslims found the challenges of the late nineteenth century transformations threatening and the celebration of change abominable. One can make better sense of this tension if we view Kerimî's fascination with the secular progress of Europe against the background of İsmâ'îl Efendi's travel account that the Volga-Ural Muslims had read and re-read for more than a century. Perhaps added to the text subsequently as it circulated in popular literature, the highlights of İsmâ'îl Efendi's travel account were the depictions of the tombs of prophets and saints he had visited throughout his journey. In the Volga-Ural Muslims' social imaginary, the narrated record of those tombs rendered faith real as materialized on geography and geography familiar as revealed in religious tradition.[91] Here was Kerimî, however, revealing a new imaginary brought from the West and evidently powerful. It posed an alternative not only in Kerimî's narrative suggestion, but also as experienced on the streets of Orenburg, Ufa, and Kazan, not to mention in an otherwise insulated Bashkir village when a son one day returned home in "Russian" clothes, smelling of tobacco.

This alternative imaginary had many daring advocates, but what made it most challenging was its mundane ubiquity. One could avoid the progressive propaganda but avoiding the convenience of sturdy boots, comfortable and fashionable garments, cigarette lighters, sewing machines, fast-running trains, pesticides and perfumed soaps, and the profits of commercial agriculture – in a word, the sea-change – was another matter. This transformation originated in western Europe, spread through Russia in an eastward direction, and engulfed the Volga-Ural region, forcing its Muslims into what we may call a "pan-European domain" where vectors of exchange and interaction moved globally, in all directions, but also unevenly, warped by the centripetal power of western Europe. One could despise and reject the appearances and dictates of this modern life, admire its novel opportunities and embrace it wholeheartedly, or choose a way in between, but the challenge was there to be faced.[92] In the following three chapters, we will examine how the Volga-Ural Muslims faced it.

---

[90] Fatih Kerimi, *Avrupa Seyahatnamesi* (1901; reprint in modern Turkish adaptation, Istanbul: Çağrı Yayınları, 2001). For a study of this travel account, see Ayşe Azade-Rorlich, "'The Temptation of the West': Two Tatar Travellers' Encounter with Europe at the End of the Nineteenth Century," *Central Asian Survey*, 1985 4(3): 39–58.

[91] See Kemper, "Ismails."   [92] For a similar view, see Kotkin, "Modern Times," 114.

6   The wealthy
Prospering with the sea-change and giving back

I know a few among our Muslim Tatars who speak Russian perfectly
and read Russian-language books although they have not studied it,
neither in government nor in private Russian educational
institutions.   Vasilii Vasil'evich Grigor'ev
                                        Report on Muslim Education, 1869[1]

Some live on earth, die, and their names are completely forgotten, but
some start to live with an even greater impact after they die ... Their
bodies pass away from this world, but their names last, and therefore,
their lives continue. Those are the fortunate.   Şâkir Ramiyef in front of
                                          Goethe's statue in Berlin, 1899[2]

As a result of the gradual expulsion of Muslims from the most productive lands after the Muscovite expansion into Muslim territories in
the mid sixteenth century, the wealthy among Volga-Ural Muslims
(*bays* in Turkic) were mostly merchants and entrepreneurs, rather
than landowners. Their numbers, wealth, and social impact started to
increase slowly during the reign of Catherine II and expanded notably in
the second half of the nineteenth century, paralleling Russia's great
transformation. They encountered the new world emerging from the
expansion of European modernity firsthand as they traded in the ethnically and religiously mixed markets of the empire, beyond the comfort
zone of insulated Muslim communities. A relatively elaborate literature
in Russian and Turkic sketches the high points of this encounter either in
a Marxist register, as the bourgeois stage in the historical evolution of
the Volga-Ural Muslim nationalities, or in a nationalist register, as an
epic moment of national awakening.[3] The Western literature, on the

---

[1] V. V. Grigor'ev, "Zapiska," in *Sbornik dokumentov i statei po voprosu ob obrazovanii inorodtsev*, ed. Ministerstvo narodnogo prosveshcheniia (St. Petersburg: V Tip. T-va Obshchestvennaia Pol'za, 1869), 206.
[2] Fatih Kerimî, "Kem ide Şakir äfände," in *Bertugan Rämiyevlär: Fänni-biografik jententk*, ed. Liron Hämidullin, Raif Märdanov, and Ramil Miñnullin (Kazan: Ruhiyat, 2002), 120.
[3] For outstanding examples, see Kurat, "Kazan Türklerinde," 113–16, 120, and 170–75; Khasanov, *Formirovanie*; Salikhov, *Tatarskaia burzhuaziia*; Hämidullin, Märdanov, and

other hand, tends to mirror the nationalist version of this narrative, mostly in passing, as the backdrop to a history of nation-building or adaptation to modernity.[4] The celebratory conclusions of each of these approaches can be traced to the progressive Russian Muslim writings of the early twentieth century that eulogized the sponsorship of certain *bays* to the improvement of Muslim institutions in Russia.[5]

The prominent role that wealthy Volga-Ural Muslims played in the social and cultural evolution of their respective communities in late imperial Russia is undeniable and is supported by the similar experiences of other ethnic or religious groups in the empire such as the Jews and Armenians.[6] The progressive literature of the time offers precious insights and data too. Yet, the interpretive upshot of the current historiography reduces the contributions of wealthy Volga-Ural Muslims in the late nineteenth century to the active sponsorship of an estimated five percent among them to progressive reformism.[7] One of the most scrupulous students of the subject suggests that, a few exceptions aside, the remaining majority of wealthy Volga-Ural Muslims supported progressive reformism simply by staying out of it.[8] This is unsatisfying. This chapter acknowledges the significance and novelty of the alliance between wealth and progressive reformism in late-imperial Russian Muslim history but offers a reinterpretation by bringing the broader trends of the Volga-Ural Muslim domain and the late-nineteenth-century sea-change back into the picture. It suggests that the wealthy Volga-Ural Muslims sought adaptation to the economic, social, and political transformations of the late Russian empire with a diverse spectrum of concerns, motives, and choices that included nationalist aspirations but otherwise emerged and remained largely within the confines of the Catherinian imperial model.

Miñnullin, *Bertugan Rämiyevlär*, and Tairov, *Akchuriny*. The ideological positioning is less pronounced in these detailed yet somewhat descriptive studies that focus on the merchants of the city of Kazan regardless of religious affiliation: Liudmila M. Sverdlova, *Kupechestva Kazani: dela i liudi* (Kazan: Matbugat Yurtı, 1998); and Sverdlova, *Kazanskoe*.

[4] See, for example, Lazzerini, "Ismail Bey," 271–76; and Noack, *Muslimischer*, especially 101–8 and 400–6.

[5] In addition to numerous articles in the Muslim periodicals of the time, see Rızâeddin bin Fahreddin, *Ahmed Bay*, (Orenburg: Vaqit Matbaʿası, 1911); and Burhan Şeref, *Gani Bay* (Orenburg: Vaqit Matbaʿası, 1913).

[6] See Ronald Grigor Suny, *Looking Toward Ararat: Armenia in Modern History* (Bloomington: Indiana University Press, 1993), 37–42, and 58 on Armenians; and Nathans, *Beyond the Pale* on Jews.

[7] The estimate belongs to Mirkasım A. Usmanov, "Yañadan tanışu, yaki fidakyar xäyriyaçelärebez xakında," in *Bertugan Rämiyevlär: Fänni-biografik jientık*, ed. Liron Hämidullin, Raif Märdanov, and Ramil Miñnullin (Kazan: Ruhiyat, 2002), 26.

[8] Salikhov, *Tatarskaia burzhuaziia*, 30.

The social functions of *bays*

The social functions of wealthy Volga-Ural Muslims were closely related to Russian imperial policies. Following the fall of Kazan to Muscovy in 1552, the Russian state gradually destroyed Muslim institutions such as mosques, madrasas, and the endowments that supported them, especially in the Volga and Kama basins.[9] Catherine II allowed mosques and madrasas to be built again, but Muslim communities had to assume the expenses of construction and maintenance directly, without government subsidies or large endowments that could have otherwise grown in size over time. The Volga-Ural Muslims could endow property in the nineteenth century, but unlike in Muslim-ruled countries, their endowments received minimal legal protection and no tax benefits.[10] Consequently, their ability to sustain religious institutions depended on the continuing willingness of the *bays* and their inheritors to finance those institutions. The *bays* also provided other collective needs, such as scholarship for students or alms and employment for the poor.[11]

Moreover, it was usually the wealthy notables who paid for and, therefore, decisively influenced the selection of Islamic scholars as imams or to other religious positions. Scholars negotiated the shared norms and imaginaries of the Volga-Ural Muslim communities within the broader Muslim domain as representatives of religious authority. But the *bays* also enjoyed leverage in the moral economy of the Muslim communities thanks to their ability to pick and occasionally depose the scholar who actively gave direction to the value judgments of their coreligionists. Besides, while scholars typically traveled to the centers of Islamic scholarship in order to acquire knowledge, merchants traveled to fairs and market towns where people from diverse backgrounds exchanged information about the larger world along with commodities. Consequently, as the *bays* pursued business, they exposed their communities to influences and challenges from outside the boundaries of the Muslim domain as well.

---

[9] See Chapter 1.

[10] Azamatov, *Iz istorii*, 4–6 and 30–76 contains transcripts of several endowment charters. Also see Z. S. Minnullin, "Problemy vakfa: istoriia i sovremennost'," in *Religiia v sovremennom obshshestve: istoriia, problemy, tendentsii*, ed. R. A. Nabiev (Kazan: Zaman, 1998), 175–78; and Sverdlova, *Kazanskoe*, 276–78.

[11] For examples of how the *bays* supported their communities, see NART, f. 1, op. 3, d. 3540; İbrâhîmof, *Tercüme-yi Hâlim*, 9, 48–52, 72, and 110; Fahreddin, *Âsar*, vol. 1, 371–80, 392, 399, and 402, and vol. 2, 114–15, 199–200, 236–37, 312–20, 339–41, 344–47, 455–58, 465–66, 378–81, and 494–95.

Up from peddlers: Formation of a Muslim merchantry in the Volga-Ural region

The beginnings of the formation of a robust Muslim merchantry in the Volga-Ural region dates to the mid eighteenth century when the tsarist state actively sought to improve its eastern trade to enlarge imperial coffers and to consolidate power in its steppe borderlands, where Kazakh tribes roamed relatively independently. Russian merchants proved unsuitable for this task. They were not only unfamiliar with the region but also unable to secure entry from Transoxianian and Chinese authorities, who, in part, were retaliating against Russia's restrictions on Persian and Transoxianian merchants since the late sixteenth century. Thus, around the mid 1700s, after two centuries of repressive policies, the tsarist administration turned to select Muslim venturers, especially from the sedentary Muslim communities of the Volga and Kama basins, as intermediaries of Russia's eastern trade. This proved to be a lucrative decision. The Volga-Ural Muslims carried the cultural capital of a business tradition that dated as far back as the Volga Bulghars of the tenth century. They already relied heavily on crafts and commerce for a livelihood as a result of their expulsion from productive lands. And they enjoyed religious and linguistic affinity with the Muslim peoples of the Kazakh Steppes, Transoxiana, and Kashgaria.

As Russian presence solidified in the territories to the south and east of the Ural Mountains, sedentary Muslims from the Volga and Kama basins moved into the fortress towns of these borderlands, such as Semipalatinsk, and even established their own settlements.[12] The foundation of Qargali was an early example of this process. In 1744, following the foundation of the Orenburg fortress at the southern skirts of the Ural Mountains, the Senate authorized a Muslim merchant, Saʿîd Babay Hayalin, to settle about fifteen miles to the northwest of Orenburg and bring two hundred Muslim peasants with him. This settlement later came to be known as Qargali. As a skillful merchant, Saʿîd Babay quickly established trade relations with the Kazakhs in the steppe region. Thanks to several privileges that the Senate offered to those who settled with him,

---

[12] Tuqayef, *Tarih-i İsterlibaş*, 2–3; M. K. Rozhkova, *Ekonomicheskie sviazi Rossii so Srednei Aziei – 40–60e gody XIX veka* (Moscow: Izdatelʹstvo Akademii Nauk SSSR, 1963), 124–35; Mirkasyim A. Usmanov, "Tatarskoe kupechestvo v torgovle Rossii s vostochnymi stranami cherez Astrakhan i Orenburg," *Russian History/Histoire russe*, 1992 19(1–4): 512–13; N. A. Khalikov, *Khoziaistvo Tatar Povolzhʹia i Urala: seredina XIX – nachalo XX v.* (Kazan: Akademiia Nauk Respubliki Tatarstana, 1995), 189–90; and Allen J. Frank and Mirkasım A. Usmanov eds., *Materials for the Islamic History of Semipalatinsk* (Berlin: ANOR, 2001), 4–9.

such as tax breaks, the population of Qargali increased quickly to 1,158 males in 1761, 2,190 in 1773, and 3,180 in 1796.[13] Some other Muslim settlers even established trade colonies in China.[14] Many of these pioneers partnered with their relatives back in the Volga-Ural region for long-distance trade. By the early twentieth century, the Qara Cıyun family from the village of Sasna in Malmyzh, for instance, had built a trade network that spanned Troitsk in the southern Urals, Orsk, Qosta-nay, and Kurgan in or bordering the Kazakh Steppes, Irkutsk in Siberia, Tashkent and Bukhara in Transoxiana, Simmi by the Amur River, and Qulja in Kashgaria.[15]

Catherine II's relatively tolerant rule further improved trade oppor-tunities for the Muslim entrepreneurs. As state peasants, the Volga-Ural Muslims were typically bound to the state and not to a private landlord who could effectively limit their mobility or economic activities.[16] They were still restricted by Russia's internal passport regulations, but in 1763, Catherine II ordered local authorities not to create difficulties for those Muslim peasants who wanted to travel for trade purposes. In 1775, as she reformed the laws governing Russia's merchantry, she allowed Muslim peasants to obtain townspeople (*meshchanstvo*) or guild mer-chant (*kupechestvo*) status upon declaring specified amounts of capital. The guild merchant category was further divided into three guilds, and Muslims could enter all three depending on the amount of capital they possessed. Each of these statuses conferred certain privileges to engage in various forms of economic activity that were closed to peasants or ordinary burghers. Townspeople, for instance, could trade as peddlers or sell their crafts but could not engage in large-scale wholesale trade, especially after 1824. Or a rule that stayed in effect until 1800 allowed first and second guild merchants to own river vessels for long-distance transportation while limiting third guild merchants to boats suitable for use on smaller rivers only.[17] Most Muslims could not leave their peasant status at the beginning, because Catherine II banned peasants from registering as townspeople in 1782 and one needed a relatively higher

[13] Fahreddin, *Ahmed*, 8–9; Usmanov, "Tatarskoe kupechestvo," 510–11; and Hamamato, "Tatarskaia Kargala," 32–51.

[14] Mirkasım A. Usmanov, "Tatar Settlers in Western China (Second Half of the 19th Century to the First Half of the 20th Century)," in *Muslim Culture in Russia and Central Asia from the 18th to the Early 20th Centuries* ed. Michael Kemper, Anke von Kügelgen, and Dmitriy Yermakov (Berlin: Klaus Schwarz Verlag, 1998), 245.

[15] Fahreddin, *Âsar*, vol. 2, 452–53.

[16] A. A. Sukharev, *Kazanskie Tatary (uezd kazanskii)* (St. Petersburg, 1904), 47–48.

[17] Khasanov, *Formirovanie*, 25 and 53; and Istomina, *Vodnye puti*, 59. Also see Alfred J. Rieber, *Merchants and Entrepreneurs in Imperial Russia* (Chapel Hill: University of North Carolina Press, 1982).

capital to register in guilds. Yet, a few Muslim peasants did accumulate the required amount, entered the third merchant guild, and some even moved further to the second and first guilds. In 1821, Nicholas I allowed peasants to register as townspeople too, and Muslim peasants did so in notably large numbers.[18]

Thus, the path to accumulating wealth was open to Volga-Ural Muslims in the late eighteenth through the early twentieth centuries, and many among them, mostly peasants, yet occasionally Muslim nobles too, walked that path. The typical beginning point for peasants was small-scale peddling. They crisscrossed villages with baskets and collected unprocessed products such as honey, eggs, and fruits. They sold these items in local bazaars and purchased easy-to-carry items, such as soap, utensils, or haberdashery, in turn. Then, they went back to the villages for sale.[19] The more fortunate and astute among them would buy a horse-drawn cart and travel longer distances with heavier loads to bigger fairs or permanent city markets. Muslim peasants from the Malmyzh County of the Viatka Gubernia, for instance, bought bast, bast mat, sacks, tar, resin, fat, leather, wool, rags, and even horses from local villages and took them to Kazan or, in the nineteenth century, to the developing textile factories of the Volga and Kama Basins.[20] Further, peasants could buy sales booths in village bazaars or, after registering as townspeople, in town markets. Şâkir Zâidof and his brother Şihabuddin from the Viatka Gubernia both started business as peasants in the 1880s and purchased booths in village bazaars, where they sold tea, sugar, soap, tableware, and fabrics. By the 1910s, they had both registered as second guild merchants and entered into the construction and transportation sectors in addition to commerce. The combined property that they had accumulated included about 1,300 acres of land and many houses that they rented in addition to several booths and retail shops. Moreover, Şâkir Zâidof traded in grains, which only the most competitive merchants of the time could do.[21]

Muslim enterprisers typically excelled in commerce, but some also ventured into rural cottage industries, such as felt, soap, and candle

---

[18] Khasanov, *Formirovanie*, 25, 54, and 87; and A. N. Zorin, *Goroda i posady dorevoliutsionnogo Povolzh'ia* (Kazan: Kazan State University Press, 2001), 81–88 and 121–22.

[19] Petr Znamenskii, *Kazanskie Tatary* (Kazan, 1910), 16; Khasanov, *Formirovanie*, 37; and Khalikov, *Khoziaistvo Tatar*, 186–87.

[20] Khalikov, *Khoziaistvo Tatar*, 188.

[21] Azat Rafikov, "Torgovo-predprinimatel'skaia deiatel'nost' tatarskogo kupechestva Viatskoi gubernii na rubezhe XIX–XX vv.," *Ekho vekov*, 2009 (2): 226–33.

making, tanning, bast weaving, and coopering, or as self-employed arti-
sans, such as jewelers, carpenters, dyers, and tailors.[22] Those Muslims
who were able to register as townspeople usually carried their rural
artisanal skills to cities and towns where they produced soap, candle,
potash, tanned leather, dyed fabrics, and made typical Muslim outfits on
a larger scale. Later, some invested in producing calico as well.[23] Most
Muslim entrepreneurs lacked the linguistic and cultural skills to survive
in fields of economic activity where Russian merchants already dominated the market, and therefore they avoided those fields.[24] But especially
in the late nineteenth century, a small number of Muslim *bays* actually
crossed cultural lines and invested in sectors ranging from match or
caramel production to gold mining. The Ramiyef family, for example,
operated gold mines,[25] while Ahmedcan Seydaşef and Bâqî Subayef
dominated the glass, tea, and fur markets in central Russia, Siberia,
and the Caucasus in the 1890s.[26]

Some of these entrepreneurs made impressive fortunes in the mid-
through the late-nineteenth century. The Aqçurin family provides an
illustrative case in point. The forefather of the family, Safâ Aqçurin
collected wool from villages and sold it to cloth manufacturers in the late
eighteenth century as a state peasant. His son, Ğabdullah Aqçurin
(d. 1848) continued the business, but also started to trade in washed silk
with his two sons Quramşah (1796–1868) and Süleyman (1802–64).
Seeing the high demand for washed silk in Moscow and in the Nizhny
Novgorod Fair, the family opened a small silk-washing business in the
Simbirsk Guberniia in the 1820s. In a few decades, Quramşah and
Süleyman Aqçurin turned this business into a giant enterprise. They
increased their profit margin by buying raw silk directly from Transoxiana. Then, Süleyman Aqçurin opened a textile-manufacturing factory
in 1849 and expanded his business by selling uniform fabrics to the
Russian army during the Crimean War. Quramşah Aqçurin also entered
the textile manufacturing business in 1862. One of the factories of the
family boasted 200 steam-powered and manual looms and sold about
200,000-rubles' worth of fabric annually in the 1860s. Both Quramşah
and Süleyman Aqçurin had registered their families as first guild

[22] Znamenskii, *Kazanskie*, 16; and Sukharev, *Kazanskie*, 47–48; and Khalikov, *Khoziaistvo Tatar*, 157–86.
[23] Khasanov, *Formirovanie*, 46–51 and 85–86.   [24] Sverdlova, *Kazanskoe*, 166.
[25] Cävdät Miñnullin, "Rämievlärneñ altın priiskaları," in *Bertugan Rämiyevlär: Fänni-biografik jentık*, ed. Liron Hämidullin, Raif Märdanov, and Ramil Miñnullin (Kazan: Ruhiyat, 2002), 82–91.
[26] Sverdlova, *Kupechestva*, 113–20.

merchants by this time. Their inheritors preserved the family wealth by founding a joint stock company that continued the textile business but also invested in land.[27]

While the Aqçurin family accumulated wealth over several generations in the manufacturing sector, the Hüseyinof brothers from Qargali illustrate how the empire's eastern trade could yield sudden fortunes too. The great-grandfather of the Hüseyinof brothers, Ğabdullah, was originally from Mamadysh in the Kazan Guberniia, and he had settled in Qargali shortly after its foundation. He was a successful merchant who had enough money to build a mosque in this settlement. His son, Hüseyin, continued the business and in turn bequeathed a considerable fortune to the father of the Hüseyinof brothers, Muhammed Ğali. However, Muhammed Ğali lost this wealth while the Hüseyinof brothers were still at a younger age. He died in 1858 without leaving anything behind. The Hüseyinof brothers started to earn their living as manual laborers in Qargali while their father was still alive. One of them, Ahmed Hüseyinof (1837–1906), saved five rubles by working as a brick maker and went to Orenburg. There, he saved more money by buying and selling wooden crates. Then, he bought a horse-cart, filled it with various goods, and went to the steppes to trade with the Kazakhs. The trip was successful. When his father died, Ahmed Hüseyinof brought his younger brothers, Ğabdulganî and Mahmûd, to Orenburg, and the three brothers started to work together. They carried manufactured commodities from Orenburg to the Kazakhs and hides, wool, sheep, and cattle from the Kazakhs to Orenburg. The Kazakhs did not like to use money at this time, but they were willing to barter, and the barter turned out to be profitable for the Hüseyinof brothers.[28]

In a few years, the three brothers saved enough money to buy an apartment in Orenburg for storage and office space. They founded a trade company under the title "Ahmed Hüseyinof and Brothers" and started to send merchandise to the Nizhny Novgorod fair. Each year, one of them went to the steppes to collect goods while the other two focused on marketing them. In 1869, Ğabdulganî Bay settled in Kazalinsk by the Aral Sea in order to administer the company's trade in the Turkestan Gubernia, which had recently been established in the Kazakh Steppes. Mahmûd Bay spent winters in the steppes and returned to Orenburg in summers while Ahmed Bay stayed in Orenburg in winters and went to Kazan, Nizhny Novgorod, and Moscow in summers. They also maintained permanent agents in several other

---

[27] Tairov, *Akchuriny*, especially 15–25.
[28] Fahreddin, *Ahmed*, 11–14; and Şeref, *Ganî*, 8–11.

locations such as Aqmescit, Tashkent, Awliya Ata, Samarqand, Almaty, Şimkent, and Tokmak in Turkestan.

This trade network consisting of one person managing a team of agents collecting goods in Turkestan, one person exploring the markets in European Russia and procuring goods to exchange with the Kazakhs, and one person coordinating the overall business from Orenburg proved to be very successful. The price differences between the empire's major cities and the difficult-to-reach parts of Turkestan, where pan-European influences had a minimal impact so far, were notably high due to difficulties of transportation. The Hüseyinof brothers could make huge profits by keeping track of these differences, making bulk purchases, and moving them over long distances by camel caravans.

According to their accountant in Kazalinsk, in 1878 the Hüseyinof brothers bought 30,000 poods of wheat for 18 kopecks a pood in Tokmak, located to the east of the Aral Sea.[29] Then, they sold it in various cities for 2.5 to 2.8 rubles a pood. A transaction like this meant about eleven-to-twelve-fold profit *after* the transportation costs. Additionally, they also opened manufacturing shops in which they could process hides to increase their profit margin. In the 1870s, they would buy cowhides for 2.5 to 3 rubles a pood in Kazalinsk and, after processing, sell them for 9 to 9.5 rubles a pood in Orenburg (see Table 6.1). As a result of this lucrative trade, the Hüseyinof brothers' capital reached 80,000 rubles in 1873 and 300,000 rubles in 1878.[30] By 1896, they owned three million rubles in currency in addition to several buildings, factories, and a hotel at the Nizhny Novgorod Fair.[31]

Merchants beyond the Muslim domain

Estate privileges and the accumulation of cultural capital in multi-generational business families, along with wealth, availed *bays* with opportunities of contact beyond the Muslim domain, which were typically unavailable to Muslim peasants. Inclusion in the legally instituted merchant guilds provided a small minority of the wealthiest *bays* with access to a privileged community of elite merchants that coalesced around professional and commercial interests rather than ethnicity or

---

[29] 1 pood equals 36.11 pounds.

[30] Şeref, *Ganî*, 12–15. In the 1870s, organizing a camel caravan between Kazalinsk and Orenburg cost 50 to 55 kopecks a pood. The distance between Tokmak and the cities where the Hüseyinof brothers sold their wheat was comparable to the distance between Kazalinsk and Orenburg.

[31] Şeref, *Ganî*, 16.

Table 6.1 *Price differences for various goods between Orenburg and Kazalinsk in the 1870s*

Prices of goods supplied by the Kazakhs

	Kazalinsk	Orenburg
Sheep hide – earlier	45–60 kopecks each	90 kopecks each
Sheep hide – later	60–65 kopecks each	1.2 – 1.50 rubles each
İçag (a type of shoe)	5 kopecks each	25–30 kopecks each
Cowhide	unprocessed: 2.5–3 rubles per pood	processed: 9–9.5 rubles per pood
Horse hide	unprocessed: 1.5–2 rubles per pood	processed: 3.5–4 rubles per pood
Camel wool	3 rubles per pood	5 rubles per pood
Sheep	3.5 rubles each	6–7.5 rubles each
Camel	25–30 rubles each	Its leather and fat sold well, but it was rather bought for transportation.

Prices of goods demanded by the Kazakhs

	Orenburg	Kazalinsk
Tar	50–60 kopecks per pood	2–5 rubles per pood
Kerosene	1 ruble per pood	2–4 rubles per pood
Iron	2.2 rubles per pood	4 rubles per pood
Cast iron	1.9–2.1 rubles per pood	5–6 rubles per pood
Bath birch	3 kopecks a pair	15 kopecks a pair
Piyale (a type of cup)	7 rubles per ¼ box	16 rubles per ¼ box
Wheat flour (five poods)	7–9 rubles per 5 poods	15–16 rubles per 5 poods

Şeref, *Ganî*, 14.

religion.[32] Together with a few Muslim nobles who had been incorporated into the imperial nobility, especially during the reign of Catherine II,[33] these *bays* had front-line access to the imperial *obshchestvo* and, in the late nineteenth century, to the growing imperial domain. They often learned Russian or, at least, had their children instructed in it. Muhammed Sâdık Ramiyef, for example, hired personal tutors to teach

[32] On the inclusion of Tatar merchants in Russian merchant organizations in the nineteenth century, see Aleksandr Kaplunovskii, "Tatary musul′mane i russkie v meshchanskikh obshchinakh srednego povolzh′ia v kontse XIX-nachale XX veka," *Ab Imperio*, 2000 (1): 101–22.
[33] See Enikeev, *Ocherk istorii*, especially 136–39.

Russian to his two sons, Şâkir and Zâkir Ramiyef.[34] Being materially self-sufficient and, therefore, relatively free from the normative pressures of local Muslim communities, these *bays* could (and some of them did) borrow from the empire's elite Russian culture too.

The first-guild merchant İsmâ'îl Apakof (1823–85), for example, belonged to the third generation of a merchant family of noble origins in Kazan. He was known for his Russian aristocratic manners, including a predilection for injecting French phrases here and there as he spoke Russian. He held a membership in the Kazan Imperial Economic Society and was elected to serve in the Kazan District Court and the Kazan County Zemstvo.[35] A third-generation member of the Aqçurin Family, Timirbulat Aqçurin, was elected to the city council in Simbirsk for the 1871–75 term.[36] And, along with several European philosophers and the literary classics of the Islamic tradition, Zâkir Ramiyef, a poet in addition to being a businessman, cherished Pushkin, Gogol, Tolstoi, and Gorky.[37] Both the Aqçurin and the Ramiyef families had eschewed traditional Muslim garb, and their female members had ceased to cover their hair by the early twentieth century.[38]

The very nature of economic exchange, too, exposed high-profile Muslim merchants to interactions that transcended the insular boundaries of the Muslim domain. One of the initial incentives for the Ramiyef brothers to learn Russian was the necessity of communicating with the engineers who worked in their mines.[39] In the 1870s, when Jewish and German merchants started to travel to Orenburg in order to purchase raw materials for export to European countries, the Hüseyinof brothers quickly noticed this demand and started to procure items that these new buyers wanted in large quantities. Then, the Hüseyinof brothers figured out that the Jewish and German merchants were actually reselling their purchases to a big German commission. Thus, the Hüseyinofs contacted the German commission and started to supply it without intermediaries. In 1879, Ahmed Bay went to Hijaz in order to perform the Hajj. On the way back, he visited Germany and Britain. He wanted to bypass the German commission too and export his goods directly to Europe, but

---

[34] Fatih Kerimi, "Därdemänd," in *Bertugan Rämiyevlär: Fänni-biografik jientık*, ed. Liron Hämidullin, Raif Märdanov, and Ramil Miñnullin (Kazan: Ruhiyat, 2002), 102–5.

[35] See Sverdlova, *Kupechestva*, 63–69; and Apakova L. Ia. and Apakova L. V., "Obshchestvennaia i torgovaia deiatel'nost' Apakovykh v XVII–XIX vv.," in *Tatarskie murzy i dvoriane: istoriia i sovremennost'*, ed. F. G. Tarkhanova (Kazan: Institut Istorii im. Sh. Mardzhani, 2010), 296–307.

[36] Tairov, *Akchuriny*, 49.   [37] Kerimi, "Därdemänd," 103.

[38] See photographs in Tairov, *Akchuriny*; and Hämidullin, Märdanov, and Miñnullin, *Bertugan Rämiyevlär*.

[39] Kerimi, "Kem ide," 93.

this required more capital and connections than Ahmed Hüseyinof and Brothers could yet claim.[40]

In 1893, Ahmed Bay decided that at long last, the time was ripe for a venture in Europe. He went to Berlin, opened a shop, and stocked it with a large selection of the merchandise that the German commission usually purchased back in Russia. However, although he tried hard, finding customers proved to be nearly impossible as a result of his inability to speak German. Finally, he hired a Russian Jew to take care of the shop and returned to Orenburg. In 1894, the Hüseyinof brothers also sent 72,000-rubles' worth of sheep to Paris, but they ended up losing near half that amount in the end. The shop in Berlin did not suffer a loss, thanks to the Hüseyinof brothers' ability to decrease costs significantly by procuring items at cheap prices in Turkestan, but, in the absence of an agent with whom they could communicate effectively, the Berlin venture did not yield worthwhile profits either. In 1896, Ahmed Bay wanted to settle in Kazan permanently, and the Hüseyinof brothers separated their businesses. Ğabdulganî Bay took the shop in Berlin and closed it in 1898.[41]

Here lay the importance of the accumulation of cultural capital in multi-generational merchant families. The skills and experience that the Hüseyinof brothers had developed in the Kazakh Steppes and the fairs of Russia were not sufficient to compete in Europe or, increasingly, in the integrating markets of European Russia. This required familiarity with the intricate financial transactions, marketing strategies, and the overall business culture of the pan-European markets. The scions of a few long-established *bay* families, whom Christian Noack calls the "new entrepreneurs," such as the Aqçurins and the Ramiyefs, who commanded sizeable amounts of capital, could hire and work with management personnel, and could function in a cosmopolitan environment in general, adapted successfully.[42] To illustrate their ability to absorb new opportunities, we can note that the Aqçurins introduced electricity in their factories in 1898, and by 1911, all members of the family had telephones in their houses. Most members of the family spoke Russian. Timirbulat Aqçurin's son, Hasan Aqçurin, supported Muslim littérateurs and scholars in the Volga-Ural region in ways that indicate the assumption of a European-inspired, Renaissance-like attitude toward culture and cultural patronage. In addition to financially supporting artists and writers, he collected many items about Volga-Ural Muslim history and founded a museum with this theme.[43] A female member of the family, Hatîce Aqçurina, studied arts in Moscow and became famous

---

[40] *Fahreddin, 'Ahmed,* 17–19.   [41] *Fahreddin, Ahmed,* 17–19; and Şeref, *Ganî,* 16–17.
[42] Noack, *Muslimischer,* 105–8.   [43] Tairov, *Akchuriny,* 59–72.

for her illustrations in the Turkic press of the early twentieth century.[44] As for the Ramiyefs, their gold mines were among the most technologically advanced mining operations in Russia. They effectively managed a team of mostly Russian engineers. Şâkir Ramiyef in particular, regularly traveled to Europe to learn about and purchase new mining equipment. Both Şâkir and Zâkir Ramiyef sent their children to the best available Russian schools. One of Zâkir Ramiyef's sons, İskender Ramiyef (1886–1943), finished the St. Petersburg Gymnasium and attended an institute in Germany, where he studied mining. He returned to Russia in 1914 to work in the family business.[45]

Nonetheless, other well-established Muslim merchant families started to decline, though not disappear, as the empire's business environment transformed radically in the late nineteenth century. The Ahmerofs, who had made a fortune by producing soap and candles in the early eighteenth century, were pushed out of the manufacturing sector and had to limit their ventures to trade when the Russian-origin Krestovnikov brothers, who produced soap with newer and better technology, gained the upper hand in the region's cosmetic market in the 1860s.[46] A contributor to *Şûra* in 1911, Halîl Sultanmuhammed, claimed that there were three kinds of businessmen: those who had an innate talent for business, those who learned business in school, and those who combined talent with education. Sultanmuhammed placed the Volga-Ural Muslim merchants in the first category. For many centuries, he wrote, they carried the goods of the East to the West and the goods of the West to the East. It was possible to find them everywhere from the Baltic countries to Manchuria, but, Sultanmuhammed continued, the time was changing, and talent alone could no longer guarantee good business. He considered Russians to be a good example for the second kind of businessmen. They measured goods with precise measuring gadgets, he wrote, and registered their transactions in notebooks. One could see that they had learned business in school. Sultanmuhammed warned that the Muslims could not compete with this sort of business unless they also received education. He had the Jews in mind for the third kind of businessmen. They had talent for business and they also learned about it. He claimed that as a result, the wealthiest persons in Europe and in

[44] Anon., "Sanâyi-i nefise yulında millî adim," *Añ*, 1915 (5): 102–3.
[45] Kerimi, *Avrupa*, especially 64–67; Rızâeddin bin Fahreddin, "Muhammedşâkir Efendi Ramiyef," *Şûra*, 1913 (6): 186–87; Liron Xämidullin, "Tarixta üz ezläre bar," in *Bertugan Rämiyevlär: Fänni-biografik jientık*, ed. Liron Hämidullin, Raif Märdanov, and Ramil Miñnullin (Kazan: Ruhiyat, 2002), 59–65; Miñnullin, "Rämievlärneñ," 82–91; and Kerimî, "Kem ide," 119–22.
[46] Sverdlova, *Kupechestva*, 72–73.

America, especially big factory owners, were mostly Jews. Sultanmuham-med's conclusion was simple: the Muslims of the Volga-Ural region should also receive education and adapt their businesses to the world's new conditions.[47]

Through the lens of progressive reformism

The fallacy of Sultanmuhammed's stereotypes aside, many prominent merchants and prolific intellectuals among Russia's Muslims nurtured similar ideas about the necessity of education as a means to equip Russia's Muslims with cultural conversance beyond the Muslim domain. These merchants and intellectuals developed new maktab and madrasa curricula, opened lay schools, published periodicals and books, founded charitable societies and libraries, established theater troupes, vied for Muslim representation in the Imperial Dumas after 1905, and worked for the social and cultural improvement of Russia's Muslims in general. These were novel and certainly significant developments. They were also controversial and, therefore, highly visible. Such visibility makes it tempting to explain the history of the Volga-Ural Muslims, especially the role of the Muslim wealthy among them, in the late nineteenth century as a moment of national awakening under the leadership of progressive *bays* and intellectuals.

The progressive reformist intellectuals of the early twentieth century viewed and presented the transformations of their time in this light too. They celebrated the Ramiyef brothers, for example, for sponsoring Muslim periodicals and other publications in Russia, especially after 1905.[48] Even the socialist poet Ğabdullah Tuqay (1896–1913), who detested the wealthy Ramiyefs' leverage over young Muslim litterateurs, appreciated the fact that a "Muslim newspaper" (*İslâm gazitî*) like *Vaqit* survived thanks to their financial support.[49] Fahreddin published a book-length biography of Ahmed Hüseyinof in 1911 while another prolific intellectual of the time, Burhan Şeref, made Ğabdulganî Hüseyinof's biography available in 1913.[50] What Fahreddin chose to highlight in Ahmed Hüseyinof's life story was that according to this illiterate yet

---

[47] Halîl Sultanmuhammed, "Sevdagirlik," *Şûra*, 1911 (15): 461–62.

[48] For examples, see Ahmed Serdar, "Çin Maçin Yolunda Muhterem Şâkir Efendi Ramiyef Hazretleri," *Şûra*, 1912 (11): 349–51; Fahreddin, "Muhammadşâkir Efendi," 188–91; and Zarif Bäşiri, "Rämievlär turında istäleklär," in *Bertugan Rämiyevlär: Fänni-biografik jientık*, ed. Liron Hämidullin, Raif Märdanov, and Ramil Miñnullin (Kazan: Ruhiyat, 2002), 138–49.

[49] Hämidullin, Märdanov, and Miñnullin, *Bertugan Rämiyevlär*, 302–3.

[50] Fahreddin, *Ahmed*; and Şeref, *Ganî*.

skillful merchant, one had to know languages and the "affairs of the world" for successful business and, therefore, it was necessary to support schools that taught literacy, mathematics, and the "affairs of the world."[51] Fahreddin singled out Ahmed Bay as the merchant who contributed the highest amount of wealth to the reform of Muslim education in the Russian empire, with the exception of the South Caucasus region.[52] Indeed, when Ahmed Bay died in 1906, he had endowed 500,000 rubles, or one third of his estate (the maximum amount that one can designate for other than one's inheritors according to the Shariah), to be used toward progressive reformist purposes. A large portion of his bequest would support the Hüseyniye Madrasa, which was originally founded by the Hüseyinof brothers in Orenburg and taught with a reformed curriculum that involved secular, in addition to Islamic, subjects. He also designated funds for the upkeep of the Muhammediye Madrasa in Kazan, for the publication of madrasa textbooks or books with a religious and moral content, and to support Muslim students attending maktabs and madrasas with a reformed curriculum, as well as imperial institutions of education, such as gymnasiums, *Realschules*, commercial schools, and universities.[53] Ğabdulganî Bay, on the other hand, received Şeref's acclaim for his support to İsmâ'îl Bey Gasprinskiy's educational initiatives. Ğabdulganî Bay had met Gasprinskiy in 1893, during a trip of the latter to Transoxiana, and thereafter, he had devotedly sponsored the Crimean reformist's ideas about restructuring Muslim schooling in the Russian empire.[54]

Philanthropy and civic organization

Such sizeable contributions from individual merchants were particularly consequential for a minority population with nearly no access to government funds to support communal institutions. However, we should keep in mind that nationalism as an ideology started to emerge among Volga-Ural Muslims at the earliest in the 1880s,[55] if we consider the

---

[51] Fahreddin, *Ahmed*, 25–26.

[52] Y. A., "Ahmed Bay Vaqfi," *Şûra*, 1908 (1): 13–15. The oil tycoon from Baku, Zeynel'âbidin Tagiyef, was probably the merchant who contributed the highest amount of money for educational reform in the Russian empire. See İsmâ'îl Gasprinskiy, "Türk Yurdcularına," *Türk Yurdu*, 1327/1912; reprint, Ankara: Tutibay Yayınları, 1998: 1133.

[53] Fahreddin, *Ahmed*, 34–46. Also see Azamatov, *Iz istorii*, 42–47.

[54] Şeref, *Ganî*, 19–22 and 124–28.

[55] See Uli Schamiloglu, "The Formation of a Tatar Historical Consciousness: Shihabuddin Marjani and the Image of the Golden Horde," *Central Asian Survey*, 1990 9(2): 39–49; and Ross, "From the Minbar," 123–38.

proto-nationalist discourse of Şihâbuddin Mercânî's Volga-Ural Muslim history, *Mustafād al-akhbār*, as a beginning.[56] The wealthy Volga-Ural Muslims' patronage of communal institutions was primarily a manifest-ation of the practice of charity in the Islamic tradition. Such patronage became most pronounced starting in the late eighteenth century, when Catherine II allowed relative freedom to Muslims to construct and maintain religious institutions.[57]

Besides, we need to remember that the wealthiest Muslim *bays* had access to a community of elite merchants that coalesced around professional and commercial interests rather than ethnicity or religion. This access brought not only privileges but also an imperially imposed responsibility to share in the burden of procuring non-religious public needs, especially in larger towns and the cities. Muslim guild merchants were highly reluctant to fulfill this responsibility in the beginning. When the Kazan governorship called for contributions to public charity from guild merchants in 1820, all the Muslim guild merchants of the Kazan Gubernia together presented, an at best symbolic, 130 rubles.[58] Yet, as they interacted with the imperial administration and with their non-Muslim colleagues in the merchant guilds, these Muslim guild merchants also became habituated in the practice of donating for secular purposes and, at times, channeling their contributions directly to non-religious public services for Muslims. In 1844, for instance, the long-established Yunusof family built an orphanage for Muslim children in Kazan and donated for its upkeep the income of fourteen booths in Kazan's hay market.[59] This was an imperial practice adapted to Muslim purposes rather than an act of "bourgeois nationalism." The concept of an orphanage did not exist in the Volga-Ural Muslim tradition, but adapting it from the imperial domain ensured that the Muslim orphans of Kazan would not be left to the care of Christian charities any longer. The Russian state recognized the Yunusofs' public contribution by admitting them to the Order of St. Anna in the third class, an honor that entitled the family to wear the order's insignia: a *cross* in imperial burgundy.[60]

The Yunusofs led Kazan's *bays* in establishing a charitable society too. This was another new borrowing from the imperial domain, for although pooling resources to build and maintain communal institutions was not

---

[56] For a reprint of the second edition of this history, see Mercani, *Müstefad'ül-Ahbar*.

[57] See, for example, the history of the construction of mosques in Semipalatinsk in Frank and Usmanov, *Materials*.

[58] Sverdlova, *Kazanskoe*, 275–76.   [59] Salikhov, *Tatarskaia burzhuaziia*, 61–62.

[60] Sverdlova, *Kazanskoe*, 286–87.

an unknown practice among Volga-Ural Muslims, their *bays* typically preferred to exclude other donors from projects that they wanted to have affiliated with their names.[61] Yet, in 1884, in response to a request from the Kazan chapter of the Imperial Philanthropic Society to build an almshouse for Muslims in Kazan in the name of the heir apparent Nicholas Aleksandrovich, İbrâhim Yunusof and his brother İshâq gathered Kazan's *bays* in their house to discuss a possible charity. The two brothers offered to donate a building and the income of two booths at Kazan's hay market for this purpose. Then, other merchants together contributed 6,000 rubles. The idea of a Muslim charitable society came up as Kazan's Muslims discussed how to proceed with this project, but in the absence of an independent society, they initially transferred the money to the custody of the Imperial Philanthropic Society.[62]

Meanwhile, Gasprinskiy's *Tercüman* received a letter from Kazan about this gathering that described the initiative as an attempt to establish an endowment for another Muslim orphanage. Since collecting money for an endowment was not an established practice in the Islamic tradition, the correspondent asked the editor of *Tercüman* if this was acceptable according to the Shariah. Gasprinskiy was not a religious authority, but he still responded that this was actually a very good idea. The Russians, he explained, had the practice of pooling donations and establishing charitable societies. It would be desirable to establish a society of this kind and register it according to the laws. If the donors needed help finding the relevant laws and founding a society legally, *Tercüman* would be glad to offer help.[63] Legally establishing a Muslim charitable society proved to be more difficult than Gasprinskiy implied in this letter though. Kazan's merchants continued to collect and save money, but only fourteen years later, in January 1898, were they able to found the "Kazan Society for the Benefit of Poor Muslims" based on a new regulation from 1897.[64] Other Muslim charitable societies followed suit in various parts of Russia, and Gasprinskiy encouraged this development by announcing the foundation of new societies in *Tercüman*.[65] By the 1910s, Muslim charitable societies had become so widespread in the empire that some villages even had their own societies.[66]

---

[61] See Fahreddin, *Ahmed*, 29–31.
[62] Sverdlova, *Kupechestva*, 156–57; and Salikhov, *Tatarskaia burzhuaziia*, 68.
[63] "Kazan," *Tercüman/Perevodchik*, February 25, 1884.
[64] "Kazan Cemiyet-i Hayriyesi," *Tercüman/Perevodchik*, January 22, 1898.
[65] See "Novoe Obshchestvo," *Tercüman/Perevodchik*, February 27, 1898; and "Krymskoe Blagotvoritel'noe Obshchestvo," *Tercüman/Perevodchik*, February 27, 1898.
[66] Bishop Aleksei, *Sovremennoe dvizhenie v srede russkikh Musul'man* (Kazan: N.P., 1910), 23–24; and Salikhov, *Tatarskaia burzhuaziia*, 69–78.

Conclusion: Back to empire

We should not be so quick to associate this surge in civic organization with the awakening of some form of national consciousness. The overall communal vitality of the Volga-Ural Muslims in late imperial Russia, I suggest, will better be understood as a reflection of the world of expanded opportunities that emerged from Russia's broad transformations in the late nineteenth century. In 1890, for instance, about eighty Muslim peasants in the Mamadysh County followed Hüseyin Yunusof's advice to take loans from the zemstvo and purchase sewing machines. Many of those peasants made extra money as itinerant tailors and some also took jobs from textile factories, especially as hemmers.[67] As the Muslim communities of the Volga-Ural region, and particularly their *bays*, did better in economic terms, they could divert more money to meet communal needs. This, however, did not necessarily transform the motives and forms of charity for most Muslims. Donating remained an act of piety, an investment in life after death, or, if we assume a materialist point of view, an instrument of preserving social status, but not necessarily a fulfillment of social responsibility. This is where the under-documented ninety-five percent of the wealthy Volga-Ural Muslims in the late nineteenth century should be placed. They did not passively observe and silently approve the novel initiatives of more affluent merchants. Rather, they actively and, in fact, more robustly continued to sponsor the long-established religious institutions and other collective needs of their respective Muslim communities. The number of mosques, for instance, grew notably in the Volga-Ural region in the last decades of the tsarist regime.[68]

This being said, some *bays* did invest in novel ways of communal empowerment too. The wealthiest among them who enjoyed institutionalized links to the imperial administration and to their Russian colleagues, primarily as guild merchants, more closely observed the overall transformation of the Russian empire in the context of pan-European pressures. They aspired to energize their coreligionists in the face of such pressures with an augmented sense of urgency. But, they did not unanimously endorse an easily identifiable and ideologically charged reform program as the appropriate response to change. Rather, they pursued adaptation with a diverse spectrum of concerns, motives, and choices.

---

[67] Ğabdulqadîm Behmanî, "Mamadış Uyezinde Müslümanlar ve Anlarnıñ İqtisadî Halleri," *Şûra*, 1910 (18): 560–61.
[68] Azamatov, *Orenburgskoe*, 102.

The Yunusof family provides an illustrative example of this situation as well. In the 1870s, they bitterly conflicted with Şihâbuddin Mercânî (1818–89), who has come to be known as one of the founding fathers of progressive reformism in the Volga-Ural region.[69] The Yunusofs maintained Kazan's First Congregational Mosque, where Mercânî had been serving as an imam since 1849, and they owned the building of an affiliated madrasa, where Mercânî taught. Although a Bukhara graduate, Mercânî had fallen at odds with many of his colleagues in the Volga-Ural region for supporting the teaching of the Russian language to madrasa students and for pursuing a puritanical scholarly approach that contradicted the then prevalent Bukharan-origin traditions of the region. Probably disturbed by the resulting tension, but also frustrated by their inability to exert control over this dignified scholar, the Yunusofs stopped sponsoring Mercânî's teaching. Undeterred, Mercânî responded by moving his madrasa to a nearby building in 1871 and, in the process, set off a protracted rivalry between the Yunusof and Mercânî factions in the neighborhood.[70] However, the Yunusofs' dislike for the implications of Mercânî's puritanical and reformist position did not prevent them from actually initiating and sponsoring other reform-oriented practices and institutions. Besides their pioneering role in mobilizing Kazan's *bays* for philanthropic purposes, the elementary school that functioned in their orphanage was one of the first educational institutions that employed the phonic method of teaching literacy as promoted by Gasprinskiy in the 1880s under the name *usûl-i cedîd* or the "new method."[71] Building on this experience, they would then sponsor the opening of many new-method schools especially in the early twentieth century.[72]

The efforts of Ğabdulganî Hüseyinof's son Muhammedvelî Hüseyinof (1867–1933) and the first-guild merchant Ğabdurrahmân İşmuratof (1857–1922) negate the myth of a Muslim bourgeoisie that united around progressive reform for national awakening too. Muhammedvelî Hüseyinof had attended the Qışqar Madrasa in the Kazan Gubernia and

---

[69] Whether Mercânî was a progressive reformist is a controversial topic. See two opposing positions in Michael Kemper, "Šihābaddīn al-Marğānī als Religionsgelehrter," in *Muslim Culture in Russia and Central Asia from the 18th to the Early 20th Centuries*, ed. Michael Kemper, Anke von Kügelgen, and Dmitriy Yermakov (Berlin: Klaus Schwarz Verlag, 1996), 129–65; and Schamiloglu, "Formation," 39–49. Yet, regardless of his true position, the progressive reformist Muslims of late imperial Russia recognized him as their ideological inspiration. See Sâlih bin Sâbit 'Ubeydullin ed., *Mercânî* (Kazan: Ma'ârif, 1914–15).

[70] 'Ubeydullin, *Mercânî*, 86–110. Also see Ross, "From the Minbar," 110–18.

[71] Salikhov, *Tatarskaia burzhuaziia*, 85.

[72] Aleksei, *Sovremennoe dvizhenie*, 24 and 36–37.

then continued on to study in Bukhara and the Ottoman territories. When Ğabdulganî Bay died and Muhammedvelî Hüseyinof took over his father's business in 1902, he was already a scholar in his own right as the imam of the First Congregational Mosque of Orenburg and the affiliated madrasa that came to be known as the "Veliye." İşmuratof and Muhammedvelî Hüseyinof both opposed the progressive reformists' religious liberalism or, in some cases, secularism. İşmuratof complained that the progressives "worshipped God inadequately, did not fast, disobeyed their parents, and did not respect the elders." To counter what they perceived to be an aberration from the Islamic tradition, the two merchants and others like them promoted an alternative – we can say conservative – type of reformism. To this end, Muhammedvelî Hüseyinof sponsored the publication of several books and a biweekly journal, *Din ve Ma'işet (Religion and Life)*, between 1906 and 1917. İşmuratof, for his part, supported the teaching and the activities of a vocally conservative scholar, İşmuhammed bin Dinmuhammed (1842–1919). Yet, İşmuratof, Muhammedvelî Hüseyinof, and their peers were by no means the reactionary representatives of a bygone world. İşmuratof spoke Russian, served as an elected member of the Kazan City Duma, and he was also a member of the Kazan Society for the Benefit of Poor Muslims. Muhammedvelî Hüseyinof, on the other hand, actually carried his father's success in trade to the manufacturing sector, which required better management skills and more involvement in the integrated markets of European Russia.[73]

Moreover, both the small and more affluent Muslim merchants of the Volga-Ural region were habituated and institutionally integrated into the Catherinian imperial model. While reflecting an awareness of the surging pan-European transformations, their strategies still remained deeply embedded in the evolving structures of the Russian imperial domain. Yes, it seems that the bays who gathered at the house of the Yunusofs in 1884 to consider the opening of an almshouse in the name of the heir apparent had reservations about leaving the oversight of their contributions completely to a non-Muslim institution, the Imperial Philanthropic Society. And this is partly – only partly – why the idea never materialized.[74]

---

[73] On İşmuratov, see Salikhov, *Tatarskaia burzhuaziia*, 30–31 and 72–73; and *Tatarskaia entsiklopediia*, s.v. "Ishmuratov, Abdrakhman Akhmetovich". On Muhammedvelî Hüseyinof, see *Islam na Urale: entsiklopedicheskii slovar'*, s.v. "Khusainov Mukhammedvali Abdulganievich." On Qışqar Madrasa, see İbrâhîmof, *Tercüme-yi Hâlim*, 11–16; and Lotfi, "Kışkar," 150–70. On İşmuhammed bin Dinmuhammed and Muslim conservatism in the Volga-Ural region in general, see Muhammetshin, *Tatarskii traditsionalizm*, especially 53–75.

[74] Salikhov, *Tatarskaia burzhuaziia*, 68.

But those reservations reflect an insistence on preserving the Volga-Ural Muslim domain's mediated distance within the Catherinian imperial model, not an ideologically charged nationalist reaction against imperial authority. It was still the Imperial Philanthropic Society and its local chapters that provided the model and incentive for the empire's Muslim charitable organizations. Furthermore, one of the primary donors and a prominent member of the Kazan Society for the Benefit of Poor Muslims was Olga Sergeevna Aleksandrova-Geins: the sole heiress of a wealthy Russian merchant family, the widow of Kazan's former governor Aleksandr Konstantinovich Geins, and a munificent public benefactor.[75]

This reinterpretation does not deny the emergence of nationalist sentiments and ideas among Volga-Ural Muslims in the final decades of the tsarist regime. That, however, was one among many ideological positions espoused by the region's Muslim intellectuals, not the defining characteristic of the Muslim wealthy. Some *bays* did contribute to an emerging nationalist consciousness and, on the other end of the ideological spectrum, others espoused a socialist point of view. But these were typically intellectuals in their own right in addition to possessing wealth, often as the scions of multigenerational merchant families. To give a few illustrative examples, in 1906 Ğabdullah Apanayef of the Apanayef family, together with the future playwright Ğaliasker Kemal (1879–1933) published a social democratic journal called *Azat* (*Freedom*).[76] Zâkir Ramiyef, who financed many initiatives that targeted national awakening among Volga-Ural Muslims together with his brother Şâkir Ramiyef, was also a sophisticated poet,[77] and although a scion of the Aqçurin family, one of the founders of both the Tatar and Turkish nationalisms, Yusuf Akçura (1879–1935), had actually hailed from the Ottoman and Parisian intellectual circles of the early twentieth century.[78] Hence, to have a more complete understanding of the ideological trends among Volga-Ural Muslims and of the cultural developments that underlined those trends in late imperial Russia, we need to bring intellectuals into this narrative. That, we will do in the following chapter.

---

[75] See Anon, "Khoziaika Aleksandrovskogo passazha: materialy o zhizni i khudozhestvennoi kollektsii O. S. Geins (Aleksandrovoi)," National Museum of the Republic of Tatarstan. Available at: www.tatar.museum.ru/nm/proj_01_2.htm.

[76] R. U. Amirkhanov, *Tatarskaia demokraticheskaia pechat' (1905–1907 gg.)* (Moscow: Nauka, 1988), 71–73.

[77] See Zâkir Ramiyef's poetry in Hämidullin, Märdanov, and Miñnullin, *Bertugan Rämiyevlär*, 164–223.

[78] See Akçura's memoirs in Yusuf Akçura, *Hatıralarım* (Istanbul: Hece Yayınları, 2005).

7   The cult of progress

Zamann̄ niçek bulsa bürkiñni şulay kiy.
Wear your hat in accordance with the times.

İtek kiydem dip çabatañnı çıgarıp taşlama.
Do not discard your soft-leather shoes thinking that you now
wear boots.   Tatar proverbs

Our age is indeed the age of progress.[1]
                            Arslan Bey Taşçıoğlu and ʿAbdulvelî Qaraşayskiy
                      two Crimean Muslim noblemen to the Governor of Tavrida, 1869

If we want to exist on the face of this earth as others do, if we won't give
up on it in despair, then, without delay, we have to work on improving
our maktabs and madrasas. We have to work on turning them into
institutions of education that remain religious in character yet provide
contemporary knowledge – knowledge that is relevant to life – as in the
educational institutions of other nations. Our existence, our ability to
live on, depends solely on the existence of such maktabs. In short, if we
have maktabs that meet the necessities of the time and that are relevant
to life, we exist; if not, we don't.[2]   Hâdi Atlâsî, a progressive reformist
                                    pedagogue in a Russian Muslim journal, 1913

Beginning in the 1880s, the coming together of many trends – the sea-
change as we have analyzed it so far – increased the permeability of
Muslim communal boundaries and expanded the bundle of opportunities,
as well as aspirations, before Volga-Ural Muslims. Some of them broke out
of their insulated communities and willingly – even ambitiously – engaged
the imperial and pan-European domains. They saw change all around and
saw it in a positive light, as "progress."[3] They wanted their coreligionists to

---

[1] Arslanbey, Taşçıoğlu, and Abdulveli, "Mnenie Tavricheskikh murz Arslan-Beia-Tashchi-
Oglu i Abdulveli Murzy Karashaiskogo," in *Sbornik dokumentov i statei po voprosu ob
obrazovanii inorodtsev*, ed. Ministerstvo narodnogo prosveshcheniia (St. Petersburg:
V Tip. T-va Obshchestvennaia Pol'za, 1869), 134.
[2] Hâdi Atlasî, "Bizniñ Mekteblerimiz," *Mekteb*, 1913 1(1): 20.
[3] For a similar observation about Central Asian Muslim reformists, see Khalid, *Jadidism*,
107–8.

progress too, and, with a sense of social responsibility, they sought ways to realize this ideal. At this juncture, through *Tercüman* and also through personal contacts, Gasprinskiy offered Russia's Muslims a modest yet promising program of empowerment that focused primarily on the improvement of Muslim schooling. Before the 1880s, the voices of a few exceptional Volga-Ural Muslim reformists had hardly reverberated among the region's Muslim communities, but now, as Russia's fast modernization exposed those communities to the world at large, a small but effective minority of scholars and merchants readily welcomed Gasprinskiy's ideas. Over a period of about twenty-five years, they introduced thousands of young Volga-Ural Muslims to secular fields of knowledge and progressive ideas in reformed Muslim schools and through the print media. In the final decades of the tsarist regime, these young men – and occasionally women – grew into a visible cohort of intellectuals who passionately devoted their energies to moving the region's Muslims forward in what they imagined to be the "path of progress." The intensity of their convictions and the zeal with which they sprang into action presented the characteristics of a newly emerging cult. The eminent Kazan Tatar historian Mirkasım Usmanov describes their movement as the "cult of knowledge,"[4] but here, I would like to suggest the "cult of progress" as a broader term since they ultimately targeted progress while they sought knowledge as an instrument, albeit a necessary one, to achieve it. What follows is an outline of the evolution of this "cult of progress" in the context of Russia's sea-change in the late nineteenth and early twentieth centuries.

The idea of progress

The idea of progress already had a long genealogy and wide currency in European thought. Progressive reformist Muslims in the Russian empire and especially the Volga-Ural region adopted it from there, often through the mediation of Russian and Ottoman intellectuals and occasionally through direct contacts.[5] Once deployed in the Russian Muslim context, the idea of progress acquired new functions and connotations.[6]

---

[4] Mirkasım A. Usmanov, "O triumfe i tragedii idei Gasprinskogo," in *Rossiia i Vostok*, ed. Mirkasım A. Usmanov (Kazan: Tatarskoe Knizhnoe Izdatel'stvo, 1993), 4.

[5] For precedents in the Russian and Ottoman contexts, among many other sources see Lincoln, "Genesis," 321–30; Andrzej Walicki, *A History of Russian Thought from the Enlightenment to Marxism* (Stanford: Stanford University Press, 1979), especially 1–34, and 222–67; and İbrahim Şirin, *Osmanlı İmgeleminde Avrupa* (Ankara: Lotus, 2006).

[6] For an analysis of similar processes, see the discussion of "transculturation" in Ortiz, *Cuban*; as well as Bronislaw Malinowski's introduction to the same.

To European thinkers, progress implied either passive advancement for the better on a path that was predetermined by the laws of history, or an active search for improvement by studying the laws of nature and putting them to good use.[7] In either case, for the nineteenth-century Europeans, the idea of progress was predicated upon "striking material evidence" in immediate experience.[8] The Russian Muslim reformists' fascination with progress, on the other hand, was predicated upon the relative paucity or even perceived lack of such evidence among Russia's Muslims as inferred from comparisons with other peoples, especially the European nations and educated Russians. Thus, ironically, as the sea-change effect of the expansion of European modernity transformed Russia's Muslim communities, rendered their boundaries more permeable, and made such comparisons possible, Russian Muslim intellectuals started to find their coreligionists "left behind" and aspired to move them forward. While progress indicated optimistic projections about an unknown yet arguably predictable future for European thinkers, for progressive Russian Muslim intellectuals, it implied a compelling need to remodel Russian Muslim communities after the contemporaneous examples of European nations and educated Russians.

The threatening idea of degeneration accompanied the hope of progress; it had precedents in European thought, and it too acquired new meanings and functions among Russia's Muslims. In Europe, the idea of progress had become more pronounced after a group of French literary critics in the seventeenth century, the *Modernes*, had rejected the idea of degeneration, claiming that the works of their contemporaries could be and indeed were superior to antiquity's intellectual heritage.[9] Yet, more complex references to degeneration made their way back into European thought by the nineteenth century. If "civilizations" emerged and disappeared in cycles of rise and fall, as many historians suggested at the time, it was quite possible for the contemporary "Western civilization" to hit a downward slope at some point as well. The elation over material progress, as experienced in daily life, pushed such pessimistic prognostications to the margins in Europe, at least until the First World War.[10] But the Russian Muslim progressive reformists would judge their

---

[7] See, John Bagnell Bury, *The Idea of Progress: An Inquiry into Its Origin and Growth* (London: MacMillan and Co., 1921); and Georg G. Iggers, "The Idea of Progress: A Critical Reassessment," *The American Historical Review*, 1965 71(1): 1–17.

[8] Bury, *The Idea*, 324.

[9] Bury, *The Idea*, 78–97. Also see Joan E. DeJean, *Ancients against Moderns: Culture Wars and the Making of a Fin de Siècle* (Chicago: University of Chicago Press, 1997).

[10] See Bury, *The Idea*, 343–44; Iggers, "The Idea," 8–9; and Georges Sorel, *The Illusions of Progress*, trans. Charlotte Stanley (Berkeley: University of California Press, 1969).

contemporary coreligionists against the backdrop of an idealized yet bygone Muslim past and of Europe's example of progress. Consequently, the idea of degeneration hounded them not as a distant possibility in the future but as an ongoing process at the present. If the world changed fast for the better and the Muslims, who had lost their glorious past, did not, the Muslims would ultimately become fit no more for survival in a Spencerian sense.[11]

Thus, degeneration did not necessarily represent an inadvertent downturn on the path of progress for progressive Russian Muslim reformists: the absence of progress itself amounted to degeneration. Arslan Bey Taşçıoğlu and ʿAbdulvelî Qaraşayskiy, two Crimean Muslim noblemen who wrote to the governor of Tavrida in 1869 about the plight of their coreligionists, lamented that "the great majority of our poor Tatars are left in a primitive state of darkness, not knowing what is going on in the world." In 1881, Gasprinskiy echoed their sentiments and complained that being torn apart from the rest of humanity and deprived from "progress and civilization," Russia's Muslims eked out a lifeless life, stock-still "like a corpse."[12]

Where knowledge comes from

The combined effect of belief in the possibility of progress and of imminent ruin unless averted through immediate intervention inspired Russian Muslims who broke out of their insulated communities with a sense of urgency and social responsibility. Gasprinskiy was not the first among them, but he was a trailblazer with regard to the breadth of his cultural exposure and long-term societal impact. He had an unusual career compared to most of his contemporary Muslims in the Russian empire. He attended Russian educational institutions as the son of a recently ennobled Crimean Tatar serviceman. In 1872, he journeyed through Europe to go to Paris and stayed there for close to three years. Then, he traveled to Istanbul where he spent another year before returning to Russia.[13] Later, he would publish his observations of Europe in *Tercüman* as well as in other publications and, to a large extent, set the tone for his contemporary Russian Muslim reformists about the merits and pitfalls of emulating Europe.

[11] See Flun, *Gayaz İsxaki*, especially 27–35; and Herbert Spencer, *The Principles of Biology*, vol. 1 (London: Williams and Norgate, 1864), especially 464–77.
[12] Gasprinskii, *Russkoe*, 7–9. Also see the quote from Hâdi Atlâsî at the beginning of this chapter.
[13] Kırımer, *Gaspıralı*, 19–21.

اسماعیل بك غصپرینسکی

Измаилъ бекъ Гаспринскій.

Figure 4 İsmâʿîl Bey Gasprinskiy.

In a pamphlet that he wrote in 1885 as an attempt to cast a "balanced look" at the "European civilization," he celebrated Europe's contributions to science, technology, and overall material welfare, but he also criticized it from an equity point of view that indicates his familiarity with the socialist and pan-Slavist literatures of the time. European civilization, he asserted, was built on "deficient and fallacious foundations" for having accepted utility (*fayda*) as the basis of social and economic organization. On the other hand, socialism, as a search for a way out of this fallacy, also failed the test, in his opinion, due to its disregard for property and inheritance rights. Instead, Gasprinskiy suggested "rightfulness" (*haqqaniyet*) as an organizing principle and claimed that the rules and regulations of the Shariah were derived from this principle. Therefore, the recipe for a just and materially advanced civilization, in Gasprinskiy's opinion, required the merger of European science and technology with the values of Islam.[14] He illustrated

---

[14] İsmâʿîl Gasprinskiy, *Avrupa Medeniyetine Bir Nazar-ı Muvazene* (İstanbul: Matbaʿa-yı Ebu Ziyâ, 1302 A.H./1885). He would later publish an expanded critique of socialism too. See İsmâʿîl Gasprinskiy, "Mezheb-i İştirâkiyyûn," in *İsmail Gaspıralı: Seçilmiş Eserleri II: Fikrî Eserleri*, ed. Yavuz Akpınar (1906; reprint in Latin transcription, İstanbul: Ötüken, 2004), 190–221.

this utopic recipe, which he characterized as a "better and more complete Muslim way of life,"[15] in a serialized novel that he published in *Tercüman* between 1887 and 1889: *Frengistan Mektupları* or *Letters from Europe*.[16]

Letters from Europe starts in Odessa where the novel's protagonist, a madrasa graduate from Tashkent named Mullah Abbas, stops on his way to Hijaz to perform the Hajj. In Odessa, he meets a young French woman who convinces him to see Europe first. Although Mullah Abbas does not think that Europe might be worthy of seeing in and of itself, he justifies a sojourn by intending to visit the tombs of earlier Muslims such as Gülbaba in Hungary and Kırk Azizler in Spain – thus, at least partly incorporating Europe into the Muslim domain. He also marries the French woman to feel comfortable in her presence. As they travel through Europe and then stay in Paris, Mullah Abbas observes and appreciates the advances of the European civilization, especially the speed of trains, the erudition of scholars in Vienna and Paris, and the orderliness of Paris. He does not like everything. The French girl disappoints him from a moralistic point of view, and they separate. But he still relates the following advice from the Hungarian Turkologist Arminius Vambéry, whom he meets in Vienna, with approval:

Europe is safe and free; you can travel as you want, nobody will bother you. Since God gave you the opportunity to see these lands, do not travel them with ignorance and leave with ignorance. Acquire experience and knowledge ... Europe is the common classroom of the world in our time. It is a treasury of knowledge and learning. The light of the knowledge of famous scholars like Aristotle, Plato, Ibn Sīnā, Farābī, and others, who are forgotten in other continents, is illuminating Europe today. You won't be in loss, I believe, if you enlighten yourself with their light. You are going to Paris. It is the most notable city for acquiring knowledge.[17]

Thus, Mullah Abbas learns French and takes classes on general history, geography, zoology, physics, calculation, and the science of health while in Paris.[18]

---

[15] Gasprinskiy, "Mezheb," 213–14.

[16] İsmâ'il Gasprinskiy, "Frengistan Mektupları," *Tercüman*, January 25, 1887–April 21, 1889. Gasprinskiy later printed this serialized story as two separate novellas under the titles *Frengistan Mektupları* and *Dâr el-Rahat Müslümanları*. They are available in a new edition printed with the Turkish alphabet: İsmâ'il Gasprinskiy, *İsmail Gaspıralı: Seçilmiş Eserleri I: Edebî Eserleri*, ed. Yavuz Akpınar, Bayram Orak, and Nazım Muradov (Istanbul: Ötüken, 2005), 81–274. I will refer to this edition in my citations.

[17] İsmâ'il Gasprinskiy, "Frengistan Mektupları," in *İsmail Gaspıralı: Seçilmiş Eserleri I: Edebî Eserleri*, ed. Yavuz Akpınar, Bayram Orak, and Nazım Muradov (1887; reprint in Latin transcription, Istanbul: Ötüken, 2005), 110.

[18] İsmâ'il Gasprinskiy, "Darürrahat Müslümanları," in *İsmail Gaspıralı: Seçilmiş Eserleri I: Edebî Eserleri*, ed. Yavuz Akpınar, Bayram Orak, and Nazım Muradov (1887–89; reprint in Latin transcription, Istanbul: Ötüken, 2005), 219.

One day, a French merchant tells Mullah Abbas that the beauty, cleanliness, and some of the customs of Paris such as lighting up the streets at night, paving the roads with stones, planting rose gardens, and building fountains are inherited from the Muslims of al-Andalus and that the Europeans benefited a lot from the Muslim scholars of Cordoba, Seville, and Granada. In response, Mullah Abbas confirms that the Islamic civilization of al-Andalus had indeed contributed immensely to the progress of Europe, and he says: "May God give us the opportunity to acquire what we have given to you once again from you." Thus, European civilization and education issue from the efforts of earlier Muslims in Mullah Abbas' perception, and acquiring them once again turns into a divine duty and blessing.[19]

In the second part of the novel, which Gasprinskiy later published as *Dâr el-Rahat Müslümanları* or *Muslims of the Land of Comfort*, he takes this line of reasoning one step further and implies that had the Muslims not lost their love for knowledge, they would have achieved an even higher level of civilization than that of Europe. After two years in Paris, Mullah Abbas goes to Spain to visit the Islamic monuments of al-Andalus. One morning, while reflecting over the beauty of the architecture in the Alhambra Palace in Granada, he sees twelve Muslim girls in one of the courtyards. Being surprised by this out-of-time appearance, he follows them and comes across an Islamic scholar whom he knew from Paris. The scholar and the girls take him through a long underground passage to a hidden country similar to Eldorado in Voltaire's *Candide* and called "The Land of Comfort." It turns out that when Muslim Granada fell to the Spanish in 1492, a select group of Muslims escaped to and settled in this unknown land. Because they did not lose their love for learning, as other Muslims in other parts of the world had done according to Mullah Abbas' interpretation of history, this select group of Andalusian Muslims not only preserved their civilization but also improved it in the Land of Comfort to the extent that the civilization of Europe that Mullah Abbas had witnessed in Paris looked backward in comparison. The Muslims of the Land of Comfort live a comfortable life in a clean and healthy environment. They have electric cars and lighting, telephone lines in every room, large and beautiful houses, and tasty food. They also enjoy a rightful society in which almost nobody lies, cheats, or oppresses. They owe this moral integrity and material comfort to science and education. In an unusual case that Mullah Abbas witnesses, for instance, a seller who

[19] Gasprinskiy, "Frengistan," 118.

had cheated his customer four years ago turns out not to have received proper education in his youth because of poor health.[20]

Mullah Abbas enjoys life in the Land of Comfort, but he cannot endure the idea of staying away from his fatherland permanently and wants to leave. Initially, the rulers of the Land of Comfort hesitate about letting him go lest he would inform the rest of the world about this isolated land. Eventually, however, they decide to give him permission, because, they reason, it would be unjust to restrict the movement of a free person. In the next scene, Mullah Abbas finds himself lying down in a hospital room in Granada about forty days after the morning at Alhambra. The nurse tells him that he was found unconscious in the mountains and that he had been in the hospital for six days. Mullah Abbas cannot prove that he was not dreaming in a state of unconsciousness and that he had actually gone to a land called the Land of Comfort.[21]

Nonetheless, the implications of Mulla Abbas' story remain clear: The knowledge that enabled the creation of the nineteenth-century European civilization originally belonged to Muslims. Therefore, Muslims should acquire it again and put it to good use, while avoiding Europe's mistakes, so as to establish a rightful society of welfare. Beyond this prescription, however, Gasprinskiy does not provide an intellectual foundation for first separating Europe's scientific and technological achievements from the non-Andalusian aspects of its cultural legacy and then merging this supposedly neutral knowledge with the Islamic tradition. In Europe, the idea of progress had evolved first by breaking the mental boundaries of Christian dogma and then the political and religious boundaries of European states and societies.[22] It carried an anti-religious and iconoclastic vein at the core, and here was Gasprinskiy claiming it for the Islamic tradition.

This contradiction does not seem to have bothered Gasprinskiy or many other nineteenth-century Muslim reformists in and outside of Russia. What motivated them was not the *idea* of progress at a doctrinal level but the products of progress as observed in the cold reality of Europe's superior power and prosperity. The famous Ottoman poet and statesman Ziya Paşa (1825–80) wrote in 1870:

> I journeyed through the lands of disbelief and saw cities and
> mansions.
> I wandered in the lands where Muslims rule and saw all in ruins.[23]

---

[20] Gasprinskiy, "Darürrahat," 169–255.   [21] Gasprinskiy, "Darürrahat," 255–70.
[22] Bury, *The Idea*, especially 335–36, and 348.
[23] Önder Göçgün, *Ziya Paşa'nın Hayatı, Eserleri, Edebi Kişiliği* (Ankara: Türk Tarih Kurumu, 2001), 203.

The nineteenth-century Muslim reformists wanted Europe's prosperity but not at the expense of total cultural submission. Hence, they imagined, in the words of İbrâhîm Şinâsî (1826–71), another well-known Ottoman figure, a "fusion of Asia's sagacious intellect with Europe's innovative ideas" as a utopic way out without much probing into the practical possibility of such a fusion.[24] However, the power discrepancy between Europe and the rest of the world did not allow for an even-sided exchange where both parties contributed with equal clout. When put into practice, Şinâsî's seemingly egalitarian fusion turned into a self-civilizing mission in which Muslim reformists endeavored to popularize European-inspired yet purportedly neutral ideas and manners among Muslim populations. Among Russia's Muslims, it was Gasprinskiy who most successfully spearheaded this self-civilizing mission.

Popularizing knowledge

Print media

Popularizing knowledge required institutions. For centuries, Russia's Muslims had relied on Sufi and scholarly networks to this end. In the nineteenth century, Arabic-script print media also entered into their options and became amply available, particularly after the 1840s, when private print houses that opened in Kazan responded to popular demand by turning out inexpensive copies of the Qur'an, prayer books and sheets, folk epics with a religious theme, and calendars in large quantities. Peddlers purchased these items from publishers either in Kazan or in the Volga-Ural region's annual fairs, then distributed them locally in bazaars and Muslim villages or even to "distant places such as Siberia, the Crimea, South Caucasus, Khiva, Bukhara, Samarqand, Kapal, and Tashkent."[25]

A prolific reformist scholar from Kazan, Ğabdulqayyûm Nâsırî (1825–1902), tapped into this burgeoning print market as early as the 1860s in order to popularize various aspects of knowledge that were not offered in Russia's maktabs and madrasas but which he deemed necessary. Among Nâsırî's many publications were annual calendars, a

[24] İbrahim Şinasi, *Makaleler*, ed. Fevziye Abdullah Tansel (Ankara: Dün-Bugün Yayınevi, 1960), vol. 4, 103.
[25] See Fahreddin, "Millî Matbu'âtımız," *Şûra*, 1908 (10): 324–26; (17): 525–27; and (21): 673–75; Battal-Taymas, *Kazan Türkleri*, 103–6; Gainullin, *Tatarskaia literatura*; Karimullin, *U istokov*, especially 82–110, 132–33, 164–65; and Rezeda R. Safiullina, *Arabskaia kniga v dukhovnoi kul'ture tatarskogo naroda* (Kazan: Izdatel'stvo Alma-Lit, 2003).

Russian-language reader, a dictionary of the Russian language for Tatar speakers, collections of folk stories written in the Turkic vernacular of the Volga-Ural Muslims, and textbooks on calculation, geometry, agriculture, geography, history, and pedagogy.[26] In his memoirs, Fahreddin relates how in the early 1880s, he had chanced upon Nâsırî's *Hisablıq* (a book on calculation printed in 1873) in a local bazaar as the only source available in Volga-Ural Turkic to learn calculation at that time.[27]

While Nâsırî remained a lone star in his publication work for a long time, gradually other reformist Muslims from various parts of Russia also began experimenting with the possibilities of using print media in order to reach out to the broader population. Alphabet books, textbooks on various subjects, and even literary works started to hit Muslim bookstalls in the 1880s, and the Muslim publishing industry reached a large volume by the 1890s.[28] By the early twentieth century, dozens of Muslim printing houses in Kazan and many others in Orenburg, Ufa, Astrakhan, Bahçe-saray, Baku, Moscow, and St. Petersburg were putting out an average of 440 titles that reached a combined print count of 2.5 million volumes annually.[29] According to one Muslim journalist, the quantity of books in the languages of Russia's Muslims was second only to the Russian-language publications at St. Petersburg's annual book fair in 1911.[30]

One media that Russian Muslim reformists still longed to utilize abundantly as late as the beginning of the twentieth century was periodicals, which could create a dialogue of opinions, as they observed was happening among educated Russians and the Ottoman intellectuals.[31] Censorship shot down their attempts to publish journals and newspapers one after the other.[32] Nâsırî published annual calendars to circumvent

---

[26] Muhammednecîb bin Şerefüddin el-Kostramavî, "Ğabdulqayyûm el-Nâsırî Hazretleri Tercüme-yi Hâline 'Âid," *Şûra*, 1913 (8): 233–37; and Çağatay, *Abd-ül-Qayyum*.

[27] Märdanov, Miñnullin, and Räximov eds., *Rizaetdin Fähretdin*, 28–29.

[28] Sharafuddinov and Khanbikov, *Istoriia pedagogiki*, 76–77; İsmâ'il Gasprinskiy, "Mebâdî-yi Temeddün-i İslâmiyan-ı Rus," in *İsmail Gaspıralı: Seçilmiş Eserleri II: Fikrî Eserleri*, ed. Yavuz Akpınar (Bahçesaray: 1910; reprint in Latin transcription, Istanbul: Ötüken, 2004), 251–72.

[29] A[brar] G. Karimullin, *Tatarskaia kniga nachala XX veka* (Kazan: Tatarskoe knizhnoe izdatel'stvo, 1974).

[30] Şerîf el-Hamdi, "Matbu'at Vıstafqası," *Şûra*, 1911 (6): 190–91.

[31] For an early expression of this aspiration, see Hämidullin, Märdanov, and Miñnullin eds., *Bertugan Rämiyevlär*, 305–8. On the role of periodicals in creating opinions in the Ottoman Empire, see Fuat Süreyya Oral, *Türk Basın Tarihi*, vol. 1 (Ankara: Yeni Adım Matbaasi, 1967), especially 66–120; and in Russia, see McReynolds, *The News*.

[32] For failed attempts before 1905, see NART, f. 1, op. 3, d. 9690, ll. 1–2b-7ob; NART, f. 142, op. 1, d. 74, ll. 20–20ob; Gainullin, *Tatarskaia literatura*, 10–12; Karimullin, *U istokov*, 172–90; Äbrar Gibadulloviç Kärimullin, *Kitap Dönyasına Säyahät* (Kazan: Tatarstan Kitap Näşriyatı, 1979), 147–54; and Diliara M. Usmanova, "Die Tatarische Presse 1905–1918: Quellen, Entwicklungsetappen und Quantitative Analyse," in *Muslim*

this impediment, and Gasprinskiy published consecutive pamphlets with different titles.[33] Finally, after four years of repeated applications, Gasprinskiy received permission to publish *Tercüman* in 1883, and arguably, the presence of *Tercüman* served as the most effective forum for popularizing progressive ideas and connecting reformists in the Russian empire until the Revolution of 1905. Once Nicholas II passed press freedom into law in this year and the Russian state lost its grip on the publishing industry, the youthful cohort of progressive reformist Muslims that followed Gasprinskiy's generation moved in with a flood of periodicals in Russia's Muslim languages. Censorship officials still managed to close a few of them, particularly after 1907, and many others simply discontinued because they could not find sponsors or readers. Several others, however, survived, with print runs approximating 5,000 on occasions.[34] They gave voice to different and at times opposing opinions that represented the ideological preferences of reformist Muslims who navigated late imperial Russia's politically charged atmosphere, and they also connected members of the progressive reformist cohort to one another by building a shared idiom and imaginary of progress.

Schooling reform

As states turned to popular schooling to remake societies in the nineteenth century, so did progressive reformist Muslims in Russia; Gasprinskiy took the lead in this too. He was not the first reformist Russian Muslim who considered empowering his coreligionists by improving their educational institutions,[35] however, he was the one who devised practical plans –

Culture in Russia and Central Asia from the 18th to the Early 20th Centuries, ed. Michael Kemper, Anke von Kügelgen, and Dmitriy Yermakov (Berlin: Klaus Schwarz Verlag, 1996), 257–59. For short-lived attempts, see Bennigsen and Lemercier-Quelquejay, *La presse*, 28–35; and Ali Erol, "Türk Kültür ve Fikir Hayatında Ekinçi (1875–1877)," *Bilig*, 2006 Fall(39): 53–72.

[33] On Gasprinskiy's early publication efforts, see Lazzerini, "Ismail Bey," 11–15. A copy of his first pamphlet, *Tonguç*, was sent to Il'minskii for censorial review in 1881. See in NART, f. 1, o. 3, d. 5184. For a list of Nâsırî's publications, see el-Kostramavî, "Ğabdulqayyûm," 235–37.

[34] On the publishing boom of the early twentieth century among Volga-Ural Muslims, see Battal-Taymas, *Kazan Türkleri*, 170–73; Bennigsen and Lemercier-Quelquejay, *La presse*; Usmanova, "Die Tatarische"; Mirkasım A. Usmanov and Raif F. Märdanov eds., *Şura jurnalınıñ bibliografik kürsätkeçe* (Kazan: Milli Kitap Neşriyatı, 2000), 4–18; and Usmanova, "K voprosu o tirazhakh musul'manskikh periodicheskikh izdanii Rossii nachala 20 veka," 212.

[35] For earlier examples, see Chantal Lemercier-Quelquejay, "Un réformateur tatar du XIXe siècle, 'Abdul Qajjum Al-Nasyri,'" *Cahiers du Monde Russe et Soviétique*, 1963 4 (1–2): 117–43; Sharafuddinov and Khanbikov, *Istoriia pedagogiki*, 8–12, 30–35, 44–53, and 64–67; and Hüseyin Feyizhanof, "Reforma medrese (Islakh madaris)," in *Khusain Faizkhanov: Zhizn' i nasledie*, ed. A. M. Akhunova and I. F. Gimadeeva (Nizhny Novgorod: Medina, 2008).

Figure 5 Prominent authors and publishers of the Volga-Ural Muslim press between 1905 and 1915 as published in the first issue of *Añ* in 1916. Top from left: Ğayaz İshâqî and Seyyidgiray Alkin. Bottom from left: Ahmed-Hâdi Maqsûdî, Şeher Şeref, and Burhan Şeref.

Figure 6 Prominent authors and publishers of the Volga-Ural Muslim
press between 1905 and 1915 as published in the first issue of *Añ* in
1916 (cont.). Top from left: Rızâeddin bin Fahreddin and Ġatâullah
Ahund Bayezidof. Bottom from left: Zâkir Ramiyef, Şâkir Ramiyef, and
Fâtih Kerîmî.

Figure 7 Prominent authors and publishers of the Volga-Ural Muslim press between 1905 and 1915 as published in the first issue of *Añ* in 1916 (cont.). Top from left: Mahmûd Fuʿâd Tuqtaref, Muhammedcan Seydaşef, and Ahmedcan Seydaşef. Bottom from left: Ahmed Urmançıyef, Hâris Feyzi, and Ğaliasgar Kemâl.

ا صان ـــــــــــــــــ آنك ـــــــــــــــ ١١ بیت

اون یللق موقت مطبوعاتمزنك محرر وناشرلری.

۱۹۱۵-۱۹۰۵

Figure 8 Prominent authors and publishers of the Volga-Ural Muslim press between 1905 and 1915 as published in the first issue of *Añ* in 1916 (cont.). Top from left: Fâtih Murtazîn, Ğabdurrahman Ğumerof, and Kemâl Tuhfetullin. Bottom from left: Habîburrahman Ğaniyef, Timurşah Salavyof, and Kelîmullah Hüseyinof.

Figure 9 Prominent authors and publishers of the Volga-Ural Muslim press between 1905 and 1915 as published in the first issue of *Añ* in 1916 (cont.). Top from left: Şerefüddîn Şehîdullin, Yaʿqûb Halîlî, and Fahrulislâm Âgiyef. Bottom from left: Mahmûd Mercânî, Ğibâdullah Ğusmanof, and Zâkir Qâdirî.

reminiscent of the small-deeds liberals among educated Russians – and who managed to get many others on board to implement his plans. Initially, it seems, he thought that the burden of spreading "European sciences and knowledge" among the Muslims of Russia fell on the imperial state in return for the taxes it collected. Writing in 1881, he was already aware of the example of the MNP's Russo-Muslim schools, but he found them unlikely to succeed primarily because they taught Muslim children in Russian and not in native Turkic. Therefore, he called on the Russian government to provide education to Muslims in their own languages, but in vain.[36] By 1884, however, he had developed a plan that he set out to implement without government support. Once again, the source of his inspiration was Europe as filtered through observations of the Russian and Ottoman experiences.

Traditionally, the speakers of most languages around the world taught literacy by introducing the names of letters to students in the context of sacred texts. By the mid nineteenth century, however, this rather cumbersome method was replaced in Europe and in North America by what had come to be known as the "new method." The new method introduced letters with their phonemes – hence it is also called the "phonic method" – and relied on simpler, child-friendly texts to make learning to read and write easier for students.[37] In the mid 1860s, the famous Russian pedagogue Konstantin D. Ushinskii adapted this method to the Russian language while an Ottoman bureaucrat, Selîm Sâbit Efendi, wrote a new-method alphabet book for Ottoman Turkish. By the 1870s, Ushinskii's works had revolutionized elementary education in Russia while several pilot schools had started to teach with the new method in the Ottoman Empire, especially in Istanbul and Salonica.[38] Furthermore, in 1883, a Russian pedagogue named A. O. Cherniaevskii, whom Gasprinskiy knew personally, adapted the phonic method to the Turkic vernacular of the South Caucasus region in an alphabet book.[39]

---

[36] Gasprinskii, *Russkoe,* especially 12–13.
[37] Mitford McLeod Matthews, *Teaching to Read: Historically Considered* (Chicago: Chicago University Press, 1966), especially 31–34 and 63.
[38] Konstantin D. Ushinskii, *Rodnoe slovo* (St. Petersburg: Tipografiia I. Markova, 1865); Nafi Atuf, *Türkiye Maarif Tarihi Hakkında Bir Deneme* (Ankara: Milliyet Matbaası, 1930); Osman Ergin, *Türkiye Maarif Tarihi,* vol. 2 (Istanbul: Osmanbey Matbaası, 1940), 379–97; N. K. Goncharov, *Pedagogicheskaia sistema K.D. Ushinskogo* (Moscow: Pedagogika, 1974); Yahya Akyüz, *Türk Eğitim Tarihi: Başlangıçtan 2001'e* (Istanbul: 2001, 2001), 192–93; Fahri Temizyürek, "Osmanlı Mekteplerinde Cedidçilik Hareketi ve Gaspıralı'nın İlham Kaynakları," in *İsmail Bey Gaspıralı İçin,* ed. Hakan Kırımlı (Kırım Türkeri Kültür ve Yardımlaşma Derneği Yayınları, 2004), 277–88.
[39] Lazzerini, "Ismail Bey", 47.

In 1884, one year after the publication of Cherniaevskii's alphabet book, Gasprinskiy decided to open an experimental new-method maktab in Bahçesaray himself. Muslims of Bahçesaray showed little interest in his project, but eventually, he was able to find twelve students to teach. He followed Ushinskii's pedagogical lead in designing a program in order to teach Turkic literacy with the phonic method, along with simple calculation and the basics of religion. He also improved the student experience with a well-organized classroom, equipment such as desks and blackboard, and breaks between class hours. Forty-five days later, he invited about two hundred notable Muslims in Bahçesaray for a public examination. Only thirty turned out, but the word quickly spread that after such a short study period, each of Gasprinskiy's twelve students could read and write Tatar words in addition to being able to read randomly chosen pages from the Qur'an. As a result, about forty more parents enrolled their children in Gasprinskiy's maktab on that very day; his initiative had proven successful. He called his program *usûl-i cedîd*, the "new method," as it was already known in the Ottoman Empire. He also wrote an alphabet book to facilitate instruction: *Hoca-yı Sıbyân*, and he began to promote the new method as a model for turning Russia's maktabs into gateways of higher knowledge for Muslim children. *Tercüman* served as his primary venue for spreading the word, but he also traveled widely in the Russian empire and even to Bukhara to seek supporters.[40]

Among the Volga-Ural Muslims, progressive merchants and a burgeoning network of reform-minded scholars, many of whom were affiliated with Mercânî, enthusiastically embraced Gasprinskiy's program.[41] It is difficult to gauge the new method's impact in the region in numerical terms. In 1904, the director of public schools in the Kazan Guberniia estimated that most mullahs still taught with the old method while there were a few who had adopted the new method.[42] However, given the makeshift nature of Russia's maktabs and the MNP bureaucrats' inability to track them, any such estimates should be considered less than informed guesses. Anecdotal data suggest that the new-method maktabs

[40] On Gasprinskiy's efforts to develop and spread this new method, see İsmâ'îl Gasprinskiy, *Hoca-yı Sıbyân* (1884; reprint Bahçesaray, 1992); İsmâ'îl Gasprinskiy, *Rehber-i Mu'allimîn yaki Mu'allimlere Yoldaş* (Bahçesaray, 1898); Gasprinskiy, "Türk Yurdcularına," 109–11; and 132–34; Edward J. Lazzerini, "From Bahchisarai to Bukhara in 1893: Ismail Bey Gasprinskii's Journey to Central Asia," *Central Asian Survey*, 1984 3(4): 77–88; İbrahim Maraş, "İsmail Gaspıralı'nın Bilinmeyen Bir Risalesi: 'Mektep ve Usûl-i Cedid Nedir,'" *Emel*, 1997 (219): 10–20. For the use of the term "usûl-i cedîd" in the Ottoman Empire, see Akyüz, *Türk Eğitim*, 190–92.
[41] On Mercânî's influence, see Ross, "From the Minbar," especially 160–219.
[42] NART, f. 92, op. 2, d. 5740, l (no pagination available).

thrived where an influential scholar or merchant endorsed them, such as Sheikh Zeynullah Rasûlî in Troitsk, but they barely made an impact in the absence of such support.[43] A survey conducted in the Orenburg Gubernia in 1915 by mailing questionnaires to registered mullahs suggests that in most cases, the method of maktab instruction was a function of the mullahs' teaching skills and the instructional material that was available to them.[44] Of the 552 surveyed mullahs, 37 percent reported teaching with the new method, and their responses about course content roughly confirm this claim. However, only 6 percent of the surveyed mullahs themselves had studied with the new method, and the responses to several other questions indicate that when mullahs claimed to teach with the new method, they did not necessarily mean what Gasprinskiy had in mind in terms of classroom facilities, instructional material, class regimen, or school calendar.[45] It seems that there was a growing awareness of the phonic method's practicality, and some mullahs tried to implement it by using one of the many new-method alphabet books that had proliferated in the market.[46] However, they did so experimentally, without necessarily adopting the new method as a complete program. On the other hand, about 25 percent of the mullahs claimed to teach in the conventional way, and a significant 38 percent simply declined this question, perhaps indicating an indifference to the matter.[47]

Nevertheless, the new method made a far more significant impact among Russia's Muslims than can be assessed by the number of mullahs who used it. As Gasprinskiy announced the new method's successes in *Tercüman* and personally in reformist circles, he inspired other Russian Muslims who wanted change but did not know how with hope that schooling reform could indeed make a positive difference. This hope and the availability of *Tercüman* as a venue to negotiate collective action encouraged many scholars and especially young madrasa graduates to push the limits of progressive reform further.

The advantage of the new method, according to Gasprinskiy, was not so much in teaching literacy more efficiently than the conventional

---

[43] For two official estimates indicating the small number of new-method schools in parts of the Kazan Gubernia in 1913, see NART, f. 1, op. 4, d. 5482, ll. 99–99ob, and 103ob/04. On the failure of new-method activists in Semipalatinsk, see Frank and Usmanov eds., *Materials*, 2–3. On a contemporary observation about the high number of new-method schools in Troitsk, see el-Kazanî, *Üç Aylık*, 8, and 13–17. For a similar situation where the support of a prominent scholar promoted the new method, see Tuqayef, *Tarih-i İsterlibaş*.

[44] Anon., *Orenburg Vilayetindeki*.   [45] Ibid., 10, 21–22, and 25–26.

[46] Especially Hâdi Maqsûdî, *Risâle-yi Mu'allim-i Evvel: Usûl-i Savtiyye Buyınça Türkî Elifba* (1892; reprint Kazan: İman Neşriyatı, 1997) made many editions.

[47] Anon., *Orenburg Vilayetindeki*, 10.

maktabs, but in turning literacy in the native tongue into an instrument of pursuing knowledge – any knowledge – beyond the recitation of sacred texts in Arabic.[48] This pursuit required opportunities beyond the four years of schooling that most new-method maktabs were designed to offer. Gasprinskiy was not a madrasa scholar who could reform Muslim schooling beyond the maktab level, but in 1889, he cooperated with a scholar named Duvanköylü Habîbullah Efendi (1820–95) in order to introduce non-religious subjects into the curriculum of Zincirli Madrasa in the Crimea and also to improve its living conditions. Habîbullah Efendi had studied in Istanbul and Cairo, and together, the two progressive reformists transferred to Russia the ideas of educational reform that were intensely debated in the Ottoman Empire in the late-nineteenth century.[49] In the Volga-Ural region, scholars such as Mercânî in the city of Kazan and Muhammed Hâris Hazret in the İsterlibaş village of the Orenburg Gubernia had already started experimenting with the idea of madrasa reform before Gasprinskiy.[50] And the Zincirli Madrasa experiment fell apart with the death of Habîbullah Efendi in 1895.[51] Yet, Gasprinskiy and Habîbullah Efendi's model at Zincirli Madrasa still signalled the direction madrasa reform would take in the Russian empire and especially in the Volga-Ural region in the 1890s and after.

By the 1890s, many Ottoman publications, including periodicals, were already available in the Russian empire through subscription.[52] With the support of the Volga-Ural region's progressive merchants, several young madrasa students or graduates, who often directly communicated with Gasprinskiy, also traveled to the Ottoman territories and Egypt in order to study or, sometimes, simply to observe. Then, they returned to Russia and started teaching in reformed madrasas with curricula designed after the westernized educational institutions of Istanbul and Cairo. Until the early twentieth century, the Ottoman authorities who feared the ulamas' opposition had left maktabs and madrasas alone by and large and focused on creating new and secular schools in a parallel system of education. The Russian government would not allow Muslim reformists to open secular schools until the 1910s, but most madrasas continued to

---

[48] Gasprinskiy, "Türk Yurdcularına," 110; and Gasprinskiy, "Mebâdî," 257–58.
[49] "Zincirli Medrese," *Tercüman*, October 9, 1894; and Kırımlı, *National Movements*, 50–51.
[50] Tuqayef, *Tarih-i İsterlibaş*, especially 10–11; and 'Ubeydullin ed., *Mercânî*, 98–125. One of Mercânî's inspirations was his student Hüseyin Feyizhan, who died prematurely in 1866. See Feyizhanof, "Reforma"; and A. M. Akhunova, "Pis'ma Khusaina Faizkhanova Shigabutdinu Mardzhani," in *Khusain Faizkhanov: Zhizn' i nasledie*, ed. A. M. Akhunova and I. F. Gimadeeva (Nizhny Novgorod: Medina, 2008), 82–106.
[51] "Vefatnâme," *Tercüman*, March 26, 1895; and "Editorial," *Tercüman*, May 18, 1899.
[52] A. Battal Taymas, *Kazanlı Türk Meşhurlarından Rızaeddin Fahreddinoğlu* (İstanbul: n.p., 1958), 14–17; and Togan, *Hatıralar*, 16.

evade the potentially restrictive supervision of MNP inspectors thanks to their status as religious institutions until the end of the tsarist regime. The progressive reformists gradually introduced secular subjects such as natural history, economy, and, most importantly, the Russian language into the programs of the madrasas where they taught. By the early twentieth century, several such madrasas, especially in the cities of Kazan and Ufa but also in more provincial locations, each graduated dozens of students every year into the progressive reformist cohort of the Volga-Ural region.[53]

Alongside madrasa reform, a less documented development that arguably carried equal weight in the growth of a progressive reformist cohort was the enrollment of Russian Muslim students in government schools. As we have seen Şahbazgiray Ahmerof report in 1885 and the governor of Kazan Poltoratskii second him in 1895, Muslim students started to take this path slowly in the 1880s and increasingly in the 1890s.[54] Especially the Kazan Tatar Teachers' School, which Radloff had opened in 1876, attracted more advanced madrasa students who wanted to become conversant in the language and culture of the imperial domain.[55] While the conventional madrasas trained students to become mullahs, Russian-language education in reformed madrasas or government schools opened up a variety of more lucrative career opportunities, including further studies at university level.[56] Hence, in 1913, the reformed Muhammediye Madrasa in Kazan would advertise its program by promising that the graduates of its elementary (maktab) section would learn enough Russian to enroll in government schools,[57] and Gasprinskiy was pleased to observe shortly before his death in 1914 that even the relatively more conservative Muslims of Russian Turkestan had started to enroll their children in government schools.[58]

[53] On reformed madrasas, see Mähdiev ed. *Mädräsälärdä Kitap Kiştäse*; Tuna, "Madrasa Reform"; and Alper Alp, "*Mir İslama* Dergisine Göre 20. Asır Başında İdil-Ural Bölgesinde Mektep ve Medrese Meselesi," *Türkiyat Araştırmaları Dergisi*, 2009 (26): 327–45.

[54] See in Chapter 4. For a similar observation from 1900, see NART, f. 92, op. 1, d. 24602.

[55] L. V. Gorokhova ed. *Kazanskaia tatarskaia uchitel'skaia shkola 1876–1917 gg.* (Kazan: Izdatel'stvo Gasyr, 2005) provides a large collection of archival materials about the Kazan Tatar Teachers' School. For a detailed study of the school, see Rezeda Rifovna Iskhakova, "*Pedagogicheskoe obrazovanie v Kazanskoi gubernii vo vtoroi polovine 19-nachale 20 vv.*" (Ph.D. Dissertation, Russian Academy of Education, 2002), 139–90.

[56] Muhîddin Qurbangaliyef, "İbtidâî Mekteblerde Uqılaturgan Fenler," *Mekteb*, 1913 1(1): 24–25; and Sharafuddinov and Khanbikov, *Istoriia pedagogiki*, 9.

[57] Mahmûd Fu'âd, "Medreselerde Çuvalular," *Mekteb*, 1913 1(3): 69; and 'Ayn. Fi., "Meşhurrak Medreseleribiz Hâlinden," *Mekteb*, 1913 1(10): 954.

[58] Mahmûd Hoca Behbûdî, "İsmâ'îl Bey Hazretleri ile Sohbet," in *Tatars of the Crimea: Their Struggle for Survival*, ed. Edward Allworth (Âyine 1914 (49): 1162–64; reprint in English translation, Durham: Duke University Press, 1988), 71–74.

The progressive youth

The cohort of young progressive reformist Muslims – the "Jadidists" or *cedîdciler* in reference to *usûl-i cedîd*, i.e. "the proponents of the new," as they came to be known – had grown significantly in size and enthusiasm by the early twentieth century. In 1901, when Gasprinskiy prepared a study of the Turkic-language publications in the Russian empire, he called it "The Beginning of the Civilization of Russia's Muslims."[59] Russia's Muslims had shaken away their corpse-like torpor, Gasprinskiy thought, and the youth, who looked up to him as a respected "teacher" or a "father" figure, mostly concurred.[60] They embraced the promise of progress with hope and a sense of continued urgency at what they perceived to be a critical moment in history.

"We are living in the time of progress," wrote Mahmûd Fu'âd, a leading member of the young reformist cohort in 1913:

Of course, a nation like us that is just waking up from slumber and that has just started to stand on the first steps of progress has a lot to accomplish ... Great advances cannot be achieved without any waste or sacrifices ... The awakening of Tatars to progress and learning has also claimed and continues to claim many sacrifices and victims.

One sacrifice that Fu'âd had in mind was the efforts of progressive reformist village mullahs who toiled in villages to spread knowledge. He related the efforts of one of these mullahs who, together with his wife, would teach from dawn to late in the night, day after day. The mullah would first instruct the boys in the maktab while his wife taught the girls, then he would teach the girls to cover subjects that his wife could not, and finally he would work with his wife and other women late into the night so that the women could teach what they learned from him to the maktab girls the next morning. Moreover, while this mullah received the usual charities for his religious services, he did not receive any material compensation for teaching. On the contrary, he had personally solicited money from a *bay* in a distant location and used it to renovate the maktab building in his village, while the villagers, who ambivalently observed the initiatives of this unusual mullah, had not even contributed their labor.[61]

---

[59] Gasprinskiy, "Mebâdî," 251–72.
[60] Mustafa Özgür Tuna, "Gaspırali v. Il'minskii: Two Identity Projects for the Muslims of the Russian Empire," in *Nationalities Papers*, 2002 30(2): 278. For an example of the youth's reverence for Gasprinskiy, see Mahmûd Fu'âd, "Büyük Bababız Vefat," *Mekteb*, 1914 2(9): 197–210.
[61] Mahmûd Fu'âd, "Avıl Mullaları," *Mekteb*, 1913 1(6): 154–57.

In the Volga-Ural region, the passion that motivated this progressive mullah and others like him spread through student networks and, especially after 1905, through the booming Muslim press as the emotional bedrock of the cult of progress. Poetry and literature, which they shared not only in print but also in person at literary gatherings, gave expression to their euphoria. Ğabdullah Tuqay, who embodied the progressive youth's radical passions, wrote in a stanza:

> There comes the end of time when the sun rises from the west.
> This is one of the many omens written in the books.
> Now that the sun of science and wisdom have risen from the West
> I know not what lies for the people of the East ahead.[62]

The rising of the sun from the west is one of the signs of the end of time, according to several traditions narrated from the Prophet Muhammad.[63] Here, Tuqay was referring to that omen and urging his people, "the people of the East," to turn to the West's "sun of science and wisdom" in order to avert imminent extinction.

Even the students of İşmuhammed bin Dinmuhammed, who vocally opposed the new-method, surreptitiously joined the tide of the progressive movement. According to Rızâ Ğazîzof, who once studied at İşmuhammed Hazret's madrasa at Tünter Village in the Viatka Gubernia, it was actually İşmuhammed bin Dinmuhammed's son who brought story and poetry books of a progressive reformist nature to the village, loaned them to students, and organized literary nights. Writing in 1992, Rızâ Ğazîzof still remembered a poem that he had memorized at the Tünter Medrese at that time:

> The sun has risen, the light has shone.
> It has radiated into the house through the window.
> Lie not asleep! Wake up oh madrasa student!
> The time to reap benefits has arrived.
>
> Take advantage of it, try and endeavor.
> Think ahead as you walk to the future.
> Fight those who block your way.
> Without that you will not get your share.

---

[62] The Kazan Tatar artist Bâqî Urmançî who was a student at the reformed Muhammediye Madrasa relates this stanza in his reminiscences of the early twentieth century: Baki Urmançı, "Çıksa Mägriptän Koyaş," in *Mädräsälärdä Kitap Kiştäse*, ed. Röstäm Mähdiev (Kazan: Tatarstan Kitap Näşriyatı, 1992), 36.

[63] Abū ʿAbd Allah Muḥammad ibn Ismāʿīl al-Bukhārī, *Ṣaḥīḥ al-Bukhārī*, ed. Abū Ṣuhayb al-Karmī (Riyadh: Bayt al-Afkār al-Dawliyyah li'l-Nashr, 1998), 1247, and Abū al-Ḥusayn Muslim b. al-Ḥajjāj al-Qushayrī al-Nishābūrī al-Nishābūrī, *Ṣaḥīḥ Muslim*, ed. Abū Qutaybah Naẓar Muḥammad al-Fārābī (Riyadh: Dār Ṭaybah, 2006), 1: 82 and 2: 1327.

Wake up oh madrasa student, sleep not!
Plow the Earth's surface tooth and nail.
Disperse seeds and let them sprout.
Do not wallow on the dark earth![64]

Conclusion

Hence, by the early twentieth century, a sizeable cohort of progressive youth was joining ranks with the small network of earlier reformers who coalesced around Tercüman after 1883. The idea of progress served as the through-line that connected the two generations. However, the inherent contradictions of attempting to merge the European and Islamic traditions that the early reformers had left unresolved opened the gates for deep fractures within this evolving movement too. Most members of the earlier generation had first internalized the Islamic tradition in the insulated Muslim domain as an indispensable foundation of their subjectivity and then set out to recognize the world at large. Therefore, they sought progress through the reconciliation of what the broader world had to offer with the norms and values that they cherished in the Islamic tradition. However, as reformed madrasas increased the number of class hours for non-religious sciences in their programs at the expense of religious sciences and introduced secular rituals of socialization, such as literary nights, they not only created opportunities for learning new subjects but also established a new balance between the authorities of religion on one side and of science and civilization on the other.[65]

The progressive youth were already immersed in a cultural environment where European concepts and institutions – especially positive science – claimed authority as "controllers" of and "exemplars" for other value systems.[66] These young men – and occasionally women – could not cast a "balanced look" at the European civilization; they were fascinated by it. The travel notes of Fâtih Kerimî, who first studied in Istanbul and then, in 1898, participated in a three-month trip to Europe, illustrate this fascination. Kerimî admires and even venerates the speedy trains, giant factories, scientific achievements, orderly streets, and the well-educated and well-mannered people that he sees in Europe. But whenever he casts

---

[64] Riza Gazizov, "Uyan, şäkirt, yoqlamagıl," in *Mädräsälärdä Kitap Kiştäse*, ed. Röstäm Mähdiev (Kazan: Tatarstan Kitap Neşriyatı, 1992), 171–75.

[65] On this process of secularization, see Tuna, "Madrasa Reform." On the Ottoman precedent to this process, see M. Şükrü Hanioğlu, "Blueprints for a Future Society: Late Ottoman Materialists on Science, Religion, and Art," in *Late Ottoman Society: The Intellectual Legacy*, ed. Elisabeth Özdalga (London: Routledge, 2005), 28–116.

[66] Bayly, *The Birth*, 3.

a critical eye, he turns to Russia's Muslims, assesses their condition according to what he considers to be the European standards, and finds them lacking.[67]

As a result, the younger generation of progressive reformists conceptualized progress not as a merger between two traditions but as a linear path in which different peoples moved forward at different speeds while Europe led the way. One reader of *Şûra*, Âhundcan İskenderî, wrote: "It goes without doubt that the Russian Tatars have not grown out of adolescence in comparison to other nations." Referring to another article in *Şûra* titled "Our Progress," İskenderî commented that the Russians were also at the stage of adolescence at the time of Peter the Great, but thanks to the Europeanizing reforms of Peter the Great, they grew past adolescence.[68] Islam did not have a central role on this linear path of progress. Only rarely did members of the youth dare to renounce religion completely and publicly, but for most of them, Islam still ceased to be an indispensable foundation of their subjectivity. When they sought progress, they did so in an order that reversed the earlier generation's priorities: by attempting to reconcile the Islamic tradition with positive science and what they admired as the European civilization. If and when their attempts failed – which happened frequently in the absence of an epistemological foundation for such reconciliation – they were ready to relegate Islam to a secondary position in order to sift through a global jungle of politically charged ideologies. In the following chapter, we will turn to the tensions and rifts that this situation created between the progressive reformist cohort and the broader Muslim population.

---

[67] Kerimi, *Avrupa*. Also see Azade-Rorlich, "The Temptation," 39–58.

[68] Hâdi Atlasî, "Bizniñ Teraqqî," *Şûra*, 1910 (24): 745–48; and Fettâh Ğadlî, "İslâmlar Arasında Ğilm Niçün Lâzım Derecede Taralmıy?," *Şûra*, (19): 588–92.

8 Alienation of the Muslim intelligentsia

Gazite! Gazite! Dünya buzılırga ite!
Newspaper! Newspaper! It ruins the world![1]   Reported by Şâkir
Ramiyef as a common expression among Volga-Ural Muslims, 1881

It is time to reform all of the old life fundamentally.[2]   A young Tatar
intellectual, 1910

Gasprinskiy considered literacy a prerequisite of learning (*ma'ârif*) and learning a prerequisite of progress (*terakkî*) or becoming civilized (*temeddün*).[3] Therefore, he regarded the public examination of his first twelve students in 1884, where he had demonstrated the possibility of teaching literacy within forty-five days with the new method, a turning point for the progress of Russia's Muslims.[4] Beginning with his biographer, Cafer Seydahmet Kırımer (1889–1960), who settled in Turkey after the Bolshevik Revolution, historians of the Russian Muslim diaspora unanimously concurred with this representation by hailing Gasprinskiy's introduction of the new method, and, therefore, functional literacy among Russia's Muslims in 1884 as an epic moment in history.[5] And many European and North American historians have long shared the same view.[6]

Gasprinskiy's role in promoting functional literacy among Russia's Muslims is well acknowledged and indeed deserved, but the celebratory tone that historians have sustained (based on the progressive Muslim

---

[1] Printed in Fahreddin, "Muhammadşâkir Efendi," 189–91.
[2] Adolf, "Usûl-i Cedîdege Umûmî Bir Nazar," in *Usûl-i Cedîdge Qarşı Birinci Adım*, ed. Halîl Ebulhanef (Kazan: Ürnek Matba'ası, 1910), viii.
[3] Gasprinskiy, "Rusya'da Matbuat ve Neşriyât-ı İslâmiye," 250; and Gasprinskiy, "Mebâdî."
[4] Gasprinskiy, "Türk Yurdcularına," 132–34.
[5] Among other sources representing this view, see Kırımer, *Gaspıralı*, 206–9; Kurat, "Kazan Türklerinde," 112–13; Azade-Rorlich, *Volga Tatars*, 88; and Kırımlı, *National Movements*, 45–48.
[6] For two seminal examples, see Alexandre Bennigsen and Chantal Lemercier-Quelquejay, *Islam in the Soviet Union* (London: Pall Mall Press, 1967), 39; and Lazzerini, "Ismail Bey," 26–28.

accounts of his contributions) veils an important detail in the story of the public examination of 1884. At the time Gasprinskiy invited the Muslim notables of Bahçesaray to this examination, Russia's Muslims valued the ability to decipher Arabic letters primarily as an instrument of voicing Qur'anic verses in the original Arabic, even though very few among them could understand it, and also of accessing other religious texts, which could be in Arabic or Turkic and were often recited publicly rather than read individually.[7] They regarded the recitation of the Qur'an from memory or with the aid of a written copy to be an act that was pleasing to God, as did other Muslims around the world.[8] They sent their children to maktab not to learn reading and writing in the vernacular as the foundation of functional literacy but to acquire the skill of deciphering Arabic letters along with basic religious knowledge and cultural norms.[9] This is why about forty parents enrolled their children in Gasprinskiy's school on the very day that he demonstrated he could teach the Arabic letters much more efficiently than the mullahs did in other maktabs.

Nonetheless, here was a dormant disconnect built into Gasprinskiy's schooling initiative – the symbolic kernel of the Russian Muslim progressive reform movement. The learning that he upheld as a prerequisite of progress issued from "scientific and literary" publications that contained "general knowledge" (ma 'lûmât-ı umûmiye) of a secular nature, not from the religious texts that most Russian Muslims wanted their children to read.[10] Yet, since the Russian government would not allow Muslims to open secular schools until the 1910s, Gasprinskiy and the progressive reformist cohort took advantage of the empire's extensive network of maktabs and madrasas in order to promote "general knowledge." In doing so, they transformed the content of Muslim education in these otherwise religious institutions by introducing European-inspired, secular fields of study, such as painting or positivist history, and also secular practices of enrichment, such as singing or even theater plays. However, many of those new concepts did not fit smoothly into the Islamic traditions of the Volga-Ural Muslim domain and challenged the religious

---

[7] A list of books in Russia's Muslim book market in 1883 reflects this situation well. See Gasprinskiy, "Rusya'da Matbuat ve Neşriyât-ı İslâmiye," 247–49.

[8] On the recitation of the Qur'an in various Islamic traditions, see Ingrid Mattson, *The Story of the Qur'an: Its History and Place in Muslim Life* (Malden: Blackwell Publishing, 2008), 76–136. Also see a related prophetic tradition in Muḥammad bin ʿĪsā al-Tirmidhī, *Sunan al-Tirmidhī* (Vaduz, Liechtenstein: Jamʿiyyat al-Maknaz al-Islāmī, 2000), vol. 2, 733.

[9] For an insightful analysis of the functions of maktab education in Central Asia, which is comparable to the situation in the Volga-Ural region, see Khalid, *Jadidism*, 24–28.

[10] Gasprinskiy, "Mebâdî," 252–53. For an enlightening debate on this issue, see Anon., "Bize Qaysı Ġilmler Lazımdır," *Şûra*, 1908.

sensitivities of ordinary Muslims. The contemporaneous progressive literature and later historiography until the end of the Cold War has often discussed this problem within the context of a backlash to progressive reformism by a conservative or "traditionalist" subsection of the ulama (the "Qadimists" or "proponents of the ancient" as the progressive reformists had labeled them), especially in the years of authoritative restoration that followed the Revolution of 1905.[11] In more recent studies, Stéphane Dudoignon complicated this controversy by emphasizing its socioeconomic foundations,[12] and Adeeb Khalid analyzed it in the Central Asian context as a process of redefining Islam in response to modernity.[13] However, analyzing the tensions resulting from this reform movement in the late tsarist period exclusively as a function of contestation for authority between progressive and "traditionalist" Muslim elites conceals a larger and, in my opinion, more significant dynamic: the progressive reformist cohort's alienation from the broader Muslim population. It is the aim of this chapter to bring that dynamic to light.[14]

Reform and religion

Building on the progressive reformist literature of the early twentieth century, some historians have conceptualized progressive reformism among Volga-Ural Muslims as continuing from the critical thinking of the early-nineteenth-century scholars Qursâvî and Utız İmenî, whose ideas, in turn, fit in the context of a global surge of puritanical Islamic revival since the seventeenth century.[15] This approach is valid in the

[11] Among many sources, see İsmâ'îl Gasprinskiy, "Kadimcilik-Ceditçilik," in *İsmail Gaspıralı: Seçilmiş Eserleri II: Fikrî Eserleri*, ed. Yavuz Akpınar (1909; reprint in Latin transcription, Istanbul: Ötüken, 2004), 273–86; Mahmûd Fu'âd, "Mektebleribizniñ Mâliye Ciheti," *Mekteb*, 1913 1 (1): 30–32, and (2): 57–60; Bennigsen and Lemercier-Quelquejay, *Islam in the Soviet*, 36; and Nadir Devlet, *Rusya Türkleri'nin Millî Mücadele Tarihi* (Ankara: Türk Kültürünü Araştırma Enstitüsü, 1985), 123–24.

[12] Stéphane A. Dudoignon, "Qadîmiya as a Historiographical Category: The Question Of Social and Ideological Cleavages Between 'Reformists' and 'Traditionalists' among the Muslims of Russia and Central Asia, in the Early 20th Century," in *Reform Movements and Revolutions in Turkistan: 1900–1924*, ed. Timur Kocaoğlu (Haarlem: SOTA, 2001), 159–77. James H. Meyer, "The Economics of Muslim Cultural Reform: Money, Power, and Muslim Communities in Late Imperial Russia," in *Asiatic Russia: Imperial Power in Regional and International Contexts*, ed. Tomohiko Uyama (New York: Routledge, 2012) fleshes out this argument.

[13] Khalid, *Jadidism*, especially 5–6.

[14] For a theoretical approach to distinguishing between the contestation of authority within an Islamic tradition and moving away from that tradition, see Tuna, "Madrasa Reform," 540–42.

[15] See for instance Kurat, "Kazan Türklerinde," 100–110; Azade-Rorlich, *Volga Tatars*, 48–103; and Ahmet Kanlıdere, *Reform within Islam: The Tajdid and Jadid Movement*

sense that the Volga-Ural region did host a scholarly tradition of puritanical revivalism since the early-nineteenth century,[16] and that many of
the earlier progressive reformers of the region, especially the founders
of reformed madrasas, related their activities to this tradition, particularly
through the connecting link of Mercânî.[17] This link allowed progressive
reformers to claim the legacy of an established tradition, as opposed to
emerging as rootless innovators. Nevertheless, the progressive reforms
did not usher in a process of religious revival in the Volga-Ural region.
They contributed to the creation of a rather large cohort of secularized
intelligentsia within late imperial Russia's fast-changing context,[18] while
the revivalist tradition continued as a parallel yet marginal pursuit among
scholarly elites.

The expansion of European modernity into tsarist Russia did not
teleologically necessitate secularization among its Muslim communities.[19] Modernity could as well elicit non-rejectionist yet still conservative responses,[20] and indeed it did, if we see the conservative ulama, the
so-called Qadimists, not as "reactionaries"[21] but, following Adeeb Khalid's interpretation, as the proponents of a different kind of reform.[22]
After all, this small group of scholars, who coalesced primarily around
the journal *Din ve Ma'îşet*, defined their goal as "preserving religion"
(*din tutuv*),[23] and they turned to Islamic sources, as opposed to European
science and civilization, in order to find solutions to the challenges of a

among the Kazan Tatars, 1809–1917: Conciliation or Conflict? (Istanbul: Eren, 1997). For
general treatments of Islamic revival since the seventeenth century, see Fazlur Rahman,
"Revival and Reform in Islam," in *The Cambridge History of Islam*, ed. P. M. Holt, Ann
K. S. Lambton, and Bernard Lewis (Cambridge: Cambridge University Press, 1977),
632–56; Madeline C. Zilfi, "The Kadizadelis: Discordant Revivalism in Seventeenth-
Century Istanbul," *Journal of Near Eastern Studies*, 1986 45(4): 251–69; and Nehemia
Levtzion and John Obert Voll, *Eighteenth-Century Renewal and Reform in Islam* (Syracuse:
Syracuse University Press, 1987); Fazlur Rahman, *Revival and Reform in Islam: A Study
of Islamic Fundamentalism*, ed. Ebrahim Moosa (Oxford: Oneworld Publications, 2000),
166–203.
[16] For two excellent studies of this tradition, see Kemper, *Sufis und Gelehrte*; and Maraş,
Türk Dünyasında.
[17] See the many entries by these reformist scholars in 'Ubeydullin ed., *Mercânî*, especially
360–602.
[18] Tuna, "Madrasa Reform."
[19] On the relationship between world religions and modernity, see Bayly, *The Birth*,
325–65.
[20] For example, see Muhammad Qasim Zaman, *Modern Islamic Thought in a Radical Age:
Religious Authority and Internal Criticism* (Cambridge: Cambridge University Press,
2012).
[21] Kurat, "Kazan Türklerinde," 160–62.
[22] Khalid, *Jadidism*, 11; and Adeeb Khalid, "Review of DeWeese, Frank, and Dudoignon,"
Kritika: Explorations in Russian and Eurasian History, 2002 3(4): 737.
[23] Maraş, *Türk Dünyasında*, 22.

world in transition. The activity of the progressive youth constituted but one of those challenges.[24] In contrast, the earlier generation of progressive reformers made a deliberate choice to recognize European science and civilization as normative sources, alongside and equal to the Islamic tradition, while their younger followers went further by investing science and civilization with ultimate authority but at the expense of the authority of Islamic sources. Secularization rushed in as a result of these deliberate choices, but we should still note that it was Russia's great transformations in the late tsarist period that expanded the range of options before Russian Muslim reformists, be they conservative or progressive.

Secularization was a subtle process and did not necessarily imply a complete rejection of religion, although that happened as well. Many members of the progressive reformist youth continued to practice Islam and even served as imams, as we have seen earlier in Mahmûd Fuʿâd's example of a selfless village mullah who toiled hard to popularize "knowledge."[25] Therefore, the eminent diaspora historian Akdes Nimet Kurat (1903–1971) could claim in 1966 that although Muslim students who studied at government schools and

received Russian education had become "Europeanized," most of them had not only remained loyal to their "Muslim and Turkic identity" (*Müslümanlık-Türklük*) thanks to family upbringing but had also chosen Turk-Tatar nationalism as a response to Russian nationalism.[26]

Thus, these young men and women had preserved their religious and national identity alike according to Kurat, but we need to note that Kurat still prioritized nationalism over religion by conceptualizing Islam as an attribute of national identity rather than as faith and devotional practice. This prioritization itself was a product of Kurat's own progressive reformist background that did not necessarily reject Islam but challenged its established primacy as the organizing principle of social and personal life in the Muslim domain.[27] By the 1910s, when progressive reformists disagreed and quarreled, they tried discrediting each other with

---

[24] For a study of conservative reformism in the Volga-Ural region, see Muhammetshin, *Tatarskii traditsionalizm*.

[25] See Fuʿâd, "Avil" 154–57 in Chapter 7.

[26] Kurat, "Kazan Türklerinde," 119. Kurat later adds that madrasa students of the Kazan region were gradually becoming similar to the Muslim graduates of government schools too.

[27] On Akdes Nimet Kurat's background, see Şerif Baştav, "Kazan Türklerinden Prof. Dr. Akdes Nimet Kurat," in *Türkiye Cumhuriyeti Devletinin Kuruluş ve Gelişmesine Hizmeti Geçen Türk Dünyası Aydınları Sempozyumu Bildirileri*, ed. Abdulkadir Yuvalı (Kayseri: Erciyes Universitesi, 1996), especially 119–20. For an early-twentieth-century example that illustrates the progressive Muslim subordination of religion to national identity, see Fâtih Seyfi, "Mektebleribizde ʿÎbâdet," *Mekteb*, 1914 2(1): 26.

accusations of not being "true nationalists"[28] while nationalism remained an alien category to most ordinary Muslims who judged people according to perceived standards of piety.[29]

A topsy-turvy world

This realignment of priorities disconnected progressive reformists from the broader Muslim population's long-established repertory of norms and values. A few examples from the Kazan-based and moderately progressive, pedagogical journal *Mekteb* should illustrate this process. Instead of building their cases on Islamic sources, for instance, *Mekteb* authors commonly sought validation in the example of what they considered to be "advanced" or "civilized" nations. This proved particularly convenient for promoting practices that had positive connotations in the pan-European cultural frame but that remained controversial from an Islamic jurisprudential point of view such as music and painting.[30] "The children of advanced (*müteraqqî*) nations experience life in the heavenly harmony of music from a very young age," wrote one *Mekteb* author, Sadri Celâl,[31] and Salâhuddin Kemâluddinof contended: "Civilized nations take immense benefits from painting and pictures."[32] Yet, *Mekteb* authors could turn to models from outside the Muslim domain even to discuss inherently religious matters. Ş. Şeref encouraged Volga-Ural Muslims to celebrate Prophet Muhammad's birthday in gatherings where competent scholars would teach them about the Prophet's exemplary model. Muslims all over the world have long celebrated Prophet Muhammad's birthday in devotional gatherings called *mawlīd* in Arabic or *mevlid* in Turkic.[33] But Şeref would turn to what he called "smart nations," in order to justify his position. "Smart nations," he wrote, "respect their great people, organize festivities for them, and

---

[28] Mahmûd Fuʿâd, "Mekteb mi İşkola mı?," *Mekteb*, 1913 1(10): especially 242.

[29] See NART, f. 92, op. 1, d. 16166, l. 23; Fahreddin, *Ahmed*, 27; Sâbircan bin el-Qurmâşî, "Dinsiz Diyler," *Şûra*, 1914 (16); and Kurat, "Kazan Türklerinde," 122.

[30] On music and painting in Islam, see Osman Şekerci, *İslâm'da Resim ve Heykelin Yeri* (Istanbul: Fatih Gençlik Vakfı, 1974); Thomas Walker Arnold, *Painting in Islam: A Study of the Place of Pictorial Art in Muslim Culture* (Piscataway: Gorgias Press, 2002), especially 1–40; and Khalid Baig, *Slippery Stone: An Inquiry into Islam's Stance on Music* (Garden Grove: Open Mind Press, 2008).

[31] Sadri Celâl, "Bizde Muziqa," *Mekteb*, 1913 1(15): 372.

[32] Salâhuddin Kemâluddinof, "Bizde Resim," *Mekteb*, 1913 1(5): 125.

[33] *Türkiye Diyanet Vakfı İslâm Ansiklopedisi*, 1st edn., s.v. "mevlid." The timing of these celebrations became one of the frequent topics of the Muslim press of the Volga-Ural region after 1905. See Naganawa, "Holidays," 42–44.

express happiness on their birthdays. And our Prophet Muhammad (peace be upon him) is the greatest person of Islam."[34]

Having been immersed in the cultural frame of the Volga-Ural Muslim domain, *Mekteb* authors would sometimes write from a religious point of view too but often in a way that betrayed their alienation from or uneasiness with the established norms and practices of the Islamic tradition. In Kemâluddinof's opinion, for instance, the Islamic injunction against painting did not have an authentic foundation in the Islamic tradition. It resulted from the corruption of "Islam's pure and natural principles" by the ulama or, in Kemâluddinof's words, by "the people who have been overseeing religion among us." To prove his point, Kemâluddinof printed the gravure of a coin with a human effigy and claimed that it was struck during the time of the first four "Rightly Guided Caliphs" (632–61),[35] whose endorsement carries a strong authority in the Sunni Islamic tradition. In reality, however, the Umayyad Caliph 'Abd al-Malik (r. 685–705), whose decision does not carry a similar authority, had struck this coin in order to rival the then prevalent Byzantine coins, and ironically, he had replaced it with a script-only alternative within three years following objections to the use of the human effigy from the Prophet's remaining companions.[36]

At times when Volga-Ural Muslim norms and practices did not meet European-inspired progressive standards, Kemâluddinof was not alone in blaming the mismatch on the corruption of the Volga-Ural Muslims' otherwise "pure" religious beliefs or "national" culture by the ulama. A contributor to *Şûra* wrote in 1914 that "undeserving mullahs" ruined the "ignorant people's" religion "by proclaiming whatever suits their interests as tenets of religion, even if it has no place in religion, and by declaring whatever they do not like incompatible with religion."[37] Another *Mekteb* author, 'Iyâd, claimed that the forefathers of the Volga-Ural Muslims had created melodies that rendered a "great service to civilization," but the mullahs who could not appreciate music for its worth had led to the ruin of this achievement by banning it from maktabs, madrasas, and life in general. Rather than nourishing people's religious feelings and elevating them to the divine, as it once did in the region,

---

[34] Ş. Şeref, "Mevlid Ayı Münasebetiyle," *Mekteb*, 1914 2(2): 29–31.

[35] Kemâluddinof, "Bizde," 125–27.

[36] Anastas al-Karmalī, *Rasā'il fī al-nuqūd al-'arabīyah wa-al-islāmīyah wa-'ilm al-namīyāt* (Cairo: Maktabat al-thaqāfah al-dīniyah, 1987), 40–42. I. Schulze and W. Schulze, "The Standing Caliph Coins of al-Jazira: Some Problems and Suggestions," *Numismatic Chronicle*, 2010 (170): 331–53 provides a useful overview of the controversy on these coins.

[37] "Mullalıkdan Küñil," 1914 (6): 173–74.

'Iyâd lamented, music was now reduced to the level of a mood setter for vulgar entertainment. "Forbidding their own music to Tatar kids has diabolically served to the ruin of national civilization," he declared and asked: "Is it not sufficient to expose the atrocity of this crime that having been expelled from their own house, our national songs and melodies have taken refuge in brothels and beerhouses?"[38]

One can only imagine how this question must have hit the non-progressive ulama – and possibly many of the ordinary Volga-Ural Muslims – as a topsy-turvy representation of the matter. The Volga-Ural Muslims did possess a relatively mature musical heritage by the late nineteenth century,[39] but the permissibility of music, or more precisely musical instruments, has been a controversial issue in the Islamic tradition,[40] and several accounts suggest the existence of a sense of uneasiness among Volga-Ural Muslims about allowing music in the communal space too. Furthermore, in the late tsarist period, alcohol usage and promiscuity had increased noticeably especially among the wealthy urbanites and student cohorts of the region's Muslim population, and musical entertainment, involving a growing body of new music that evolved under Russian influence, often accompanied this kind of behavior. As students danced and drank to the tune of Russian melodies played on the fast-spreading accordion, scholars pushed back by further delegitimizing music and musical instruments in the communal space.[41] And here was 'Iyâd, putting the cart before the horse and the ulama on the spot – suggesting that the ulama's opposition to music was simply a matter of subjective misunderstanding without evidential basis in the Islamic tradition and declaring that the association of musical entertainment with promiscuous behavior among the region's Muslims had resulted from this opposition.

An anonymous article from *Mekteb* titled "Hooliganism and Our Maktabs" illustrates how this topsy-turvy line of thinking could escalate to advocating an almost burlesque reversal of religiously based communal norms while obliviously maintaining an air of piety and identification

---

[38] 'Iyâd, "Millî Kuy ve Muñlarıbız," *Mekteb*, 1914 2(5): 101–3.
[39] For examples of this heritage, see S. G. Rybakov, *Muzyka i pesni uralskikh musulman s ocherkom ikh byta* (St. Petersburg, 1897); and Fatih Urmançiev, *Başlangıcından Günümüze Kadar Türkiye Dışındaki Türk Edebiyatları Antolojisi: Tatar Edebiyatı I*, vol. 17 (Ankara: T.C. Kültür Bakanlığı, 2001), especially 365–68.
[40] Baig, *Slippery*.
[41] On increased alcohol usage and promiscuity, see Kurat, "Kazan Türklerinde," 121–22. On examples of uneasiness about musical entertainment, see İbrâhîmof, *Tercüme-yi Hâlim*, 12–15; and Raif Märdanov, Ramil Miñnullin, and Süleyman Rähimov eds., *Bertugan Butıylar Mädräsäse* (Kazan: Ruhiyat, 1999), 30. For the increased usage of European musical instruments, see Ross, "From the Minbar," 68 and 93.

with the people. The anonymous author of this article begins by complaining about the increased instances of drunkenness and violence among Volga-Ural Muslims and argues that such "hooliganism" did not happen in the old days. Because, the author explains, previously the youth entertained in mixed-gender gatherings where young women's tender emotions assuaged young men's rough impulses. Now that such mixing of genders was "forbidden in the name of the Shariah" (implying that the source of the ban was not the Shariah but its misinterpretation), young men were left to drinking and hooliganism in the absence of the taming influence of their female peers. The solution that the author proposed was using the buildings of new-method maktabs to organize "literary nights" where young men and women could mix and entertain "in a morally acceptable way."[42] Once again, one can only imagine how this line of thinking must have baffled non-progressive readers since the Islamic tradition of the region recognized the mixing of genders in spaces that could potentially facilitate intimacy in and of itself as morally unacceptable.[43]

As some of the criticisms in the above articles from *Mekteb* also indicate, some Volga-Ural Muslims did drink, play music, and engage in promiscuous behavior. They also tolerated gender mixing at varying degrees depending on the circumstances. Communities met such behaviors with complaints, reprobation, ridicule, and also disregard in recognition of the necessities of life.[44] The Kazan merchant İbrâhim Yunusof once caught two young mullahs furtively drinking wine at lunch-time. He wanted to give them a lesson and secretly nailed their shoes to the wooden floor. The scene of two drunk mullahs trying to put their shoes on in a state of clumsy confusion caused a long-lasting joke in Kazan. Yet, the Yunusofs also owned a brewery for a while: business was business.[45] Ğabdul'allâm Hazret, who operated a relatively large madrasa in the Bubi village of the Viatka Gubernia, forbade musical instruments at his madrasa. When students still sneaked them into their sleeping

---

[42] Anon., "Huliganlıq ve Mektebleribiz," in *Mekteb*, 1914 2(3): 66–69.

[43] On contemporary observations and views about gender segregation among Volga-Ural Muslims, see Fuks, *Kazanskie Tatary*, 31–36; and Muhammedzarîf ibn ʿAbdurrahmân, "Edebiyat Kiçesi Nedir?," *Din ve Maʿîşet*, 1910 (16): 251–52. For a scholarly view on the subject, see Damir Iskhakov, *Etnografiia tatarskogo naroda* (Kazan: Magarif, 2004), 118. On gender segregation in the Islamic tradition in general, see Judith E. Tucker, *Women, Family, and Gender in Islamic Law* (Cambridge: Cambridge University Press, 2008), 175–200.

[44] For examples of complaints and reprobation, see *Sbornik tsirkuliarov* [Russian section], 95 in the Tatar-language section; and Fahreddin, *Âsar*, vol. 2, 200–1, 337–38, 357–58, and 384–86.

[45] Sverdlova, *Kupechestva*, 40 and 43.

quarters, however, he preferred to feign ignorance.[46] Zeki Velidî Togan's father, who was a pious scholar, would also pretend ignorance at times when Togan's mother drank a lightly alcoholic beverage made from honey.[47] Finally, while the womenfolk of richer urban families lived a carefully segregated life, peasant women in villages or poorer women in the city who had to work could move around relatively freely, although modesty and a certain degree of gender separation were still expected.[48]

As communal strategies of coping with aberrant behavior, complaints, reprobation, ridicule, and disregard moderated life experience without undermining the society's moral norms. When a madrasa student who furtively played music and perhaps drank alcohol came of age and took a mullah position, he could disavow his earlier behaviors as youthful excesses and uphold the moral standards of his congregation without coming across as duplicitous.[49] Ğabdurreşîd İbrâhim's father could not help drinking, but in his state of drunkenness, he would withdraw to a room and start crying while he pleaded God for forgiveness.[50] Acknowledging aberrant behavior as "sinful" enabled the preservation of norms and values even as people continued to "sin."

The progressive reformists usually carried themselves in an upright manner, worked hard with a sense of self-sacrifice in order to benefit their coreligionists, and avoided impulsive excesses. However, they questioned the very wisdom and validity of the Muslim communities' religiously based moral standards. When they drank, they did not consider it impulsive excess but personal choice.[51] When they played music or broke gender lines on literary nights or at theater plays, they did so with a claim to the legitimacy or even patriotic utility of their actions. Ğabdul'allâm Hazret's two sons, Ğubeydullah and Ğabdullah Bubî, reformed their father's madrasa after 1895. They encouraged students to learn to play at least one musical instrument, such as violin, accordion, or flute, and they also organized musical spectacles, theater plays, and literary nights with the students. When the inhabitants of the village where their madrasa was located objected to theater plays, the two brothers, who had scholarly credentials, tried to convince the villagers by preaching from the mosque pulpit during congregational Friday prayers.[52]

---

[46] Märdanov, Miññullin, and Rähimov eds., *Bertugan*, 30.   [47] Togan, *Hatıralar*, 17–18.
[48] Fuks, *Kazanskie Tatary*, 31–36.
[49] See the case of İşmuhammed bin Zâhid in Chapter 1.
[50] İbrâhimof, *Tercüme-yi Hâlim*, 3.   [51] Togan, *Hatıralar*, 68–73.
[52] Märdanov, Miññullin, and Rähimov eds., *Bertugan*, 43–44. Also see the story of how Zâhide Ahmerova, a young woman of noble origin in Kazan, agreed to perform in a theater play "for the nation's sake." Goldberg, "Tatar Theater," 42.

The Muslim intelligentsia and its alienation

With such endorsement from their scholar teachers, the reformed madrasa students – or the young reformist cohort in general – adopted a completely new way of life that was at odds with the Volga-Ural Muslim repertory of norms and values and, therefore, that alienated them from the region's broader Muslim population. Many members of this cohort studied at madrasas and took positions as village imams or madrasa instructors, but even as they carried the "mullah" title, they did not operate in the traditional ulama networks.[53] Other young progressive reformists taught in village maktabs but did so without a certified mullah position, in a structure separate from the mosque building, and with a new title, *mu'allim*, designating their distinctive function as new-method teachers. The progressive reformist mullahs and the new-method teachers, together with their numerous peers who made a living in various other ways, such as journalists, Russo-Muslim school teachers, white-collar workers, and even lawyers, doctors, and professional revolutionaries, belonged to a new web of relations: a new social class that became increasingly more vocal and visible especially after 1905: the "Muslim intelligentsia."

While the earlier reformers, such as Rızâeddin bin Fahreddin or the founder of the reformed Muhammediye Madrasa in Kazan, Gâlimcan Barudî (1857–1921), usually continued to identify with the ulama, the progressive youth self-consciously marked themselves apart as "intellectuals," or *ziyâlılar* in Turkic and "intelligenty" in Russian. The Russian-language bylaw of the "Muslim Circle of Petersburg Students," a text prepared during the revolutionary tide of 1905 and preserved in Fâtih Kerimî's personal archive, is illustrative in this regard. The authors of this bylaw classify the objectives of the Muslim Circle of Petersburg Students in three categories as regarding the circle's "members," the "intelligentsia," and the "popular mass together with its men of religion (*dukhovenstvo*)." A reading of these objectives indicates that while the authors of the bylaw envisioned the circle's student members as joining the intelligentsia upon graduation, they regarded the ulama and the broader Muslim population as permanent others. "The members," the bylaw stipulated, "are required to maintain active relations with the men

---

[53] On the criticism of early progressive reformist ideas by the younger generation, see Noack, *Muslimischer*, 426–33, and 461–73; and Tuna, "Madrasa Reform." For a study that emphasizes this process in the context of Transoxiana, see Ahmet Salih Bıçakçı, "Bukharan Madrassahs: Usul-i Kadim," in *Reform Movements and Revolutions in Turkistan: 1900–1924*, ed. Timur Kocaoğlu (Haarlem: SOTA, 2001), 135–49.

of religion" in order "to earn the confidence and sympathy" of the people, the "dark mass."[54]

The "Muslim intelligentsia" of the Volga-Ural region, as it evolved in the early twentieth century, comprised a motley group. Until the 1905 Revolution, progressive reformist Muslims in Russia had one major forum to discuss their issues and to follow for guidance: *Tercüman*. Press freedom and political mobilization opened a Pandora's box in the years following the revolution. Many regional and ideological differences arose, further highlighting the otherwise obscure generational split between the earlier reformers and their youthful students. The idea of progress still provided a connecting paradigm for the progressive reformists. However, the pursuit of progress required commitment to a subjectively defined process of improvement rather than to a definite blueprint for the future. While the process of improvement typically implied turning to the contemporaneous examples of European nations and educated Russians, those examples offered not one but many paths to follow. In the end, the pursuit of progress remained a hollow aspiration that could be filled in many different ways, and that is what the Muslim progressive youth of the early twentieth century did.

The generational split between the progressive youth and the earlier reformers usually remained concealed behind the younger generation's display of respect for the age and pioneering role of the earlier reformers. Occasionally, however, the youth's growing impatience with the small-deeds liberalism of Gasprinskiy's generation could burst out as attacks on the new-method from a progressive point of view, ironically, for being "traditionalist." In 1910, for instance, a certain Halîl Ebulhanef started a series of pamphlets, called *The First Step against the New Method*, in which he promised to criticize the Jadidist program from a progressive reformist standpoint.[55] The first work he published in this series was a critical analysis of the new-method alphabet books that were in circulation. The author, who signed his name as Adolf, suggested that the old and the new methods were the same in essence, because they both focused on the improvement of religious and moral character. Therefore, he wrote, the contents of the progressive and the conservative literatures

---

[54] NART, f. 1370, op. 1, d. 1, l. 7. For similar references to a Muslim intelligentsia that stands in distinction to the ulama, see a petition written by thirty-five prominent Volga-Ural Muslims to the mufti of the Orenburg Spiritual Assembly in NART, f. 1370, op. 1, d. 2, ll. 8–9; and an "Address to All Muslims of Russia" in NART, f. 1370, op. 1, d. 1, ll. 23–23ob, both written in 1905.

[55] Halîl Ebulhanef, *Usûl–i Cedîdge Qarşı Birinci Adım* (Kazan: Ürnek Matbaʿası, 1910), i–ii. I was unable to find further publications in this series. Ebulhanef also contributed to *Mekteb*. See Halîl Ebulhanef, "Mekteblerde ʿUlûm-ı Tabiʿiyye," *Mekteb*, 1913 1(1): 28–30.

were also alike. A book by Fahreddin (*Edebli Şâkird*) and another by Barudî (*Tekmîle*), for instance, were both translations of excerpts from earlier Arabic texts according to Adolf's observation. The only difference he found between the new method and the conventional way of instruction was that while proponents of the new method relied on written translations, non-progressive scholars used Arabic-language texts and offered oral translations in class. Otherwise, Adolf stressed, the students of both methods learned the same trivial details in the name of religion and they were both taught to follow the elders blindly in all affairs. The "Jadidists" were no different from the "Qadimists," in his opinion, for they both opposed "the present Tatar intellectuals [*ziyalı*]." Adolf pictured the "Jadidists" as having "declared war on" the intellectuals, fearing that the intellectuals would "harm the new method with [their] ideas." At this point, Adolf started to write with exclamation marks: "As if they reformed the Tatar society in any way! ... To the contrary, they fear reform now ... They are not Jadidists [proponents of the new] ... Now is the time to follow the real new [*cedîd*] without being deceived by the name Jadidist. It is time to reform all of the old life fundamentally."[56]

While the ever-diplomatic Gasprinskiy typically countered such caustic outbursts and the radicalism of young Muslim intellectuals with measured explanations of what he considered to be their ideological fallacies,[57] other members of the earlier generation could not always be as patient. In 1911, a *Şûra* reader, Fettâh Ğadlî, described young Muslim intellectuals as "some members of the youth who sell philosophies" that are "far from being in tandem with the sacred feelings of our people." He wrote:

Although they are very few in number, they are very bold, and they defend their position powerfully ... However, the people do not accept their philosophy, which they express with a language that is a mixture of the Russian and Tatar vocabularies and which they themselves understand only superficially.[58]

Comparably bitter comments by Ğabdurrahmân bin Ğatâullah, a progressive mullah from Kazan who had long settled in Yarkend, may illustrate the regional differences among the Muslim intelligentsia. In 1911, as Ğatâullah approached Kazan during a trip back to the Volga-Ural region, he was astonished to see some Muslims, whom he called "monkey-like

---

[56] Adolf, "Usûl-i Cedîdege", iii–viii . For Mahmûd Fu'âd's rebuttal to a similar attack by İbrâhim Bikqulef on the new-method schools in 1913, see Fu'âd, "Mekteb mi."

[57] See for instance, Gasprinskiy, "Mezheb"; or his many articles on the linguistic unity of Turkic peoples in İsmâ'îl Gasprinskiy, *İsmail Gaspıralı: Seçilmiş Eserleri III: Dil-Edebiyat-Seyahat Yazıları*, ed. Yavuz Akpınar (İstanbul: Ötüken, 2008), 25–199.

[58] Fettâh Ğadlî, "İslâmlar Arasında," 1911 (19): 588.

imitators," in "the clothing of European people."[59] The cosmopolitan-
ism of Kazan's youth was too much even for Fahreddin, who otherwise
considered the change of clothing styles in time to be a natural process.[60]
In 1904, following an entry in Âsar on an early-nineteenth-century
scholar who had diligently copied books all his life, he wrote with resent-
ment and sarcasm:

> The children of such fathers who burnt burning sticks [for light] and wrote two
> hundred volumes of books should have been engineers, who filled Siberia with
> railways, and teachers, who filled the entire world with books and knowledge.
> Alas, they became wild animals in the guise of human beings ... Here, I am
> referring to the Muslims of the Ural region to which my tribe and people belong.
> May the Muslims in the Kazan region and Kazan city not be offended by my
> words ... They are exempted from these words since they have progressed in
> accordance with the time! It is said that one cannot tell their gold jewelry, fine
> fur caps, walking canes, expensive watches, bicycles, and summer houses even
> from those of the French. Moreover, some young bays and owners of fashionable
> beards are said to deserve even the praise of independent observers who are found
> in café chantants and who say: "They are so perfect, so exemplary that one wants
> to become a Tatar." This is what one calls progress![61]

Perhaps a counterpart to this sarcastic view was a verse from Ğabdullah
Tuqay, who lived in Kazan while many of his friends accepted offers
from the Ramiyef brothers' press enterprise and left for Orenburg in the
years following the 1905 Revolution. Tuqay, a socialist who considered
working for big money a betrayal to the cause, wrote in a poem that soon
became controversial and famous:

> The gold of the Ramiyefs lifts the youth of Kazan away.[62]

The ideological spectrum of the progressive youth spanned from various
forms of nationalism to various forms of socialism and also involved
eclectic mixtures of the two. One of Gasprinskiy's most cherished
aspirations was the unity of Russia's Muslims as indicated by the motto
he chose for Tercüman in 1912: "Unity in Language, Thought, and
Action."[63] Yet, while those who remained close to Gasprinskiy's ideas
imagined a widespread Turkic (Türk) nation, many young Muslim intellectuals espoused ethnically or regionally defined nationalisms at the

---

[59] el-Kazanî, Üç Aylık, 12.
[60] Fahreddin, "Kiyümler," 1915 (8): 225–28, (9): 258–60, 10: 289–92.
[61] Fahreddin, Âsar, vol. 1, 456–57.   [62] Bäşiri, "Tarixta," 147–49.
[63] On Gasprinskiy's views about unity, see Lazzerini, "Ismail Bey," especially 207–29; and
Hakan Kırımlı, "İsmail Bey Gaspıralı ve 'Birlik' Kavramı Üzerine," in İsmail Bey
Gaspıralı İçin, ed. Hakan Kırımlı (Ankara: Kırım Türkleri Gençlik ve Yardımlaşma
Derneği, 2004), 55–70. Gasprinskiy used this motto for the first time when Tercüman
became a daily newspaper on October 7, 1912.

expense of wider unity.[64] On the left side of the aisle, one could find both Socialist Revolutionaries, who often combined socialism with nationalist ideals, and Social Democrats.[65] Especially during the 1905 Revolution, the students of some of the reformed madrasas and the Kazan Tatar Teachers' School fraternized with the revolutionary youth and became unruly. The reformed madrasa students challenged their teachers to offer more secular curricula and also to involve students in the administration of their madrasas.[66] The teachers' school students, on the other hand, escaped from the school premises and participated in revolutionary activities so often that the school's pedagogical council had to cease classes for two months, expel all students, and require them to reapply for admission.[67]

The new ideologies, revolutionary activity, and the "Europeanized" manners of the progressive youth were unfamiliar and usually repulsive to ordinary Muslims. The pedagogical council of the Kazan Tatar Teachers' School noted in October 1905 that as their students participated in revolutionary rallies with red flags in their hands and sang revolutionary songs together with reformed madrasa students, "the Tatars of the bazaar such as salesmen, small traders, workers, etc." had begun to express their anger about the situation. Rumors were circulating that these Muslim urbanites would physically harm the school, causing the school's pedagogical council to rush their decision for temporary closure.[68]

Radloff had recognized the possibility of this alienation early in the 1870s when he planned on teaching secular subjects and the Russian language to Muslim students at the Kazan Tatar Teachers' School. As a

---

[64] See the illustrative debate over the choice of Turkic vs. Tatar identities in *Şûra*: Ğâlimcan İbrâhimof, "Biz Tatarmız," *Şûra*, 1011 (8): 236–38; and Türkoğlu, "Biz Türkmiz," *Şûra*, 1911 (8): 238–41, (11): 327–29, 1912 (1): 19–21, (2): 55–56, and (3): 79–80; and Tataroğlu, Ali Akış, Saadet Çağatay, and Ğâlimcan İbrâhimof, "'Biz Kim?' Bahisi," *Şûra*, 1912 (9): 267–68. Also see Daniel Evan Schafer, *"Building Nations and Building States: The Tatar-Bashkir Question in Revolutionary Russia, 1917–1920"* (Ph. D. Dissertation, University of Michigan, 1995).

[65] For two prominent examples, see the biographies of Hüseyin Yamaşev and Ğayaz İshaqî in Khusain Khasanovich Khasanov, *Revolutsioner-internatsionalist: zhizn i deiatel'nost' bolshevika Khusaina Iamasheva* (Kazan: Tatarskoe Knizhnoe Izdatel'stvo, 1971); Tahir Çağatay, Ali Akış, Saadet Çağatay, and Hasan Agay eds., *Muhammed Ayaz İshaki: Hayatı ve Faaliyeti* (Ankara: Ayyıldız Matbaası, 1979); and Flun, *Gayaz İsxaki.*

[66] Galimdzhan İbragimov, *Tatary v revoliutsii 1905 goda* (Kazan: Izd-vo TS, 1926), especially 179–94; Khusain Khasanovich Khasanov, *Revoliutsia 1905–1907 gg v Tatarii* (Moscow: Nauka, 1965), 313–19; Ämirxan, "Möhämmädiyä," 22–24; and Märdanov, Miñnullin, and Rähimov eds., *Bertugan*, 137–38.

[67] NART, f. 142, op. 1, d. 72, ll. 116–17ob printed in Gorokhova ed. *Kazanskaia*, 166–170.

[68] Ibid.

precaution, he had required the teachers' school students to observe prayers and other Muslim rituals, attend congregational prayers at the mosque on Fridays, and maintain the "external appearance and outfit of a true Muslim." He and the other teachers' school administrators remained cognizant of the fact that each of these religiously defined acts, or their absence, carried a normative value in the social imaginary of the Volga-Ural Muslims. Conscious or unconscious failure to show due respect to those values could easily discredit the school, or any party that transgressed for that matter.[69] However, a police report submitted to the governor of Kazan in 1889 indicates that by the end of the 1880s, the teachers' school students had already made a reputation for drinking vodka, smoking, not fasting, rarely attending the mosque, and behaving in a manner that the "simple folk" among Muslims found to be inappropriate.[70] In 1900, a graduate of the teachers' school who taught at a Russo-Muslim school in a Muslim village of the Ufa Gubernia complained that the villagers followed "each of his steps with suspicion." "The following curious occasion happened in my short experience of teaching," he wrote:

I read a booklet about savages (*dikar'*) in the classroom and explained: "Earlier, we were all savages like this, then we became half savages, and finally, we started to become somewhat similar to humans. There will be a time when we will have no difference from the real enlightened people that we call Europeans. Russia is also a European country, but only less enlightened."

I finished my reading about savages in this way.

I was sitting that night peacefully and enjoying the hot samovar. Suddenly, the figure of a furious old man appeared at the door. I recognized him as N., a Muslim man well respected by all the villagers.

"Will you make our children '*Uros*' [Russian]? What do you mean that we are savages? Are we an '*İvrupiiskii*' [European] country after all?" – stood the enraged old man at the door.

Before I was able to open my mouth, the figure of the honorable guardian of the old man who was hiding behind the door slammed it with a big noise.

Now, they took the grandson of that old man from the school. The old man ceased to recognize me [in the street]. And the grandson, of course not without pressure from the old man, does not greet me anymore.

I have one more enemy.[71]

As reformed madrasa students joined ranks with the students of the Kazan Tatar Teachers' School or with Muslim students at other imperial

---

[69] NART, f. 92, op. 1, d. 16166, l. 23.   [70] NART, f. 1, op. 3, d. 7797, ll. 4–5.
[71] Gorokhova ed. *Kazanskaia*, 96.

institutions of education, the Volga-Ural Muslims watched them with suspicion too.[72] In the 1890s, when Ğabdulganî Hüseyinof financed the organization of a summer school for new-method teachers in Qargali and opened new-method maktabs in various locations, rumors spread suggesting that he was indeed a hidden missionary and that his money was coming from missionaries.[73] Fahreddin relates that many Volga-Ural Muslims prayed for Ahmed Hüseyinof's death as he opened new-method maktabs and supported madrasa reform.[74] Given this environment of suspicion, even a seemingly simple item that the progressive reformists introduced like blackboards in classrooms could raise concerns about religiosity since some Muslims found erasing the name of God from the blackboard with a dirty sponge sacrilegious.[75]

Despite this environment of suspicion and the overall disconnect between the progressive Muslim intelligentsia and ordinary Muslims, the progressive intellectuals thought of themselves as serving and even representing the "people" or the "nation" (millet) – however one would define it. Yet, similar to Russian populists in the early Great Reforms era, the people often rejected the young progressive reformists.[76] In an illustrative case from 1903, a Muslim noblewoman, Sûfiyebike Canturina, endowed 200 desiatinas of land to a village mosque in the Ufa Guberniia. She allocated the income from thirty desiatinas of the property to pay for the two mullahs serving at the mosque and designated the remainder for general maintenance and supporting students in an affiliated madrasa. Then, she brought several new-method teachers to the village and asked the old mullahs to limit their instruction to the older students so that the new-method teachers could start teaching younger kids with a reformed madrasa curriculum. When the two mullahs opposed Canturina's initiative, the disagreement quickly escalated into a serious conflict involving the villagers who sided with the old mullahs. The tension continued for several years until the villagers finally resolved the issue for good by chasing the new-method teachers out of the village in late 1907.[77]

---

[72] See Mahmûd Fu'âd's example of a hardworking reformist mullah in Fu'âd, "Avıl," 154–57 in Chapter 7. Also see the letters of two progressive reformist mullahs to Fâtih Kerimî in NART, f. 1370, op. 2, d. 11; and NART, f. 1370, op. 1, d. 20, ll. 21–23; also quoted in detail in Meyer, "Turkic Worlds," 107–9.

[73] M. V. Gainetdinov, "Gani Hösäyinov häm yana mäktäb öçin köriş," in Narodnoe prosveshcheniie u Tatar v dooktiabr'skii period, ed. R. M. Amirkhanov and I. A. Giliazov (Kazan: Kazan IIaLI im. G. Ibragimova, 1992), 134–41.

[74] Fahreddin, Ahmed, 32–33.   [75] NART, f. 92, op. 2, d. 19435, ll. 12–14ob.

[76] On the populists' relations with the people, see Richard Wortman, The Crisis of Russian Populism (London: Cambridge University Press, 1967), especially 1–34.

[77] Azamatov, Iz istorii, 64–66.

Ulama as scapegoats

Such defeats did not lead progressive reformists to reevaluate their alienation from the norms and values of the people that they wanted to serve. Instead, in a manner similar to the reactions of imperial agents to the Muslim peasants' resistance to Russo-Muslim schools, the progressive reformists blamed mullahs who did not subscribe to progressive ideas for agitating the people against reform. The people would embrace progressive reform initiatives, they thought, had it not been for the reactionary mullahs. Mahmûd Fu'âd wrote: "The entire Tatar nation sees its salvation in the reform and improvement (teraqqî) of its maktabs. That means, the ideal of all of our people is the continuation, reform, and improvement of these maktabs."[78] Opposing the new-method, Fu'âd wrote in an earlier article, would amount to "betraying the nation and religion."[79]

Yet, not opposing was also insufficient; the progressive reformists expected the ulama to contribute actively to the "reform and improvement" of Muslim schooling. A series of readers' letters published in Şûra in 1913 and 1914 discussing the position of mullahs in the Volga-Ural region illustrate how the progressive reformists expected the ulama to actively support their reform programs. Becoming a mullah, according to one author, Ahund Ğabdulhâdî el-Mecidî, was a perfect opportunity "to serve the people." He wrote: "Good mullahs open schools, teach religion and literacy to all of the children (girls and boys) in the neighborhood, [and] open people's minds."[80] Ahmed Latîf Bikqulef asserted that among the occupations that young Muslims could choose, the most promising one was becoming a mullah, for it came "closest to achieving the goal of ameliorating the people's social and economic circumstances while also improving their religion and morals."[81] Bikqulef's representation was not grossly incompatible with the mullahs' traditionally accepted duties, but some Şûra readers had a notably broad understanding of what the mullahs could and should do in order to improve the Muslims' social and economic circumstances. Feyzürrahman Raqay wrote: "It is the knowledgeable mullahs who initiate mutual aid societies in villages. Although not many, there are mullahs who set an example to the villagers by

---

[78] Fu'âd, "Mekteb mi," 239.   [79] Fu'âd, "Mektebleribizniñ," (1): 31.
[80] "Mullalıkdan Küñil," 1913 (20): 622–23.
[81] "Mullalıkdan Küñil," 1914 (8): 241–42. For another similar expression, see "Mullalıkdan Küñil," 1914 (6): 169–71.

improving gardens and introducing beehives too."[82] Another reader,
Ğabdullah Bigî, objected to defining the mullahs' responsibilities in such
a broad way and wrote: "If we ask [the mullahs] to deal with trade, banks,
and agriculture in order to set examples for the people, their duty will
become too big and the product of their works will look too small." Yet,
even Bigî considered it incumbent upon the mullahs to inform their
congregations that Islam was "not an obstacle before progress and
advancement (terakkî ve te'âlî)."[83] Perhaps, the mullahs did not have to
lead the people in all arenas of life, but the progressive reformists expected
them to espouse the progressive cause at the minimum.

When non-progressive scholars stayed aloof to reform or, in some
cases, actively opposed it, the progressive reformists attacked them with
a barrage of derision in the print media. Another *Şûra* reader, Seyyid Şerif
Cihanşin, wrote:

> The national press looks at [the mullahs] from above. You cannot find a page that
> does not reproach the mullahs. Journals of satire are full of their pictures. Wall
> calendars make fun of them every other day if not every day. Our national novels
> [and] theaters are filled with their criticism. Our young new-method teachers
> always [teach] children about [the mullahs'] faults.[84]

Hundreds of satirical cartoons published in the Baku-based illustrated
journal *Molla Nasreddin*, which circulated throughout the empire after
1906, epitomized such attacks on the ulama by portraying non-progressive
mullahs as dark, parochial, ignorant, greedy, and intimidating figures.
Molla Nasreddin's cartoonists tended to target the Shiite scholars of the
South Caucasus region relatively more than the Sunnite ulama in the rest
of the empire, but this distinction lost significance beyond the South Caucasus. In November 1911, for instance, *Molla Nasreddin*'s cover portrayed
a fat Shiite mullah who was pleasantly holding his big belly and expressing
gratefulness to God for being able to feed himself by reciting elegies at
funerals. Next to his figure was an emaciated and contemplative Sunnite
mullah with a book in his hand (Figure 10). When this issue of *Molla
Nasreddin* was featured in the annual publication fair of St. Petersburg in
1911, an author who reported about the fair in *Şûra* narrated his amusement
upon seeing the illustration of the Shiite mullah but did not bother to
mention the picture of the Sunnite mullah that conveyed a positive image.[85]

As a matter of fact, the Sunnite reformists portrayed non-progressive
Sunnite scholars exactly as the Shiite mullah on *Molla Nasreddin*'s cover.
Ahund Ğârifullah Kiköf, who contributed to the *Şûra* discussion about

---

[82] "Mullahkdan Küñil," 1914 (1): 18–21.   [83] "Mullahkdan Küñil," 1914 (2): 44.
[84] "Mullahkdan Küñil," 1914 (3): 73–75.   [85] el-Hamdi, "Matbu'at," 1011 (6): 191.

Figure 10 The cover of the 41st issue of *Molla Nasreddin* in 1911.

the position of mullahs, wanted "ignorant mullahs who [did] not know
the world or the religion" to vanish.[86] Even as he criticized the negative
portrayal of the ulama in the "national press," another *Şûra* contributor,

---

[86] "Mullalıkdan Küñil," 1914 (8): 239.

Figure 11 Şihâbuddin Mercânî.

Hüccetülhakîm Mahmûdof, proclaimed that if the mullahs wanted to restore their prestige, they had to stop being like the "dignitaries (*hazrets*) with big stomachs and big turbans who sell sophistries."[87]

Thus, in the Muslim intelligentsia's discourse against non-progressive scholars, the very signs of piety in the Volga-Ural Islamic tradition such as large, Bukharan-style turbans and long robes, which Radloff had required from the Kazan Tatar Teachers' School students and Mercânî had worn to the end of his life, had turned into indications of presumed deceitfulness (see Figure 11). The ulama did not epitomize piety any more, according to the progressive authors, but showed it off. If some mullahs opposed the new method, this just meant that they were ignorant of the new method's benefits or jealous about its achievements, and if not that, they were concerned about losing income, i.e. the charities of their congregations, to the new-method teachers.[88]

---

[87] "Mullalıkdan Küñil," 1914 (5): 135–36.

[88] Among many examples, see Kerimî, *Bir Şakird*; el-Kazanî, *Üç Aylık*; Âhund el-Mes'ûdî, "Tertibli Mektebge Başlab Qarşuçıları Kimler?," *Mekteb*, 1913 1(7): 173–75; and Fu'âd, "Mektebleribizniñ," (1): 30–32, and (2): 57–60.

For many members of the ulama, such attacks remained a distant nuisance that they did not need to worry about as long as they stayed away from the progressive publications. In regions where Muslim intellectuals showed a meager presence, the ulama dismissed the new-method as a superficial and passing experiment.[89] In other regions, many mullahs approached the new method not as a matter of ideological preference but as a practical contribution to their teaching functions. They used new-method techniques and, when available, materials selectively, as they felt comfortable with them.[90] A smaller group of non-progressive scholars, whom we may refer to as the "conservative reformists," challenged progressive reformists in the print media, primarily in *Din ve Ma'işet* but also with separate publications such as İşmuhammed bin Dinmuhammed's numerous works.[91] And finally, in the years following the 1905 Revolution, when imperial authorities started to clamp down on progressive activists with suspicions of separatism – as we shall see more in the coming chapters – some non-reformist mullahs tried to eliminate rivalry from progressive reformists by denouncing them to the police or to various government offices, including the spiritual assembly.[92]

The conservative reformist opposition annoyed the progressive reformists while the denunciations hurt them, and both responses sharpened their attacks on the non-progressive ulama further. The result was a battle of slurs fought in print between the progressive and conservative reformists. By 1909, even Gasprinskiy was complaining about the lack of understanding between the two parties and the superficial nature of their disputes. He wrote:

Our Jadidists attack the Qadimists very severely. Our Qadimists do not let this go either and respond with a bigger effort. The two sides come to a point where they cannot understand each other, and the people (*cema'at*) are left without knowing what to do.[93]

In 1913, Mahmûd Fu'âd raised a similar concern in *Mekteb* and suggested that resolving this controversy required instituting more predictable ways

---

[89] Frank, *Muslim Religious Institutions*, 248–49; and Frank and Usmanov eds., *Materials*, 2–3.

[90] See in Chapter 7.

[91] For a list of İşmuhammed bin Dinmuhammed's publications, some of which were printed in *Din ve Ma'işet*, see Muhammetshin, *Tatarskii traditsionalizm*, 156–62. For sample anti-progressive articles from *Din ve Ma'işet*, see Muhammed el-Sâdıq el-Osmânî, "Mûsa Bigiyef'ge Reddiye," *Din ve Ma'işet*, 1910 (2): 22–25; Anon., "Hankirman İmamlarınıñ Reddiyesi," *Din ve Ma'işet*, 1910 (5): 70; and Anon., "Raport," *Din ve Ma'işet*, 1910 (16): 250–51.

[92] Meyer, "The Economics," especially 259–62.

[93] Gasprinskiy, "Kadimcilik," 273–78. For a similar and later remark in the Muslim press, see Patinskiy, "Millî Matbû'atımız," *Şûra*, 1915 (20): 630–31.

of paying the village mullahs and new-method teachers. Because, he reasoned, when a new-method teacher moved into a village, the villagers started to divert some of their charity to the teacher, therefore reducing the village mullah's income.[94]

Conclusion

The problem with such analyses offered by early-twentieth-century progressive authors or the historiographic studies that build on such analyses is that they deny content to the dispute and voice to the non-progressive ulama along with the Volga-Ural region's broader Muslim population.[95] Ordinary Volga-Ural Muslims did not passively stand by and wait for the print battles of the progressive and conservative factions to come to a resolution so that they would know whom to follow. Neither did they instinctively long for progress as a neutral proposition. As the Catherinian imperial boundaries, which had long kept Volga-Ural Muslims at a mediated distance from outside influences, eroded in late imperial Russia and as the comfort zone of the Volga-Ural Muslim domain gradually blurred into the imperial and pan-European domains, most ordinary Muslims wanted to preserve the norms and values that they had inherited from their ancestors.

The foremost predicament of the progressive reformists was that they challenged those norms and values and therefore failed to enlist large segments of the Muslim population on their side. The non-progressive mullahs' apathy or opposition to the progressive cause was just the tip of this deep iceberg: a side note to the more serious problem of alienation from the broader Muslim population. Yet it was still a significant side note, because more than representing the pushback of a materially constricted social class, the ulama's opposition reflected their inherent function as custodians of the Islamic tradition from which the Volga-Ural Muslim norms and values had long originated. The young Volga-Ural Muslim intellectuals jeopardized the progressive movement's ability to transform the broader Muslim population by challenging those norms and values and, therefore, moving away from the cultural epicenter of the Volga-Ural Muslim domain.

Historical experience offers many examples of small but determined and dedicated networks of activists who mobilize large and initially antagonistic population groups and eventually transform their way of life and thinking. However, this typically calls for more than mere

---

[94] Fuʾâd, "Mektebleribizniñ," (1): 30–32, and (2): 57–60.
[95] For instance, see Dudoignon, "The Question"; and Meyer, "The Economics."

contestation of authority within the existing social fabric. It requires enlisting governmental power on the side of the activist cause either through a metamorphosis of power dynamics, as in the examples of the Bolshevik and Kemalist takeovers in the Soviet Union and modern Turkey, or through the backing of existing power structures, as in the American federal government's support for the Civil Rights Movement in the 1960s. The Central Asian Jadidists too achieved some of their goals by infusing local revolutionary discourse with their progressive ideas and functionalizing state power to promote them in the early Soviet period.[96] The Volga-Ural region's progressive Muslim intellectuals in late tsarist Russia, on the other hand, contested the ulama's authority within the Volga-Ural Muslim domain but did not have access to governmental power. Their efforts still bore results, but as we shall see in the following chapters, primarily in the sense that their vocal presence in the imperial domain contributed to the government's increasingly more heavy-handed treatment of Volga-Ural Muslims by stoking the suspicions of tsarist officials.

---

[96] Marianne Kamp, *The New Woman in Uzbekistan: Islam, Modernity, and Unveiling under Communism* (Seattle: University of Washington Press, 2006), especially 32–52.

9   Imperial paranoia

The Muslim press, as it is probably known to you, belongs completely to the Muslims and it serves as a glaring mouthpiece for the ideas and tendencies that are promoted by the Muslim intelligentsia. Since the tendencies of the Muslim intelligentsia pass to the broader masses of the Muslim population in the most diverse ways and the most persistent forms, the police officers have to familiarize themselves with the above mentioned tendencies of the Muslim intelligentsia so that we can come closer to shedding light on the Muslim movement, which, unfortunately, as far as I am convinced, has not been understood as necessary yet.[1]   From the Governor of Kazan, Mikhail Vasil'evich Strizhevskii to Police Masters and Chiefs in the Kazan Gubernia, 1911

The Russian empire treated confessions as administrative categories.[2] Robert Crews has highlighted this practice within a "paradigm of toleration" and has cautioned that toleration, as introduced into Russian imperial practice officially by Catherine II, "did not mean official indifference or neutrality toward non-Orthodox religious affairs." Rather, it entailed relating to each faith depending on "its utility to the state."[3] A practical implication of this utilitarian approach, somewhat obscured in the narrative of Crews, was that as the Russian monarchs and most state functionaries identified with Orthodox Christianity; the rights of all other confessions started where the interests of Orthodoxy ended. Concerns of stability moderated the initiatives of the Orthodox Church at times but not a genuine care for the interests of other confessions.[4] As estates were unequal so were confessions, and Islam ranked regressively lower in Russia's hierarchy of religions by the early twentieth century.

The image that progressive Muslim intellectuals projected to the imperial domain, primarily through the press, had an important role in this regression. Their energy and jubilant activism, especially in the

---

[1] NART, f. 1, op. 4, d. 6189, l. 3.   [2] See Chapter 3.
[3] Crews, "Empire," 50–83, quotes from 57–58. Also see, Crews, *For Prophet*; and Dolbilov, "Russifying Bureaucracy," especially 113–15.
[4] Werth, "Coercion," 543–69.

relatively liberal and liberating atmosphere of the years following the
1905 Revolution irritated the officials and self-appointed agents of the
empire. Yet, the liberal atmosphere of 1905 started to fade into an
authoritarian regime after June 1907, when Pyotr Arkadievich Stolypin,
Nicholas II's Chairman of the Council of Ministers, dissolved the
Second State Duma and launched a concerted pushback against the tide
of revolution.[5] This pushback reinforced a long-existing alliance against
Muslim activism between the state establishment and the Volga-Ural
region's Orthodox missionary circles.[6] Stuck in the conservative spin
that the concept of unmediated governance had acquired in the 1860s,[7]
the members of this alliance believed in the possibility and ultimate
necessity of molding Russia's many peoples into ideal subjects for the
empire. Frustratingly, however, after many decades of effort and investment since Count Tolstoi and his advisors had first designed schools to
mold ideal subjects from Muslims in the 1870s, the Muslim image that
progressive Muslim intellectuals projected into the imperial domain
hardly matched the missionary-state alliance's standards of ideal
subjects.

Meanwhile, a growing number of Russian nationalists perceived the
assertiveness of non-Russian minorities, including the Volga-Ural
Muslims, as a challenge to Great Russian primacy in the empire. Fueled
by a sense of indignation, they promoted teaching the Russian language
to non-Russians more vigorously in order to bring them closer to the
"Russian core," while the missionaries continued to highlight the utility
of Orthodox indoctrination for the same purpose. Hence, the nationalist
and missionary factions hardly saw eye to eye in their suggested solutions
to the "Muslim question," but their anxieties about the potential dangers
of Muslim activism converged.[8] Until 1907, the government generally
maintained its calm even as it worked closely with the missionaries on

---

[5] On this pushback, see Ascher, *Authority Restored*. For a survey of government policies
regarding Muslims in this period, see Noack, *Muslimischer*, 350–93.

[6] On this alliance, see Wayne Dowler, "Pedagogy and Politics: Origins of the Special
Conference of 1905 on Primary Education for Non-Russians in the East," *Nationalities
Papers*, 1998 26(4): 761–75; Robert P. Geraci, "Russian Orientalism at an Impasse:
Tsarist Education Policy and the 1910 Conference on Islam," in *Russia's Orient:
Imperial Borderlands and Peoples, 1700–1917*, ed. Daniel Brower and Edward J. Lazzerini
(Bloomington: Indiana University Press, 2001), 138–61; and Geraci, "Russian
Orientalism," 264–308.

[7] See Chapter 3.

[8] Dowler, *Classroom and Empire*, 160–87 and 215–34; Robert P. Geraci, "Going Abroad or
Going to Russia? Orthodox Missionaries in the Kazakh Steppe," in *Of Religion and
Empire: Missions, Conversion, and Tolerance in Tsarist Russia*, ed. Robert P. Geraci and
Michael Khodarkovsky (Ithaca: Cornell University Press, 2001), 274–310; and
Campbell, *Muslim Question*, 137–94.

the affairs of non-Russians in the Volga-Ural region. But as Stolypin overturned the revolutionary tide during this year and conservative voices gained the upper hand in imperial governance, nationalist pressures on the missionary-state alliance increased, and together, the government and its conservative allies in society slipped into a state of paranoia. The following offers an analysis of the sources and policy implications of this paranoia and points out how paranoid perceptions and responses ultimately hurt the tsarist state by hampering its ability to understand, relate to, and benefit from the empire's Muslim subjects.

The missionary-state alliance

Mikhail Dolbilov suggests that the "Russifying bureaucracy" (i.e. those who implemented the policies of molding ideal subjects) in the tsarist empire's northwestern territories habitually focused on "a symbolic emphasis on completion" rather than "the dynamic of change," and therefore, often lost trust in the processes of Russification that they had introduced as imperial projects.[9] Robert Geraci suggests that this was the attitude of "many Russians" with regard to "the Russification of the Tatars."[10] On closer look, we might see that until the late 1880s, the russifying bureaucrats of the Volga-Ural region, especially the MNP officials, *did* focus on the process, and they remained hopeful about the eventual Russification of Muslims – including Tatars – through schooling. Radloff played a key role in maintaining this optimism. Even when he left Kazan for an academic position in St. Petersburg in 1884, his frustration reflected the curtailment of his authority more than the resistance of Muslims to Russo-Muslim schools.[11] Alternatively, Nikolai Ivanovich Il'minskii and the Orthodox missionary circle that coalesced around his ideas maintained that the Volga-Ural Muslims were too resistant to Christian suggestion to justify being targeted for immediate russificatory projects,[12] but they did not dismiss the process of russifying Muslims entirely either. Rather, they thought that the Volga-Ural Muslims'

---

[9] Mikhail Dolbilov, "Russification and the Bureaucratic Mind in the Russian Empire's Northwestern Region in the 1860s," *Kritika: Explorations in Russian and Eurasian History*, 2004 5(2): 247.

[10] Geraci, *Window*, 248. [11] See Chapter 4.

[12] There were other missionaries in the Volga-Ural region who disagreed with this position, but they were less influential. See Geraci, *Window*, 86–115; and Saime Selenga Gököz, *Yevfimiy Aleksandroviç Malov: İdil-Ural'da İslam Karşıtı Rus Misyon Siyaseti* (Ankara: KÖKSAV, 2007). Il'minskii and his followers erroneously considered Kazakhs as only nominally Muslim, and therefore, they did target Kazakhs for long-term cultural transformation. See Alektorov, "Iz istorii," 154–91. On the confusions about the religion of Kazakhs, see Frank, *Muslim Religious Institutions*, 274–313.

commitment to and immersion in the Islamic tradition had to be weakened first before they could become subjects of direct Russification.[13]

That said, the immediate and primary concern of Il'minskii and his followers regarding Muslims in Russia was the influence of Volga-Ural Muslims and especially the Tatars over the empire's other non-Russian peoples. Il'minskii and his followers founded an umbrella organization, the Brotherhood of St. Gurii, to provide schooling and church services to animist and recently baptized non-Russian peoples and repeatedly pointed fingers to the influence of Volga-Ural Muslims as large numbers of baptized non-Russians in the region forsook Orthodoxy for Islam throughout the nineteenth and the early twentieth centuries.[14] Not only Il'minskii and his followers but also Russian Orthodox missionaries in general dreaded Muslim influence over other non-Russian peoples so much that they imagined a "war with Muhammadanism" (*bor'ba s magometanstvom*) as a necessary extension of their missionary – and russificatory – work. The more prosperous did Muslim communities appear in Russia, often as observed from the activities of the Muslim intelligentsia, the more hawkishly the missionaries as well as secular nationalist circles wished, advised, and demanded government officials to restrict the Muslims' margin of movement. Supposedly, such restrictions would limit the Muslims' cultural affluence, undermine their commitment to the Islamic tradition, and prepare the ground for their future Russification while also saving other non-Russian peoples from Muslim influences.[15]

Advised by missionaries such as Il'minskii and conservative academics such as Vasilii Vasil'evich Grigor'ev, the Russian administration presumed the existence of a "Muslim question" in Russia at least from the 1860s on.[16] Bureaucrats usually exercised caution in approaching

---

[13] See Chapter 3 for more on this.

[14] Sophy Bobrovnikoff, "Moslems in Russia," *The Moslem World*, 1911 1(1): 5–31; Kreindler, "Educational Policies"; Werth, *At the Margins*, 147–99; and Johnson, "Imperial Commission."

[15] On the attitudes of the region's Orthodox missionaries about Volga-Ural Muslims, see Kreindler, "Educational Policies", 102–12; Geraci, *Window*, 107–15, and 264–308; Werth, *At the Margins*, especially 178–99; and Tuna, "Gaspirali v. Il'minskii," 265–89. For contemporary references to "war with Muhammadanism," see Nikolai Ivanovich Il'minskii, "Iz neizdannykh pisem N. I. Il'minskogo," *Sotrudnik bratstva sviat. Guriia*, 1909 (December 12): 24–32; A. Semenov, "Vozmozhna li bor'ba s Islamom i kakimi sredstvami," *Sotrudnik bratstva sviat. Guriia*, 1909 (December 25): 54–57; Bishop Andrei, "Krupnaia novost' v dele inorodcheskogo Prosveshcheniia," *Sotrudnik bratstva sviat. Guriia*, 1911 (February 6): 83–89; and Geraci, *Window*, 283.

[16] Daniel Brower, "Islam and Ethnicity: Russian Colonial Policy in Turkestan," in *Russia's Orient: Imperial Borderlands and Peoples, 1700–1917*, ed. Daniel Brower and Edward J. Lazzerini (Bloomington: Indiana University Press, 1997), especially 117–18; and Elena I. Campbell, "The Muslim Question in Late Imperial Russia," in *Russian Empire: Space,*

measures that could incite the Muslim population or damage Russia's foreign image as a multiconfessional empire. They viewed the Muslim question primarily as a religious matter that needed to be dealt with within the paradigm of enlightenment without escalating to a matter of security.[17] However, as imperial officials lost composure in the vortex of the unsettling events that marked the turn of the twentieth century for Russia, their caution gave way to a hawkish approach, therefore bringing officials and missionary circles into closer alliance and cooperation. A special conference that the MNP convened in 1905 in order to study the schooling of non-Russian peoples in Russia's east provided Volga-Ural missionaries with ample opportunity to inform government policies regarding Muslims. Especially after this conference, the imperial bureaucracy started to view Russia's Muslims through an ever-thickening lens of distrust and turned against them as a security threat.[18]

Pan-Islamism

Meanwhile, a number of broader developments – from the anti-European Boxer Rebellion in China to Russia's growing involvement in the governance of recently conquered territories in Transoxiana, and from exposure to anti-Muslim literature in European languages to renewed memories of Muslim resistance in the Caucasus – further sensitized Russian educated elites against Muslim activism.[19] The outcome of this publicly resonating sensitivity was an environment more conducive to hawkish statements and policies against Muslims, where the government had to respond not only to potential threats from Muslim activists but also to concerns arising from public perceptions of such threats. The concept of "pan-Islamism," coined in Europe in the 1870s and defined by the *Imperial Dictionary of the English Language* in 1883 as "a sentiment or movement in favour of a union or confederacy of the Mohammadan nations,"[20] entered from the growing European literature on the subject into the repertoire of Russian public and bureaucratic anxieties in this period.[21] In 1898, a Naqshbandi sheikh, Muhammed

---

People, Power, 1700–1930, ed. Jane Burbank, Mark von Hagen, and Anatoly Remnev (Bloomington: Indiana University Press, 2007), 322–25.

[17] Campbell, *Muslim Question*, 91–99.

[18] See N. Miropiev, "Russko inorodcheskie shkoly sistemy N. I. Il'minskogo," *Zhurnal Ministerstva Narodnogo Prosveshcheniia*, 1908 new series (13): 183–210; Dowler, "Pedagogy and Politics," 761–75; and Dowler, *Classroom and Empire*, 172–87.

[19] Campbell, *Muslim Question*, 147–58.

[20] *The Imperial Dictionary of the English Language*, new edn., 1883, s.v. "Panislamism".

[21] For early examples of references to "pan-Islamism" in European literature, see "The Eastern Question," *The Times*, June 5, 1876; George Stokes, "Panislamism and the

'Ali Sâbir, and his followers attacked a garrison in Andijan in the recently annexed Ferghana valley of Russian Turkestan hoping to start a rebellion and expel Russians from "Muslim territory." Russian forces repelled the attack and suppressed the rebellion before it started. Investigators found in Muhammed 'Ali's possession an edict addressed to him from the Ottoman Sultan and connected this aborted rebellion to pan-Islamism, which they conceptualized as a transregional Islamic conspiracy organized by the Ottoman sultan and caliph in order to unite world Muslims under caliphal authority. This edict was later found out to be forged, but the "specter of Panislamism" continued to haunt Russian officials both in Russian Turkestan and elsewhere in the empire. The rumors of Ottoman involvement in the incident proved more enduring than the facts disclosed in the investigation.[22]

As Muslim notables from most parts of Russia convened congresses during the 1905 Revolution, organized a somewhat united political movement, ran electoral campaigns, and sent deputies to the State Duma, and as Muslim deputies of the Duma overwhelmingly sided with the liberal Constitutional Democrats, all against the background of the specter of pan-Islamism, Russian officials and their conservative allies in society felt further justified in their fears of a transregional Muslim political movement that was pro-Ottoman and therefore anti-Russian and separatist.[23] When Young Turks took over the government in the Ottoman Empire with a coup d'etat in 1908 and the progressive Muslim intellectuals of the Volga-Ural region inundated the Muslim press with vaguely defined references to a "nation" or

---

Caliphate," *The Contemporary Review*, 1883 43(January–June): 57–68; Gabriel Charmes, *L'Avenir de la Turquie: Le panislamisme* (Paris: Lévy, 1883); and Ármin Vámbéry, "Pan-Islamism," *The Living Age*, 1906 251(3253): 356–63.

[22] On the Andijan Uprising and the concerns it raised about pan-Islamism, see Konstantin Konstanovich Pahlen, *Mission to Turkestan: Being the Memoirs of Count K. K. Pahlen, 1908–1909*, ed. Richard A. Pierce (London: Oxford University Press, 1964), 41–59; Alexander Morrison, "Sufism, Pan-Islamism and Information Panic: Nil Sergeevich Lykoshin and the Aftermath of the Andijan Uprising," *Past & Present*, 2012 214(1): 255–304; Brower, "Russian Roads," 567–84; and Lâle Can, *"Trans-Imperial Trajectories: Pilgrimage, Pan-Islam, and Ottoman Central Asian Relations, 1865–1914"* (Ph.D. Dissertation, New York University, 2012).

[23] On the political activism of Russia's Muslims in the early twentieth century, see, among many other sources, A. Arsharuni and Kh. Gabidullin, *Ocherki panislamizma i pantiurkizma v Rossii* (Riazan: Izdatel'stvo Bezbozhnik, 1931), 3–75; Zenkovsky, *Pan-Turkism*, 37–138; Bennigsen and Lemercier-Quelquejay, *Islam in the Soviet*, 3–80; Devlet, *Rusya Türkleri'nin*; Kırımlı, *National Movements*; Noack, *Muslimischer*, 218–349; and Giray Saynur Bozkurt, *1905–1907 Yılları Rusya Müslümanları'nın Siyasi Kimlik Arayışı* (Istanbul: Doğu Kütüphanesi, 2008).

"nationalism," the fears of yet another transregional conspiracy led by the Ottoman Empire, "pan-Turkism," joined and even surpassed the specter of pan-Islamism.[24]

Moreover, within five years of Nicholas II declaring freedom of conscience in April 1905, approximately 49,000 Russian subjects who were officially registered as Orthodox Christians in the Volga-Ural region forsook Christianity to be recognized as Muslims, further justifying the efforts of Il'minskii's followers.[25] Not only baptized Tatars, whose ancestors were Muslim before Russian occupation, but also the members of other non-Russian peoples such as the Chuvash and even some Russians were converting to Islam.[26] The circumstances were ripe for the followers of Il'minskii, as well as a growing cohort of concerned Russian nationalists, to push for more restrictive policies targeting Muslims in the Volga-Ural region. In line with their long-held position, Il'minskii's followers singled out Tatars as the primary instigators of trouble among Russia's Muslims. In 1908, Bishop Andrei, a prominent figure in the Brotherhood of St. Gurii, called Stolypin's attention to "the development of 'Tatar-Muhammadan' propaganda in the Volga region."[27] In the same year, Iakov Dmitrievich Koblov, a school inspector in the Kazan Educational Circuit and a sympathizer of missionary purposes, although at times he was at odds with Il'minskii's followers, published a booklet about the role of the new-method schools in promoting "Tatar-Muslim" nationalism in Russia.[28] In 1910, Il'minskii's biographer Petr Znamenskii wrote:

Tatars are the most enduring one among the peoples of the eastern non-Russian borderlands ... For three hundred years, they lived with the Russians under Russian authority, and they did not become Russianized as other non-Russian peoples have done. To the contrary, they themselves acquired a significant

[24] On the Russian fears of pan-Islamism and pan-Turkism, see Geraci, *Window*, 277–84. For a contemporary essay that represents these fears, see Nikolai Petrovich Ostroumov, "K istorii musul'manskogo obrazovatel'nogo dvizheniia v Rossii v XIX i XX stoletiiakh," *Mir Islama*, 1913 2(5): 302–26. On pan-Turkism in general, see Jacob M. Landau, *Pan-Turkism in Turkey: A Study of Irredentism* (Hamden: Archon Books, 1981).

[25] Geraci, "Russian Orientalism," 140.

[26] Prot. Taras' Ivanitskii, "Kakie i ch'i vliianiia inorodtsy ispytyvaiut na sebe," *Sotrudnik bratstva sviat. Guriia*, 1909 (November 29): 10–13; N. Nikol'skii, "Kak uderzhat' Chuvash ot tatarizatsii," *Sotrudnik bratstva sviat. Guriia*, 1909 (November 1): 5–10; and R. D., "Neobkhodimost' shkol'nogo obucheniia dlia devits kreshchenykh Tatar," *Sotrudnik bratstva sviat. Guriia*, 1910 (January 23): 125–26.

[27] Campbell, "The Muslim Question," 332.

[28] Iakov Dmitrievich Koblov, *Mechty tatar-magometan o natsional'noi obsheobrazovatel'noi shkole* (Kazan: Tipo-Litografiia Imperatorskogo Universiteta, 1908).

influence over the neighboring non-Russian peoples by converting them to Muhammadanism and gradually Tatarizing them.[29]

The link between this missionary discourse and the imperial bureaucracy was thick with followers and sympathizers of Il'minskii's ideas filling many of the MNP positions in the Volga-Ural region and having the ears of both MVD and MNP officials. In March 1911, for instance, the trustee of the Kazan Educational Circuit wanted the director of public schools in the Kazan Gubernia to provide information about a number of Muslim schools that an article in the publication organ of the Brotherhood of St. Gurii, *Sotrudnik*, had mentioned as suspicious.[30] Or, when the Muslim peasants in a mixed Tatar–Cheremis village wanted a Brotherhood of St. Gurii teacher who operated a school in the village to stop teaching, again in March 1911, Bishop Andrei wrote directly to the governor of Kazan, Mikhail Vasil'evich Strizhevskii, to intervene. Following investigation, the governor ordered the arrest of three Muslims in the village.[31]

In the higher echelons of the bureaucracy, another special conference that Stolypin convened in January 1910 to "work out measures to counteract the Tatar-Muslim influence in the Volga Basin" enabled Il'minskii's followers to further inform and shape government policies regarding Muslims. Nikolai A. Bobrovnikov, Il'minskii's adopted son and the head of the Brotherhood of St. Gurii, was in attendance – as he was in the MNP conference in 1905 – and so were Governor Strizhevskii and Bishop Andrei.[32] The workings of the conference reflected all the anxieties and demands of the Volga-Ural region's missionary circles, singling out Tatars as the troublemakers among Russia's Muslims and the activities of progressive Muslims as signals of a pro-Ottoman and anti-Russian political movement. When Stolypin reported these findings to the Council of Ministers, he highlighted that the developments among Russia's Muslims were not accidental and that they were in agreement with the "Pan-Islamists' program."[33]

With a green light from the Council of Ministers, the MVD issued a circular in December 1910 to the empire's security organs to alert them to the dangers of pan-Islamism. "This fanatic movement," the circular read:

which is supported by Young Turk and Young Persian committees, started to become especially strong in Russia ... [It aims] to unite Muslims all over the world politically and economically under the protection of Turkey with the ultimate goal of establishing an all-Turkic republic in the future ... Their

---

[29] Znamenskii, *Kazanskie*, 32.   [30] NART, f. 92, op. 2, d. 12614, ll. 1–2ob.

[31] NART, f. 1, op. 4, d. 4688, ll. 2–3, 6–6ob, and 16–29.

[32] On this conference, see A. Arsharuni, "Iz istorii natsional'noi politiki tsarizma," *Krasnyi arkhiv*, 1929 4(35): 107–27; and Geraci, "Russian Orientalism."

[33] Arsharuni, "Iz istorii," 108.

immediate goal is to join all conscientious Muslims for political war against the current governmental structure of the empire, which the Pan-Islamists view as the main obstacle before the national self-determination of Muslims.

Following this introduction, the MVD circular instructed police, gendarme, and Okhrana (secret police) units to:

(1) immediately take measures in order to acquire agents to unveil the criminal activities of the Pan-Islamists and their revolutionary organizations with the simultaneous purpose of suppressing them,
(2) assiduously follow the mood of the Muslim population, paying special attention to the activities of the pedagogical personnel in Muslim schools and of the Muslim men of religion, who are closely interacting with the Muslim population thanks to their positions (Periodically report on this issue.), and finally,
(3) follow the activities of Pan-Islamist publishers as well as the Pan-Islamist literature in all its versions and report articles that are relatively worthy of attention.[34]

Thus, the government was poised to crack down on the progressive Muslim movement. The raid and closure of the Bubi Madrasa in the Viatka Gubernia by the police has long epitomized this crackdown in the minds of Volga-Ural Muslims. On the night of January 30, 1911, several policemen surrounded the Bubi Madrasa, searched the houses of the mullahs and teachers in the village, confiscated religious books and textbooks, arrested five mullahs and nine teachers, including the Bubî brothers who owned the madrasa, and took them to Sarapul, where they were put in jail. An officer came back to the village later, in March, and closed the madrasa officially. For several months, the villagers repeatedly petitioned the MNP to reopen their madrasa but to no avail. The Bubi Madrasa remained closed, and, fearing further repression, the Bubî brothers moved to Qulja in Eastern Turkestan once they were released from jail after a few months.[35]

Imperial paranoia

Three days after the Bubi Madrasa was officially closed, Sadri Maqsûdî, a Muslim deputy to the Third State Duma from the Kazan Guberniia,

---

[34] NART, f. 1, op. 4, d. 6189, ll. 1–2ob; also reproduced partly in Arsharuni and Gabidullin, *Ocherki*, 110–11.
[35] See NART, f. 92, op. 2, d. 14852, ll. 24–25; Möhämmät Mähdiev, "Bubi Mädräsäse," in *Mädräsälärdä Kitap Kiştäse*, ed. Röstäm Mähdiev (Kazan: Tatarstan Kitap Näşriyatı, 1992), 38–72; Alta Kh Makhmutova, *Lish' tebe narod, sluzhen'e!: istoriia tatarskogo prosvetitel'stva v sud'bakh dinastii Nigmatullinykh-Bubi* (Kazan: Magarif, 2003), 231–362; Märdanov, Miñnullin, and Rähimov eds., *Bertugan*, 61–89 and 180–207; and Ross, "From the Minbar," 363–80.

gave a long speech at the Duma and criticized the government's mounting assault on Muslim educational institutions and progressive reformists. He reported that only within the past one year "better informed mullahs and mu'allims" had been subjected to criminal investigation in over 150 locations, and over seventy big Muslim schools, several newspapers and journals with large print counts, as well as several Muslim societies had been closed. There were two ways to explain this situation according to Maqsûdî:

Either the Russian government does not want us to progress and become civilized, and therefore, it wants to stop this somehow, or it mistakenly assumes the presence of a movement and ideas among Muslims against the Russian state, and it wants to counter them with extraordinary measures. Both of these explanations are accurate in my opinion ... The government does not want Muslims in Russia to advance and progress ... In response to the question "Is there a harmful movement, a faction organized against the state among Muslims?" they [the authorities] say "Yes, there is." and we say "No, there is not."

In the rest of his speech, Maqsûdî tried to prove that assuming the presence of a pan-Islamist movement among Russia's Muslims was absurd and it reflected the prejudices of Kazan's missionaries, especially the members of the Brotherhood of St. Gurii, more than reality.[36]

Nonetheless, Maqsûdî's words fell on deaf ears. A report that the MVD commissioned in response to his Duma speech reasserted that not only did a worldwide pan-Islamist movement exist but also it was rapidly growing in Russia. Maktabs, madrasas, Muslim periodicals, and Muslim charitable societies, the report claimed, were all venues for the spread of this movement.[37] Governor Strizhevskii took a personal interest in suppressing pan-Islamist and pan-Turkist propaganda in the Kazan Gubernia. He had already on multiple occasions warned the security personnel under his command of the "seriousness of the Muslim movement that," he claimed, "constitute[d] a highly visible threat to the Russian government."[38] Following the special conference in St. Petersburg in 1910, he passed the conference findings on to his subordinates and ordered them to be vigilant especially regarding the activities of progressive Muslims, who, he explained, should not be allowed to become "mullahs, teachers, or official functionaries in matters involving the administration of peasants."[39]

---

[36] The speech is reproduced in Märdanov, Miññullin, and Rähimov eds., *Bertugan*, 113–28.

[37] Arsharuni and Gabidullin, *Ocherki*, 101–10.   [38] NART, f. 1, op. 4, d. 6189, l. 107.

[39] NART, f. 1, op. 4, d. 6189, ll. 3–4ob, the report in 5–25ob.

Each time security officers received a circular like this one, a witch-hunt started in the Volga-Ural region. The MVD was informing its agents that there was a subversive Muslim movement, and police officers had to find the perpetrators. Although maktabs remained in a legal limbo up until the end of the tsarist regime, administrative practice gradually criminalized instruction with the new method and created an environment in which Muslims, especially mullahs, could settle local disputes by denouncing their rivals to the authorities as proponents of the new method. Such denunciations rarely led to real charges, but following them up helped police officers to show their superiors that they were working on the Muslim question.[40]

The police also reported potentially anti-government rumors among Muslim communities. The Balkan Wars, in which the Ottoman Empire lost most of its Balkan territories to Greece, Bulgaria, Montenegro, and Serbia, which Russia favored as its Slavic and/or Orthodox protégés,[41] particularly alerted Russian security forces to possible Ottoman influences among Volga-Ural Muslims. In November 1912, shortly after the beginning of the First Balkan War, the Mamadysh police reported the circulation of rumors in the county that suggested that if Russia and the Ottoman Empire fought and Tatars were conscripted, the Tatar soldiers would first shoot their officers or, in another version of the rumor, they would not shoot at Turkish soldiers.[42] One issue that particularly troubled the authorities was the collection of donations among Russia's Muslims for the Ottoman Red Crescent. Governor Strizhevskii warned his subordinates that the Tatars planned on collecting donations "under the pretext of helping the Red Crescent," but "without doubt, under this pretext, there [would] be collections for the Turkish army and navy too." Therefore, Strizhevskii ordered, any attempts for collecting donations should be considered against the law and dealt with accordingly.[43] Later in 1912, Strizhevskii received information on three individuals in Kazan who had allegedly collected 200 rubles, but a search of their houses did not reveal any evidence with which to charge them. The governor wrote to the MVD: "Be that as it may, I do not suspect the reliability of my intelligence ... if it has not been possible to expose the illegal collection of donations ... that is simply because

---

[40] For examples of such denunciations, see NART, f. 1, op. 4, d. 4667; NART, f. 199, op. 1, d. 772, ll. 57–59; and NART, f. 1, op, 4, d. 5191. One of the rare cases in which such denunciations proved consequential was the closure of the Bubi Madrasa.
[41] See Jacob Gould Schurman, *The Balkan Wars* (Princeton: Princeton University Press, 1916), especially 4–29.
[42] NART, f. 1, op. 4, d. 6978, l. 82.   [43] NART, f. 1, op. 4, d. 6978, ll. 11ob-12.

of the utmost conspiratorial way in which [the collectors] have furnished their activities."[44]

Governor Strizhevskii's warped logic was not exceptional. The overall interpretive scheme that grew out of the missionary-state alliance in the overly sensitized atmosphere of the post-revolutionary period recognized even the invisibility of a Muslim conspiracy as "proof of its existence," as Robert Geraci has pointed out.[45] False denunciations, rumors, and intelligence tips failed investigators again and again. Sometimes, even official reports on the Muslim question admitted that pan-Islamism as a political movement would not amount to any more than a pipedream.[46] Yet, partly pumped by the right-wing Russian press,[47] suspicion continued to accumulate. The same report that characterized pan-Islamism as a pipedream concluded after a lengthy narrative that the Russian empire did face a pan-Islamist threat. It was the way the missionary-state alliance generated knowledge about Muslims more than, or rather than, the acts of Russia's Muslims that produced this paranoia in a Saidian Orientalist paradigm.[48]

The distorted lens

The ever-thickening lens of distrust through which the Russian state viewed its Muslim subjects was cast in the correspondence of imperial authorities with experts on Muslim affairs, who tended to be either missionaries or sympathizers of the Orthodox missionary cause, and this lens suffered from at least two major distortions. First, the imperial authorities and experts often assumed that they could follow Muslim affairs from the Muslim press. Strizhevskii wrote in 1911: "In the war of ideas, press appears to be the most powerful instrument in the hands of the fighters. One can assess the size and popularity of the ideas that underline a movement among a specific population group by evaluating the volume of [their presence in] the press."[49] With this hyperbolic belief in the ability of press to represent or shape public opinion, the government mobilized experts to follow Muslim publications in order to "know" what the Muslims were up to. However, given the progressive Muslim intellectuals' disproportionately large presence in the Muslim press along with their alienation from the broader Muslim population, relying on the press to follow Muslim affairs reified the role of progressive intellectuals in representing or shaping the views

[44] NART, f. 1, op. 4, d. 6978, ll. 62ob-63.   [45] Geraci, "Russian Orientalism," 155–56.
[46] NART, f. 41, op. 11, d. 8, l. 34.   [47] Noack, *Muslimischer*, 446.
[48] See Said, *Orientalism*.
[49] NART, f. 1, op. 4, d. 6189, l. 3. Also see the quote from him at the beginning of this chapter.

and inclinations of Russia's Muslims. Furthermore, with a mission to catch anti-state conspiracies, expert readers searched through printed material looking for potential threats to the state while skipping over the mundane and the unthreatening.[50]

And second, from Il'minskii's letters to Count Tolstoi, to published works or formal reports that government offices commissioned from experts, the content of the state–missionary discourse on Muslims grew in a sedimentary manner. Earlier reports and publications informed later ones, and opinions turned into "facts" as they sank deeper in the resulting body of "knowledge." Many scholars of Russia's encounter with the "East" have insisted that Russian Orientalism was unique, that with a keen sense of themselves being between the East and the West, Russian "Orientologists" (as opposed to "Orientalists") "did not reduce the object of their inquiry to some uniform, Saidian other," and that Russian Orientalist scholarship did not directly link to governance. These studies usually focus on the works of lay scholars, such as Grigor'ev or Vasilii Vladimirovich Barthold, and they miss the crucial role that missionaries or the missionary concerns of lay scholars played in generating knowledge about the tsarist empire's non-Russian peoples.[51] Missionary experts benefited from the works of lay scholars, and both missionaries and missionary concerns informed Russian imperial policies. Grigor'ev, for instance, had personally mentored Il'minskii earlier in Il'minskii's career,[52] and Nikolai Petrovich Ostroumov, a close disciple of Il'minskii, served both as an expert on Muslim affairs and as one of the most influential lay authorities of Russian Turkestan.[53]

A look at the above-mentioned lengthy report on Russia's Muslim question should illustrate those points. The Kazan Circuit Court had commissioned this report in 1911 to find answers to two sets of questions, one about the nature of pan-Islamism and the other about the new-method movement's connections to pan-Islamism.[54] The report's

---

[50] NART, f. 1, op. 4, d. 6978, ll. 92–96ob; NART, f. 1, op. 4, d. 5482, ll. 90–96, and 207–10; and NART, f. 1, op. 4, d. 6189, ll. 3–4.

[51] Knight, "Grigor'ev", 74–100; Nathaniel Knight, "On Russian Orientalism: A Response to Adeeb Khalid," *Kritika: Explorations in Russian and Eurasian History*, 2000 1(4): 701–15; David Schimmelpenninck van der Oye, *Russian Orientalism: Asia in the Russian Mind from Peter the Great to the Emigration* (New Haven: Yale University Press, 2010), quote from 238; Vera Tolz, *Russia's Own Orient: The Politics of Identity and Oriental Studies in the Late Imperial and Early Soviet Periods* (Oxford: Oxford University Press, 2011). On Russia's in betweenness, also see Etkind, *Internal Colonization*.

[52] Kreindler, "Educational Policies," 56–59 and 120.

[53] Alexander Morrison, "'Applied Orientalism' in British India and Tsarist Turkestan," *Comparative Studies in Society and History*, 2009 51(3): 640–44.

[54] NART, f. 41, op. 11, d. 8, ll. 11, and 36.

author, Aleksandr Vasil'evich Goriachkin, had first-hand experience with Muslims for he had traveled extensively among them as an inspector of public schools for the Kazakh Inner Horde.[55] However, while commenting on the question of pan-Islamism, he relied primarily on earlier reports and the works of Russian and French historians. Quoting a published report on the Andijan Rebellion by Sergei Mikhailovich Dukhovskoi, the governor of Russian Turkestan at the time of the rebellion,[56] Goriachkin wrote that the Ottoman Empire had started to "establish moral protectorate over our Tatars of the Volga Basin" at least since the time of Catherine II.[57] He referenced another report, submitted by Bishop Aleksei to the MVD in 1909, as evidence for the existence of a worldwide movement to unite all Muslims under the leadership of the Ottoman Empire. Then, he provided an historical survey of the evolution of the Caliphate to elucidate the "role and meaning [of pan-Islamism] for Muslims living under the sovereignty of the Russian emperor." His sources for this survey were the historical works of Agafangel Efimovich Krymskii and Barthold along with several articles from the French *Revue du monde musulman*.[58]

Goriachkin's account of the caliphate confirmed the long-vocalized position of Il'minskii and his followers that Russia's troubles with its Muslim subjects had started with Catherine II. When the empress had forced the Ottoman Empire to recognize the Crimean Khanate as an independent state in 1774, she had in turn acknowledged the Ottoman sultan's religious authority as the caliph over the Crimean Muslims. This, according to Goriachkin, was a grave mistake for, on the authority of the works of Barthold and Krymskii, the Ottomans were not actually entitled to the caliphate at that time.[59] Russia had managed to avoid references to the caliphate in the Treaty of Paris, signed in 1856 after the Crimean War, but by then, Goriachkin lamented, the Ottomans had already consolidated the idea of the "Ottoman sultan's spiritual leadership among the believers of the Muslim world."[60]

---

[55] See one of his reports to the trustee of the Kazan Educational Circuit in 1910. NART, f. 92, op. 1, d. 10972, ll. 3–4.

[56] *Vsepoddanneishii doklad Turkestanskogo general-gubernatora gen. ot infanterii Dukhovskogo: Islam v Turkestane* (Tashkent, 1899). Goriachkin mistakenly dates the report to 1908.

[57] NART, f. 41, op. 11, d. 8, ll. 12–12ob.

[58] NART, f. 41, op. 11, d. 8, l. 14. Agafangel Efimovich Krymskii, *Musul'manstvo i ego budushchnost"* (Moscow: Knizhnoe delo, 1899). Although not referenced by Goriachkin, Krymskii later published an extended history of Islam largely based on the works of European Orientalists Reinhart Dozy and Ignác Goldziher. See Agafangel Efimovich Krymskii, *Istoriia Musul'manstva*, 2nd edn. (Moscow: Tipografiia Varvary Gattsuk, 1904). See Vasilii Vladimirovich Bartol'd, *Teokraticheskaia ideia i svetskaia vlast' v musul'manskom gosudarstve* (St. Petersburg: Tipo-litogr. B. M. Vol'fa, 1903).

[59] This view has since been refuted in the scholarship. See for instance Hasan Gümüşoğlu, *İntikalinden İlgasına Osmanlı'da Hilafet* (Istanbul: Kayıhan Yayınları, 2011), 32–64.

[60] NART, f. 41, op. 11, d. 8, ll. 13–23, quote from 21.

Pan-Islamism, as Goriachkin described it, had evolved around this spiritual leadership as a political movement that aimed to unite world Muslims against non-Muslims. According to Krymskii, Goriachkin continued to relate, since Abdulhamid II's accession to the throne in 1876, the pan-Islamists had focused on propagating Islam "among animists and the less cultured tribes" while attempting "to unite Muslims more strongly around Constantinople – the abode of the Caliphate." As a result, Islam was spreading among the animist peoples of Siberia without bounds, the danger of China turning Muslim was not too far, the "Brahman religion" countered Islam in India, but Islam still claimed one-eighth of the subcontinent's population, and finally, Malaysia and Africa were quickly becoming Muslim too. The peril that Krymskii warned about and Goriachkin conveyed in his report was the destruction of "our civilization" as a result of the growth of Islam in all corners of the world.[61]

Goriachkin noted that according to the French Orientalist Alfred Le Châtelier, pan-Islamism did not aim to unite all Muslims in a single state, and even if it did, a united Muslim state was not possible as long as the great powers – such as Russia, England, Germany, and France – opposed it.[62] However, events could take a more risky turn if Krymskii's worries about the spread of Islam in China came true. Furthermore, even without the spread of Islam in China or the rest of the world, Goriachkin thought that if the "twenty million" Muslims in Russia united, they would already pose a significantly serious threat to the Russian state.[63]

Goriachkin began his response to the Kazan Circuit Court's second set of questions about the new-method movement's connections to pan-Islamism with a description of conventional maktabs and madrasas based on the works of Krymskii, Ostroumov, and a physician in Tashkent, Aleksandr Shishov, who in turn was quoting the Russian Orientalist and bureaucrat Vladimir Petrovich Nalivkin.[64] But when Goriachkin

---

[61] NART, f. 41, op. 11, d. 8, ll. 23–32ob; and Krymskii, *Musul'manstvo*, 105–20. Ostroumov had expressed similar concerns about the spread of Islam earlier in 1884. See NART, f. 968, op. 1, d. 43. Goriachkin also quoted Octave Victor Houdas, *L'islamisme* (Paris: Dujarric, 1904) in this section.

[62] Alfred Le Châtelier, "Politique musulmane," *Revue du monde musulman*, 1910 12(9): 1–165.

[63] NART, f. 41, op. 11, d. 8, ll. 32ob-35.

[64] NART, f. 41, op. 11, d. 8, ll. 38–47ob. For the works quoted by Goriachkin in this section, see Krymskii, *Musul'manstvo*, 85–86; Aleksandr Polikarpovich Shishov, "Sarty: etnograficheskie i antropologicheskie issledovanie," in *Sbornik materialov dlia statistiki Syr-Darinskoi oblasti*, vol. 11 (Tashkent: Izdanie A. L. Kirsnera, 1904), 441–46; and Nikolai Petrovich Ostroumov, *Sarty: Etnograficheskie materialy* (Tashkent: Tipo-Litografiia Lakhtina, 1908), 240–71.

wrote about the new method, he turned to police reports and the progressive Muslim press, especially periodicals, such as *Tercüman*, *Vaqit*, *İrşâd*, and *Teraqqî*, and pamphlets about the Russian Muslim congresses of 1905 and 1906.[65] He cited *Tercüman*'s jubilant announcements of newly opening new-method maktabs as evidence for the spread of the new method among Russia's entire Muslim population. He considered this a sign of progress but still, a negative development. Since the new-method maktabs were established without administrative oversight, Goriachkin cautioned, it was difficult to estimate which direction they would take in the future. Yet, one thing was clear: the new-method maktabs' mission was incompatible "with the goals of the Russian government." To prove his point, Goriachkin quoted the following words from an article in *Tercüman*:

Bitter experience has taught us that we should not appropriate customs of the Europeans or their external forms of life, but we should take their science, knowledge, work methods, business structures, and social philanthropy.

The article was actually published first in a journal in Egypt and then reprinted in *Tercüman*, but in Goriachkin's view, it was sufficient to expose the position of "the leaders of the Muslim masses" in Russia. Even though these leaders wanted progress, they did not see "rapprochement with the Russians on the grounds of the Russian state's common interests" as the basis of that progress.[66]

Reading through the resolutions of the Third All-Russian Muslim Congress,[67] Goriachkin suggested that following a long period of "silent fermentation," the Muslim movement in Russia had entered a new phase with the Russo-Japanese War and the following revolution in 1905. The delegates of the Muslim congress, he asserted, had shown their aspiration for a state-like organization within the Russian state by dividing the Muslim-inhabited parts of the empire into regions, by electing representatives for those regions "in the model of a cabinet," and by founding an organization named the "Union of Muslims" (*İttifâq-ı Müslimîn*).[68] The delegates, Goriachkin asserted, aimed for a pan-Islamist unity and not for participation in the Russian political system through the formation of an official party.[69] Referring to an article by Gasprinskiy where he invited Muslim deputies in the Duma to be concerned with the question of "nationality" (*natsional'nost'*), regardless of where they stood in the

---

[65] *İrşâd* and *Teraqqî* were both published by Ahmet Agayef in Baku. Bennigsen and Lemercier-Quelquejay, *La presse*, 106–8.
[66] NART, f. 41, op. 11, d. 8, ll. 48ob-62ob.
[67] Bigiyef, *Islâhat* provides detailed information on this congress.
[68] NART, f. 41, op. 11, d. 8, ll. 63–68ob.   [69] NART, f. 41, op. 11, d. 8, l. 69.

political spectrum, Goriachkin inferred: "Thus we see that at the foundation of the program of the Union of Muslims lies the 'question of nationality,' which is the alpha and omega of the program of this party."[70]

Goriachkin was convinced that an "anti-state movement" existed among Russia's Muslims, and it had "already been continuing for decades." "The cultural, nationalist, and political movement of Muslims in central Russia, Crimea, the Caucasus, and the South Caucasus," he wrote:

has reached a significant level and so did that of the Muslims of the Turkestan Borderlands, where Tatars from central Russia have been spreading the propaganda of cultural and national progress along with the ideas of unification and separatism, and where the number of local agitators have reached impressive numbers as well.[71]

The main instrument of the unification of Russia's Muslims, according to Goriachkin, was the creation of a common Turkic language through print media and through schooling in the new-method maktabs.[72] Therefore, maktabs and madrasas could not be considered institutions of religious instruction only; rather, they had to be treated as political institutions.[73] In these maktabs and madrasas, Goriachkin wrote, one could find the "common-Turkic language as an attribute of the political unification of all peoples with Turkic roots." "The Muslim movement," he warned:

is founded upon anti-state ideas and is without doubt an extreme threat to the Russian state ... It is quite likely that the Muslim national new-method schools, which are constructed according to European models, which follow the principle of national and religious exclusiveness, and which are left alone [by the government], can turn the twenty-million-strong Muslim population into enemies of Russia in no time.

No single umbrella organization formally united Muslims, according to Goriachkin, but "several cultural and educational (*prosvetitel'nyi*) Muslim societies that [had] opened with the permission of local author-ities according to the law on societies and unions fulfill[ed] the task of such an organization successfully."[74] The Muslim movement had not yet matured enough to "target the foundation of an independent Muslim state." The efforts of its leaders were still limited to "preparing the Muslim masses" for that idea, but in the future, Goriachkin concluded:

as possible complications in the West or in the East or social changes in China, such as conversion to Islam, allow, and as the twenty-million-strong Muslim population of Russia progresses culturally, unites with a single language, becomes

---

[70] NART, f. 41, op. 11, d. 8, l. 70.   [71] NART, f. 41, op. 11, d. 8, ll. 88, and 90.
[72] NART, f. 41, op. 11, d. 8, ll. 111–17.   [73] NART, f. 41, op. 11, d. 8, l. 154.
[74] NART, f. 41, op. 11, d. 8, ll. 157–58.

fully organized, and receives education in the spirit of the Ottoman Empire, then it goes without doubt that [Russia's Muslims] will not think twice for taking advantage of a suitable moment at a time of difficulty for Russia in order to restore political independence or, at a single signal, to raise a common banner of rebellion.[75]

The archival file that contains Goriachkin's report does not offer information about who might have read the report, but the notes and underlining on the text indicate that it was read, probably by a member of the Kazan Circuit Court. The themes that the reader has consistently underlined include Muslim nationalism, the connection of educational reform to Muslim nationalism, Muslim political mobilization, calls for Muslim unity, the role of a common Turkic language in providing unity among Russia's Muslims, grievances expressed by Muslim authors against the Russian state, earlier court cases and police investigations in which Muslim activists were involved, and possible connections between Russia's Muslims and the Ottoman Empire. Hence, it appears that the reader was primarily interested in the question of whether the Muslim progressive movement posed a political threat to the Russian state and that the text left him with the impression that it did.[76]

The process through which Goriachkin prepared his report and the court reader underlined certain sections in it reveals how the Russian imperial paranoia about an anti-state movement among Russia's Muslims was born and sustained. Once again, the pieces that Goriachkin selected from the Muslim press and that attracted his reader's attention constituted only a small fraction of the content of the publication boom in Muslim languages in the Russian empire after 1905. An earlier report that Goriachkin had submitted to the Trustee of the Kazan Educational Circuit in 1910 shows that when he started his research for the Kazan Circuit Court, he already viewed new-method schools and the Muslim progressive movement as a threat to Russian state interests.[77] All that was left for him to convince the court about this opinion was to handpick and present corroborating material from the existing secondary literature and Muslim publications. The court reader, on the other hand, was not concerned about objectively observing and evaluating the developments among Muslims. That was the expert's job, and the court reader was willing to take the expert's claims as authoritative.

---

[75] NART, f. 41, op. 11, d. 8, ll. 191–91ob.
[76] NART, f. 41, op. 11, d. 8, ll. 70–191ob. (A female reader in the court was highly unlikely.)
[77] NART, f. 92, op. 2, d. 12614, ll. 3–4.

Hindsight

With hindsight, we know that the global threat of pan-Islamism (or pan-Turkism) was fiction, at least until the First World War, and that no concerted Russian Muslim movement against the tsarist state ever existed. The idea of pan-Islamism indirectly contributed to the adoption of the idea of self-determination in the Muslim anti-colonial movements of Europe's Asian colonies during and after the First World War, but this hardly affected Russia's Muslims.[78] On the Ottoman side, as Michael Reynolds has forcefully demonstrated, the Young Turks prioritized geopolitics over utopian idealism in matters of pan-Islamism and pan-Turkism even when the Russian empire disintegrated in the wake of the October Revolution in 1917.[79] Furthermore, the crumbling Ottoman Empire lacked the resources to organize a worldwide movement of any sorts by this point in its existence. The most the Young Turks could attempt beyond the Ottoman Empire's immediate borders was to send a few patriotic adventurers to Transoxiana and Eastern Turkestan, some of whom eventually contributed their military expertise to, but did not instigate, an anti-Russian rebellion in 1916.[80]

In fact, the Young Turk administration itself was uneasy about utopian "pan" ideals that would possibly damage its already delicate geopolitical standing. In 1913, the Ottoman Minister of Cadaster, Mahmud Esad Efendi, toured Russia and Finland, visiting local Muslim communities along his way. Russian journalists asked him about pan-Islamism and pan-Turkism. He responded that if pan-Islamism referred to uniting all Muslims in the world politically, this was impractical and pursuing it would only bring harm. "There is no real power to realize this idea," he explained:

And therefore, the noise raised by its imprudent and heedless proponents will turn Christian peoples against Muslims in the worst possible way. Being carried away with the ideas of pan-Islamism would lead all Muslims to disaster and should be

---

[78] On the connections between pan-Islamism and anti-colonial movements, see Cemil Aydın, *The Politics of Anti-Westernism in Asia: Visions of World Order in Pan-Islamic and Pan-Asian Thought* (New York: Columbia University Press, 2007), especially 93–110 and 127–60.

[79] Michael A. Reynolds, *Shattering Empires: The Clash and Collapse of the Ottoman and Russian Empires, 1908–1918* (New York: Cambridge University Press, 2011), especially 167–251. Also see Can, "Trans-Imperial."

[80] For the memoirs of one of these adventurers, see Adil Hikmet, *Asya'da Beş Türk* (Istanbul: Ötüken, 1998), 17–24, and 126–226. On the 1916 Rebellion, see Steven Sabol, *"The 1916 Russian-Central Asian Revolt: Its Causes, Consequences, and Reinterpretation"* (paper presented at the 4th Biannual Conference: The International Society for First World War Studies, Washington, DC).

considered a big crime against Turkey's Muslims. It would be unforgivable if the Turkish politicians endangered the [Ottoman] empire by following the absurd utopia of a chimerical union of Muslims in the name of pan-Islamism.

On the other hand, if pan-Islamism meant "establishing spiritual connections among all Muslims," that was unnecessary according to Mahmud Esad Efendi, for such connections already existed. The caliphate united world Muslims in a spiritual family, but without political implications, similar to the way the papacy united world Catholics.

As for pan-Turkism, if it implied "uniting the seventy to eighty million Turkic peoples who live[d] in Turkey, Russia, Iran, and China in a single state," Mahmud Esad Efendi commented: "frankly, this is an impossible utopia that only the inexperienced youth can dream of." However, if pan-Turkism meant "creating a shared culture and literature among the Turkic peoples of the world and improving their common economic interests," this would harm no one and only contribute to the improvement of art and literature globally.[81]

True, there were progressive Russian Muslim intellectuals who espoused pan-Turkist and pan-Islamist ideals in a political sense. Yusuf Akçura was one. He promoted pan-Turkism in an oft-quoted and controversial essay that he published in Egypt in 1904 and later in the journal *Türk Yurdu*, which he edited from Istanbul on and off between 1911 and 1917.[82] Ğabdurreşîd İbrâhîm, who played an important role in organizing Muslim congresses in Russia after the 1905 Revolution and devoted most of his life to "pan" movements ranging from pan-Islamism to pan-Asianism, was another one.[83] There were also strong connections between the reformist movement in the Russian empire and the westernizing elites of the Ottoman Empire, including the Young Turks.[84] Yet, these individual pipedreams or reformist connections hardly amounted to a trans-imperial political movement. In fact, when war broke out

---

[81] Anon., "Mahmud Esad Efendi v Rossii," *Mir Islama*, 1913 2(7): 476–79. For a detailed study of this tour, see Alper Alp, "Defter-i Hakani Nazırı Mahmud Esad Efendi'nin Gözüyle 20. Asır Başında Türk Dünyası," *Cumhuriyet Tarihi Araştırmaları Dergisi*, 2006 2(3): 18–42.

[82] For an analysis of this essay and examples of its refutations in the contemporary Ottoman press, see Enver Ziya Karal ed., *Yusuf Akçura: Üç Tarz-ı Siyaset* (Ankara: Türk Tarih Kurumu, 1976).

[83] *Te'ârüf-i Müslimîn*, a journal that Ğabdurreşîd İbrâhîm published in 1908 in Istanbul, represents his pan-Islamist views well. For a biography of İbrâhîm, see Türkoğlu, *Abdürreşid İbrahim*. On İbrâhîm's involvement in pan-Asianist movements, see Aydın, *The Politics of Anti-Westernism*, especially 177.

[84] For works investigating these connections, see Tuna, "Madrasa Reform"; Meyer, "Turkic Worlds"; and Mustafa Gökçek, *"A Kazan Tatar Contribution to the Late Ottoman Debates on Nationalism and Islam: The Life and Works of Halim Sabit Şibay"* (Ph.D. Dissertation, University of Wisconsin, 2008).

between Russia and the Ottoman Empire in 1914, the Volga-Ural Muslims loyally served in the tsarist army.[85] Even as the Russian empire disintegrated in 1917, the cultural and political leaders of Russia's Muslims neither followed a pan-Turkist or pan-Islamist ideal nor did they act in unity. Rather, they were divided on many political issues. A minority among them considered an all-Russian political movement, but most others reckoned local political mobilization to be more feasible.[86]

Conclusion: Knowledge is weakness

The tsarist authorities and their expert consultants on Muslim affairs did not have the advantage of hindsight, but their prejudiced positions led them to systematically disregard contemporary pieces of information that could have otherwise helped them better understand Russia's Muslims. In the face of the recent attempts to salvage Russian Oriental studies from the pejorative connotations that Oriental studies have accrued following Edward Said, the findings of this chapter build on an earlier lead by Adeeb Khalid and suggest that Russia's imperial discourse about Muslims at the turn of the twentieth century was Orientalist through and through.[87] Regardless of where Russian imperial agents perceived themselves between the East and the West, their discourse about Muslims reduced Muslims to a scorned other while informing policy in many direct and indirect ways.

However, if we pose the question as to whether the tsarist imperial agents' selective and sedimentary knowledge of Muslims yielded power to the Russian state, as Said suggests the "knowledge of subject races or Orientals" does,[88] we may have to part from the Saidian paradigm. The Russian authorities' prejudiced knowledge of Muslims constituted a notable weakness in their ability to relate to and, therefore, successfully manage the empire's Muslim population. When push came to shove, the imperial state still had the ability to deploy armed forces in order to shut down maktabs and madrasas or to suppress rebellions. It possessed power in the form of physical force regardless of the utility of Orientalist

---

[85] Norihiro Naganawa, "Musul'manskoe soobshchestvo v usloviiakh mobilizatsii: uchastie volgo-ural'skikh musul'man v voinakh poslednego desiatiletiia sushchestvovaniia Rossiiskoi imperii," in *Volgo-Uralskii region v imperskom prostranstve xviii–xx vv.*, ed. Norihiro Naganawa, Diliara M. Usmanonova, and Mami Hamamato (Moscow: Vostochnaia Literatura, 2011), 198–228; and Campbell, *Muslim Question*, 195–214.
[86] See Schafer, "Building"; and Kırımlı, *National Movements*.
[87] See Khalid, "Russian History".
[88] Said, *Orientalism*, especially 31–49; quote from 36.

knowledge to justify its use. However, if the inter-imperial context of the late nineteenth century dictated empires to maximize resources, if resource maximization required unmediated governance, and if the success of unmediated governance depended on the ability of states to build bonds with their subjects,[89] then the policies of the Russian state–missionary alliance in the early twentieth century were self-defeating.[90] The paranoia that built through the correspondence networks of this alliance in the overly sensitized atmosphere of the post-revolutionary period came with the opportunity cost of depriving the Russian empire of maximizing the contributions of its Muslim subjects. Lest the image of a Hobbesian Russian state pounding on Muslim activists as presented in this chapter be conceived as yet another prelude to the end of the tsarist regime, we will turn to an investigation of the possibilities for such contributions in the following chapter.

---

[89] Dominic Lieven, "Dilemmas of Empire 1850–1918: Power, Territory, Identity," *Journal of Contemporary History*, 1999 34(2): 163–200 elaborates on such challenges that empires faced in the late nineteenth century.

[90] For similar conclusions primarily in the case of Russian presence in Transoxiana, see Morrison, "Applied Orientalism."

10   Flexibility of the imperial domain and the limits of integration

> In fact, there are people who claim that Muslims are seeking separation. This may be a possibility, but in my entire life, I have not seen a single Muslim involved in a separatist movement.[1]   A. N. Baraninskii, member of the educational commission of the Kazan County Zemstvo, 1912

> We teach the Qur'an, we teach only the Qur'an.[2]   Lebībe Hüseyinova, owner of a reformed madrasa for girls in Kazan, 1911

> Will this multi-million Tatar-Muhammadan population of Russia that is richly gifted by nature continue to remain long in an ossified ignorance by refusing the means of moving out of that ossification into the path of intellectual and moral progress that is offered to them by the Great Russian people!?[3]   O. R-v., an inspector of public schools in the Spassk Gubernia, 1916

In his revisionist historical snapshot *Russia in 1913*, Wayne Dowler concludes that despite "severe stresses and tensions ... the clear trend before the war was toward cooperation and integration."[4] The state–missionary alliance's hostility toward progressive Muslim intellectuals and the Volga-Ural Muslims in general contradicts this view, but we should not be so quick to interpret that hostility as evidence for the tsarist regime's dysfunctionality in its last years. Merely looking at the binary relations between Russia's Muslim communities and the central state establishment cannot provide a complete account of the imperial situation that surrounded Volga-Ural Muslims by the early twentieth century. The imperial domain allowed for the interplay of a multitude of agents and attitudes in a multitude of encounters that incorporated but were not necessarily dominated by the actions of the central state establishment. The flexibility resulting from this interplay *did* create many opportunities

[1] Anon., *Qazan Uyezdindeki*, 5.
[2] Alta Mähmutova, "Kazandagı Kızlar Öçen Mäktäp-Mädräsälär," in *Mädräsälärdä Kitap Kiştäse*, ed. Röstäm Mähdiev (Kazan: Tatarstan Kitap Näşriyatı, 1992), 137.
[3] R-v., O., *K voprosu o magometanskikh i russko-tatarskikh uchilishchakh* (Kazan: Tsentral'naia Tipografiia, 1916), 27.
[4] Dowler, *Russia in 1913*, 279.

for cooperation, but not necessarily for integration. Admittedly, those opportunities were not always realized. Some of the failures could be chalked up among the opportunity costs of the state–missionary alliance's paranoia about Muslims. Others relate to the progressive intellectuals' alienation from the broader Muslim population. We have no way of knowing whether the aggregate of opportunities for cooperation or the hostility of the state–missionary alliance would have eventually defined the Volga-Ural Muslims' long-term experience had it not been for the disruption of wars, revolutions, and Socialist restructuring after 1914. However, we still need to recognize that despite the bitterness characterizing the Russian state's relations with Volga-Ural Muslims in the last decades of the tsarist regime, the flexibility of the imperial domain moderated the overall experience of Volga-Ural Muslims as subjects of an empire ruled by non-Muslims. This final chapter delves into some key aspects and examples of that moderation while also questioning its limits.

Separate but equal

Jane Burbank reminds us that despite the Great Reforms and the ensuing transformations and even a revolution in 1905, long-established imperial institutions and categories, or the habit of "thinking like an empire," proved resilient in the Russian empire. Peasants, for instance, preferred "their own local, and locally elected, judges against a new definition of universal justice that would include nobles and peasants in the same legal structure." Their response to egalitarian suffrage that would cross long-established estate boundaries in electing judges was "better separate than equal."[5]

Nevertheless, the functions and nature of these long-established institutions could change even as they continued to define the empire's structures. An illustrative example of such change in the case of the Volga-Ural Muslims relates to the tsarist state's use of confessional categories as instruments of identification and governance. The Volga-Ural Muslims cherished the mediated distance that the recognition of their faith by the "confessional state" accorded them. Gasprinskiy was an exception when he complained in 1881 that the Russian state collected taxes from Muslims, as it collected from Russians, but did not provide educational services to Muslims, as it provided to Russians.[6] In fact, the Catherinian imperial model's allowance for leaving Volga-Ural Muslims

---

[5] Burbank, "Thinking," 196–217, quotes from 212; and Burbank, *Russian Peasants*, 44.
[6] Gasprinskii, *Russkoe*, 12–13.

alone in most communal affairs, including education, helped them justify their subjection to a non-Muslim power. By 1905, however, the tsarist regime had left the Catherinian imperial model behind, and many Volga-Ural Muslims, especially the progressive intellectuals, had started to view Muslims in Russia as well as Russia itself within the family of world empires in a comparative perspective. They found the inferior status of Muslims in the empire's hierarchy of peoples, and the resulting neglect in terms of the resources allocated to their needs, to be unfair. As might be gleaned from the contemporaneous Muslim press and the petitions of many Muslim communities to the tsarist state after 1905, their response to this perceived injustice could be summarized as "better separate *and* equal."[7]

The concern for being treated equally in a comparative perspective while continuing to be recognized and accommodated in a separate confessional, or increasingly ethnic, category permeated the discourse of the Volga-Ural Muslim elites – both the progressive intellectuals and others – during the 1905 Revolution and persisted thereafter. The Third All-Russian Muslim Congress that convened in Nizhny Novgorod in August 1906 and was attended primarily by progressive Muslim notables resolved to attain the equality of Muslims "with Russians in all aspects of all political, social, and religious rights."[8] In another illustrative example, the representatives of five Bashkir villages in the Orenburg Guberniia petitioned the Council of Ministers to be granted full equality with the "core Russian people" and, therefore, for the unlimited implementation of the newly announced state reforms to the Bashkirs.[9] Then, in the 1910s, one could find the Muslim elites of the city of Kazan struggling to obtain official recognition for Muslim holidays and to have Muslim shop owners excluded from "the prohibition against trading on Christian holidays."[10]

The scope of the Volga-Ural Muslims' publicly voiced demands for equality expanded over time from equality in legal rights to equality in receiving services from the state. Mark Raeff writes that Russia's "directive and interventionist welfare state," which had become "an end unto itself" by the late nineteenth century, commanded "every

---

[7] For an overview of Muslim demands during the 1905 Revolution, see Bozkurt, *1905*, 153–81.

[8] Bigiyef, *Islâhat*, 175–78.   [9] NART, f. 1370, op. 1, d. 2, ll. 49–50.

[10] Robert P. Geraci, *"Sunday Laws and Ethno-Commercial Rivalry in the Russian Empire, 1880s–1914,"* National Council for Eurasian and East European Research, 2006. Available at: www.ucis.pitt.edu/nceeer/2006_819_Geraci.pdf. See also Naganawa, "Holidays," 25–48.

citizen" to "serve the state's requirements of ongoing modernization."[11] After the 1905 Revolution, however, many of the empire's subjects, including Muslims and especially the progressive intellectuals among them, turned the table on the state and expected it to provide services for their wellbeing as *they* saw fit. Muhîddin Qurbangaliyef, a contributor to the journal *Mekteb* in 1913, wrote: "In the view of experienced educators and those who serve the society, the raison d'être of a state is to protect its people, benefit them, increase their happiness, and meet their needs."[12] Another Muslim author concurred: "the government is an institution that has been created to meet the people's needs."[13]

Given the central state establishment's unconcealed hostility toward them, one remaining option for the Volga-Ural Muslims was to channel their expectations and appeals for government services to the zemstvos and other bodies of local governance. In an address to the Muslims of Russia in 1905, "the Organizing Circle of the Muslim Intelligentsia in St. Petersburg" protested that while in the second half of the nineteenth century, Russia had entered a path of development in which all peoples benefited from the services of courts, zemstvos, and city governments, the situation of Muslims had deteriorated paradoxically due to policies of "assimilation and spiritual annihilation."[14] Hâdi Atlasî, reported in *Mekteb* in 1913 that the zemstvos had received two rubles for each individual living in the area of their jurisdiction in 1911 and had spent 52 kopecks out of this amount on public education. Hence, the Kazan Zemstvo had diverted to public education approximately 364,000 rubles from the taxes of near 700,000 Muslims who lived in the Kazan Gubernia. Yet, zemstvo investment in the education of Muslims had remained negligible. While Muslims had paid their taxes under the same conditions as other peoples, Atlasî concluded, they had not benefited from zemstvo services equally. He acknowledged that the zemstvo schools admitted Muslim students, but the students entering zemstvo schools would have to study in the Russian language with a program that the MNP officials had prepared with the needs of Orthodox Russians in mind. This was not what Atlasî asked for; he wanted the zemstvos to support Muslim maktabs as they supported the Russian schools.[15]

---

[11] Marc Raeff, "The Well-Ordered Police State and the Development of Modernity in Seventeenth-and-Eighteenth-Century Europe: An Attempt at a Comparative Approach," *American Historical Review*, 1975 80(5): 1221–43.

[12] Qurbangaliyef, "İbtidâî," 24.

[13] M. 'Ali, "Mekteb mi? İşqola mı?," *Mekteb*, 1913 1(8): 192.

[14] NART, f. 1370, op. 1, d. 1, l. 21.

[15] Hâdi Atlasî, "Zemstva ve Bizniñ Mektebler," *Mekteb*, 1913 1(15): 361–63.

Thus, by the turn of the twentieth century, even as the Volga-Ural Muslims continued to cherish their distinctive confessional category as Muslims, one could encounter voices among them that demanded to receive equal rights and services with other confessional categories, including the Russians. Members of the state–missionary alliance followed this development mostly via the progressive Muslim literature and scorned it as a sign of the failure of government efforts to mold Muslims into ideal subjects. Yet, when viewed without the distortion of imperial anxieties about Muslim fanaticism and separatism, I would suggest that such calls for separate and equal treatment actually indicated an increasing willingness among Volga-Ural Muslims to engage the imperial domain and to identify with the tsarist state more directly, without the protection that the Volga-Ural Muslim domain's mediated distance accorded.

Representation and local governance

The Volga-Ural Muslims, or at least the vocal elite among them, wanted not only to be treated equally while preserving their distinctiveness but also to participate in the empire's governance. Between 1905 and 1907, the representatives of Muslim communities from many parts of the empire inundated local authorities, the spiritual assemblies, and the Council of Ministers in St. Petersburg with hundreds of petitions. One of their outstanding demands was to be given a voice in administrative matters particularly when those matters concerned Muslims directly.[16] When the Council of Ministers commissioned Mufti Muhammedyâr Sultanof to prepare a report about the affairs of the Orenburg Spiritual Assembly in 1905 and the mufti invited prominent members of the ulama to a special conference for this purpose, lay Muslim notables from various locations under his jurisdiction petitioned him for admittance to the conference.[17] In another example, the representatives of Orsk Bashkirs, who were excluded from the electorate due to their special military service status, petitioned the Chairman of the Council of Ministers Sergei Witte in 1906 to be able to send representatives to the State Duma since "peoples with a much smaller population size than the Bashkirs, such as the Kalmyks and Buriats," were allowed to do so.[18]

[16] The copies of many of these petitions are preserved in NART, f. 1370, op. 1, d. 2. Also see Bozkurt, *1905*, 142–79.
[17] NART, f. 1370, op. 1, d. 2, ll. 8–9ob and 10–11ob.
[18] NART, f. 1370, op. 1, d. 2, ll. 19–20ob, also see ll. 49–50 for a similar petition. For other examples of calls for equality during the 1905 Revolution, see NART, f. 1370, op. 1, d. 1, ll. 27–29; NART, f. 1370, op. 1, d. 2, ll. 17–18ob, 49–50, 56–61, and 62–64; as well

Having been already included in the electorate, many other Muslim communities organized politically, went to the ballot, and sent twenty-five representatives to the first State Duma in 1906 and thirty-seven to the second Duma in 1907. About half of these Muslim deputies were elected from the Volga-Ural region.[19]

Despite this promising start, representation at the State Duma turned into a disappointing experiment for the Volga-Ural Muslims. Nicholas II closed each of the first two Dumas after a few months in session and, with Stolypin's advice, changed the electoral law to favor conservative Russian representatives thereafter. Consequently, the number of Muslim deputies dropped to ten in the third State Duma (1907–12) and six in the fourth (1912–17).[20] Moreover, in all Dumas, Muslim deputies remained a marginal minority whose effectiveness depended on supporting the initiatives of other parties rather than promoting their own initiatives. As the center of weight shifted from the liberal left to the conservative right in the third and fourth Dumas, Muslim interests lost any chance of receiving positive consideration despite the energetic efforts of a few Muslim deputies such as Sadri Maqsûdî or İbniemîn Ebusuʿûdoviç Ahtyamof.[21]

At this juncture, however, zemstvos and other bodies of local governance, such as the city Dumas and various local commissions, provided an alternative venue where Muslims could promote their interests. The confessional and ethnic prejudices of the Romanov regime that favored Orthodox Russians over other peoples restricted Muslim representation in these institutions too. Some Muslim-inhabited parts of the Volga-Ural region, such as the Orenburg and Astrakhan gubernias received zemstvo administration only in the 1910s, partly because their demographics did not favor ethnic Russians. Where the imperial government instituted zemstvos earlier, such as in the Kazan Gubernia in 1865 and the Ufa Gubernia in 1874, Muslim nobles and big merchants energetically participated in the zemstvo affairs to promote Muslim interests. Yet, in general, Muslim representation remained limited in the zemstvos too. Even when it started to pick up with a new law in 1906 allowing peasants

---

as the program of the "Union of Russian Muslims" as passed in the First All-Russian Muslim Congress in 1905 in Anon., *1906 Sene 16–21 Avgustda İctima' İtmiş Rusya Müslümanlarınıñ Nedvesi* (Kazan: Matbaʿa-yı Kerîmiyye, 1906), addendum 1–18.

[19] Diliara M. Usmanova, *Musulʹmanskaia fraktsiia i problemy "svobody sovesti" v Gosudarstvennoi Dume Rossii (1906–1917)* (Kazan: Izdatelʹstvo Master Lain, 1999), 128–38 (Table 2); and Bozkurt, *1905*, 259–61, and 333–50.

[20] Ascher, *Authority Restored*, 162–215, and 337–68; Usmanova, *Musulʹmanskaia fraktsiia*, 41–48; and Meyer, "Turkic Worlds," 172–78.

[21] Usmanova, *Musulʹmanskaia fraktsiia*, 64–71.

to join zemstvo boards, governors often limited the participation of elected Muslim representatives in board activities due to concerns of separatism. In the end, as Hâdi Atlasî's earlier comments in this chapter also indicate, zemstvo contributions to the welfare of Muslims remained far from satisfactory. However, both the zemstvos and other bodies of local governance offered a variety of opportunities to Muslims, and compared to the achievements of Muslim deputies in the State Dumas, the work of the few Muslim representatives who took part in local governance usually yielded more effective outcomes.[22]

The businesslike approach of many – though not all – institutions of local governance to the task of providing services to Muslims (countering the central state establishment's hostility) contributed to this relative efficacy. As a result, Muslims engaged local bodies of governance more easily. In January 1911, for instance, three Muslim members of the Kazan city educational commission proposed opening a Russo-Muslim school for girls in Kazan's fourth district. The MNP representative at the meeting was the inspector of public schools in the Kazan Gubernia, Aleksandr Sergeevich Rozhdestvin. As a proponent of Il'minskii's ideas, he was sympathetic to initiatives that provided secular schooling in the Russian language to Muslims.[23] He readily consented to the proposal, and the educational commission agreed to allocate money from its annual budget for the expenses of the new girls' school. This allocation still needed to be sanctioned by the trustee of the Kazan Educational Circuit Aleksei Nikolaevich Derevenskii, who was the most senior MNP

---

[22] On Muslim participation in zemstvo affairs, see Noack, *Muslimischer*, 92–94, and 433–37; Gul'naz Bulatovna Azamatova, *Ufimskoe zemstvo, 1874–1917: sotsial'nyi sostav, biudzhet, deiatel'nost' v oblasti narodnogo obrazovaniia* (Ufa: Gilem, 2005), 138–51, Charles Robert Steinwedel, "Polozhenie Bashkirii v sostave Rossii: regional'nye osobennosti, paralleli, obsheimperskii kontekst (1552–1917)," in *Volgo-Ural'skii region v imperskom prostranstve XVIII–XX vv.*, ed. Mami Hamamato, Norihiro Naganawa, and Diliara Usmanova (Moscow: Vostozhnaia literatura, 2011), 71–72; Il'dus Zagidullin, "Tatary v organakh samoupravleniia: zemskikh, gorodskikh, i krest'ianskikh," in *Istoriia Tatar s drevneishikh vremen: Formirovanie tatarskoi natsii XIX-nachalo XX v.*, ed. Ildus Zagidullin (Kazan: Akademiia Nauk Respubliki Tatarstan, 2013), 477–81. For examples of zemstvo involvement in providing services to Muslims, see NART, f. 92, op. 1, d. 12347, ll. 1–1ob and 20–21; NART, f. 92, op. 1, d. 23263, l. 4; NART, f. 92, op. 2, d. 14852, ll. 1–1ob and 8; NART, f. 92, op. 2, d. 19438, ll. 1–5; NART, f. 92, op. 2, d. 17120, l. not paginated ; NART, f. 1370, op. 1, d. 2, ll. 43–47; Märdanov, Miñnullin, and Rähimov eds., *Bertugan*, 37–39, and 136–37.

[23] On Il'minskii's ideas regarding Muslim education, see Chapter 3. On Rozhdestvin's ideas about the Il'minskii system, see Aleksandr Sergeevich Rozhdestvin, *Nikolai Ivanovich Il'minskii i ego sistema inorodcheskogo obrazovaniia v Kazanskom krae* (Kazan: Tipo-litografiia Imperatorskogo Universiteta, 1900); and Aleksandr Sergeevich Rozhdestvin, *Rodnoi iazyk kak osnova shkol'nogo obucheniia* (Kazan: Tipo-litografiia Imperatorskogo Universiteta, 1903).

representative in the Volga-Kama region. Therefore, Rozhdestvin informed the director of public schools in the Kazan Guberniia, Mikhail Nikolaevich Pinegin, who in turn passed the information on to Derevenskii. Pinegin knew Tatar, had taught at the Kazan Tatar Teachers' School, and had served as its principal before becoming the director of public schools in 1907. His secret reports to higher authorities on Muslim affairs and his decisions in the various administrative positions that he had held reveal him as a relatively hawkish imperial agent who was committed to the idea of providing Russian education to Muslims while limiting the activism of progressive Muslims through administrative fiat.[24] Hence, his letter to Derevenskii was approving of the new school initiative too.

Yet, Derevenskii's response was bitterly negative. He asked Pinegin how he could consider a school for Muslim girls "indispensable" while Russian inhabitants in other parts of the city of Kazan lacked schooling facilities "even for boys." Fortunately for him, Pinegin retired from government service before he had to answer this question. By the time a new director of public schools was appointed in his place and managed to respond to Derevenskii's letter later in November, Rozhdestvin and the Kazan city educational commission had already opened the girls' school and enrolled thirty-eight students. Normally, they should have waited for a final authorization from the new director, Aleksandr Vasil'evich, before they used their funds for a new school, but when questioned on the matter, Rozhdestvin apologetically explained that he did not know the procedure. Vasil'evich assured Derevenskii that he did not favor the school either, but closing it at this point could potentially cause unrest among the city's Muslim inhabitants and was therefore unadvisable.[25] Meanwhile, Derevenskii left Kazan to become the trustee of the Kiev Educational Circuit,[26] and the new school for Muslim girls remained open. Had Kazan's Muslim notables approached the MNP directly to open this school, Derevenskii would have learned about their request earlier on and declined to allocate funds for it. However, the school opened and remained open thanks

---

[24] For examples of Pinegin's views, see NART, f. 142, op. 1, d. 39, ll. 21–23; NART, f. 142, op. 1, d. 74, ll. 20–20ob printed in Gorokhova ed. *Kazanskaia*, 146–47; and NART, f. 1, op. 4, d. 5482, ll. 89–96.

[25] NART, f. 92, op. 2, d. 14852, ll. 27–31. It seems the letter was first written by the assistant of Derevenskii in his absence but then Derevenskii had approved and sent it.

[26] I. E. Krapotkina, "Administrativnaia deiatel'nost' popechitel'ia uchebnogo okruga (iz istorii Kazanskogo uchebno-okruzhnogo tsentra," in *Izvestiia Altaiskogo gosudarstvennogo universiteta*, 2010 (68): 24.

to the Kazan city educational commission's involvement in the decision making process and, of course, its funds.

The minutes of a meeting organized over two days in January 1912 by the Kazan County Zemstvo in order to develop a strategy for opening Russo-Muslim schools also illustrates the dynamics of the relations among local bodies of governance, Muslim notables, and the representatives of the central state establishment in the last years of the tsarist regime.[27] To this meeting, the Kazan county zemstvo had invited thirty-one prominent Muslims, including newspaper editors, publishers, attorneys, mullahs, and merchants, of whom twenty-one attended. On the second day of the meeting, the inspector of public schools in the Kazan Educational Circuit Iakov Dmitrievich Koblov joined in. An article published by Koblov in 1905 indicates his sympathy for missionary work among non-Russians, although he had disagreements with Il'minskii's followers regarding the methods of proselytization.[28] Moreover, as we have seen earlier, Koblov had authored several influential works against Muslim activism in the Volga-Ural region too.[29] Therefore, we can safely consider him on the side of the state–missionary alliance against Muslim activism. As such, his exchanges with the Muslim representatives of the meeting reflect tension and mutual irritation, especially when compared to the zemstvo board's noticeable efforts to find common ground with the Muslim representatives. The contrast between the tones of these two sets of dialogue shows how cooperation and confrontation were both possible in the late Russian empire depending on the position of each party involved in an exchange.

The meeting of the Kazan County Zemstvo opened with the presentation of a report that the zemstvo had commissioned from Koblov on Russo-Muslim schools. The report suggested that the Volga-Ural Muslims, and especially the Tatars, opposed Russo-Muslim schools and that Muslim newspapers propagated separatism. When this presentation finished, Muhammedcan Seydaşef, a reporter of the Muslim

---

[27] The meeting minutes were published in Turkic translation in 1912, Anon., *Qazan Uyezdindeki*; and a detailed police report about the meeting in NART, f. 199, op. 1, d. 772, ll. 62–66 provides corroborating information.

[28] Iakov Dmitrievich Koblov, "O neobkhodimosti inorodcheskikh missionerov v dele prosveshcheniia inorodtsev," *Pravoslavnyi sobesednik*, 1905 (April): 705–16; and (May): 108–18.

[29] Some of these works include Iakov Dmitrievich Koblov, *Graf L. N. Tolstoi i musul'mane* (Kazan: Tipo-Litografiia Imperatorskogo Universiteta, 1904); Koblov, *O magometanskikh*; and Koblov, *Mechty*; Iakov Dmitrievich Koblov, *O tatarizatsii inorodtsev privolzhskogo kraia* (Kazan: Tsentrtipogr, 1910). Another book that Koblov published a few years after this meeting was *Konfessional'nyia shkoly*.

newspaper *Beyânü'l-Haq*, announced that as the representative of a
Muslim newspaper, he was against separatism and wanted Russo-
Muslim schools to open. Other members also declared that they were
not against Russo-Muslim schools and if there was some degree of
opposition among the broader Muslim population, this should be attrib-
uted to the disregard of the Muslims' demands for attention to religious
education in the preparation of the Russo-Muslim school curricula.
Following the Muslim representatives' comments, a member of the
board's school commission, A. N. Baraninskii, announced that he did
not think the Tatars nurtured ideas of separatism and, according to
Nicholas II's October Manifesto from 1905, which implied equality
among the empire's subjects, nor could they be considered enemies of
the state. Baraninskii gradually softened the meeting's atmosphere. He
added that the Tatars were children of the Russian empire, just as the
Russians were, and they should be expected to serve the empire with
sincerity. Nowhere in the world could the Tatars find a better place to
preserve their religion and way of life, Baraninskii continued, and many
Tatars had sacrificed their lives to protect Russia in the past. Following
this calming introduction, he finally opened the details of the zemstvo
projects for Russo-Muslim schools to discussion.[30]

The zemstvo projects called for three main issues to be discussed and
decided: the language of instruction, the place of Islamic subjects in the
programs of government schools for Muslims, and the timing of class
hours for religious subjects in the daily regimen of these schools. The
zemstvo needed the Muslim notables' support to have Russo-Muslim
schools embraced by the Muslim population. Baraninskii ensured that
the Tatar language and Islam would be taught throughout the duration
of schooling, which was planned to be six to eight years, and only the
subjects of general knowledge would be taught in Russian. Following
a break during which the Muslim representatives discussed these issues
among themselves, the first day of the meeting ended with the Muslim
representatives declaring formally that they were not against opening
Russo-Muslim schools and preferred the Tatar language and religious
subjects to be taught in the morning, when students were fresh. They
also endorsed an idea by the zemstvo board to publish a periodical
informing the Muslim population about government schools for
Muslims.[31]

Koblov joined the meeting on the second day. He read the official
programs for Russo-Muslim schools according to the law of March 26,

---

[30] Anon., *Qazan Uyezdindeki*, 1–7.   [31] Ibid., 8–13.

1870 and a more recent law from 1907.[32] Seydaşef asked what would happen if the attending Muslim representatives endorsed Russo-Muslim schools, but the law changed afterwards without their involvement. Koblov, with a stately demeanor that one can sense from the minutes, answered that the new law would take effect. Baraninskii once again tempered the mood by informing the participants about the ongoing discussions on this issue in the State Duma and concluded that even if the law changed, it would be in a way that should please the Muslims. Two main controversial issues came up during the rest of the meeting: the obligation to have singing classes in government schools for non-Russians, including Muslims, as required by the law of 1907, and the choice of teachers for Russo-Muslim schools. The singing classes were included in the school programs for non-Russians mainly because singing hymns was an important part of Orthodox religious education in the Il'minskii system. Koblov solved this problem by conceding that singing in Russo-Muslim schools could be interpreted as Qur'anic recitation although he would not drop the clause altogether since it was already in the law.

The choice of teachers was a more contentious issue that simultaneously cut through the progressive-conservative controversy among Volga-Ural Muslims and highlighted the missionary-state alliance's concerns about the Muslims' activism. Some of the Muslim representatives at the zemstvo meeting wanted mu'allims and not mullahs to teach the Tatar language and religious subjects in the Russo-Muslim schools. Members of the zemstvo board did not know the distinction very well and seemed to consider this a matter to be decided among Muslims. Baraninskii related the discussion to the choice of priests versus lay teachers in Orthodox Russian schools. He considered religion to be a matter of emotions more than knowledge and, therefore, opposed substituting priests with lay teachers in Russian schools. Likewise, he thought that the mullahs must have stronger emotions than mu'allims and, therefore, should make better teachers of religion. However, Baraninskii was primarily concerned with opening schools for Muslims, not with identity politics, and he seemed ready to concede his point if he was given sufficient explanation.[33]

On the other hand, Koblov knew very well that mu'allims and mullahs had comparable educational backgrounds and the main distinction between them lay in their position regarding the progressive reform

---

[32] On these laws, see Anon., *Pravila o nachal'nykh uchilishchakh dlia inorodtsev* (Orenburg: Kerîmof-Hüseyinof, 1908).

[33] Anon., *Qazan Uyezdindeki*, 13–19.

movement among Muslims. He had already expressed publicly that he was worried about the influence of Muslims, and especially the Muslim men of religion, over other non-Russian peoples in the Volga-Ural region. Moreover, he saw reformist Muslim activism as a serious threat to the empire's interests. Hence, he announced that he would prefer mullahs over muʿallims, because, he explained, the mullahs were certified by the Muslim spiritual assemblies whereas the muʿallims had no certification. In addition, the mullahs would teach for 60 rubles a year, since they already had income as imams, but the appointment of a muʿallim as the religion teacher of a Russo-Muslim school would cost 360 rubles. Finally, the Muslim representatives' demand did not make sense to him since the mullahs had long taught religion and the Tatar language to Muslim children in maktabs. He preferred religious subjects and the Tatar language to be taught by the mullahs while leaving the subjects of general education to Russian teachers or the graduates of the Muslim teachers' schools.

Later in the day, one of the Muslim representatives, Sheikh Ğattar Îmanayef, raised this issue again. Among the three possible candidates for teaching in Russo-Muslim schools, the mullahs, muʿallims, and the graduates of the Muslim teachers' schools, he considered graduates of the teachers' schools unfit for the job for not knowing the Tatar language well. He did not find the mullahs reliable either due to their lack of pedagogical skills and the grammatical knowledge of the Tatar language. This left him with the muʿallims, whom he proposed to be the ideal candidates for the job as adept pedagogues and users of the Tatar language. He wanted muʿallims to teach all subjects at the Russo-Muslim schools, including religion, the Tatar language, and the subjects of general education.

Koblov lost his nerve at this point. The teachers' schools for Muslims were under his jurisdiction. He declared that the primary teachers of Russo-Muslim schools had to be versed first and foremost in the general sciences and it was the graduates of the teachers' schools who could claim the best credentials in this regard. They studied both the subjects of general education and the Tatar language extensively. With regard to the muʿallims, he asked rhetorically, "Who are they?" and answered: "People aspiring to become mullahs." They graduated from madrasas just as the mullahs did, and with regard to their knowledge about general sciences, they had to be considered equal to the mullahs. "How can we assume that the mullahs are not capable of teaching but the muʿallims are?" he asked rhetorically again, and continued, "In any case, it is possible to appoint muʿallims as teachers of religion and the Tatar language but not to teach the subjects of general knowledge."

Here, the debate turned to the quality of religious and Tatar-language education that the Muslim teachers' schools offered. At some point, one of the Muslim representatives explained that the teachers of Russo-Muslim schools should be trained to teach "the Russian language, the Tatar language, religion, and the general subjects of knowledge as due." Thinking in more practical terms than both the Muslim representatives and Koblov, members of the zemstvo board took this statement as a compromise point. Instead of getting lost in the specifics of which graduates to hire from what type of schools, they suggested registering these necessary qualifications and worrying about the rest on a case-by-case basis. With all in agreement on this solution, the meeting could finally move on with the discussion of other, less controversial topics.[34]

Mundane encounters and occasions

One more factor that moderated the overall experience of Volga-Ural Muslims as subjects of the Russian empire emerged as the happenings of life unfolded in mundane encounters and occasions. Even as hawkish imperial functionaries tried to restrict the activism of Muslims, the outcomes of the interventions of these functionaries depended on the dynamics of an intricate web of human relations taking place in the context of the multiconfessional and multiethnic empire that Russia was. The story of how a reformed girls' madrasa in Kazan survived in the 1910s thanks to the possibly unintended support of Pinegin, despite his overall opposition to the activities of progressive Muslims, well illustrates this point.

The girls' madrasa in question belonged to Lebîbe Hüseyinova (1880–1920). Born to the family of a village mullah from the Chistai County of the Kazan Gubernia, Hüseyinova first studied with her father and then continued her education under the instruction of her elder brother who had progressive reformist ideas. At fifteen years of age, she started teaching at a maktab that the famous Muslim merchant family, the Akçurins, opened at the site of one of their factories in Penza. Then, Mâhrû Abıstay, Gâlimcan Barudî's wife and the head of the female section of his reformed madrasa, the Muhammediye, hired her as an assistant teacher. Here, Hüseyinova both studied and taught until 1903, when she got married and left. However, when Mâhrû Abıstay died the following year, many of her students sought Hüseyinova's assistance to continue their education, and in 1906, Hüseyinova opened her own

---

[34] Ibid., 19–29.

maktab in a two-story building in the city of Kazan with support from the female members of several merchant families. By the 1910s, she had hired other female teachers and started to teach at the madrasa level with a program that was comparable to the programs of the best reformed madrasas in the region. Her school was now known as the "Lebîbe Hanım Madrasa," and in addition to the traditional subjects of religion, it offered instruction in the Tatar language and literature, the Russian language and literature, the Arabic and Persian languages, mathematics, geometry, geography, history, botany, zoology, anatomy, painting, hygiene, singing, and pedagogy.

In 1911, as the imperial government started to clamp down on progressive maktabs and madrasas, it required private Muslim schools to register their programs with the MNP. Being located prominently in the city of Kazan, the Lebîbe Hanım Madrasa could not simply ignore this requirement, as did many other Muslim maktabs and madrasas in rural areas. Yet, the MNP was unlikely to approve a reformed madrasa program either, for it now required maktab and madrasa programs to be limited to religious subjects alone. Thus, Lebîbe Hüseyinova submitted a conventional maktab program for authorization while in reality she continued to follow her reformed madrasa program. Yet, the advanced level of her teaching was too conspicuous to escape notice, and the suspecting MNP inspectors raided her madrasa six times in the 1911–12 school year. Hüseyinova, her assistant teachers, and her students survived each of these raids successfully without giving the inspectors evidence for closure. All that the inspectors could find during their visits was the appearance of a conventional girls' maktab that taught nothing but basic religious subjects in a larger than conventional building.

This is how it happened. Lebîbe Hüseyinova was friends with Zöhre Alkina, a Muslim Tatar woman from a merchant family of noble origins, and Zöhre Alkina lived in domestic union with Pinegin, who remained well-connected in Kazan's administrative circles even after his retirement in late 1911. Alkina would learn about upcoming inspections through Pinegin's connections and pass the information on to Hüseyinova. Hüseyinova and her assistants would then prepare the madrasa for inspection by hiding geographic maps and globes in the attic and non-religious books under the floor. They would leave only religious books on the desks. All of the students would gather in one room to give the impression that only one type of elementary education was provided in the school. The eldest students, who could sometimes be in their fifties, would leave the premises temporarily. With one of the girls keeping watch on the street, the students would start reading religious books as soon as the inspectors appeared on the corner. Lebîbe Hüseyinova would meet the inspectors at the door, and not knowing Russian, she would constantly repeat the Russian-language words *"Koran uchim, tol'ko Koran uchim"* (We teach the Qur'an, we teach only the Qur'an). Then Sûfiye Şâkircan, one of her assistants, would escort the inspectors through the building speaking in Russian.[35]

While such occasions of evasion – or other tactics that may fall under the rubric of "everyday forms of resistance" – helped Volga-Ural Muslims absorb the pressures of restrictive tsarist policies, the moderating mundane encounters spread through a broader range of life experiences. The Volga-Ural Muslim domain, as it had evolved in the Catherinian imperial model, served Muslims not only as a refuge for religious identity but also as a comfort zone, where they could confine their interactions to familiar language and practices. Yet the inventions and amenities that became available as the expansion of European modernity transformed imperial Russia offered them numerous temporal comforts outside of the Volga-Ural Muslim domain. In 1879, for instance, Ğabdurreşîd İbrâhim, who was still an obscure madrasa student, boarded a train that took him from Orenburg to Perm in less than a day. He was on his way to Hijaz, as we have seen in an earlier chapter, and he had previously covered the distance from Petropavl to Orenburg on foot. He did not know that such a thing as a train existed to travel further. An imam he met in Petropavl informed him about the newly launched railway service, purchased a ticket, and sent him off to Perm.[36] As other obscure Volga-Ural Muslims boarded trains, admired the urban amenities of cities such as Kazan and Nizhny Novgorod,[37] or gradually became involved in the market revolutions of the late nineteenth century, say, by buying rubber boots or selling surplus grain,[38] they pushed the boundaries of their comfort zones, one amenity at a time, beyond the confines of the Volga-Ural Muslim domain. In an article that he wrote in 1915, Fahreddin narrates how a prominent Islamic scholar in Kazan had threatened his congregation with not conducting their funeral services if they continued to dress in short jackets (*kazakin*), a particular type of fur cap (*börk*), and boots, which the Volga-Ural Muslims traditionally did not wear.[39] All the same, Kazan's Muslims continued to wear these new and convenient outfits that made Russians, Muslims, and everyone else look more

---

[35] Mähmutova, "Kazandagı," 134–37.
[36] İbrâhîmof, *Tercüme-yi Hâlim*, 54. Also see Chapter 5.
[37] On such urban amenities, see Brower, *Russian City*, especially 73–74.
[38] Fahreddin, "Kiyümler," 225–28; and Frank, *Muslim Religious Institutions*, 48–49.
[39] Fahreddin, "Kiyümler," 225–28.

like each other, while also attending prayers at the mosque and therefore, marking their distinctiveness as Muslims.

Limits on integration

Expectations of equal treatment, more inclusive representation, and
mundane encounters and occasions moderated the Volga-Ural Muslims
experience as subjects of a non-Muslim ruled empire, but equating the
resulting flexibility to a foundation for genuine integration would be
overly optimistic. Most Volga-Ural Muslims rarely engaged the world
beyond the confines of the regional or trans-regional Muslim domains
in ways meaningful enough to create familiarity with Russians or other
non-Muslims. With few exceptions, such as the big merchants of
Kazan who had a multigenerational history of participation in imperial
institutions, or the alienated intellectuals who chose a cosmopolitan way
of life, the average Volga-Ural Muslim confined his or her personal
attachments to a world of Muslims even while physically moving among
the empire's multi-confessional and multi-ethnic crowd. The comfort
zone that expanded beyond insulated Muslim communities through the
incorporation of temporal amenities in daily life rarely reached far
enough to include personal relations with non-Muslims. Here, a barrier
of unfamiliarity marked the limits of the Volga-Ural Muslims' integration
into the increasingly more cosmopolitan Russian society. Yes,
Ğabdurreşîd İbrâhîm was excited about riding a train in 1879, and during
his sojourns as a young and broke student, he would occasionally engage
Russians for small purposes, such as for asking for a piece of bread
or getting on a boat, but he would always seek fellow Muslims for more
meaningful assistance and interaction. He learned enough Russian to
communicate at a reasonable rate only when he was put in jail for
traveling without a valid passport and sent to his hometown, Tara,
among many non-Muslim convicts in an exile convoy that walked in
chains through Siberia.[40] Or take the example of Ğabdurrahmân bin
Ğatâullah el-Kazanî who relates no account of an exchange with non-
Muslims in his travel notes of a three-month journey between Yarkend
and Nizhny Novgorod in 1901, although, as we have seen earlier, he was
a well-educated intellectual with progressive ideas and evidently spoke
Russian too.[41]

A curious story from a small book published in 1916 further illustrates
this barrier of unfamiliarity. The anonymous author of the book appears

---

[40] İbrâhîmof, *Tercüme-yi Hâlim*, especially 19–32.
[41] el-Kazanî, *Üç Aylık*. Also see in Chapter 5.

to have served as a school inspector in the Simbirsk Gubernia in the 1910s. Following complaints about the separatism of Muslims and the deplorable condition of government education among them, this author identifies the root cause of the Muslims' indifference to government schooling as the mutual suspicion and uneasiness characterizing the relations between Muslims and government officials. Then, he provides an example by recounting one of his visits to a madrasa. "I approached the madrasa," he writes:

Many curious eyes rushed to the windows of the upper floor of the big building. I was convinced that these were the madrasa students. I entered the hallway that led to a long corridor. The entire school stirred up in agitation, but soon, all became quiet. Then, four young Tatars between the ages of twenty-five and thirty appeared from somewhere and surrounded me. On their faces, I did not notice fear, bewilderment, or distrust but suspicion.

Speaking in Russian, the author explained to the young men that he was traveling to learn about schools and teachers. Then, he asked for the mullah who operated the madrasa. When the mullah arrived, the young men stopped talking and responded to the author's questions with a silent expression of incomprehension on their faces, leaving the mullah to speak for them all. As the mullah showed the author one of the rooms in the building, the author noticed the room's "neatness and cleanness" and asked who lived there. The mullah pointed to two of the young men who had met the author upon his arrival. Then the author asked what the young men did. After a long hesitation, the mullah replied that they simultaneously taught and studied at the madrasa. The author then started questioning the young men in order to learn where they had studied previously and in what capacity they were serving at the madrasa, but a sense of even stronger suspicion filled the air. After exchanging looks among each other, the mullah and the young men announced that they knew Russian badly and therefore could not understand the author's questions. "I realized that the school's functionaries, who had never been reviewed by the authorities of the schooling administration before, decided to proceed carefully in conversing with me," remarks the author. He asked for a translator, and the village scribe, "who was also Muslim," came to translate. But the author could not break his interlocutors' reticence with the translator either. The mullah and the young men exchanged comments among themselves in Tatar and then responded to him with evasive and inconsistent answers. At some point, when the translator attempted to explain an issue, the mullah even stopped him and instructed that he should only translate.

The author continued this futile exchange for a while before he suddenly announced that he actually knew Tatar. "The mullah blushed and smiled in a good-natured way. He livened up," the author writes, and the tone of their conversation changed entirely. The mullah started answering the author's questions willingly and clearly. The author found out that this was a new-method madrasa with an eight-year program. Aside from the building, the mullah showed the author the books used for instruction at the madrasa, which included several Russian-Tatar dictionaries and Russian-language readers in addition to textbooks written by progressive Muslim intellectuals and scholars. When the author finished his inspection and wanted to leave, the mullah "amiably" invited him to his house for tea. The author agreed, and the two became so engrossed in conversation over tea that by the time the author left, it was late in the evening.[42]

Thus, the author of this small book was able to break the barrier of unfamiliarity by speaking Tatar, but that was an exception that proved the rule. Only rarely did a Russian official speak to Muslims in their language, and when one did, it was the surprise effect of this extraordinary occurrence that broke the ice. Although many Volga-Ural Muslims started to make an effort to learn Russian by the 1910s, speaking Russian often remained a survival tool in an unfamiliar, unpredictable, and precarious world, as illustrated by the attitude of the four young men who met the anonymous author of the above story upon his arrival at their madrasa. They obviously spoke Russian but still felt compelled to avoid prolonged conversation lest what they divulged would hurt the madrasa. Learning Russian helped Volga-Ural Muslims navigate the imperial domain and take advantage of the many opportunities it offered, but this did not necessarily translate into grounds for familiarity and comfort in personal relations.

In the last chapter of *Window on the East*, Robert Geraci describes how the Kazan Imperial University professor Nikolai Fedorovich Katanov's ethnic origin as a Khakas had constrained his integration into Russian public life, despite his command of the Russian language, brilliant academic career, and voluntary conversion to Orthodoxy. Katanov's Russian peers were simply unwilling or unable to accept him as one of their own.[43] The limits on the Volga-Ural Muslims' integration into Russian society in the late Russian empire point to the flipside of this stalemate. Russia's imperial domain expanded in the late nineteenth and the early twentieth centuries, releasing "thousands of invisible threads" that connected Russians, Muslims, and others to "a vast state" beyond

---

[42] R-v., O., *K voprosu o magometanskikh*, 10–27.   [43] Geraci, *Window*, 309–42.

their local communities.[44] Yet a comforting aura of familiarity preserved the priority of connections to other Muslims for most Volga-Ural Muslims, while a distressing sense of unfamiliarity, or even strangeness, limited the quality of their connections to non-Muslims, even as those connections increased quantitatively. The invisible threads that connected Volga-Ural Muslims to the imperial domain were many but not strong enough to bring down the invisible boundaries of the Volga-Ural Muslim domain.

Conclusion

By studying court cases and other conflict situations in which individual Muslims have resorted to the intervention of Russian authorities to resolve disputes with other Muslims, Robert Crews and Stefan B. Kirmse have identified several politically significant examples of Muslim engagement with the tsarist state. Crews, especially, suggests that by applying what Russian officials had considered to be the "Islamic law" in adjudicating such disputes, the Russian state transformed "Muslims into active participants in the daily operation of the autocracy and the local construction and maintenance of the empire."[45] However, the high-stake conflict situations that escalated beyond the ability of local communities to settle without external enforcement or that involved only particular factions of a Muslim community cannot embody the Volga-Ural Muslims' overall experience. One could alternatively study other conflict situations in which tensions arose between the tsarist state and Muslim factions – such as the defiance of Russian authority after the 1860s by the Vaisovs,[46] a puritanist, increasingly sectarian, and relatively small group of Volga-Ural Muslims, or the closure of new-method schools in the 1910s – and in the end, one could find evidence for antagonism and alienation as well. The first one of these approaches supports the paradigm of an empire ever able to accommodate differences and therefore resilient in the face of turmoil while the second supports an interpretation of the entire pre-revolutionary Russian history as a prelude to the Bolshevik takeover in 1917.

A more complete understanding of the overall experience of Volga-Ural Muslims in late imperial Russia, as well as the imperial situation that characterized the tsarist empire more broadly, calls for evaluating the

---

[44] On the evolution of these new state–subject bonds in the Russian empire, see Steinwedel, "Invisible", quote from 1.

[45] Crews, *For Prophet*, quotation from 3; and Kirmse, "Dealing with Crime," 209–42.

[46] Usmanova, *Musul'manskoe* offers a detailed analysis of the Vaisov movement.

evidence from such conflict situations in the context of more mundane relations and processes as described in this chapter. This is difficult, for the mundane relations and processes leave little documentary trail. What this chapter, or this book in general, has been able to recover suggests that the Volga-Ural Muslims faced a complex situation in the late Russian empire. Their experiences involved instances of cooperation but also tension while the imperial domain's mundane flexibility moderated the intensity of both situations. This complexity needs to be appreciated on its own terms, rather than as an arsenal of evidence for either of the "toleration" or "prelude" paradigms.

Conclusion

[A]ll religious organizations of Muslims are on the verge of total destruction and effacement from the face of the earth.[1]   Rızâeddin bin
Fahreddin, the Mufti of Inner Russia and Siberia, 1930

The Soviet reconstruction of society was painful for the Volga-Ural Muslims as it was for many other peoples of the former Russian empire. The Bolsheviks preserved the Orenburg Spiritual Assembly under the name of "the Spiritual Assembly of Inner Russia and Siberia," but destroyed the Muslim institutions that the assembly had come to regulate since the time of Catherine II. By 1926, there were only 969 legally existing maktabs and madrasas left in the over 13,650 Muslim mahalles (neighborhoods with a mosque) under the assembly's jurisdiction, indicating that over ninety percent of the mullahs could not teach legally in "inner Russia and Siberia." The state had transferred the schooling of Muslim children to the Soviet educational system, which promoted atheism and ridiculed religion as superstitious and backward. In 1929, a resolution of the All-Union Central Executive Committee limited the activity of "religious organizations merely to the satisfaction of the religious needs of believers inside places of worship." Fahreddin, who was elected the mufti of the spiritual assembly in 1923, reported in 1930 that the vast majority of the mahalles under his jurisdiction had ceased to exist as administrative units due to the closure of local offices linking neighborhood imams to the spiritual assembly.[2] If the mullahs continued to serve their neighborhoods, they did so without guidance from the mufti.

Practicing religion was increasingly criminalized in the 1930s. Ten Muslim peasants in the Ul'ianovsk *oblast* who publicly celebrated the most important Muslim holiday of the year (*kurban bäyrämi*) were sentenced to death in 1930 while several of their co-celebrators were sent to labor camps.[3] Mullahs and prominent Muslim intellectuals particularly

---

[1] Quoted in Möhämmätshin, "Tatar Intelligentsia," 36.   [2] Ibid.
[3] İldus Tagirov, "Uchastnikov Kurban-bairama prigovorili k rasstrelu...," *Ekho vekov*, 1999 1(2): 126–35.

suffered from the purges of this period. One source estimates that about 30,000 members of the ulama in Soviet Russia were killed during Stalin's rule.[4] Soviet police archives hold the "confessions" of many Volga-Ural Muslim intellectuals who, after being forced to admit their involvement in "a pan-Turkist and pan-Islamist insurgent counterrevolutionary organization," were executed or sent to labor camps.[5]

One of those intellectuals was Ahmed-Hâdi Maqsûdî, the brother of Sadri Maqsûdî. Having led the aborted political mobilization of Tatars in the chaotic period following the October Revolution, Sadri Maqsûdî had escaped to Europe first and then settled in Turkey in 1925. His daughter and biographer Adile Ayda relates how her father was cut off from Russia in this period and even had to stop writing to his brother in Kazan upon learning from a random traveler from the Soviet Union that following each of his letters, the police would interrogate Hâdi Maqsûdî for several months in jail.[6] One can only imagine the frustration of Russian Muslim intellectuals in exile such as Sadri Maqsûdî, as they followed the news from abroad about the catastrophic uprooting of Muslim institutions and people in the Soviet Union.

Those diaspora intellectuals established the tone of Turkish and Western historiography on the Volga-Ural Muslims until the end of the Cold War. With already bitter memories from the inter-revolutionary period, they viewed Soviet policies as building on tsarist precedents and exposed Russian imperial treatment of Muslims as reactionary and repressive. Especially after the Second World War, this representation resonated with European and American scholars and politicians who were interested in exploring the possibility of a disaffected and potentially subversive Muslim contingent in the Soviet Union.[7] Yet, the disintegration of the Soviet Union in 1992 rendered that quest obsolete. Since then, a fresh cohort of researchers, who enjoyed relatively easy access to Soviet and tsarist archives, joined the "imperial turn" and challenged the

---

[4] A. A. Alov and N. G. Vladimirov, *Islam v Rossii* (Moscow: Institut Naslediia, 1996), 60. See Il'nur. R. Minnullin, *Musul'manskoe dukhovenstvo Tatarstana v usloviiakh politicheskikh repressii 1920–1930-kh gg.* (Nizhny Novgorod: Id. Mädina, 2007) for a survey of the persecution of the Volga-Ural ulama in the 1920s and 1930s.

[5] On these purges, see S. T. Rakhimov, "Akhmet-Khadi Maksudi," *Ekho vekov*, 1995 1(1): 185–95; S. T. Rakhimov, "Dzh. Validi: 'U menia raznoglasiia s sovvlast'iu'," *Ekho vekov*, 1996 1(2): 150–73; and İldus Tagirov, "O chem rasskazyvaet sledstvennoe delo Iliasa Alkina," in *Ekho vekov*, 2001 3(4): 142–48.

[6] Adile Ayda, *Sadri Maksudi Arsal* (Ankara: Kültür Bakanlığı Yayınları, 1991), 206–7.

[7] For a detailed overview and critique of the Western historiography on Volga-Ural Muslims, see Mustafa Tuna, "Zapadnaia literatura istorii Tatar 18go-nachala 20go vv.," in *Istoriia Tatar s drevneishikh vremen*, ed. Il'dus Zagidullin (Kazan: Institut istorii im. Sh. Mardzhani, 2013), 42–46.

paradigm of the Russian empire as a "prison of nations" by exploring the notions of diversity, accomodation, and variations in local practice in the histories of the tsars' Muslim as well as other non-Russian subjects.[8] As Christopher Bayly writes: "Historians keep themselves in a job by overthrowing received wisdom once a generation or so. This is a task which can usually be achieved quite simply, because all historical writing is a question of assigning emphasis."[9] The post-Cold War "imperial turn" among the historians of Russia's minorities reflects this tendency: the sharp contradictions in the historiography before and after the disintegration of the Soviet Union demonstrate how scholars have observed the historical past from different vantage points, rather than representing a mired confusion about what transpired.

In this book, I have sought not to overthrow the received wisdom but to build on and move beyond its two seemingly contradictory positions in order to attain a more sophisticated understanding of imperial situations such as the one that shaped the experiences of Volga-Ural Muslims in late tsarist Russia. I have pursued this goal with a fluid model of observation made possible by the revealing lens of the concept of "domains," which we might define as shared worlds emerging from patterns of human exchange that are sufficiently continuous and intense to offer a common cultural frame and comfort zone to their participants. Prioritizing exchange in identifying human categories frees the narrative from the rigid constraints of temporal and spatial boundaries as well as that of conventional identifiers, such as political subjecthood, ethnicity, and religion. Such boundaries and identifiers remain significant, and I have paid close attention to them, for they bear upon the formation and evolution of domains, but only as one among many contributing factors. Thinking with domains helps illuminate the overarching processes as they evolve through the interaction of those particular factors that notably include contingency as well.

In this study, I have identified and weaved together the stories of four domains: the transregional Muslim domain, the Volga-Ural Muslim domain, the Russian imperial domain, and the pan-European domain. It is worth repeating that the idea of a "domain" would best be understood as an "open concept" and since exchange patterns shift, intersect,

---

[8] A pioneering work representing this approach was Andreas Kappeler, *Russland als Vielvölkerreich: Entstehung, Geschichte, Zerfall* (Munich: Beck, 1992). Some other noteworthy contributions are Geraci, *Window*; Dowler, *Classroom and Empire*; Nathans, *Beyond the Pale*; Werth, *At the Margins*; Crews, *For Prophet*; and Mikhail Dolbilov, *Russkii krai, chuzhaia vera: etnokonfessional'naia politika imperii v Litve i Belorussii pri Aleksandre II* (Moscow: Novoe literaturnoe obozrenie, 2010).
[9] Bayly, *The Birth*, 399.

and merge so do domains. Therefore, these four domains are not to be interpreted as rigid building blocks of a still mosaic but rather, as the entangled and evolving plots of a complicated motion picture. Each plot – that is each of the four domains explored in this study – reveals a larger scenario – the imperial situation that shaped the experiences of Volga-Ural Muslims in late tsarist Russia – from a different vantage point, and overlaying the images obtained from those multiple perspectives has offered a significantly expanded scope of historical analysis and interpretation to this book.

Viewed from those multiple perspectives, the Russian empire appears as a vast arena of exchange and sharing that was embedded within even broader patterns of transregional exchange. Individual subjects, communities, and state agents did not simply act their wills out in this arena but responded to the actions and perceived positions of each other. Hence, the complexity of the imperial situation that shaped the lives of Volga-Ural Muslims in late tsarist Russia (or of imperial situations in general) emanated from both the multiplicity of involved parties and the reflexive nature of their relations.

The level of comfort with which imperial agents approached this reflexivity determined their willingness to accomodate the needs and sensitivities of subject communities, and that willingness played an important role in the maintenance of relatively peaceful relations between the tsarist state and Volga-Ural Muslims in the Catherinian imperial model. By stopping the missionary interventions of the earlier centuries and allowing Volga-Ural Muslims to maintain a mediated distance from the tsarist state, Catherine II opened up an insulated safe space for them within the empire. The Volga-Ural Muslim domain, as I have described it in this study, evolved in that safe space. Islamic scholars played a crucial role in facilitating and, more importantly, giving meaning to the exchange that brought this domain into existence, and they also connected Volga-Ural Muslims to a broader, transregional Muslim domain. The preservation and in some respects, reinforcement of the ulama's centrality in communal affairs, as well as the mediating role of the muftis between the tsarist state and the Volga-Ural Muslim domain, secured a relatively agreeable situation for Volga-Ural Muslims roughly between the late eighteenth and the mid nineteenth centuries.

Yet, the escalation of rivalries among major empires for global mastery or regional influence in the second half of the long nineteenth century compromised the Catherinian imperial model's appeal for the Romanov regime. Competing in the race of empires required imperial states to maximize their internal resources, which in turn called for better strategies of accomodation to encourage the mobilization of imperial subjects behind imperial ideals. However, this was easier said than done. Setbacks in Russia's performance in the race of empires, such as the two embarrassing defeats in the Crimean and the Russo-Japanese wars, uncertainties accompanying the epochal transformations of the Great Reforms era, and the uncontainable spread of European modernity across imperial boundaries heightened the anxieties of tsarist authorities and elites about the subversive potentials of minorities. As these developments expanded the imperial domain by opening more inclusive channels of contact and communication among the empire's subjects and between those subjects and the tsarist state, official and self-appointed agents of the empire grew less comfortable with reflexivity. Instead, they wanted to create ideal subjects in a new, increasingly state-centered, and supposedly more competitive imperial model based on unmediated governance. This, however, could turn into a self-defeating endeavor, especially as the expansion of the pan-European domain exposed Russia's subjects to previously unavailable or nonexistent opportunities and aspirations that contradicted centrally defined ideals. Moreover, the attempts at socially engineering subject population groups into ideal subjects ran the risk of inciting those groups against the imperial state by disrupting the long-established social contracts on which they had come to rely. The resulting tensions were likely to hurt, if not completely impair, the Russian empire's viability.

In the Volga-Ural region, local concerns, such as the demands of baptized non-Russians to be registered as Muslims, escalated the anxiety of the members of a conservative alliance among central state bureaucrats and local missionaries to a detrimentally paranoid anti-Muslim stance. In the 1870s, the tsarist state sought to "russify" Volga-Ural Muslims through the instruction of the Russian language in special government schools. However, this strategy yielded meagre results after decades of trial (and error). Meanwhile, a small but highly active group of Muslim reformists began to introduce European-inspired schooling alternatives for Muslim children in the Russian empire. They worked to disseminate progressive ideas among their coreligionists, and following the 1905 Revolution, they even organized all-Russian congresses to represent Muslims in imperial politics. In the Volga-Ural region, their ability to mobilize the broader population of Muslim peasants remained highly limited, for not only did they lack the executive muscles of a state to back their projects, but also they fell at odds with the region's ulama and Islamic traditions, therefore challenging the Volga-Ural Muslim domain's long-established repertory of norms and values. However, the instruments they employed in pursuing their objectives, such as the print media, theater performances, and philanthropic societies, functioned in a modern paradigm that the Russian government agents and elites also shared. As a result, these otherwise disengaged intellectuals obtained a disproportionately vocal presence in the imperial domain, further stoking the fears of the state–missionary alliance about the Volga-Ural Muslims' resistance to Russification and, even worse, influence over other non-Russian peoples. Already frustrated by the failure of the government's earlier efforts to mold Muslims into ideal subjects, the members of this alliance pushed for increasingly restrictive and even repressive measures against Muslims in the region. Hence, the Volga-Ural Muslim experience in the last decades of the tsarist regime was actually replete with tensions.

Nevertheless, looking beyond the binary of relations between central state agents and local Muslim communities reveals a far more complicated web of exchange relations that defined the experiences of Volga-Ural Muslims in late tsarist Russia. The estate privileges of the Volga-Ural Muslim merchants and nobility, for instance, connected them to institutions and networks functioning in the imperial domain, which in turn was highly receptive to European influences. Thanks to such connections, these notables learned about and responded to the happenings of a broader world beyond the Volga-Ural Muslim domain, and they promoted the interests of their coreligionists in that world. The emergence or consolidation of local bodies of governance in the Great Reforms era created alternative venues for state–subject interactions, rendering the imperial domain more readily accessible to local Muslim communities and therefore, moderating their experience as subjects of a non-Muslim-ruled empire. And perhaps most importantly, the expansion of European modernity and concomitant transformations in Russia's social and economic landscape, such as infrastructural improvements, urbanization, and the integration of markets, extended mundane opportunities of a new kind to the empire's subjects, providing Volga-Ural Muslims with further sources of moderation even in the face of an increasingly repressive regime.

Empires enable us to frame certain groups of peoples and the lands they inhabited in recognizable units governed by a single, although multifaceted, apparatus. This provides a useful alternative to nation-states in conceiving history on a global scale, as exemplified in Jane Burbank and Frederick Cooper's remarkable survey, *Empires in World History*.[10] Yet, substituting empires for nation-states still preserves the centrality of the state in historical analysis, and the evidence provided in

---

[10] Burbank and Cooper, *Empires*.

this book points to the significance of metatopical exchange systems – or "domains" – in shaping people's lives along with, if not regardless of, imperial policies and state institutions.[11] This, however, is not an "either/or" question. Imperial states existed simultaneously with multiple domains and interacted with them in consequential ways.

By integrating the perspectives of several domains into telling the history of Volga-Ural Muslims in late imperial Russia, this book sheds light on two important probes of the imperial turn: the ability of empires to accommodate diversity and relatedly, their viability in the face of modern challenges. However, the reader may notice that the narrative withholds a definitive answer to either question. This is deliberate, since the evolving and multifaceted nature of empires, as highlighted throughout this study, defies easy generalizations that could have otherwise offered a resolution to the ongoing discussion that ultimately judges the merits and shortcomings of empires as institutions of governance. Therefore, instead of making a nostalgic case for empire, this book calls for a recognition of the complexity of imperial situations that simultaneously hosted possibilities of accomodation and confrontation, as do the nation-states of the post-imperial world we live in today. Inter-imperial competition and the uncertainties resulting from the fast-transforming impact of the expansion of European modernity aggravated the "tensions of empire" in the second half of the long nineteenth century,[12] but they also created opportunities of moderation. The final judgment on the ability of each empire to accommodate diversity or readily adapt to circumstances and therefore remain viable depended on the competence of its rulers to manage the multitude of exchange patterns that produced complex imperial situations. Less was sometimes more in this regard, as the relative success of the Catherinian imperial model testifies, but less and smart government was not necessarily tantamount to the ideal type of an empire, as indicated by the pursuit of tsarist agents for unmediated governance in the second half of the long nineteenth century.

---

[11] For a similar argument that focuses on "regional orders," see Cemil Aydın, *Beyond the Imperial and the Global: The Persistence of Regions in the Political History of the Long Nineteenth Century, 1750–1924* (unpublished manuscript draft). I would like to thank Cemil Aydın for sharing his unfinished work with me.

[12] I borrow this phrase from Frederick Cooper and Ann Laura Stoler, *Tensions of Empire: Colonial Cultures in a Bourgeois World* (Berkeley: University of California Press, 1997).

Bibliography

FONDS OF THE NATIONAL ARCHIVE OF THE REPUBLIC OF TATARSTAN
(NART)

Fond 1: Office of the Governor of Kazan
Fond 41: Kazan Circuit Court
Fond 92: Trustee of the Kazan Educational Circuit
Fond 142: Kazan Tatar Teachers' School
Fond 199: Gendarme Administration of the Kazan Gubernia
Fond 322: Inspector of Public Schools in the Kazan Gubernia
Fond 968: Personal Archive of Nikolai Ivanovich Il'minskii
Fond 1370: Personal Archive of Fâtih Kerîmî

PRIMARY SOURCES IN TURKIC

Anon. "Bankta Aqça Artuvu." *Şûra*, 1906 (6): 1
"Bize Qaysı Ğilmler Lazımdır." *Şûra*, 1908 (7): 197–99, (11): 338–43, (12):
    370–72, (13): 317–20, (14): 434–36, (15): 470–73
"Bugünki Meselemiz." *Şûra*, 1909 (8): 236–37
"Hankirman İmamlarınıñ Reddiyesi." *Din ve Ma'işet*, 1910 (5): 70
"Huliganlıq ve Mektebleribiz." *Mekteb*, 1914 2(3): 66–69
"Iz Bukhary." *Tercüman*, February 28, 1886
"Kazan Cemiyet-i Hayriyesi." *Tercüman/Perevodchik*, January 22, 1898
"Kazan." *Tercüman/Perevodchik*, February 25, 1884
"Raport." *Din ve Ma'işet*, 1910 (16): 250–51
"Sanâyi-i nefise yulında millî adım." *Añ*, 1915 (5): 102–3
Orenburg Vilayetindeki Mektebler. Orenburg: Orenburgskoe Gubernskoe
    Zemstvo, 1916
Osmanlı Belgelerinde Kazan. Ankara: Başbakanlık Devlet Arşivleri Genel
    Müdürlüğü, 2005
*Qazan Uyezdindeki Müslüman Avıllarında Rusça-Tatarça Mektebler Açuv
    Hususında*. Kazan: Beyanü'l-Haq Matbaası, 1912
1906 Sene 16–21 Avgustda İctima' İtmiş Rusya Müslümanlarınıñ Nedvesi. Kazan:
    Matba'ayı Kerîmiyye, 1906
"Yazı Maşinası." *Tercüman*, May 29, 1883
A., Y. "Ahmed Bay Vaqfı." *Şûra*, 1908 (1): 13–15

ʿAbdurrahmân, Muhammedzarîf ibn. "Edebiyat Kiçesi Nedir?" *Din ve Maʿîşet*, 1910 (16): 251–52

Adolf. "Usûl-i Cedîdege Umûmî Bir Nazar." In: *Usûl-i Cedîdge Qarşı Birinci Adım*, (ed.) Halîl Ebulhanef. Kazan: Ürnek Matbaʿası, 1910

Akçura, Yusuf. *Hatıralarım*. Istanbul: Hece Yayınları, 2005

ʿAli, M. "Mekteb mi? İşqola mı?" *Mekteb*, 1913 1(8): 192–97

Atlasî, Hâdi. "Bizniñ Mekteblerimiz." *Mekteb*, 1913 1(1): 19–20

Atlasî, Hâdi. "Bizniñ Teraqqî." *Şûra*, 1910 (24): 745–48

Atlasî, Hâdi. "Zemstva ve Bizniñ Mektebler." *Mekteb*, 1913 1(15): 361–63

Ayuhanof, Zâkir. "Ribâ Haqqında." *Şûra*, 1915 (1–19)

Bäşiri, Zarif. "Rämievlär turında istäleklär." In: *Bertugan Rämiyevlär: Fänni-biografik jentık*, (ed.) Liron Hämidullin, Raif Märdanov, and Ramil Miññullin, 138–49. Kazan: Ruhiyat, 2002

Behmanî, Ğabdulqadîm. "Mamadış Uyezinde Müslümanlar ve Anlarnıñ İqtisadî Halleri." *Şûra*, 1910 (18): 560–61

Bigiyef, Mûsa Cârullah. *Islâhat Esasları*. Petrograd: Tipografiia M-A Maksutova, 1915

Celâl, Sadri. "Bizde Muziqa." *Mekteb*, 1913 1(15): 369–73

Ebulhanef, Halîl. "Mekteblerde ʿUlûm-ı Tabiʿiyye." *Mekteb*, 1913 1(1): 28–30

Usûl-i Cedîdge Qarşı Birinci Adım. Kazan: Ürnek Matbaʿası, 1910

el-Hamdi, Şerîf. "Matbuʿat Vıstafqası." *Şûra*, 1911 (6): 190–91 and (7): 208–9

el-Kazanî, Ğabdurrahmân bin Ğatâullah. *Üç Aylık Seyahat*. Orenburg: Kerimof Matbaası, 1905

el-Kostramavî, Muhammednecîb bin Şerefüddin. "Ğabdulqayyûm el-Nâsırî Hazretleri Tercümeyi Hâline ʿÂid." *Şûra*, 1913 (8): 233–37

el-Mesʿûdî, Âhund. "Tertibli Mektebge Başlab Qarşuçıları Kimler?" *Mekteb*, 1913 1(7): 173–75

el-Osmânî, Muhammed el-Sâdıq. "Mûsa Bigiyefʿge Reddiye." *Din ve Maʿîşet*, 1910 (2): 22–25

el-Qurmâşî, Sâbircan bin. "Dinsiz Diyler." *Şûra*, 1914 (16): 503

Fahreddin, Rızâeddin bin. *Ahmed Bay*. Orenburg: Vaqit Matbaʿası, 1911

Âsar: Üz Memleketimizde Ulgan İslâm ʿÂlimleriniñ Tercüme ve Tabaqaları. 2 vols. Kazan: Tipo-litografiia imperatorskogo universiteta, 1900–8

İslâmlar Haqqında Hükûmet Tedbirleri. Vol. 1. Orenburg: Kerimof, Hüseyinof ve Şürekâsı, 1907

(ed.) *İsmâʿîl Seyahati*. Kazan: Tipo-Litografiia İ. N. Kharitonova, 1903

(ed.) "Kiyümler Haqqında." *Şûra*, 1915 (8): 225–28, (9): 258–60, 10: 289–92

(ed.) "Millî Matbuʿâtımız." *Şûra*, 324–26, 525–27, 673–75

(ed.) "Muhammedşâkir Efendi Ramiyef." *Şûra*, 1913 (6): 186–88

Fi., ʿAyn. "Meşhurrak Medreseleribiz Hâlinden." *Mekteb*, 1913 1(10): 952–54, (11): 261–64, (12): 290–91

"Tabîʿiyyattan Ders Kitablarıbız." *Mekteb*, 1913 1(12): 294–97

Fuʿâd, Mahmûd. "Avıl Mullaları." *Mekteb*, 1913 1(6): 154–57

"Büyük Bababız Vefat." *Mekteb*, 1914 2(9): 197–210.

"Medreselerde Çuvalular." *Mekteb*, 1913 1(3): 68–71

"Mekteb mi İşkola mı?" *Mekteb*, 1913 1(10): 237–42

"Mektebleribizniñ Mâliye Ciheti." *Mekteb*, 1913 1: (1): 30–32, (2): 57–60
Ğadlî, Fettâh "İslâmlar Arasında Ğilm Niçün Lâzım Derecede Taralmıy?" *Şûra*,
    1911 (18): 552–56, (19): 588–92, (20): 614–16
Gasprinskiy, İsmâ'îl. *Avrupa Medeniyetine Bir Nazar-ı Muvazene*. İstanbul:
    Matba'a-yı Ebu Ziyâ, 1302 A.H./1885
"Darürrahat Müslümanları." In: *İsmail Gaspıralı: Seçilmiş Eserleri I: Edebî
    Eserleri*, (ed.) Yavuz Akpınar, Bayram Orak, and Nazım Muradov, 167–
    274. Reprint, in Latin transcription, Istanbul: Ötüken, 2005
"Editorial." *Tercüman*, January 7, 1885
"Frengistan Mektupları." In: *İsmail Gaspıralı: Seçilmiş Eserleri I: Edebî Eserleri*,
    (ed.) Yavuz Akpınar, Bayram Orak, and Nazım Muradov, 81–166. Reprint,
    in Latin transcription, Istanbul: Ötüken, 2005
"Kadimcilik-Ceditçilik." In: *İsmail Gaspıralı: Seçilmiş Eserleri II: Fikrî Eserleri*, (ed.)
    Yavuz Akpınar, 273–86. Reprint, in Latin transcription, Istanbul: Ötüken, 2004
"Mebâdî-yi Temeddün-i İslâmiyan-ı Rus." In: *İsmail Gaspıralı: Seçilmiş Eserleri
    II: Fikrî Eserleri*, (ed.) Yavuz Akpınar, 251–72. Reprint, in Latin
    transcription, Istanbul: Ötüken, 2004
"Mezheb-i İştirâkiyyûn." In: *İsmail Gaspıralı: Seçilmiş Eserleri II: Fikrî Eserleri*,
    (ed.) Yavuz Akpınar, 190–221. Reprint, in Latin transcription, İstanbul:
    Ötüken, 2004
"Rusya'da Matbuat ve Neşriyât-ı İslâmiye." In: *İsmail Gaspıralı: Seçilmiş Eserleri
    II: Fikrî Eserleri*, (ed.) Yavuz Akpınar, 245–50. Reprint, in Latin
    transcription, İstanbul: Ötüken, 2004
"Türk Yurdcularına." *Türk Yurdu*, 1: (7): 109–11 and (8):132–34
Hoca-yı Sıbyân. Reprint, Bahçesaray, 1992
Gasprinskiy, İsmâ'îl. *İsmail Gaspıralı: Seçilmiş Eserleri III: Dil-Edebiyat-Seyahat
    Yazıları*, (ed.) Yavuz Akpınar. İstanbul: Ötüken, 2008
Rehber-i Mu'allimîn yaki Mu'allimlere Yoldaş. Bahçesaray, 1898
Gazizov, Rıza. "Uyan, şäkirt, yoqlamagıl." In: *Mädräsälärdä Kitap Kiştäse*, (ed.)
    Röstäm Mähdiev, 171–75. Kazan: Tatarstan Kitap Neşriyatı, 1992
"Geçdi Zaman, Geldi Zaman." *Tercüman*, October 29, 1904
Hämidullin, Liron, Raif Märdanov, and Ramil Miñnullin (eds.). *Bertugan
    Rämiyevlär: Fännibiografik jentık*. Kazan: Ruhiyat, 2002
Hikmet, Adil. *Asya'da Beş Türk*. Istanbul: Ötüken, 1998
İbrâhimof, Abdürreşid. *Çoban Yıldızı*. St. Petersburg: Abdürreşid İbrâhimof
    Elektrik Basmahanesi, 1907
Tercüme-yi Hâlim yaki Başıma Kilenler. St. Petersburg: Elektro-pechati A. O.
    Ibragimova, 1883
İbrâhimof, Ğâlimcan. "'Biz Kim?' Bahisi." *Şûra*, 1912 (9): 267–68
"Biz Tatarmız." *Şûra*, 1911 (8): 236–38
İshakî, Ayaz. *İki Yüz Yıldan Suñ İnqıraz*. Kazan: I. N. Kharitopov Tipografiyası,
    1904
'Iyâd. "Millî Kuy ve Muñlarıbız." *Mekteb*, 1914 2(5): 101–3
Kemâluddinof, Salâhuddin. "Bizde Resim." *Mekteb*, 1913 1(5): 125–27
Kerimi, Fatih. *Avrupa Seyahatnamesi*. Reprint, in modern Turkish adaptation,
    Istanbul: Çağrı Yayınları, 2001
Bir Şakird ile Bir Student. Kazan: Tipografiia B. L. Dombrovskogo, 1903

"Därdemänd." In: *Bertugan Rämiyevlär: Fänni-biografik jientık*, (ed.) Liron Hämidullin, Raif Märdanov, and Ramil Miñnullin, 102–9. Kazan: Ruhiyat, 2002

"Kem ide Şakir äfände." In: *Bertugan Rämiyevlär: Fänni-biografik jientık*, (ed.) Liron Hämidullin, Raif Märdanov, and Ramil Miñnullin, 119–22. Kazan: Ruhiyat, 2002

Maqsûdî, Hâdi. *Risâle-yi Mu'allim-i Evvel: Usûl-i Savtiyye Buyınça Türkî Elifba.* Reprint, Kazan: İman Neşriyatı, 1997

Märdanov, Raif F. "*Vakıt* gazetası." In: *Bertugan Rämiyevlär: Fänni-biografik jientık*, (ed.) Liron Hämidullin, Raif Märdanov, and Ramil Miñnullin, 161–63. Kazan: Ruhiyat, 2002

Märdanov, Raif, Ramil Miñnullin, and Süleyman Rähimov (eds.). *Bertugan Bubıylar Mädräsäse.* Kazan: Ruhiyat, 1999

(eds.) *Fatih Kärimi.* Kazan: Ruhiyat, 2000

(eds.) *Rizaetdin Fähretdin: Fänni-biografik jientık.* Kazan: Ruhiyat, 1999

Mercani, Şehabeddin. *Müstefad'ül-Ahbar Fi Ahval-i Kazan ve Bulgar.* 2 vols. Reprint, Ankara: Türk Kültürünü Araştırma Enstitüsü Yayınları, 1997

Mir Haydar, Mutahhir ibn Mulla. *İski Qışqı Tarihi.* Orenburg: Din ve Ma'îşet Matbaası, 1911

Muzafferof, Muhammed Kemal. "Bizde Şâkirdler Sabırlılar." *Şûra*, 1912 (18): 568–69

Patinskiy. "Millî Matbû'atımız." *Şûra*, 1915 (20): 630–31

Qurbangaliyef, Muhîddin. "İbtidâî Mekteblerde Uqılaturgan Fenler." *Mekteb*, 1913 1(1): 24–25

Rasûlî, Zeynullah. *Troyski Ğuleması ve Usûl-i Cedîde.* Orenburg: Kerimof Hüseynof Matba'ası, 1907

Salaviyof, Timurşah. *Mekteb ve Medreselerni Duhovniy Sobraniyege Birüv.* Orenburg: Kerimof, Hüseyinof, ve Şürekâsı, 1908

Serdar, Ahmed. "Çin Maçin Yolunda Muhterem Şâkir Efendi Ramiyef Hazretleri." *Şûra*, 1912 (11): 349–51

Şeref, Burhan. *Ganî Bay.* Orenburg: Vaqit Matba'ası, 1913

Şeref, Ş. "Mevlid Ayı Münasebetiyle." *Mekteb*, 1914 2(2): 29–31

Seyfi, Fâtih. "Mektebleribizde 'İbâdet." *Mekteb*, 1914 2(1): 26–28

Seyfülmülükef, Mustafa. "İqtisâdî Tarihte Ribâ Meselesi." *Şûra*, 1915(14–24), 1916(6–9)

Şinasi, İbrahim. *Makaleler.* Ankara: Dün-Bugün Yayınevi, 1960

Süleymanof, Niyaz Muhammed. *Mektublarım.* Orenburg: Kerimof, Hüseyinof ve Şürekâsı, 1908

Sultanmuhammed, Halîl. "Sevdagirlik." *Şûra*, 1911 (15): 461–62

Tataroğlu. "Biz Kim." *Şûra*: 1911 (2): 2, (4): 2

Togan, Zeki Velidi. *Hatıralar: Türkistan ve Diğer Müslüman Doğu Türklerinin Milli Varlık ve Kültür Mücadeleleri.* Ankara: Türkiye Diyanet Vakfı Yayınları, 1999

Tuqayef, Muhammed Şakir Mahdum. *Tarih-i İsterlibaş.* Kazan: B. L. Dombrovskogo Tipografiyası, 1899

Türkoğlu. "Biz Türkmiz." *Şûra*, 1911 (8): 238–41, (11): 327–29, 1912 (1): 19–21, (2): 55–56, (3): 79–80

'Ubeydullin, Sâlih bin Sâbit, (ed.). *Mercânî.* Kazan: Ma'ârif, 1914–15

Urmançı, Baki. "Çıksa Mägriptän Koyaş." In: *Mädräsälärdä Kitap Kiştäse*, (ed.) Röstäm Mähdiev, 33–37. Kazan: Tatarstan Kitap Näşriyatı, 1992

PRIMARY SOURCES IN RUSSIAN

Anon. "Krymskoe Blagotvoritel'noe Obshchestvo." *Tercüman/Perevodchik*, February 27, 1898
"Mahmud Esad Efendi v Rossii." *Mir Islama*, 1913 2(7): 462–78
"Novoe Obshchestvo." *Tercüman/Perevodchik*, February 27, 1898
Pravila o nachal'nykh uchilishchakh dlia inorodtsev. Orenburg: Kerîmof-Hüseyinof, 1908
Abdrafikova, G. Kh. and V. Iu. Gabidullina (eds.). *Materialy k biobibliografii Rizy Fakhretdinova*. Ufa: IIIaL UNTs RAN, 2010
Aleksei, Bishop. *Sovremennoe dvizhenie v srede russkikh Musul'man*. Kazan, 1910
Alektorov, A. "Iz istorii razvitiia obrazovaniia sredi Kirgizov Akmolinskoi i Semipalatinskoi Oblastei." *Zhurnal Ministerstva Narodnogo Prosveshcheniia*, 1905 362 (December): 154–91
Andrei, Bishop. "Krupnaia novost' v dele inorodcheskogo Prosveshcheniia." *Sotrudnik bratstva sviat. Guriia*, 1911 (February 6): 83–89
Arsharuni, A. "Iz istorii natsional'noi politiki tsarisma." *Krasnyi arkhiv*, 1929 4(35): 107–27
Bartol'd, Vasilii Vladimirovich. *Teokraticheskaia ideia i svetskaia vlast' v musul'manskom gosudarstve*. St. Petersburg: Tipo-litogr. B. M. Vol'fa, 1903
Bobronikov, Nikolai. "Sovremennoe polozhenie uchebnogo dela u inorodcheskikh plemen vostochnoi Rossii." *Zhurnal Ministerstva Narodnogo Prosveshcheniia*, 1917 novaia seriia 135 (May): 51–84
D., R. "Neobkhodimost' shkol'nogo obucheniia dlia devits kreshchenykh Tatar." *Sotrudnik bratstva sviat. Guriia*, 1910 (January 23): 125–26
Fuks, Karl. *Kazanskie Tatary v statisticheskom i etnograficheskom otnosheniiakh*. Reprint, Kazan: Fond TIaK, 1991
Gasprinskii, Ismail Bei. *Russkoe Musul'manstvo: mysli, zametki, nabliudenie musul'manina*. Simferopol: Spiro, 1881
Gorokhova, L. V. (ed.). *Kazanskaia tatarskaia uchitel'skaia shkola 1876–1917 gg.* Kazan: Izdatel'stvo Gasyr, 2005
Grigor'ev, V. V. "Zapiska." In: *Sbornik dokumentov i statei po voprosu ob obrazovanii inorodtsev*, (ed.) Ministerstvo narodnogo prosveshcheniia, 204–6. St. Petersburg: V Tip. T-va Obshchestvennaia Pol'za, 1869
Il'minskii, Nikolai Ivanovich. "Iz neizdannykh pisem N. I. Il'minskogo." *Sotrudnik bratstva sviat. Guriia*, 1909 (December 12)
Opyty perelozheniia khristianskikh verouchitel'nykh knig na Tatarskii i drugie inorodcheskie iazyki v nachale tekushchogo stoleiia. Kazan: Tipografiia Imperatorskogo Universiteta, 1883
Ivanitskii, Prot. Taras'. "Kakie i ch'i vliianiia inorodtsy ispytyvaiut na sebe." *Sotrudnik bratstva sviat. Guriia*, 1909 (November 29): 10–13
Koblov, Iakov Dmitrievich. *Graf L. N. Tolstoi i musul'mane*. Kazan: Tipo-Litografiia İmperatorskogo Universiteta, 1904
Konfessional'nyia shkoly kazanskikh tatar. Kazan: Tsentral'naia tip., 1916

Mechty tatar-magometan o natsional'noi obsheobrazovatel'noi shkole. Kazan: Tipo-Litografiia Imperatorskogo Universiteta, 1908

O magometanskikh mullakh: religiozno-bytovoi ocherk. Kazan: Izdatel'stvo Iman, 1907. Reprint, 1998.

"O neobkhodimosti inorodcheskikh missionerov v dele prosveshcheniia inorodtsev." *Pravoslavnyi sobesednik*, 1905 (April): 705–16; (May): 108–18.

O tatarizatsii inorodtsev privolzhskogo kraia. Kazan: Tsentrtipogr, 1910

Krymskii, Agafangel Efimovich. *Istoriia Musul'manstva.* 2nd edn. Moscow: Tipografiia Varvary Gattsuk, 1904

Musul'manstvo i ego budushchnost'. Moscow: Knizhnoe delo, 1899

Malov, Efimii. "O tatarskikh mechetiakh v Rossii." *Pravoslavnyi sobesednik*, 1867 (3): 285–320 and 1868 (1): 3–45

Materialy po istorii Bashkirskoi ASSR. Vol. 5. Moskva: Izd-vo Akademii nauk SSSR, 1960.

Miropiev, N. "Russko inorodcheskie shkoly sistemy N. I. Il'minskogo." *Zhurnal Ministerstva Narodnogo Prosveshcheniia*, 1908 new series (13): 183–210

Morozov, I. L. and N. N. Semenova. *Agrarnyi vopros i krest'ianskoe dvizhenie 50–70x godov XIX v.* Moscow: Izdatel'stvo Akademii Nauk SSSR, 1936

Nikol'skii, N. "Kak uderzhat' Chuvash ot tatarizatsii." *Sotrudnik bratstva sviat. Guriia*, 1909 (November 1): 5–10

O., R-v. *K voprosu o magometanskikh i russko-tatarskikh uchilishchakh.* Kazan: Tsentral'naia Tipografiia, 1916

Ostroumov, Nikolai Petrovich. "K istorii musul'manskogo obrazovatel'nogo dvizheniia v Rossii v XIX i XX stoletiiakh." *Mir Islama*, 1913 2(5): 302–26

Sarty: Etnograficheskie materialy. Tashkent: Tipo-Litografiia Lakhtina, 1908

Pol'noe sobranie zakonov Rossiiskoi Imperii: sobranie tret'e. St. Petersburg: Gosudarstvennaia Tipografiia, 1885–1916

Postnikovii, N. N. (ed.). *Sistematicheskii sbornik postanovlenii Kazanskoi Gorodskoi Dumy za 22 goda.* Kazan: Kazanskaia Gorodskaia Uprava, 1898

Radlov, Vasilii V. "Eshche neskol'ko slov ob uchebnikakh russkogo iazyka dlia tatarskikh narodnykh shkol." *Zhurnal Ministerstva Narodnogo Prosveshcheniia*, 1877 194: 99–119

Rakhimov, S. T. "Akhmet-Khadi Maksudi." *Ekho vekov*, 1995 1(1): 177–95

"Dzh. Validi: 'U menia raznoglasiia s sovvlast'iu'." *Ekho vekov*, 1996 1(2): 150–73

Rozhdestvin, Aleksandr Sergeevich. *Nikolai Ivanovich Il'minskii i ego sistema inorodcheskogo obrazovaniia v Kazanskom krae.* Kazan: Tipo-litografiia Imperatorskogo Universiteta, 1900

Rodnoi iazyk kak osnova shkol'nogo obucheniia. Kazan: Tipo-litografiia Imperatorskogo Universiteta, 1903

Sbornik dokumentov i statei po voprosu ob obrazovanii inorodtsev. (Ed.) Ministerstvo narodnogo prosveshcheniia. St. Petersburg: V Tip. T-va Obshchestvennaia Pol'za, 1869

Sbornik postanovlenii po ministerstvu narodnogo prosveshcheniia: tsarstvovanie imperatora Aleksandra II, 1865–70. Vols. 4, 6, 10. St. Petersburg: Tipografiia imperatorskoi akademii nauk, 1871, 1878, 1892

Sbornik tsirkuliarov i inykh rukovodiashikh rasporiazhenii po okrugu Orenburgskogo Magometanskogo dukhovnogo sobraniia 1841–1901 g. Russian-language part. Ufa, 1902

Semenov, A. "Vozmozhna li bor'ba s Islamom i kakimi sredstvami." *Sotrudnik bratstva sviat. Guriia,* 1909 (December 25): 54–57

Shishov, Aleksandr Polikarpovich. *"Sarty: etnograficheskie i antropologicheskie issledovanie."* Tashkent: Izdanie A. L. Kirsnera, 1904

Smirnov, Vasilii D. "Neskol'ko slov ob uchebnikakh russkogo iazyka dlia tatarskikh narodnykh shkol." *Zhurnal Ministerstva Narodnogo Prosveshcheniia,* 1877 189(4): 1–25

"Po voprosu o shkol'nom obrazovanii inorodtsev-musul'man." *Zhurnal' Ministerstva Narodnogo Prosveshcheniia,* 1882 222(3): 1–24

Sukharev, A. A. *Kazanskie Tatary (uezd kazanskii).* St. Petersburg, 1904

Taşçıoğlu, Arslanbey. *"Mnenie Tavricheskikh murz Arslan-Beia-Tashchi-Oglu i Abdulveli Murzy Karashaiskogo."* In: *Sbornik dokumentov i statei po voprosu ob obrazovanii inorodtsev,* (ed.) Ministerstvo narodnogo prosveshcheniia, 134–37. St. Petersburg: V Tip. T-va Obshchestvennaia Pol'za, 1869

Tolstoi, Dmitrii A. "Po voprosu ob obrazovanii inorodtsev." In: *Sbornik dokumentov i statei po voprosu ob obrazovanii inorodtsev,* (ed.) Ministerstvo narodnogo prosveshcheniia, 157–60. St. Petersburg: V Tip. T-va Obshchestvennaia Pol'za, 1869

Ushinskii, Konstantin D. *Rodnoe slovo.* St. Petersburg: Tipografiia I. Markova, 1865

Znamenskii, Petr. *Kazanskie Tatary.* Kazan, 1910

PRIMARY SOURCES IN OTHER LANGUAGES

Anon. "The Eastern Question." *The Times,* June 5, 1876, 7

Observations on the Objects and Prospects of the Russian Railway Enterprise. London: T.F.A. Day, 1857

Aini, Sadriddin. *Pages From My Own Story.* Moscow: Foreign Languages Pub. House, 1958

al-Bukhārī, Abū ʿAbd Allah Muḥammad ibn Ismāʿīl. *Ṣaḥīḥ al-Bukhārī.* Riyadh: Bayt al-Afkār al-Dawliyyah li'l-Nashr, 1998

al-Nishābūrī, Abū al-Ḥusayn Muslim b. al-Ḥajjāj al-Qushayrī al-Nishābūrī. *Ṣaḥīḥ Muslim.* Riyadh: Dār Ṭaybah, 2006

al-Tirmidhī, Muḥammad bin ʿĪsā. *Sunan al-Tirmidhī.* Vaduz: Jamʿiyyat al-Maknaz al-Islāmī, 2000

Behbûdî, Mahmûd Hoca. "Ismâ'îl Bey Hazretleri ile Sohbet." In: *Tatars of the Crimea: Their Struggle for Survival,* (ed.) Edward Allworth, 71–73. Reprint, in English translation, Durham: Duke University Press, 1988

Bobrovnikoff, Sophy. "Moslems in Russia." *The Moslem World,* 1911 1(1): 5–31

Catherine II. *The Memoirs of Catherine the Great,* (ed.) Moura Budberg and Dominique Maroger. New York: Collier Books, 1961

Charmes, Gabriel. *L'Avenir de la Turquie: Le panislamisme.* Paris: Lévy, 1883

Frank, Allen J. and Mirkasyim A. Usmanov. *An Islamic Biographical Dictionary of the Eastern Kazakh Steppe, 1770–1912.* Boston: Brill, 2005

(eds.) *Materials for the Islamic History of Semipalatinsk*. Berlin: ANOR, 2001
Ogilvie, John Annandale Charles. "Panislamism." In: *The Imperial Dictionary of the English Language*. London: Blackie & Son, 1883
Pahlen, Konstantin Konstanovich. *Mission to Turkestan: Being the Memoirs of Count K. K. Pahlen, 1908–1909*, (ed.) Richard A. Pierce. London: Oxford University Press, 1964
Peacock, N. (ed.). *The Russian Year-Book: 1916*. London: Eyre and Spottiswoode, Ltd., 1916
Stokes, George. "Panislamism and the Caliphate." *The Contemporary Review*, 1883 43 (January–June): 57–68
Sultangalieva, Gulmira S. "The Russian Empire and the Intermediary Role of Tatars in Kazakhstan: The Politics of Cooperation and Rejection." In: *Asiatic Russia: Imperial Power in Regional and International Contexts*, (ed.) Tomohiko Uyama, 52–79. New York: Routledge, 2012
Vámbéry, Ármin. "Pan-Islamism." *The Living Age*, 1906 251(3253): 356–67

SECONDARY SOURCES

Abu-Manneh, Butrus. "The Naqshbandiyya-Mujaddidiyya in the Ottoman Lands in the Early 19th Century." *Die Welt des Islam*, 1982 22(1): 1–36
Akgündüz, Hasan. *Klasik Dönem Osmanlı Medrese Sistemi*. Istanbul: Ulusal Yayınları, 1997
Akhunova, A. M. "Pis'ma Khusaina Faizkhanova Shigabutdinu Mardzhani." In: *Khusain Faizkhanov: Zhizn' i nasledie*, (ed.) A. M. Akhunova and I. F. Gimadeeva, 82–106. Nizhny Novgorod: Medina, 2008
Akyüz, Yahya. *Türk Eğitim Tarihi: Başlangıçtan 2001'e*. Istanbul: Alfa Yayinlari, 2001
al-Karmalī, Anastas. *Rasā'il fī al-nuqūd al-'arabīyah wa-al-islāmīyah wa-'ilm al-namīyāt*. Cairo: Maktabat al-thaqāfah al-dīniyah, 1987
Algar, Hamid. "The Naqshbandi Order: A Preliminary Survey of Its History and Significance." *Studia Islamica*, 1976 (44): 123–52
"Shaykh Zaynullah Rasulev: the Last Great Naqshbandi Shaykh of the Volga-Ural Region." In: *Muslims in Central Asia*, (ed.) Jo-Ann Gross, 112–33. Durham: Duke University Press, 1992
Alov, A. A. and N. G. Vladimirov. *Islam v Rossii*. Moscow: Institut Naslediia, 1996
Alp, Alper. "Defter-i Hakani Nazırı Mahmud Esad Efendi'nin Gözüyle 20. Asır Başında Türk Dünyası." *Cumhuriyet Tarihi Araştırmaları Dergisi*, 2006 2(3): 18–42
"*Mir İslama* Dergisine Göre 20. Asır Başında İdil-Ural Bölgesinde Mektep ve Medrese Meselesi." *Türkiyat Araştırmaları Dergisi*, 2009 (26): 327–45
Amirkhanov, R. U. "Nekotorye osobennosti razvitiia narodnogo obrazovaniia u Tatar v dooktiabrskii period." In: *Narodnoe prosveshcheniie u Tatar v dooktiabr'skii period*, (ed.) R. M. Amirkhanov and I. A. Giliazov, 22–60. Kazan: Institut Iazyka, Literatury i Istorii im. G. Ibragimova, 1992
Tatarskaia demokraticheskaia pechat' (1905–1907 gg.). Moscow: Nauka, 1988
Ämirxan, Ravil. "Möhämmädiyä Mädräsäse." In: *Mädräsälärdä Kitap Kiştäse*, (ed.) Röstäm Mähdiev, 12–33. Kazan: Tatarstan Kitap Näşriyatı, 1992

Arapov, D. Iu. (ed.). *Islam v Rossiiskoi Imperii (Zakonadatel'na'ia akty, opisaniia, statistika)*. Moscow: Akademkniga, 2001

Arnold, Thomas Walker. *Painting in Islam: A Study of the Place of Pictorial Art in Muslim Culture*. Piscataway: Gorgias Press, 2002

Arsharuni, A. and Kh. Gabidullin. *Ocherki panislamizma i pantiurkizma v Rossii*. Riazan: Izdatel'stvo Bezbozhnik, 1931

Asad, Talal. *The Idea of an Anthropology of Islam*. Washington, DC: Georgetown University Center for Contemporary Arab Studies, 1986

Ascher, Abraham. *The Revolution of 1905: Authority Restored*. Stanford, CA: Stanford University Press, 1992

Atuf, Nafi. *Türkiye Maarif Tarihi Hakkında Bir Deneme*. Ankara: Milliyet Matbaası, 1930

Avrutin, Eugene M. *Jews and the Imperial State: Identification Politics in Tsarist Russia*. Ithaca: Cornell University Press, 2010

Ayda, Adile. *Sadri Maksudi Arsal*. Ankara: Kültür Bakanlığı Yayınları, 1991

Aydın, Cemil. *Beyond the Imperial and the Global: The Persistence of Regions in the Political History of the Long Nineteenth Century, 1750–1924*. Unpublished manuscript draft.

The Politics of Anti-Westernism in Asia: Visions of World Order in Pan-Islamic and Pan-Asian Thought. New York: Columbia University Press, 2007

Azade-Rorlich, Ayşe. "Rızaeddin Fahreddin and the Debate over 'Muslim Dress' among the Volga-Ural Muslims." *International Journal of Turkish Studies*, 2005 11(1–2): 95–105

"'The Temptation of the West': Two Tatar Travellers' Encounter with Europe at the End of the Nineteenth Century." *Central Asian Survey*, 1985 4(3): 39–58

The Volga Tatars: A Profile in National Resilience. Stanford: Hoover Institution Press, 1986

Azamatov, Daniel D. *Iz istorii musul'manskoi blagotvoritel'nosti: vakufy na territorii evropeiskoi chasti Rossii i Sibiri v kontse XIX – nachale XX veka*. Ufa: Bashkir University, 2000

"The Muftis of the Orenburg Spiritual Assembly in the 18th and 19th Centuries: The Struggle for Power in Russia's Muslim Institution." In: *Muslim Culture in Russia and Central Asia from the 18th to the Early 20th Centuries*, Vol. 2, (ed.) Anke von Kügelgen, Michael Kemper and Allen J. Frank. Berlin: Klaus Schwarz Verlag, 1998

Orenburgskoe Magometanskoe Dukhovnoe Sobranie v kontse XVIII–XIX vv. Ufa: Gilem, 1999

"Russian Administration and Islam in Bashkiria (18th–19th Centuries)." In: *Muslim Culture in Russia and Central Asia from the 18th to the Early 20th Centuries*, (ed.) Anke von Kügelgen, Michael Kemper, and Dmitriy Yermakov. Berlin: Klaus Schwarz Verlag, 1996

"Waqfs in the European Part of Russia and Siberia in the Beginning of the XXth Century." In: *Islamic Civilisation in the Volga-Ural Region*, (ed.) Ali Çaksu and Rafik Muhammetshin, 257–60. Istanbul: Organisation of the Islamic Conference, 2004

Azamatova, Gul'naz Bulatovna. *Ufimskoe zemstvo, 1874–1917: sotsial'nyi sostav, biudzhet, deiatel'nost' v oblasti narodnogo obrazovaniia*. Ufa: Gilem, 2005

Babadžanov, Baxtiyor M. "On the History of the Naqšbandīya Muğaddidīya in Central Māwarāannahr in the Late 18th and Early 19th Centuries." In: *Muslim Culture in Russia and Central Asia from the 18th to the Early 20th Centuries*, (ed.) Michael Kemper, Anke von Kügelgen, and Dmitriy Yermakov, 386–413. Berlin: Klaus Schwarz Verlag, 1996

Baibulatova, Liliia. *Asar Rizy Fakhreddina: istochnikovaia osnova i snachenie svoda.* Kazan: Tatar. kn. izd-vo, 2006

Baig, Khalid. *Slippery Stone: An Inquiry into Islam's Stance on Music.* Garden Grove: Open Mind Press, 2008

Bairoch, Paul. "Europe's Gross National Product: 1800–1975." *The Journal of European Economic History*, 1976 5(2): 273–340

Barkey, Karen. *Empire of Difference: The Ottomans in Comparative Perspective.* Cambridge, New York: Cambridge University Press, 2008

Baştav, Şerif. "Kazan Türklerinden Prof. Dr. Akdes Nimet Kurat." In: *Türkiye Cumhuriyeti Devletinin Kuruluş ve Gelişmesine Hizmeti Geçen Türk Dünyası Aydınları Sempozyumu Bildirileri*, (ed.) Abdulkadir Yuvalı, 119–26. Kayseri: Erciyes Universitesi, 1996

Battal-Taymas, Abdullah. *Kazan Türkleri: Türk Tarihinin Hazin Yaprakları.* Ankara: Türk Kültürünü Araştırma Enstitüsü, 1966

Bauer, Henning, Andreas Kappeler, and Brigitte Roth. *Die Nationalitäten des Russischen Reiches in der Volkszählung von 1897.* Vol. 1. Stuttgart: F. Steiner, 1991

Bayly, Cristopher Alan. *The Birth of the Modern World, 1780–1914: Global Connections and Comparisons.* Malden: Blackwell Publications, 2004

Becker, Seymour. *Russia's Protectorates in Central Asia: Bukhara and Khiva, 1865–1924.* Cambridge, MA: Harvard University Press, 1968

Bennigsen, Alexandre and Chantal Lemercier-Quelquejay. *Islam in the Soviet Union.* London: Pall Mall Press, 1967

La presse et le mouvement national chez les musulmans de Russie avant 1920. Paris: Mouton, 1964

Berkey, Jonathan Porter. *The Transmission of Knowledge in Medieval Cairo: A Social History of Islamic Education.* Princeton: Princeton University Press, 1992

Bıçakçı, Ahmet Salih. "Bukharan Madrassahs: Usul-i Kadim." In: *Reform Movements and Revolutions in Turkistan: 1900–1924*, (ed.) Timur Kocaoğlu, 135–49. Haarlem: SOTA, 2001

Blackwell, William L. *The Beginnings of Russian Industrialization, 1800–1860.* Princeton: Princeton University Press, 1968

The Industrialization of Russia: An Historical Perspective. New York: Crowell, 1970

Bogoroditzkaia, N. A. "Torgovlia inostrannymi tovarami na Nizhegorodskoi iarmarke vo vtoroi polovine XIX-Nach. XX vv." In *Makar'evsko-Nizhegorodskaia iarmarka: ocherki istorii*, (ed.) N. F. Filatov, 134–49. Nizhnii Novgorod: Nizhegorodkii gosudarstvennii universitet, 1997

Bourdieu, Pierre and Loïc J. D. Wacquant. *An Invitation to Reflexive Sociology.* Chicago: University of Chicago Press, 1992

Bozkurt, Giray Saynur. *1905–1907 Yılları Rusya Müslümanları'nın Siyasi Kimlik Arayışı.* Istanbul: Doğu Kütüphanesi, 2008

Bradley, Joseph. *Muzhik and Muscovite: Urbanization in Late Imperial Russia.* Berkeley: University of California Press, 1985

Brooks, Jeffrey. *When Russia Learned to Read: Literacy and Popular Literature, 1861–1917.* Evanston: Northwestern University Press, 2003

Brower, Daniel. "Islam and Ethnicity: Russian Colonial Policy in Turkestan." In: *Russia's Orient: Imperial Borderlands and Peoples, 1700–1917,* (ed.) Daniel Brower and Edward J. Lazzerini, 115–37. Bloomington: Indiana University Press, 1997

"Russian Roads to Mecca." *Slavic Review,* 1996 55(3): 567–84

The Russian City between Tradition and Modernity, 1850–1900. Berkeley: University of California Press, 1990

Bukharaev, Ravil. *Islam in Russia: The Four Seasons.* New York: St. Martin's Press, 2000

Burbank, Jane. *Russian Peasants Go to Court: Legal Culture in the Countryside, 1905–1917.* Bloomington: Indiana University Press, 2004

"Thinking Like an Empire: Estate, Law, and Rights in the Early Twentieth Century." In: *Russian Empire: Space, People, Power, 1700–1930,* (ed.) Jane Burbank, Mark von Hagen, and Anatoly Remnev, 196–217. Bloomington: Indiana University Press, 2007

Burbank, Jane, and Frederick Cooper. *Empires in World History: Power and Politics of Difference.* Princeton: Princeton University Press, 2010

Burbank, Jane, and Mark von Hagen. "Coming into the Territory: Uncertainty and Empire." In: *Russian Empire: Space, People, Power, 1700–1930,* (ed.) Jane Burbank, Mark von Hagen, and Anatoly Remnev, 1–29. Bloomington: Indiana University Press, 2002

Burds, Jeffrey. "The Social Control of Peasant Labor in Russia: The Response of Village Communities to Labor Migration in the Central Industrial Region, 1861–1905." In: *Peasant Economy, Culture, and Politics of European Russia, 1800–1921,* (ed.) Jeffrey Burds, Esther Kingston-Mann, and Timothy Mixter, 52–100. Princeton: Princeton University Press, 1991

Burds, Jeffrey, Esther Kingston-Mann and Timothy Mixter (eds.). *Peasant Economy, Culture, and Politics of European Russia, 1800–1921.* Princeton: Princeton University Press, 1991

Burns, Russell W. *Communications: An International History of the Formative Years.* London: Institute of Electrical Engineers, 2004

Burton, Audrey. *Bukharan Trade, 1558–1718.* Bloomington: Indiana University, Research Institute for Inner Asian Studies, 1993

Bury, John Bagnell. *The Idea of Progress: An Inquiry into Its Origin and Growth.* London: MacMillan and Co., 1921

Çağatay, Saadet. *Abd-ül-Qayyum Nasırî.* Ankara: Türk Tarih Kurumu, 1952

Çağatay, Tahir, Ali Akış, Saadet Çağatay, and Hasan Agay (eds.). *Muhammed Ayaz İshaki: Hayatı ve Faaliyeti.* Ankara: Ayyıldız Matbaası, 1979

Calhoun, Craig, Joseph Gerteis, James Moody, Steven Pfaff, and Indermohan Virk (eds.). *Contemporary Sociological Theory,* 2nd edn. Malden, MA: Blackwell Publishing, 2008

Campbell, Elena I. *Muslim Question and Russian Imperial Governance.* Bloomington: Indiana University Press, 2015

"The Muslim Question in Late Imperial Russia." In: *Russian Empire: Space, People, Power, 1700–1930*, (ed.) Jane Burbank, Mark von Hagen, and Anatoly Remnev, 320–47. Bloomington: Indiana University Press, 2007.

Can, Lâle. *Trans-Imperial Trajectories: Pilgrimage, Pan-Islam, and Ottoman Central Asian Relations, 1865–1914*. Ph.D. Dissertation, New York University, 2012

Clowes, Edith W., Samuel D. Kassow and James L. West (eds.). *Between Tsar and People: Educated Society and the Quest for Public Identity in Late Imperial Russia*. Princeton: Princeton University Press, 1991

Colonna, Fanny. "Educating Conformity in French Colonial Algeria." In: *Tensions of Empire: Colonial Cultures in a Bourgeois World*, (ed.) Frederick Cooper and Ann Laura Stoler, 346–70. Berkeley: University of California Press, 1997

Cooper, Frederick and Ann Laura Stoler. *Tensions of Empire: Colonial Cultures in a Bourgeois World*. Berkeley: University of California Press, 1997

Coronil, Fernando. "Introduction: Transculturation and the Politics of Theory: Countering the Center, Cuban Counterpoint." In: Fernando Ortiz, *Cuban Counterpoint: Tobacco and Sugar*, ix–lvi. Durham: Duke University Press, 1995

Crews, Robert. "Empire and the Confessional State: Islam and Religious Politics in Nineteenth-Century Russia." *American Historical Review*, 2003 108(1): 50–83

For Prophet and Tsar: Islam and Empire in Russia and Central Asia. Cambridge, MA: Harvard University Press, 2006

David-Fox, Michael, Alexander M. Martin, and Peter Holquist. "The Imperial Turn." *Kritika: Explorations in Russian and Eurasian History*, 2006 7(4): 705–12

Davidheiser, Evelyn B. *The World Economy and Mobilizational Dictatorship: Russia's Transition, 1846–1917*. Ph.D. Dissertation, Duke University, 1990

de Vries, Jan. "The Industrial Revolution and the Industrious Revolution." *The Journal of Economic History*, 1994 54(2): 249–70

The Industrious Revolution: Consumer Behavior and the Household Economy, 1650 to the Present. Cambridge: Cambridge University Press, 2008

DeJean, Joan E. *Ancients against Moderns: Culture Wars and the Making of a Fin de Siècle*. Chicago: University of Chicago Press, 1997

Dennison, Tracy and Steven Nafziger. "Living Standards in Nineteenth-Century Russia." *Journal of Interdisciplinary History*, 2013 43(3): 397–441

Deringil, Selim. *The Well-Protected Domains: Ideology and the Legitimation of Power in the Ottoman Empire, 1876–1909*. New York: I. B. Tauris, 1998

Devlet, Nadir. *Rusya Türkleri'nin Millî Mücadele Tarihi*. Ankara: Türk Kültürünü Araştırma Enstitüsü, 1985

Dikhtiar, G. A. *Vnutrenniaia torgovlia v dorevoliutsionnoi Rossii*. Moscow: Izdatel'stvo Akademii Nauk SSSR, 1960

Dillon, Michael. *China's Muslim Hui Community: Migration, Settlement and Sects*. London: Curzon Press, 1999

Dolbilov, Mikhail. "Russification and the Bureaucratic Mind in the Russian Empire's Northwestern Region in the 1860s." *Kritika: Explorations in Russian and Eurasian History*, 2004 5(2): 245–71

"Russifying Bureaucracy and the Politics of Jewish Education in the Russian Empire's Northwest Region (1860s–1870s)." *Acta Slavica Iaponica*, 2007 (24): 112–43

Russkii krai, chuzhaia vera: etnokonfessional'naia politika imperii v Litve i Belorussii pri Aleksandre II. Moscow: Novoe literaturnoe obozrenie, 2010

Dowler, Wayne. *Classroom and Empire: the Politics of Schooling Russia's Eastern Nationalities, 860–1917.* Montreal: McGill-Queen's University Pess, 2001

"Pedagogy and Politics: Origins of the Special Conference of 1905 on Primary Education for Non-Russians in the East." *Nationalities Papers*, 1998 26(4): 761–75

Russia in 1913. DeKalb: Northern Illinois Press, 2010

Dronin, N. M. and Bellinger E. G. *Climate Dependence and Food Problems in Russia, 1900–1990: The Interaction of Climate and Agricultural Policy and Their Effect on Food Problems.* Budapest: Central European University Press, 2005

Dudoignon, Stéphane A. "Qadîmiya as a Historiographical Category: The Question Of Social and Ideological Cleavages Between 'Reformists' and 'Traditionalists' among the Muslims of Russia and Central Asia, in the Early 20th Century." In: *Reform Movements and Revolutions in Turkistan: 1900–1924*, (ed.) Timur Kocaoğlu, 159–77. Haarlem: SOTA, 2001

Ejrnæs, Mette, Karl Gunnar Persson, and Søren Rich. "Feeding the British: Convergence and Market Efficiency in the Nineteenth-Century Grain Trade." *The Economic History Review*, 2008 61(S1): 140–71

Eklof, Ben. *Russian Peasant Schools: Officialdom, Village Culture, and Popular Pedagogy, 1861–1914.* Berkeley: University of California Press, 1986

"Ways of Seeing: Recent Anglo-American Studies of the Russian Peasant (1861–1914)." *Jahrbucher für Geschichte Osteuropas*, 1988 36(1): 57–79

Emirhan, Ravil. *İmanga Tugrılık.* Kazan: Tatarstan Kitap Neşriyatı, 1997

Engel, Barbara Alpern. *Between the Fields and the City: Women, Work, and Family in Russia, 1861–1914.* New York: Cambridge University Press, 1994

Enikeev, Said Murza Kniaz'. *Ocherk istorii tatarskogo dvorianstva.* Ufa: Izdatel'stvo Gilem, 1999

Ergin, Osman. *Türkiye Maarif Tarihi.* Vol. 2. Istanbul: Osmanbey Matbaası, 1940

Ernst, Carl W. "Ideological & Technological Transformations of Contemporary Sufism." In: *Muslim Networks from Hajj to Hip Hop*, (ed.) Miriam Cooke and Bruce B. Lawrence, 191–207. Chapel Hill: The University of North Carolina Press, 2005

Erol, Ali. "Türk Kültür ve Fikir Hayatında Ekinçi (1875–1877)." *Bilig*, 2006, Fall (39): 53–72

Etkind, Aleksandr. *Internal Colonization: Russia's Imperial Experience.* Malden: Polity Press, 2011

Falkus, Malcolm E. *The Industrialisation of Russia, 1700–1914.* London: Macmillan, 1972

Fedor, Thomas Stanley. *Patterns of Urban Growth in the Russian Empire during the Nineteenth Century.* Chicago: University of Chicago Dept. of Geography, 1975

Feyizhanof, Hüseyin. "Reforma medrese (Islakh madaris)." In: *Khusain Faizkhanov: Zhizn' i nasledie*, (ed.) A. M. Akhunova and I. F. Gimadeeva, 12–28. Nizhny Novgorod: Medina, 2008

Fisher, Alan W. "Enlightened Despotism and Islam under Catherine II." *Slavic Review*, 1968 (4): 542–53

Fitzpatrick, Anne Lincoln. *The Great Russian Fair: Nizhnii Novgorod, 1840–90*. London: The Macmillan Press, 1990

Fleischer, Cornell H. *Bureaucrat and Intellectual in the Ottoman Empire: The Historian Mustafa Ali (1541–1600)*. Princeton: Princeton University Press, 1986

Flun, Musin. *Gayaz İshaki*. Kazan: Tatarstan Kitap Näşritatı, 1998

Frank, Allen J. *Bukhara and the Muslims of Russia: Sufism, Education, and the Paradox of Islamic Prestige*. Leiden: Brill, 2012

Islamic Historiography and "Bulghar" Identity among the Tatars and Bashkirs of Russia. Boston: Brill, 1998

"Islamic Shrine Catalogues and Communal Geography in the Volga-Ural Region: 1788–1917." *Journal of Islamic Studies*, 1996 7(2): 265–286

Muslim Religious Institutions in Imperial Russia: the Islamic World of Novouzensk District and the Kazakh Inner Horde, 1780–1910. Boston: Brill, 2001

Fraser, Nancy. "Transnationalizing the Public Sphere: On the Legitimacy and Efficacy of Public Opinion in a Post-Westphalian World." *Theory, Culture, and Society*, 2007 24(4): 7–30

Freeze, Gregory L. "Bringing Order to the Russian Family: Marriage and Divorce in Imperial Russia, 1760–1860." *The Journal of Modern History*, 1990 62(4): 709–46

"Handmaiden of the State? The Church in Imperial Russia Reconsidered." *Journal of Ecclesiastical History*, 1985 36(1): 82–102

The Parish Clergy in Nineteenth-Century Russia: Crisis, Reform, Counter-Reform. Princeton: Princeton University Press, 1983

"The Soslovie (Estate) Paradigm and Russian Social History." *The American Historical Review*, 1986 91(1): 11–36

Gainetdinov, M. V. "Gani Hösäyinov häm yana mäktäb öçin köriş." In: *Narodnoe prosveshcheniie u Tatar v dooktiabr'skii period*, (ed.) R. M. Amirkhanov and I. A. Giliazov, 129–46. Kazan: Kazan IIaLI im. G. Ibragimova, 1992

Gainullin, Muhamed Kh. *Tatarskaia literatura XIX veka*. Kazan: Tatarskoe Knizhnoe Izdatel'stvo, 1975

Garipova, Rozaliya. The Transformation of the Ulama and the Shari'a in the Volga-Ural Muslim Community under Russian Imperial Rule. Ph.D. Dissertation, Princeton University, 2013

Gatrell, Peter. "The Meaning of the Great Reforms in Russian Economic History." In: *Russia's Great Reforms, 1855–1881*, (ed.) Ben Eklof, John Bushnell, and Larisa Georgievna Zakharova. Bloomington: Indiana University Press, 1994

The Tsarist Economy, 1850–1917. New York: St. Martin's Press, 1986

Geraci, Robert P. "Going Abroad or Going to Russia? Orthodox Missionaries in the Kazakh Steppe." In: *Of Religion and Empire: Missions, Conversion, and Tolerance in Tsarist Russia*, (ed.) Robert P. Geraci and Michael Khodarkovsky, 274–310. Ithaca: Cornell University Press, 2001

"Russian Orientalism at an Impasse: Tsarist Education Policy and the 1910 Conference on Islam." In: *Russia's Orient: Imperial Borderlands and Peoples, 1700–1917*, (ed.) Daniel Brower and Edward J. Lazzerini, 138–61. Bloomington: Indiana University Press, 2001

Sunday Laws and Ethno-Commercial Rivalry in the Russian Empire, 1880s–1914. Washington DC: National Council for Eurasian and East European Research, 2006.

Window on the East: National and Imperial Identities in Late Tsarist Russia. Ithaca: Cornell University Press, 2001

Gerasimov, Ilya. "In Search of a New Imperial History." *Ab Imperio*, 2005 (1): 33–56

Giddens, Anthony. *The Consequences of Modernity.* Stanford: Stanford University Press, 1990

Gleason, Abbott. "The Terms of Russian Social History." In: *Between Tsar and People: Educated Society and the Quest for Public Identity in Late Imperial Russia*, (ed.) Edith W. Clowes, Samuel D. Kassow, and James L. West. Princeton: Princeton University Press, 1991

Gobäydullin, Sälman, Kulipin-Gobäydullin Eduard, Raif Märdanov and Irek Hadiev (eds.). *Gaziz Gobäydullin.* Kazan: Ruhiyat, 2002

Göçgün, Önder. *Ziya Paşa'nın Hayatı, Eserleri, Edebi Kişiliği.* Ankara: Türk Tarih Kurumu, 2001

Gökçek, Mustafa. A Kazan Tatar Contribution to the Late Ottoman Debates on Nationalism and Islam: The Life and Works of Halim Sabit Şibay. Ph.D. Dissertation, University of Wisconsin, 2008

Gököz, Saime Selenga. *Yevfimiy Aleksandroviç Malov: İdil-Ural'da İslam Karşıtı Rus Misyon Siyaseti* Ankara: KÖKSAV, 2007

Goldberg, Madina V. Russian Empire-Tatar Theater: The Politics of Culture in Late Imperial Kazan. Ph.D. Dissertation, University of Michigan, 2009

Goncharov, N. K. *Pedagogicheskaia sistema K.D. Ushinskogo.* Moscow: Pedagogika, 1974

Goodwin, Barry K. and Thomas J. Grennes. "Tsarist Russia and the World Wheat Market." *Explorations in Economic History*, 1998 35(4): 405–30

Gramsci, Antonio. *Selections from the Prison Notebooks of Antonio Gramsci.* (Ed.) Quintin Hoare and Geoffrey Nowell-Smith. New York: International Publishers, 1971

Gregory, Paul R. "Grain Marketings and Peasant Consumption, Russia, 1885–1913." *Explorations in Economic History*, 1980 17(2): 135–64

Russian National Income, 1885–1913. Cambridge: Cambridge University Press, 1982

Gümüşoğlu, Hasan. *İntikalinden İlgasına Osmanlı'da Hilafet.* Istanbul: Kayıhan Yayınları, 2011

Gündüz, İrfan. *Gümüşhânevî Ahmed Ziyâüddin (ks): Hayatı-Eserleri-Tarîkat Anlayışı ve Hâlidiyye Tarîkatı.* Ankara: Seha Neşriyat, 1984

Habermas, Jürgen. *The Structural Transformation of the Public Sphere: An Inquiry into a Category of Bourgeois Society.* Trans. Thomas Bürger and Frederick Lawrence. Cambridge: Polity Press, 1992

Hamamato, Mami. "Tatarskaia Kargala in Russia's Eastern Policies." In: *Asiatic Russia: Imperial Power in Regional and International Contexts*, (ed.) Tomohiko Uyama, 32–51. New York: Routledge, 2012

Hanioğlu, M. Şükrü. "Blueprints for a Future Society: Late Ottoman Materialists on Science, Religion, and Art." In: *Late Ottoman Society: The Intellectual Legacy*, (ed.) Elisabeth Özdalga, 28–116. London: Routledge, 2005

Hanway, Jonas. *An Historical Account of the British Trade over the Caspian Sea: with a Journal of Travels from London through Russia into Persia; and Back Again through Russia, Germany and Holland.* London: Dodsley, 1753

Haxthausen, Baron von. *The Russian Empire: Its People, Institutions, and Resources*, 2 vols. Trans. Robert Farie. London: Chapman and Hall, 1856

Haywood, Richard Mowbray. "The Development of Steamboats on the Volga River and its Tributaries, 1817–1856." In: *Research in Economic History: A Research Annual*, (ed.) Paul Uselding, 142–86. Greenwich: Jai Press, 1981

Horn, Antoine E. "A History of Banking in the Russian Empire." In: *A History of Banking in All the Leading Nations*, 338–435. New York: The Journal of Commerce and Commercial Bulletin, 1896

Hosking, Geoffrey A. *Russia: People and Empire, 1552–1917.* Cambridge, MA: Harvard University Press, 1997

Houdas, Octave Victor. *L'islamisme.* Paris: Dujarric, 1904

Humphreys, R. Stephen. *Islamic History: A Framework for Inquiry.* Princeton: Princeton University Press, 1991

Ia., Apakova L. and Apakova L. V. "Obshchestvennaia i torgovaia deiatel'nost' Apakovykh v XVII–XIX vv." In: *Tatarskie murzy i dvoriane: istoriia i sovremennost'*, (ed.) F. G. Tarkhanova, 296–307. Kazan: Institut Istorii im. Sh. Mardzhani, 2010

İbragimov, Galimdzhan. *Tatary v revoliutsii 1905 goda.* Kazan: Izd-vo TS, 1926

Iggers, Georg G. "The Idea of Progress: A Critical Reassessment." *The American Historical Review*, 1965 71(1): 1–17

Iskhakov, Damir. *Etnografiia tatarskogo naroda.* Kazan: Magarif, 2004

Iskhakova, Rezeda Rifovna. Pedagogicheskoe obrazovanie v Kazanskoi gubernii vo vtoroi polovine 19-nachale 20 vv. Ph.D. Dissertation, Russian Academy of Education, 2002

Islaev, F. G. *Islam i pravoslavie v Povolzh'e XVIII stoletiia ot konfrontatsii k terpimosti.* Kazan: Kazan University Press, 2001

Istomina, E. G. *Vodnye puti Rossii vo vtoroi polovine XVIII-nachale XIX veka.* Moscow: Nauka, 1982

Johnson, Michael W. Imperial Commission or Orthodox Mission: Nikolai Il'minskii's Work among the Tatars of Kazan, 1862–1891. Ph.D. Dissertation, University of Illinois at Chicago, 2005

Kahan, Arkadius. *Russian Economic History: The Nineteenth Century.* Chicago: University of Chicago Press, 1989

Kamp, Marianne. *The New Woman in Uzbekistan: Islam, Modernity, and Unveiling under Communism.* Seattle: University of Washington Press, 2006

Kanatchikov, Semën Ivanovich. *A Radical Worker in Tsarist Russia: The Autobiography of Semën Ivanovich Kanatchikov.* (Ed.) Reginald E. Zelnik. Stanford: Stanford University Press, 1986

Kanlıdere, Ahmet. *Reform within Islam: The Tajdid and Jadid Movement among the Kazan Tatars, 1809–1917: Conciliation or Conflict?* Istanbul: Eren, 1997

Kaplunovskii, Aleksandr. "Tatary musul'mane i russkie v meshchanskikh obshchinakh srednego povolzh'ia v kontse XIX-nachale XX veka." *Ab Imperio*, 2000 (1): 101–22

Kappeler, Andreas. *The Russian Empire: A Multiethnic History*. Harlow: Longman, 2001

Kara, Mustafa. "Ahmed Ziyaüddin-i Gümüşhanevî'nin Halifeleri." In: *Ahmed Ziyaüddin Gümüşhanevî Sempozyum Bildirileri*, (ed.) Necdet Yılmaz, 121–29. İstanbul: Seha Neşriyat, 1992

Karal, Enver Ziya (ed.). *Yusuf Akçura: Üç Tarz-ı Siyaset*. Ankara: Türk Tarih Kurumu, 1976

Karimullin, A[brar] Gibadulloviç. *U istokov tatarskoi knigi: ot nachala do 60-kh godov XIX veka*. Kazan: Tatarskoe Knizhnoe Izdatel'stvo, 1992

Kitap Dönyasına Säyahät. Kazan: Tatarstan Kitap Näşriyatı, 1979

Tatarskaia kniga nachala XX veka. Kazan: Tatarskoe knizhnoe izdatel'stvo, 1974

Kefeli-Clay, Agnès. Kräshen Apostasy: Popular Religion, Education, and the Contest over Tatar Identity (1856–1917). Ph.D. Dissertation, Arizona State University, 2001

Kellner-Heinkele, Barbara. "Crimean Tatar and Nogay Scholars of the 18th Century." In: *Muslim Culture in Russia and Central Asia from the 18th to the Early 20th Centuries*, (ed.) Michael Kemper, Anke von Kügelgen, and Dmitriy Yermakov, 279–96. Berlin: Klaus Schwarz Verlag, 1996

Kemper, Michael. "Dahestani Shaykhs and Scholars in Russian Exile: Networks of Sufism, Fatwas and Poetry." In: *Daghestan and the World of Islam*, (ed.) Moshe Gammer and David J. Wasserstein, 95–107. Helsinki: Academia Scientiarum Fennica, 2006

"Entre Boukhara et la Moyenne-Volga: 'Abd an-Naṣīr al-Qursāwī (1776–1812) en conflit avec les oulémas traditionalistes." *Cahiers du Monde Russe*, 1996 37(1–2): 41–51

"The History of Sufism in the Volga-Urals." In: *Islamic Civilisation in the Volga-Ural Region*, (ed.) Ali Çaksu and Rafik Muhammetshin, 35–39. Istanbul: Organisation of the Islamic Conference, 2004

"Ismails Reisebuch als Genremischung." In: *Istochniki i issledovaniia po istorii Tatarskogo naroda*, (ed.) Mirkasım A. Usmanov and Diliara M. Usmanonova. Kazan: Kazan State University, 2006

Muslim Culture in Russia and Central Asia. Vol. 4, Die Islamgelehrten Daghestans und ihre arabischen Weke. Berlin: Schwarz, 2004

"Review of *For Prophet and Tsar: Islam and Empire in Russia and Central Asia*." *Die Welt des Islams*, 2007 47(1): 126–29

"Šihābaddīn al-Marğānī als Religionsgelehrter." In: *Muslim Culture in Russia and Central Asia from the 18th to the Early 20th Centuries*, (ed.) Michael Kemper, Anke von Kügelgen, and Dmitriy Yermakov, 129–65. Berlin: Klaus Schwarz Verlag, 1996

"Šihābaddīn al-Marğānī über Abū n-Naṣr Qūrsāwīs Koflikt mit den Gelehrten Bucharas." In: *Muslim Culture in Russia and Central Asia: Arabic Persian and Turkic Manuscripts (15th–19th Centuries)*, (ed.) Anke von Kügelgen, Aširbek Muminov, and Michael Kemper, 353–71. Berlin: Klaus Schwarz Verlag, 2000

Sufis und Gelehrte in Tatarien und Baschkirien, 1789–1889: der islamische Diskurs unter russischer Herrschaft. Berlin: K. Schwarz, 1998

Khalid, Adeeb. *The Politics of Muslim Cultural Reform: Jadidism in Central Asia.* Berkeley: University of California Press, 1998

"Review of DeWeese, Frank, and Dudoignon." *Kritika: Explorations in Russian and Eurasian History,* 2002 3(4): 728–38

"Russian History and the Debate over Orientalism." *Kritika: Explorations in Russian and Eurasian History,* 2000 1(4): 691–99

"'Tolerating Islam.' Review of *For Prophet and Tsar: Islam and Empire in Russia and Central Asia.*" *London Review of Books,* May 24, 2007

Khalikov, N. A. *Khoziaistvo Tatar Povolzh'ia i Urala: seredina XIX—nachalo XX v.* Kazan: Akademiia Nauk Respubliki Tatarstana, 1995

Khanbikov, Iakub I. *Russkie pedagogi Tatarii.* Kazan: Kazan State Pedagogical Institute, 1968

Khasanov, Khusain Khasanovich. *Formirovanie tatarskoi burzhuaznoi natsii.* Kazan: Tatarskoe knizhnoe izdatel'stvo, 1977

Revoliutsia 1905–1907 gg v Tatarii. Moscow: Nauka, 1965

Revolutsioner-internatsionalist: zhizn i deiatel'nost' bolshevika Khusaina Iamasheva. Kazan: Tatarskoe Knizhnoe Izdatel'stvo, 1971

Khodarkovsky, Michael. "Review of *For Prophet and Tsar: Islam and Empire in Russia and Central Asia.*" *The American Historical Review,* 2007 112(5): 1491–93

"'Not by Word Alone': Missionary Policies and Religious Conversion in Early Modern Russia." *Comparative Studies in Society and History,* 1996 38(2): 267–93

King, Charles. *The Black Sea: A History.* Oxford: Oxford University Press, 2004

Kingston-Mann, Esther. "Breaking the Silence: An Introduction." In: *Peasant Economy, Culture, and Politics of European Russia, 1800–1921,* (ed.) Jeffrey Burds, Esther Kingston-Mann, and Timothy Mixter, 3–19. Princeton: Princeton University Press, 1991

Kırımer, Cafer Seydahmet. *Gaspıralı İsmail Bey.* Istanbul: Türk Anonim Şirketi, 1934

Kırımlı, Hakan. "İsmail Bey Gaspıralı ve 'Birlik' Kavramı Üzerine." In: *İsmail Bey Gaspıralı İçin,* (ed.) Hakan Kırımlı, 55–70. Ankara: Kırım Türkleri Gençlik ve Yardımlaşma Derneği, 2004

National Movements and National Identity among the Crimean Tatars, 1905–1916 Leiden: Brill, 1996

Kirmse, Stefan B. "Dealing with Crime in Late Tsarist Russia: Muslim Tatars Go to Court." In: *One Law for All?: Western Models and Local Practices in (Post-)Imperial Contexts,* (ed.) Stefan B. Kirmse, 209–42: Campus Verlag, 2012

"Law and Empire in Late Tsarist Russia: Muslim Tatars Go to Court." *Slavic Review,* 2013 72(4): 778–801

Knight, Nathaniel. "Grigor'ev in Orenburg, 1851–1862: Russian Orientalism in the Service of Empire?" *Slavic Review,* 2000 59(1): 74–100

"On Russian Orientalism: A Response to Adeeb Khalid." *Kritika: Explorations in Russian and Eurasian History,* 2000 1(4): 701–15

"Was the Intelligentsia Part of the Nation? Visions of Society in Post-Emancipation Russia." *Kritika,* 2006 7(4): 733–58

Kocaoğlu, Timur. "Tercüman Gazetesi'nin Dili ve Coğrafyası." In: *İsmail Bey Gaspıralı İçin*, (ed.) Hakan Kırımlı, 215–27. Ankara: Kırım Türkleri Kültür ve Yardımlaşma Derneği Yayınları, 2004

Kotkin, Stephen. "Modern Times: The Soviet Union and the Interwar Conjuncture." *Kritika: Explorations in Russian and Eurasian History*, 2001 2(1): 111–64

"Mongol Commonwealth? Exchange and Governance across the Post-Mongol Space." *Kritika: Explorations in Russian and Eurasian History*, 2007 8(3): 487–531

Kraidy, Marwan. *Hybridity, or the Cultural Logic of Globalization*. Philadelphia: Temple University Press, 2005

Krapotkina, I. E. "Administrativnaia deiatel'nost' popechitel'ia uchebnogo okruga (iz istorii Kazanskogo uchebno-okruzhnogo tsentra)." *Izvestiia Altaiskogo gosudarstvennogo universiteta*, 2010 (68): 123–32

Kreindler, Isabelle Teitz. Educational Policies Toward the Eastern Nationalities in Tsarist Russia: A Study of Il'minskii's System. Ph.D. Dissertation, Columbia University, 1969

Kurat, Akdes Nimet. "Kazan Türklerinde 'Medeni Uyanış' Devri." *Ankara Üniversitesi Dil ve Tarih-Coğrafya Fakültesi Dergisi*, 1966 24(3–4): 95–194

Landau, Jacob M. *Pan-Turkism in Turkey: A Study of Irredentism*. Hamden: Archon Books, 1981

Latham, Robert Gordon. *Russian and Turk*. London: William H. Allen and Co., 1878

Lazzerini, Edward J. "From Bahchisarai to Bukhara in 1893: Ismail Bey Gasprinskii's Journey to Central Asia." *Central Asian Survey*, 1984 3(4): 77–88

Ismail Bey Gasprinskii and Muslim Modernism in Russia, 1878–1914. Ph. D. Dissertation, University of Washington, 1973

"Ismail Bey Gasprinskii's Perevodchik/Tercüman: A Clarion of Modernism." In: *Central Asian Monuments*, (ed.) Hasan B. Paksoy, 143–56. Istanbul: Isis Press, 1992

Le Châtelier, Alfred. "Politique musulmane." *Revue du monde musulman*, 1910 12(9): 1–165

Lemercier-Quelquejay, Chantal. "Les missions orthodoxes en pays musulmans de moyenne-et basse-Volga, 1552–1865." *Cahiers du Monde Russe et Soviétique*, 1967 8(3): 369–403

"Un réformateur tatar du XIXe siècle, 'Abdul Qajjum Al-Nasyri." *Cahiers du Monde Russe et Soviétique*, 1963 4(1–2): 117–43

Levi, Scott Cameron. *The Indian Diaspora in Central Asia and Its Trade, 1550–1900*. Leiden: Brill, 2002

Levtzion, Nehemia and John Obert Voll. *Eighteenth-Century Renewal and Reform in Islam*. Syracuse: Syracuse University Press, 1987

Lieven, Dominic. "Dilemmas of Empire 1850–1918: Power, Territory, Identity." *Journal of Contemporary History*, 1999 34(2): 163–200

Lincoln, W. Bruce. "The Genesis of an Enlightened Bureaucracy in Russia." *Jahrbücher für Gesichte Osteuropas*, 1972 20(3): 321–30

The Great Reforms: Autocracy, Bureaucracy, and the Politics of Change in Imperial Russia. DeKalb: Northern Illinois University Press, 1990

In the Vanguard of Reform: Russia's Enlightened Bureaucrats, 1825–1861.
DeKalb: Northern Illinois University Press, 1982
Lotfi, Gasim. "Kışkar Mädräsäse." In: *Mädräsälärdä Kitap Kiştäse*, (ed.) Röstäm
Mähdiyäv. Kazan: Tatarstan Kitap Näşriyatı, 1992
Lotfullin, İskhak M. and F. G. Islaev. *Dzhikhad tatarskogo naroda.* Kazan, 1998
Mähdiev, Möhämmät. "Bubi Mädräsäse." In: *Mädräsälärdä Kitap Kiştäse* (ed.)
Röstäm Mähdiev, 38–72. Kazan: Tatarstan Kitap Näşriyatı, 1992
Mähdiev, Röstäm (ed.). *Mädräsälärdä Kitap Kiştäse.* Kazan: Tatarstan Kitap
Näşriyatı, 1992
Mähmutova, Alta. "Kazandagı Kızlar Öçen Mäktäp-Mädräsälär." In:
Mädräsälärdä Kitap Kiştäse, (ed.) Röstäm Mähdiev, 129–50. Kazan:
Tatarstan Kitap Näşriyatı, 1992
Makhmutova, Alta Kh. *Lish' tebe narod, sluzhen'e!: istoriia tatarskogo
prosvetitel'stva v sud'bakh dinastii Nigmatullinykh-Bubi.* Kazan: Magarif, 2003
*Stanovlenie svetskogo obrazovaniia u tatar: bor'ba vokrug shkol'nogo voprosa,
1861–1917.* Kazan: Izd-vo Kazanskogo universiteta, 1982
Maraş, İbrahim. "İdil-Ural Bölgesinin Cedidci Dinî Lideri Zeynullah Rasûlî'nin
Hayatı ve Görüşleri." *Dinî Araştırmalar*, 1998 1(1): 76–92
"İsmail Gaspıralı'nın Bilinmeyen Bir Risalesi: 'Mektep ve Usûl-i Cedid
Nedir'." *Emel*, 1997 (219): 10–20
Türk Dünyasında Dinî Yenileşme, 1850–1917. Istanbul: Ötüken, 2002
Matthews, Mitford McLeod. *Teaching to Read: Historically Considered.* Chicago:
Chicago University Press, 1966
Mattson, Ingrid. *The Story of the Qur'an: Its History and Place in Mulim Life.*
Malden: Blackwell Publishing, 2008
Mäxmutov, Xuçiäxmät (ed.). *Kayum Nasıyri: Saylanma Äsärlär.* Vol. 3. Kazan:
Tatarstan Kitap Näşriyatı, 2005
McCarthy, Frank T. "The Kazan Missionary Congress." *Cahiers du monde russe et
sovietique*, 1973 14(3): 308–32
McReynolds, Louise. *The News under Russia's Old Regime: The Development of a
Mass-Circulation Press.* Princeton: Princeton University Press, 1991
Russia at Play: Leisure Activities at the End of the Tsarist Era. Ithaca: Cornell
University Press, 2003
Mel'nikov, A. P. *Ocherki bytovoi istorii Nizhegorodskoi iarmarki (1817–1917).*
Nizhny Novgorod: Nizhegorodskii kompiuternyi tsentr, 1993
Mel'nikova, V. V. *Iz istorii razvitiia pochtovo-telegrafnoi sviazi v krae v XVIII-
pervoi chetverti XX v.* Volgograd: Volgogradskoe nauchnoe izdatel'stvo,
2004
Metzer, Jacob. "Railroad Development and Market Integration: The Case of
Tsarist Russia." *The Journal of Economic History*, 1974 34(3): 529–50
Meyer, James H. "The Economics of Muslim Cultural Reform: Money, Power,
and Muslim Communities in Late Imperial Russia." In: *Asiatic Russia:
Imperial Power in Regional and International Contexts*, (ed.) Tomohiko
Uyama, 252–70. New York: Routledge, 2012
*Turkic Worlds: Community Representation and Collective Identity in the
Russian and Ottoman Empires, 1870–1914.* Ph.D. Dissertation, Brown
University, 2007

Mikhail, Alan and Christine M. Philliou. "The Ottoman Empire and the Imperial Turn." *Comparative Studies in Society and History*, 2012 54(04): 721–45

Miller, Alexei. "Between Local and Inter-imperial: Russian Imperial History in Search of Scope and Paradigm." *Kritika*, 2004 5(1): 7–26

The Romanov Empire and Nationalism. Budapest: Central European University, 2008

Mills, James Cobb. Dmitrii Tolstoi as Minister of Education in Russia, 1866–1880. Ph. D. Dissertation, Indiana University, 1967

Minnullin, Z. S. "Problemy vakfa: istoriia i sovremennost'." In: *Religiia v sovremennom obshshestve: istoriia, problemy, tendentsii*, (ed.) R. A. Nabiev, 175–78. Kazan: Zaman, 1998

"Rämievlärneñ altın priiskaları." In: *Bertugan Rämiyevlär: Fänni-biografik jientık*, (ed.) Liron Hämidullin, Raif Märdanov, and Ramil Miñnullin, 82–91. Kazan: Ruhiyat, 2002

Minnullin, Il'nur. R. *Musul'manskoe dukhovenstvo Tatarstana v usloviiakh politicheskikh repressii 1920–1930-kh gg*. Nizhny Novgorod: Id. Mädina, 2007

Mironov, Boris Nikolaevich. *The Standard of Living and Revolutions in Russia, 1700–1917*. New York: Routledge, 2012

Mixter, Timothy. "The Hiring Market as Workers' Turf: Migrant Agricultural Laborers and the Mobilization of Collective Action in the Steppe Grainbelt of European Russia, 1853–1913." In: *Peasant Economy, Culture, and Politics of European Russia, 1800–1921*, (ed.) Jeffrey Burds, Esther Kingston-Mann, and Timothy Mixter, 294–340. Princeton: Princeton University Press, 1991

Moon, David. "Reassessing Russian Serfdom." *European History Quarterly*, 1996 26(4): 483–526

The Russian Peasantry, 1600–1930: The World the Peasants Made. New York: Longman, 1999

Morrison, Alexander. "'Applied Orientalism' in British India and Tsarist Turkestan." *Comparative Studies in Society and History*, 2009 51(03): 619–47

"Review of *For Prophet and Tsar: Islam and Empire in Russia and Central Asia*." *The Slavonic and East European Review*, 2008 86(3): 553–57

"Sufism, Pan-Islamism and Information Panic: Nil Sergeevich Lykoshin and the Aftermath of the Andijan Uprising." *Past & Present*, 2012 214(1): 255–304

Muhammetshin, Rafik. *Tatarskii traditsionalizm: osobennosti i formy proiavleniia*. Kazan: Meddok, 2005

"The Tatar Intelligentsia and the Clergy, 1917–1937." In: *In Devout Societies vs. Impious States?*, (ed.) Stéphane A. Dudoignon, 29–38. Berlin: Klaus Schwarz Verlag, 2004

Mullagulov, M. G. *Bashkirskii narodnyi transport, xix-nachalo xx v.* Ufa: Ural'skogo otdeleniia RAN, 1992

Naganawa, Norihiro. "The Hajj Making Geopolitics, Empire and Local Politics: A View from the Volga Ural Region at the Turn of the Nineteenth and Twentieth Centuries." In: *Central Asian Pilgrims: Hajj Routes and Pious Visits between Central Asia and Hijaz*, (ed.) Alexandre Papas, Thomas Welsford, and Thierry Zarcone, 168–98. Berlin: Klaus Schwarz Verlag, 2012

"Holidays in Kazan: The Public Sphere and the Politics of Religious Authority among Tatars in 1914." *Slavic Review*, 2012 71(1): 25–48

"Maktab or School? Introduction of Universal Primary Education among the Volga-Ural Muslims." In: *Empire, Islam, and Politics in Central Eurasia*, (ed.) Tomohiko Uyama, 65–97. Hokkaido: Slavic Research Center, 2007

"Molding the Muslim Community through the Tsarist Administration: Mahalla under the Jurisdiction of the Orenburg Muhammedan Spiritual Assembly after 1905." *Acta Slavica Iaponica*, 2006 (23): 101–23

"Musul'manskoe soobshchestvo v usloviiakh mobilizatsii: uchastie volgo-ural'skikh musul'man v voinakh poslednego desiatiletiia sushchestvovaniia Rossiiskoi imperii." In: *Volgo-Uralskii region v imperskom prostranstve xviii–xx vv.*, (ed.) Norihiro Naganawa, Diliara M. Usmanonova, and Mami Hamamato, 198–228. Moscow: Vostochnaia Literatura, 2011

Nasyrova, I. R. (ed. and trans.). *Sheikh Zeinulla Rasuli (Rasulev) an-Nakshbandi: izbrannye proizvedeniia*. Ufa, 2001

Nathans, Benjamin. *Beyond the Pale: The Jewish Encounter with Late Imperial Russia*. Berkeley: University of California Press, 2002

Noack, Christian. *Muslimischer Nationalismus im russischen Reich: Nationsbildung und Nationalbewegung bei Tataren und Baschkiren: 1861–1917*. Stuttgart: Franz Steiner Verlag, 2000

O'Rourke, Kevin H. "The European Grain Invasion, 1870–1913." *The Journal of Economic History*, 1997 57(4): 775–801

O'Rourke, Kevin H. and Jeffrey G. Williamson. *Globalization and History: The Evolution of a Nineteenth-Century Atlantic Economy*. Cambridge, MA: MIT Press, 1999

Oral, Fuat Süreyya. *Türk Basın Tarihi*. Vol. 1. Ankara: Yeni Adım Matbaasi, 1967

Ortiz, Fernando. *Cuban Counterpoint: Tobacco and Sugar*. New York: A. A. Knopf, 1947

Papas, Alexandre, Thomas Welsford and Thierry Zarcone (eds.). *Central Asian Pilgrims: Hajj Routes and Pious Visits between Central Asia and Hijaz*. Berlin: Klaus Schwarz Verlag, 2012

Pomeranz, Kenneth. *The Great Divergence: Europe, China, and the Making of the Modern World Economy*. Princeton: Princeton University Press, 2000

Quelquejay, Chantal. "Le 'Vaisisme' a Kazan: Contribution a l'etude des confreries musulmanes chez les tatars de la volga." *Die Welt des Islams*, 1959 6(1/2): 91–112

Raeff, Marc. *Origins of the Russian Intelligentsia: The Eighteenth-Century Nobility*. New York: Harcourt Brace & Harvest, 1966

"The Well-Ordered Police State and the Development of Modernity in Seventeenth- and Eighteenth-Century Europe: An Attempt at a Comparative Approach." *American Historical Review*, 1975 80(5): 1221–43

Rafikov, Azat. "Torgovo-predprinimatel'skaia deiatel'nost' tatarskogo kupechestva Viatskoi gubernii na rubezhe XIX–XX vv." *Ekho vekov*, 2009 (2): 226–33

Rahman, Fazlur. "Revival and Reform in Islam." In: *The Cambridge History of Islam*, (ed.) P. M. Holt, Ann K. S. Lambton, and Bernard Lewis, 632–56. Cambridge: Cambridge University Press, 1977

Revival and Reform in Islam: A Study of Islamic Fundamentalism. Oxford: Oneworld Publications, 2000

Rashin, A. G. *Naselenie Rossii za 100 let (1811–1913 gg.).* Moscow: Gosudarstvennoe Staticheskoe Izdatel'stvo, 1956

Reynolds, Michael A. *Shattering Empires: The Clash and Collapse of the Ottoman and Russian Empires, 1908–1918.* New York: Cambridge University Press, 2011

Riasanovsky, Nicholas V. *Nicholas I and Official Nationality in Russia, 1825–1855.* Berkeley: University of California Press, 1959

  A Parting of Ways: Government and the Educated Public in Russia, 1801–1855. Oxford: Clarendon Press, 1976

Rieber, Alfred J. "Alexander II: A Revisionist View." *The Journal of Modern History,* 1971 43(1): 42–58

  "Bureaucratic Politics in Imperial Russia." *Social Science History,* 1978 2(4): 399–413

  Merchants and Entrepreneurs in Imperial Russia. Chapel Hill: University of North Carolina Press, 1982

Ro'i, Yaacov. *Islam in the Soviet Union: From the Second World War to Gorbachev.* London: Hurst & Co., 2000

Rosen, William. *The Most Powerful Idea in the World: A Story of Steam, Industry, and Invention.* New York: Random House, 2010

Ross, Danielle M. From the Minbar to the Barricades: The Transformation of the Volga-Ural 'Ulama into a Revolutionary Intelligentsia. Ph.D. Dissertation, University of Wisconsin, Madison, 2011

  In Dialogue with the Shadow of God: Imperial Mobilization, Islamic Revival and the Evolution of an Administrative System for the Tatars, Bashkirs and Mishars of Eighteenth-Century. M.A. Thesis, University of Wisconsin, Madison, 2007

Rozhkova, M. K. *Ekonomicheskie sviazi Rossii so Srednei Aziei – 40–60e gody XIX veka.* Moscow: Izdatel'stvo Akademii Nauk SSSR, 1963

Ruane, Christine. *The Empire's New Clothes: A History of the Russian Fashion Industry, 1700–1917.* New Haven: Yale University Press, 2009

Rybakov, S. G. *Muzyka i pesni uralskikh musulman s ocherkom ikh byta.* St. Petersburg, 1897

Sabol, Steven. "The 1916 Russian-Central Asian Revolt: Its Causes, Consequences, and Reinterpretation." In: *4th Biannual Conference: The International Society for First World War Studies.* Washington DC, 2007

Safiullina, Rezeda R. *Arabskaia kniga v dukhovnoi kul'ture tatarskogo naroda.* Kazan: Izdatel'stvo Alma-Lit, 2003

  Istoriia knigopechataniia na arabskom iazyke v Rossii i musulman Povolzh'ia. Kazan, 2003. Available at: www.tataroved.ru/publication/nacobr/7

Said, Edward W. *Orientalism.* New York: Vintage Books, 1994

Salikhov, Radik. *Tatarskaia burzhuaziia Kazani i natsional'nye reformy vtoroi poloviny XIX nachala XX v.* Kazan: Izdatel'stvo Master Lain, 2000

Schafer, Daniel Evan. Building Nations and Building States: The Tatar-Bashkir Question in Revolutionary Russia, 1917–1920. Ph.D. Dissertation, University of Michigan, 1995

Schamiloglu, Uli. "The Formation of a Tatar Historical Consciousness: Shihabuddin Marjani and the Image of the Golden Horde." *Central Asian Survey*, 1990 9(2): 39–49

Schimmelpenninck van der Oye, David. *Russian Orientalism: Asia in the Russian Mind from Peter the Great to the Emigration.* New Haven: Yale University Press, 2010

Schivelbusch, Wolfgang. *The Railway Journey: The Industrialization of Time and Space in the 19th Century.* Berkeley: University of California Press, 1986

Schulze, I. and W. Schulze. "The Standing Caliph Coins of al-Jazira: Some Problems and Suggestions." *Numismatic Chronicle*, 2010 (170): 331–53

Schurman, Jacob Gould. *The Balkan Wars.* Princeton: Princeton University Press, 1916

Schwarz, David. *Culture & Power: The Sociology of Pierre Bourdieu.* Chicago: The University of Chicago Press, 1997

Scott, James C. *Weapons of the Weak: The Everyday Forms of Peasant Resistance.* New Haven: Yale University Press, 1985

Şekerci, Osman. *İslâm'da Resim ve Heykelin Yeri.* Istanbul: Fatih Gençlik Vakfı, 1974

Sharafuddinov, Z. T., and Iakub Iskhak Khanbikov. *Istoriia pedagogiki Tatarstana.* Kazan: Kazan State Pedagogical University, 1998

Sinel, Allen. *The Classroom and the Chancellery: State Educational Reform in Russia under Count Dmitry Tolstoi.* Cambridge, MA: Harvard University Press, 1973

Şirin, İbrahim. *Osmanlı İmgeleminde Avrupa.* Ankara: Lotus, 2006

Smith, Douglas. "Freemasonry and the Public in Eighteenth Century Russia." In: *Imperial Russia: New Histories for the Empire*, (ed.) Jane Burbank and David L. Ransel, 281–304. Bloomington: Indiana University Press, 1998

Sorel, Georges. *The Illusions of Progress.* (Trans.) Charlotte Stanley. Berkeley: University of California Press, 1969

Spannaus, Nathan. "The Decline of the Ākhūnd and the Transformation of Islamic Law under the Russian Empire." *Islamic Law and Society*, 2013 20(3): 202–41

Spencer, Herbert. *The Principles of Biology.* Vol. 1. London: Williams and Norgate, 1864

Steinwedel, Charles Robert. Invisible Threads of Empire: State, Religion, and Ethnicity in Tsarist Bashkiria, 1773–1917. Ph.D. Dissertation, Columbia University, 1999

    "Making Social Groups, One Person at a Time: The Identification of Individuals by Estate, Religious Confession, and Ethnicity in Late Imperial Russia." In: *Documenting Individual Identity: The Development of State Practices in the Modern World*, (ed.) Jane Caplan and John Torpey, 67–82. Princeton: Princeton University Press, 2001

    "Polozhenie Bashkirii v sostave Rossii: regional'nye osobennosti, paralleli, obsheimperskii kontekst (1552–1917)." In: *Volgo-Ural'skii region v imperskom prostranstve XVIII–XX vv.*, (ed.) Mami Hamamato, Norihiro Naganawa, and Diliara Usmanova. Moscow: Vostozhnaia literatura, 2011

Suny, Ronald Grigor. *Looking Toward Ararat: Armenia in Modern History.* Bloomington: Indiana University Press, 1993

Sverdlova, Liudmila M. *Kazanskoe kupechestvo: sotsial'no-ekonomicheskii portret*. Kazan: Tatarskoe Knizhnoe Izdatel'stvo, 2011 *Kupechestva Kazani: dela i liudi*. Kazan: Matbugat Yurtı, 1998

Tagirov, İldus. "O chem rasskazyvaet sledstvennoe delo Iliasa Alkina." *Ekho vekov*, 2001 3(4): 142–48 "Uchastnikov Kurban-bairama prigovorili k rasstrelu" *Ekho vekov*, 1999 1(2): 126–31

Tairov, Nail'. *Akchuriny*. Kazan: Tatarskoe Knizhnoe Izdatel'stvo, 2002

Taylor, Charles. *Modern Social Imaginaries*. Durham: Duke University Press, 2004

Taylor, Charles. *Modernity and the Rise of the Public Sphere*. (Ed.) Grethe B. Peterson, 203–60. Salt Lake City: University of Utah Press, 1993 *A Secular Age*. Cambridge, MA: The Belknap Press of Harvard University Press, 2007

Taymas, A. Battal. *Kazanlı Türk Meşhurlarından Rızaeddin Fahreddinoğlu*. İstanbul, 1958

Tazhibaev, T. T. *Prosveshchenie i shkoly Kazakhstana vo vtoroi polovine XIX veka*. Alma-Ata: Kazakhskoe gosudarstvennoe izdatel'stvo politichesckoi literatury, 1962

Temir, Ahmet. *Türkoloji Tarihinde Wilhelm Radloff Devri: Hayatı, İlmî Kişiliği, Eserleri*. Ankara: Türk Dil Kurumu, 1991

Temizyürek, Fahri. "Osmanlı Mekteplerinde Cedidçilik Hareketi ve Gaspıralı'nın İlham Kaynakları." In: *İsmail Bey Gaspıralı İçin*, (ed.) Hakan Kırımlı, 277–88. Ankara: Kırım Türkeri Kültür ve Yardımlaşma Derneği Yayınları, 2004

Togan, Ahmed Zeki Velidi. *Bugünkü Türkili: Türkistan ve Yakın Tarihi*. Istanbul: Arkadaş, Ibrahim Horoz ve Güven Basımevleri, 1942

Tolz, Vera. *Russia's Own Orient: The Politics of Identity and Oriental Studies in the Late Imperial and Early Soviet Periods*. Oxford: Oxford University Press, 2011

Tucker, Judith E. *Women, Family, and Gender in Islamic Law*. Cambridge: Cambridge University Press, 2008

Tuna, Mustafa Özgür. "Gaspırali v. Il'minskii: Two Identity Projects for the Muslims of the Russian Empire." *Nationalities Papers*, 2002 30(2): 265–89 "Madrasa Reform as a Secularizing Process: A View from the Late Russian Empire." *Comparative Studies in Society and History*, 2011 53(3): 540–70 "Zapadnaia literatura istorii Tatar 18go-nachala 20go vv." In: *Istoriia Tatar s drevneishikh vremen*, (ed.) İl'dus Zagidullin. Kazan: Institut istorii im. Sh. Mardzhani, 2013

Türkoğlu, İsmail. *Rusya Türkleri Arasında Yenileşme Hareketinin Öncülerinden Rızaeddin Fahreddin*. Istanbul: Ötüken Neşriyat, 2000 *Sibiryalı Meşhur Seyyah Abdürreşid İbrahim*. Ankara: Türkiye Diyanet Vakfı Yayınları, 1997

Urmançiev, Fatih. *Başlangıcından Günümüze Kadar Türkiye Dışındaki Türk Edebiyatları Antolojisi: Tatar Edebiyatı I*. Vol. 17. Ankara: T.C. Kültür Bakanlığı, 2001

Usmanov, Mirkasım A. "O triumfe i tragedii idei Gasprinskogo." In: *Rossiia i Vostok*. Kazan: Tatarskoe Knizhnoe Izdatel'stvo, 1993

"Tatarskoe kupechestvo v torgovle Rossii s vostochnymi stranami cherez Astrakhan i Orenburg." *Russian History/Histoire russe*, 1992 19(1–4): 505–13

"Tatar Settlers in Western China (Second Half of the 19th Century to the First Half of the 20th Century)." In: *Muslim Culture in Russia and Central Asia from the 18th to the Early 20th Centuries*, (ed.) Michael Kemper, Anke von Kügelgen, and Dmitriy Yermakov, 243–70. Berlin: Klaus Schwarz Verlag, 1998

"Yañadan tanışu, yaki fidakyar xäyriyaçelärebez xakında." In: *Bertugan Rämiyevlär: Fänni-biografik jientık*, (ed.) Liron Hämidullin, Raif Märdanov, and Ramil Miñnullin, 5–33. Kazan: Ruhiyat, 2002

Usmanov, Mirkasım A. and Raif F. Märdanov (eds.). *Şura jurnalınıñ bibliografik kürsätkeçe*. Kazan: Milli Kitap Neşriyatı, 2000

Usmanova, Diliara M. "Die Tatarische Presse 1905–1918: Quellen, Entwicklungsetappen und Quantitative Analyse." In: *Muslim Culture in Russia and Central Asia from the 18th to the Early 20th Centuries*, (ed.) Michael Kemper, Anke von Kügelgen, and Dmitriy Yermakov. Berlin: Klaus Schwarz Verlag, 1996

"K voprosu o tirazhakh musul'manskikh periodicheskikh izdanii Rossii nachala 20 veka." Paper presented at Ismail Gasprinskii – prosvetitel' naraodov Vostoka, k 150-letiiu co dnia rozhdeniia, Moscow, 2001

Musul'manskaia fraktsiia i problemy "svobody sovesti" v Gosudarstvennoi Dume Rossii (1906–1917). Kazan: Izdatel'stvo Master Lain, 1999

Musul'manskoe "sektantstvo" v Rossiiskoi imperii: "Vaisovskii Bozhii polk staroverov-musul'man" 1862–1916 gg. Kazan: Fen, 2009

Verhoeven, Claudia. *The Odd Man Karakozov: Imperial Russia, Modernity, and the Birth of Terrorism*. Ithaca: Cornell University Press, 2009

Verner, Andrew. "Discursive Strategies in the 1905 Revolution: Peasant Petitions from Vladimir Province." *Russian Review*, 1995 54(1): 65–90

Von Laue, Theodore H. *Sergei Witte and the Industrialization of Russia*. New York: Columbia University Press, 1963

Walicki, Andrzej. *A History of Russian Thought from the Enlightenment to Marxism*. Stanford: Stanford University Press, 1979

Weber, Max. *The Theory of Social and Economic Organization*. (Trans) A. M. Henderson and Talcott Parsons. New York: Oxford University Press, 1947

Weeks, Theodore R. *Nation and State in Late Imperial Russia: Nationalism and Russification on the Western Frontier, 1863–1914*. DeKalb: Northern Illinois University Press, 1996

"Russification and the Lithuanians, 1863–1905." *Slavic Review*, 2001 60(1): 96–114

"Russification: Word and Practice 1863–1914." *Proceedings of the American Philosophical Society*, 2004 148(4): 471–89

Werth, Paul W. *At the Margins of Orthodoxy: Mission, Governance, and Confessional Politics in Russia's Volga-Kama Region, 1827–1905*. Ithaca: Cornell University Press, 2002

"Coercion and Conversion: Violence and the Mass Baptism of the Volga Peoples, 1740–55." *Kritika: Explorations in Russian and Eurasian History*, 2003 4(3): 543–69

Westwood, John Norton. *A History of Russian Railways*. London: George Allen and Unwin Ltd., 1964

Wilbur, Elvira M. "Peasant Poverty in Theory and Practice: A View from Russia's 'Impoverished Center' at the End of the Nineteenth Century." In: *Peasant Economy, Culture, and Politics of European Russia, 1800–1921*, (ed.) Jeffrey Burds, Esther Kingston-Mann, and Timothy Mixter, 101–27. Princeton: Princeton University Press, 1991

Wortman, Richard. *The Crisis of Russian Populism*. London: Cambridge University Press, 1967

Scenarios of Power: Myth and Ceremony in Russian Monarchy. Vol. 2. Princeton: Princeton University Press, 1995

Xämidullin, Liron. "Tarixta üz ezläre bar." In: *Bertugan Rämiyevlär: Fänni-biografik jentık*, (ed.) Liron Hämidullin, Raif Märdanov, and Ramil Miñnullin, 34–68. Kazan: Ruhiyat, 2002

Yücer, Hür Mahmut. *Osmanlı Toplumunda Tasavvuf [19. Yüzyıl]*. Istanbul: İnsan Yayınları, 2003

Yusupov, Munir. *Galimdzhan Barudi*. Kazan: Tatarskoe Knizhnoe Izdatel'stvo, 2003

Zagidullin, I. K. *Perepis' 1897 goda i Tatary Kazanskoi Gubernii*. Kazan: Tatarskoe Knizhnoe Izdatel'stvo, 2000

Zagidullin, Il'dus. "Tatary v organakh samoupravleniia: zemskikh, gorodskikh, i krest'ianskikh." In: *Istoriia Tatar s drevneishikh vremen: Formirovanie tatarskoi natsii XIX-nachalo XX v.*, (ed.) Ildus Zagidullin, 477–81. Kazan: Akademiia Nauk Respubliki Tatarstan, 2013

Zaman, Muhammad Qasim. *Modern Islamic Thought in a Radical Age: Religious Authority and Internal Criticism*. Cambridge: Cambridge University Press, 2012

Zäynullin, Zäki. "Ästärlebaş Mädräsäse." In: *Mädräsälärdä Kitap Kiştäse*, (ed.) Röstäm Mähdiev, 175–85. Kazan: Tatarstan Kitap Näşriyatı, 1992

Zenkovsky, Serge A. *Pan-Turkism and Islam in Russia*. Cambridge, MA: Harvard University Press, 1960

Zilfi, Madeline C. "The Kadizadelis: Discordant Revivalism in Seventeenth-Century Istanbul." *Journal of Near Eastern Studies*, 1986 45(4): 251–69

Zorin, A. N. *Goroda i posady dorevoliutsionnogo Povolzh'ia*. Kazan: Kazan State University Press, 2001

Index

Afghanistan, 20, 26, 106
agency, 69, 102
Ahmerof, Şahbazgiray, 91, 98, 166
ahund, 39–40, 42–43, 45, 47–48, 188–89.
    See also ulama
Alexander I, 58
Alexander II, 5, 61, 64, 71, 76–77,
    86, 109
Alexander III, 86, 91, 141
Andijan Rebellion, 199, 208. *See also*
    paranoia about Islam
Andrei, Bishop, 201–2
Apanayef, Ğabdullah, 145
Aqçurin family, 131–32, 135–36, 145
    Yusuf Akçura, 145, 214
Asad, Talal, 13

Balkan Wars, 205
banking. *See* Great transformation
baptism. *See* Christianization
Baptized Tatars. *See* Christianization
Baraninskii, A. N., 226–27
Barudî, Ğâlimcan, 181, 183, 229
Bashkir, 4, 40–41, 123–24, 219, 221
bay. See merchants
Bigî, Ğabdullah, 189
Bikkenin, Muhammed Safâ, 83
Bikqulef, Ahmed Latîf, 188
Bolsheviks, 59, 171, 194, 235, 237
Bourdieu, Pierre, 11
Bubi Madrasa, 203

Caliphate, 208–9, 214
Cârullah bin Bikmuhammed, 23
Catherine II, 5, 36–37, 41–43, 57, 59, 68,
    84, 125, 127, 129–30, 134, 140, 195,
    208, 237, 240
Catherinian imperial model, 15, 17, 62, 70,
    77, 126, 144–45, 193, 218, 231, 240,
    243. *See also* governance: mediated
Caucasus, 4, 13, 57, 199, 211
Celâl, Sadri, 176

Celâleddin bin Burhâneddin, 107–9
Cherkasov, Leonid Ivanovich, 87–90
China, 4, 7, 129, 199, 209, 211, 214
Christianization
    Baptized Tatars, 5, 63, 67, 86, 201
    missionary work, 187, 196–99, 201–2,
        206–7, 217, 225
    missionary work, Brotherhood of St.
        Gurii, 198, 201–2, 204
    religious coercion, 40–41
Cihanşin, Seyyid Şerif, 189
clergy. *See ulama*
clothing
    female, 122
    traditional vs. European style, 122–24,
        183–84, 231–32
comfort zones, 11, 15, 99, 125, 193,
    231–32, 239. *See also* domains
conservative Muslim reformists, 144,
    173–75, 192–93, 222
Cooper, Frederick, 242
Crews, Robert, 9, 39, 84, 195, 235
Crimea, 4–5, 13, 69, 71, 154, 165, 211
    Crimean Khanate, 41, 208
Crimean War, 50, 57, 84, 131, 208, 241

Daghestan, 20, 27, 33
el-Daghestani, Muhammed bin 'Ali, 27
Delianov, Ivan Davydovich, 61, 63, 86–87,
    97
Derevenskii, Aleksei Nikolaevich, 223–24
Diderot, 41
Dolbilov, Mikhail, 197
domains
    definition, 10–14
    ethnic Russian domain, 13
    pan-European domain, 14–15, 124, 146,
        193, 241
    Russian imperial domain, 13–14, 57,
        59–62, 82, 89, 94, 99–101, 134,
        140–41, 144, 166, 194–96, 217–18,
        221, 234–36, 239–42

domains (cont.)
  transregional Muslim domain, 13, 35,
    240
  Volga-Ural Muslim domain, 13–15, 54,
    89, 99, 116, 126, 145, 172, 177,
    193–94, 221, 231, 235, 240
Dowler, Wayne, 59, 217
drinking, 18, 179–80, 186

Efendi, Mahmud Esad, 213–14
Efendi, Muhammed, 28
Egypt, 20, 26, 165, 210, 214
emancipation of serfs. See Great Reforms
empires
  complexity of, 236, 240, 243
  imperial situations, 2, 4, 10, 12, 59–60,
    217, 235, 239–40
  rivalry among, 240
  viability of, 241, 243. See also governance
enlightenment, 15–16, 41, 60–66, 70, 186,
    199. See also progress, cult of;
    schooling
estates, 12, 46, 60, 62, 70, 115, 133, 139,
    195, 242
ethnicity and religion, 239
Etkind, Alexander, 62
Europe
  economic comparisons with, 148
  as model, 6–7, 116, 156–62
everyday forms of resistance, 80, 231
exchange, 1, 11–14, 19, 35, 56, 60, 104,
    111, 124, 239–40, 242–43. See also
    domains

Fahreddin, Rızâeddin bin, 1–2, 20–21, 24,
    27–28, 32, 42, 105–9, 116–17, 123,
    138, 155, 181, 183–84, 187, 231, 237
fanaticism, 66–67, 69, 77, 88, 100, 202,
    221. See also paranoia about Islam
Fayḍhan bin Hiḍrkhan, 32
Freeze, Gregory, 38
Fuʾâd, Mahmûd, 167, 175, 188, 192–93

Ğabdulhâlıq bin Ğabdulkerîm, 29
Ğabdulvâhid bin Süleyman, 50–51, 84
Ğabdurrahmân bin Ğatâullah, 183
Ğadlî, Fettâh, 183
Gasprinskiy, İsmâʿîl Bey, 117, 139, 143,
    147, 149–50, 171–72, 192, 210, 218
  Letters from Europe, 151–54
  Tercüman, 116–22, 141, 147, 156,
    163–64, 169, 184, 210. See also
    schooling: maktabs
Gâziyef, Ğârifullah, 98
Geraci, Robert, 206, 234

Goriachkin, Aleksandr Vasil'evich, 207–12
governance
  bureaucracy, 45, 49, 52, 100, 115,
    197–203
  bureaucracy, liberal vs. conservative,
    60–62
  central vs. local, 6
  equality, 218–21, 226
  flexibility, 217–18, 232, 236
  ideal subjects, 15, 58–63, 66, 86, 196–97,
    221, 241–42
  mediated (Catherinian imperial model),
    5, 9, 15, 38, 55, 62, 81, 89, 93, 145,
    193, 195, 218, 221, 240
  representation, 221–29
  unmediated (new imperial model), 5, 15,
    76–77, 81–96, 196, 216, 241, 243
Gramsci, Antonio, 6
Great Reforms, 5, 15, 57–60, 62, 65,
    70–71, 77, 99, 113, 187, 218, 241–42
Great transformation, 103–5, 123–24
  communications, 110–11
  economy, 111–13
  European Russia vs. Asian Russia, 105
  material life, 114–16
  Muslims in, 116–23
  transportation, 109–10
  urbanization, 113–14
Grigor'ev, Vasilii Vasil'evich, 65, 67–68,
    198, 207
Gümüşhânevî, Ahmed Ziyaüddin, 33
Ğusmanova, Bîbicemal, 83

Habermas, Jürgen, 12, 60
Habîbullah Efendi, Duvanköylü, 165
Hajj. See traveling: Hajj
Halîl Sultanmuhammed, 137–38
Hayalin, Saʿîd Babay. See Qargali
Hijaz, 27, 106–7, 135, 151, 231
historiography, 4, 12, 79, 113, 126, 173,
    238–39
  conventional, 7
  revisionist interventions, 8, 217
Hocaşef, Muhammed İbrahimoğlu, 47
Hüseyinof, Muhammedvelî, 143–44
Hüseyinova, Lebîbe, 229–31

İbrâhîm bin Hocaş, 30
İbrâhîm, Ğabdurreşîd, 28, 34, 109, 232
Igel'strom, Baron Osip A., 41–43, 46
Il'minskii, Nikolai Ivanovich, 63–64,
    66–68, 71, 74, 77, 197–98, 201–2,
    207–8, 223, 225, 227
India, 20, 26–27, 106, 209
inorodtsy. See non-Russian

insulated safe space. *See* domains: Volga-
  Ural Muslim domain
integration, 99, 101, 217
  limits on, 232–35
  and markets, 231–32
  of Muslims, 4, 50, 80, 94
intelligentsia, 59, 79, 174
  Muslim intelligentsia, 16, 181–87, 191,
    195, 198. *See also* progressive Muslim
    reformists
intermediaries. *See* governance: mediated
  governance
invisible boundaries, 10, 235. *See also*
  domains
Islamic scholars. *See ulama*
İsmâ'îl Efendi, 105–8, 124
İşmuhammed bin Dinmuhammed, 144,
  168, 192
İşmuhammed bin Zâhid, 18–19
İşmuratof, Ğabdurrahmân, 143
İttifâq-ı Müslimîn (Union of Muslims), 210.
  See also Muslim congresses

Jadidism. See progressive Muslim reformists

Karakazov, Dmitrii Vladimirovich, 61
Karaşayskiy, Abdulveli, 69
Kashgaria, 4, 106, 128–29
Kazakh Steppes, 4, 106, 109–10, 128–29,
  132, 136
Kazakhs, 4, 40, 67, 128, 132–34
Kazan
  city, 18, 22, 24, 26, 31, 43, 63, 75–76,
    88
  city duma, 83, 98, 144
  Kazan Gubernia, 88, 91–93, 95, 97, 132,
    140, 143, 163, 202–4, 222–24, 229
  zemstvo, 99, 135, 220, 225–27
Kazan Tatar Teachers' School. *See*
  schooling: Kazan Tatar Teachers'
  School
el-Kazânî, Ğabdurrahmân bin Ğatâullah,
  116, 232
Kemâluddinof, Salâhuddin, 176
Kerîm, Muhammed, 31
Kerimî, Fâtih, 117, 123–24, 169, 181
Khalid, Adeeb, 9, 90, 173–74, 215
Kirmanî, Ercümend, 31
knowledge, secular vs. religious, 90, 139,
  165, 172–76, 185–86
Koblov, Iakov Dmitrievich, 201, 225–29
Kurat, Akdes Nimet, 175

language
  common Turkic, 211–12

Russian language, 43, 57, 67–69, 76, 79,
  89, 99–100, 143, 155, 162, 166, 185,
  196, 220, 223, 241
Tatar language, 74, 163, 229–30, 233.
  See also nationalism; Russification;
  schooling
Law of July 16, 94–96
Law of March 26, 72, 74–75, 82, 85–86, 94,
  227
Lincoln, Bruce, 60
literacy, 30, 58, 143, 162–65, 171–72. *See
  also* schooling: maktabs

madrasa. *See* schooling
mail. *See* Great transformation:
  communications
maktab. *See* schooling
Maqsûdî, Ahmed-Hâdi, 238
Maqsûdî, Sadri, 203–4, 238
markets
  advertisements, 117–22
  consumers, 112–14
  integration of, 15, 99, 103, 111, 114,
    136, 144, 242
  urban, 114
Mecca, 2, 18, 27–29, 105–9
Medina, 28–29, 107, 109
merchants, 127–30
  and conservatism, 144
  business networks, 129, 132
  entrepreneurship, 83, 114, 125, 129,
    131–33, 136–37
  integration in imperial domain, 140–41
  and nationalism, 139–40
  philanthropy and communal patronage,
    15, 139–41
  and progressive Muslim reformists,
    138–39
  and townspeople (*meshchanstvo*), 129
Mikhail Vasil'evich, 204
military, 47–49, 213, 221
Ministry of Internal Affairs (MVD), 42, 45,
  50, 52, 67, 72, 74, 76, 84–85, 89
Ministry of Public Enlightenment (MNP),
  61
  jurisdiction over Muslim schools, 63–69,
    86. *See also* schooling
modernity, 6–7, 105, 116, 125, 148,
  173–74, 241–43definition, 6
  innovation and technology, 231. *See also*
  Great transformation
moral economy, 9, 53–54, 127
mosques, 21–22, 29, 35, 37, 45, 51, 53,
  73–74, 127, 142–44
mu'allim, 181, 204, 227–28

mufti. *See* Orenburg Spiritual Assembly
Muhammed Ğali, 132
Muhammed Hâris Hazret, 70, 165
Muhammedcan bin el-Hüseyin, 42, 99
Mullah Abbas. *See* Gasprinskiy: *Letters from Europe*
mundane encounters, 229–32
music, 176–80
Muslim congresses, 42, 200, 210–11, 214, 219, 241
Muslim holidays, 37, 40, 219, 237
Muslim notables, 14, 81, 86, 91, 101, 122, 127, 163, 172, 200, 219, 221, 224, 226, 242. *See also* governance: mediated; merchants; *ulama*
Muslim question, 196, 198, 205–7. *See also* paranoia about Islam
Muslim social imaginaries, 91, 124, 186
Müslim, Ğabdullah, 40

Naqshbandi Sufi order. *See* Sufism
Nâsırî, Ğabdulqayyûm, 154–56
Nathans, Benjamin, 10
nationalism, 15–16, 201, 212
    Great Russian, 62, 64, 78, 196
    and Russification, 71
    Russian Muslim vs. ethnic, 175, 184–85.
        See also paranoia about Islam
new method (*usûl-i cedîd*). *See* schooling: *maktabs*, reform of
Neziroğlu, 47–48
Nicholas I, 58–59, 130
Nicholas II, 61, 97, 156, 196, 201, 222, 226
Nizhny Novgorod Fair, 2, 24–25, 95, 112, 116, 131–33
nobility, 19, 69, 130, 134–35, 149, 187, 218, 222, 230, 242. *See also* estates
non-Russian, 15, 57, 60, 63–71, 79–81, 101, 196–99, 201–2, 207, 225, 227–28, 241–42

obshchestvo. See public
Orenburg Spiritual Assembly, 2, 20, 38–39, 42–56, 67, 72, 81, 90, 92, 95, 97, 221, 237
    certification at, 43–45, 52–53, 96–97, 228. *See also* ulama
Orientalism, 207, 215–16
Ottoman Empire, 4

painting, 172, 176–77
Pan-islamism, 199–203
Pan-turkism, 201, 204, 213–15
paranoia about Islam
    missioinary-state alliance, 197–99

separatism, 192, 200, 211, 221, 223, 225, 233
Tatarization, 202. *See also* governance; pan-Islamism; pan-Turkism
peasants
    nomads, 19, 40
    rationalism, 92
    rationalism of, 89
    serfs vs. state peasants, 58
Peter III, 41
petition movement. *See* schooling: Russo-Muslim schools
Pinegin, Mikhail Nikolaevich, 224, 229–30
Poltoratskii, Petr Alekseevich, 94–95, 97–98, 166
Pomeranz, Kenneth, 104
print media, 156
    and censorship, 16, 155–56
    and transregional connections, 19–20
    in Turkic, 117
    periodical press, 115, 122, 155–56, 165, 210
progress, cult of, 146–54
    education, 156–66
    science, 150–53. *See also* progressive Muslim reformists
progressive Muslim reformists
    alienation, 181–87
    conflict with mullahs, 177–78
    generations, 169–70, 175
    secularization, 174–76
    student networks, 168–70
public, 12, 58–59, 115, 134
    imperial public, 59–60. *See also* domains

Qadimism. See conservative Muslim reformists
Qaraşayskiy, 'Abdulvelî, 149
Qargali, 106, 128–29, 132, 187
Qur'an recitation, 19, 21–22, 172
Qursâvî, Ebunnasr Ğabdunnasîr, 34, 173

Radloff, Wilhelm (V. V. Radlov), 77, 82–88, 166, 185–86, 191, 197
railways. *See* Great transformation: transportation
Ramiyef family, 123, 131, 134–35, 137–38, 145, 184
    Şâkir Ramiyef, 135, 137, 145
    Zâkir Ramiyef, 135, 137, 145
Raqay, Feyzürrahman, 188
reform and religion, 173–76
Revolution of 1905, 14, 117, 156, 173, 181–82, 185, 196, 200, 210, 214, 218–20, 241

Revolution of 1917, 59, 171, 213, 235
Romanov regime, 57, 60–64, 68, 70, 78,
    101, 222, 240. *See also* governance
Russification, 197–98
    and language, 67–76, 80–82
    and Orthodoxy, 15, 59, 61, 66, 70,
    195–98. *See also* Christianization;
    schooling
Russo-Muslim (native/Tatar) schools. *See*
    schooling

Sâbir, Muhammed ʿAli, 199
schooling
    and governance, 223–29
    Kazan Tatar Teachers' School, 91, 166,
    186, 191, 224
    madrasas, 16, 22–26, 29–31, 67–76, 97
    madrasas, Bukharan, 25
    madrasas, reform of, 139, 143–44,
    165–66, 187
    madrasas, Volga-Ural, 22–25
    maktabs, 16, 22, 67–68, 71–75, 85–87,
    90–91, 97–98
    maktabs, reform of, 143, 162–65, 171,
    182–83, 191–92, 205, 210
    non-Russian schools, 63–64
    public schools, 71–72, 90, 97–98
    Russo-Muslim schools, 71, 74, 76,
    80–84, 86, 91, 97–101, 162, 225–29
    Russo-Muslim schools, resistance to,
    75–77, 80, 188, 197
    of women, 167, 223–24, 229–30
Şeref, Burhan, 138–39
Şeref, Ş., 176
Seydaşef, Ahmedcan, 83, 131, 227
Seydaşef, Muhammedcan, 99, 225
Seyfeddin bin Ebubekir, 31
Siberia, 5, 7, 33, 43, 93, 110, 113, 129, 131,
    154, 184, 209, 232, 237
Smirnov, Vasilii Dmitrievich, 87
smoking, 123–24
socialism, 145, 150, 184–85, 218
South Caucasus, 5, 139, 154, 162, 189, 211
Soviet Union, 4, 19–20, 35, 42, 194,
    237–39
St. Petersburg, 2, 40, 42, 45, 53, 69–70, 81,
    86–87, 90–91, 96, 137, 155, 189, 197,
    220
State Dumas, 138, 222–23
steamboats. *See* Great Transformation:
    transportation
Stolypin, Pyotr Arkadievich, 196–97,
    201–2, 222
Strizhevskii, Mikhail Vasil'evich, 202,
    205–6

studying. *See* schooling
Subayef, Bâqî, 131
Sufism, 26–27, 29, 32–33, 35, 38. *See also*
    ulama
Sultanof, Muhammedyâr, 48, 51, 84, 221

Taşçıoğlu, Arslanbey, 69, 149
Tatars, 4–5, 66–67, 205. *See also*
    Christianization: Baptized Tatars;
    language: Tatar language
Taylor, Charles, 11–12
telegraph. *See* Great transformation:
    communication
Tercüman. *See* Gasprinskiy; print media
Tevkelef, Selimgerey, 72–73, 82, 97
theater, 116, 138, 172, 180, 241
Timashev, Aleksandr Egorovich, 72–73, 82,
    86
Togan, Zeki Velidî, 123, 180
toleration. *See* governance: mediated; moral
    economy
Tolstoi, Count Dmitrii A., 61–75, 77, 86,
    89. *See also* schooling
Transoxiana, 2, 4, 13, 20, 24–26, 106, 111,
    128–29, 131, 199, 213. *See also*
    schooling: *madrasa*, Bukharan
traveling, 2, 28, 106
    Hajj, 18, 27–29, 31, 35, 47, 107–9, 135,
    151
    passport regulation, 114, 129. *See also*
    Great transformation: transportation
Tuqay, Ğabdullah, 138, 168, 184
el-Türkmânî, Niyazqul, 32

Ufa, 2, 20, 29, 42, 71, 74–76, 166
Ufa Gubernia, 29, 48, 51, 101, 186, 222
ulama
    definition and communal authority, 30
    hierarchy, 52–53
    in imperial service, 39–52
    networks, 29–34
    traveling for studying, 24–32
United States, 119–20, 138, 194
Ural Mountains, 7, 110, 115, 128
Utız İmenî, Ğabdurrahîm bin Ğusman, 34

Vasil'evich, Aleksandr, 224
Velîd bin Maqsûd, 40
Volga-Ural Muslims
    diaspora, 3–4, 171, 238
    significance, 3–5, 19–20
Voltaire, 41, 152

waqf (religious endowment), 22, 25, 35
West. *See* Europe

Witte, Sergei, 109, 115, 221
women, 179
    dress, 122
    segregation, 179–80. *See also* schooling:
        of women

Ya'qub Ağa, 106–7
Yûnus bin İvanay, 24

Yunusof family, 140–44, 179
    İbrâhim Yunusof, 141, 179
Yusupof, Ğumerbay, 85

*zemstvo*s, 5, 80, 99, 101, 110, 220, 222
Znamenskii, Petr, 201–2
Zolotnitskii, Nikolai Ivanovich, 63,
    66–67